The Forgotten Generation

The Forgotten Generation

The Status and Challenges of Adults with Mild Cognitive Limitations

edited by

Alexander J. Tymchuk, Ph.D.
School of Medicine
University of California, Los Angeles

K. Charlie Lakin, Ph.D.
College of Education and Human Development
University of Minnesota, Minneapolis

and

Ruth Luckasson, J.D.
College of Education
University of New Mexico, Albuquerque

·P A U L·H·
BROOKES
PUBLISHING C?

Baltimore · London · Toronto · Sydney

Paul H. Brookes Publishing Co.
Post Office Box 10624
Baltimore, Maryland 21285-0624

www.brookespublishing.com

Typeset by A.W. Bennett, Inc., Hartland, Vermont.
Manufactured in the United States of America by Versa Press, East Peoria, Illinois.

Chapter 16 copyright © by Robert Silverstein, 2000. This chapter is a reprint of Appendix 1, "An Overview of the Emerging Disability Policy Framework: A Guidepost for Analyzing Public Policy." 85 *Iowa Law Review* 1757 (2000).

Portions of Chapter 6 are reprinted by permission from Wehman, P. (1999). Development of business supports for persons with mental retardation in the workplace. *Journal of Vocational Rehabilitation, 13*(3).

Various passages in Chapter 4 are excerpted from MENTAL RETARDATION: DEFINITION, CLASSIFICATION, AND SYSTEMS OF SUPPORTS, by LUCKASSON, RUTH A., Copyright 1992 by AM ASSN ON MENTAL RETARDATION/AAMR. Reproduced with permission of AM ASSN ON MENTAL RETARDATION/AAMR in the format Textbook via Copyright Clearance Center.

The case stories in this book are composites of the authors' actual experiences. In all instances, names have been changed; in some instances, identifying details have been altered to protect confidentiality.

Library of Congress Cataloging-in-Publication Data

Tymchuk, Alexander J.
    The forgotten generation : the status and challenges of adults with mild cognitive
limitations / edited by Alexander J. Tymchuk, K. Charlie Lakin, and Ruth Luckasson.
        p.   cm.
    Includes bibliographical references and index.
    ISBN 1-55766-499-4
        1. Mentally handicapped—United States—Social conditions.   2. Mentally handicapped—
    Services for—United States.   3. Learning disabled—United States—Social conditions.
    4. Learning disabled—Services for—United States   I. Lakin, K. Charlie   II. Luckasson,
    Ruth.   III. Title.
    HV3006.A4 T95 2001
    362.3'0973—dc21   2001025795

British Library Cataloguing in Publication data are available from the British Library.

Contents

About the Editors viii
About the Contributors x
Acknowledgments xx
Introduction xxiii

I   **Background, Challenges, and Key Concepts in the
    Lives and Struggles of Adults with Mild Cognitive
    Limitations**

    1   The Hidden Majority of Individuals with Mental
        Retardation and Developmental Disabilities
        Robert B. Edgerton 3

    2   Life at the Margins: Intellectual, Demographic,
        Economic, and Social Circumstances of Adults with
        Mild Cognitive Limitations
        *Alexander J. Tymchuk, K. Charlie Lakin, and
        Ruth Luckasson* 21

    3   Renegotiating the Social Contract: Rights,
        Responsibilities, and Risks for Individuals with Mild
        Cognitive Limitations
        Robert M. Gettings 39

    4   Community and Culture: World Views and Natural
        Affiliations as the Basis of Understanding, Trust,
        Assistance, and Support
        *William M. Kane, Magdalena M. Avila, and
        Everett M. Rogers* 55

II **Income Security, Employment, and Career Development**

    5   Promoting Employment Opportunities for Individuals
        with Mild Cognitive Limitations: A Time for Reform
        John Kregel. 87

    6   Corporate-Initiated Workplace Supports
        *Paul Wehman, Pamela Sherron Targett, Michael D. West,
        Helen Eltzeroth, J. Howard Green, and Valerie Brooke* 99

    7   Career Development: Helping Youth with Mild
        Cognitive Limitations Achieve Successful Careers
        Patricia Rogan, Richard G. Luecking, and Mary Held 119

III Housing and Community Living

  8 A Home of One's Own: The Role of Housing and
     Social Services Agencies
     Suellen Galbraith 141

  9 Social and Community Participation: How to Enhance
     Supports for People with Mild Cognitive Limitations
     Valerie J. Bradley, John M. Agosta, and
     Madeleine Kimmich 169

 10 Building Stronger Communities for All: Thoughts
     About Community Participation for Individuals with
     Developmental Disabilities
     Robert Bogdan and Steven J. Taylor 191

IV Health and Well-Being

 11 Access to Health Services: Improving the Availability
     and Quality of Health Services for People with Mild
     Cognitive Limitations
     Deborah M. Spitalnik and Sheryl White-Scott 203

 12 The Healthy People 2010 Process: Difficulties
     Related to Surveillance and Data Collection
     Vincent A.Campbell and Holly J. Fedeyko 221

V Familial, Psychological, and Spiritual Well-Being

 13 Family Life: Experiences of People with Mild
     Cognitive Limitations
     Alexander J. Tymchuk 249

 14 People with a Dual Diagnosis: America's Powerless
     Population
     Steven Reiss 275

 15 Spirituality and Self-Actualization: Recognizing
     Spiritual Needs and Strengths of Individuals with
     Cognitive Limitations
     William Gaventa and Roger K. Peters 299

VI Citizenship and Civil Rights

 16 An Overview of the Emerging Disability Policy
     Framework: A Guidepost for Analyzing Public Policy
     Robert Silverstein 323

 17 The Criminal Justice System and People with Mild
     Cognitive Limitations
     Ruth Luckasson 347

18   Enhancing Understanding, Opportunity, and Social
     Support through Community Programs and Social
     Policy
     Alexander J. Tymchuk, Ruth Luckasson, and
     K. Charlie Lakin. 357

Index 367

About the Editors

Alexander J. Tymchuk, Ph.D., is Professor of Medical Psychology in the psychiatry and biobehavioral sciences department in the School of Medicine at the University of California, Los Angeles (UCLA). Advised by Bill Gaddes, Bob Knights, Carl Haywood, Sam Ashcroft, and Nick Hobbs, Dr. Tymchuk assisted in establishing a clinical service, training, and research program related to childhood disorders, including mental retardation, at UCLA. He has served in a number of administrative, clinical, training, and consultation roles at UCLA as well as nationally and internationally. A licensed psychologist, Dr. Tymchuk also maintains a clinical practice. Known for his work with parents with cognitive limitations and their families, Dr. Tymchuk recently completed a random clinical trial of two approaches to health and safety education for young and expectant mothers with mild cognitive limitations. He also was instrumental in establishing the first public school classes for children with autism. Dr. Tymchuk's interests include examination of ethical decision-making processes used by professionals, particularly as they relate to vulnerable populations; development of methods related to ensuring full treatment and research assent/consent with vulnerable populations, including an examination of concordance of treatment and research participation decisions made by an individual with mental retardation in comparison to those made by a surrogate decision maker on the individual's behalf; and examination of competence determination related to parenting. By necessity, this work has led Dr. Tymchuk to examine and address legal and policy issues related to each of these areas. In addition, Dr. Tymchuk served as an expert witness in the recent litigation in Alberta, Canada, regarding involuntary sterilization of institutionalized individuals presumed to have cognitive limitations. Currently, Dr. Tymchuk and his students are examining injury events involving children with developmental or related disabilities in order to test suitable interventions. In addition to his other positions, Dr. Tymchuk serves as one of the coordinators of the Developmental Disabilities Immersion Program at UCLA.

K. Charlie Lakin, Ph.D., is Director of the Rehabilitation Research and Training Center (RRTC) on Community Living at the University of Minnesota in Minneapolis. Dr. Lakin has more than 25 years of experience in providing services to individuals with intellectual and developmental disabilities as a teacher, researcher, trainer, consultant, and advocate. He is principal investigator of numerous research and/or training centers and projects and has authored or co-authored more than 175 books, monographs, journal articles, book chap-

and technical reports. Dr. Lakin has been a frequent consultant to federal and state agencies on matters of policy, research, and evaluation, including the Administration on Developmental Disabilities, the Health Care Financing Administration, the Assistant Secretary for Planning and Evaluation (U.S. Department of Health and Human Services), the National Center on Health Statistics, the National Institute on Disability and Rehabilitation Research, the Congressional Research Service, the General Accounting Office, and the Centers for Disease Control and Prevention. Dr. Lakin has worked actively as a director or consultant for nonprofit organizations and agencies focused on community services, arts, outdoor recreation and adventure, integrated sports, and advocacy for individuals with disabilities. He has collaborated with universities, private research companies, and foundations in national evaluation and research programs. Dr. Lakin currently is an associate editor of *Mental Retardation* and an editorial board member of the *Journal of The Association for Persons with Severe Handicaps* (JASH), the *Journal of Intellectual and Developmental Disability,* and the *Journal of Social Science and Disability.* Among the recognitions afforded Dr. Lakin are the Dybwad Humanitarian Award of the American Association on Mental Retardation and an appointment by former President Clinton to the President's Committee on Mental Retardation.

Ruth Luckasson, J.D., is Regent's Professor and Professor of Special Education and Coordinator of Mental Retardation and Severe Disabilities in the College of Education at the University of New Mexico in Albuquerque. Professor Luckasson is Vice President of the American Association on Mental Retardation (AAMR). She served on former President Clinton's Committee on Mental Retardation, serves on the Litigation and Human Rights Committee of The Arc of the United States, and is the chair of the American Association on Mental Retardation's Committee on Terminology and Classification. Professor Luckasson formerly served as Chair of the American Bar Association Commission on Mental and Physical Disability Law. She has published widely in the areas of legal rights of people with disabilities, people with mental retardation as defendants and victims in the criminal justice system, the definition of mental retardation, and children in special education.

About the Contributors

John M. Agosta, Ph.D., is a vice president at the Human Services Research Institute (HSRI) and has worked with people with disabilities since the 1970s. Dr. Agosta completed his doctorate in rehabilitation research at the University of Oregon, specializing in research methods and community supports for people with disabilities. In addition, he has extensive experience with community supports, having worked in direct services and administrative positions within agencies offering early intervention and residential, vocational, or family support services. Employed at HSRI since 1983, Dr. Agosta has worked under contract with state and federal agencies on a variety of projects focusing on community integration for individuals with disabilities. He has been involved at HSRI with nearly all efforts surrounding family support issues, conducted analyses of entire state systems for people with developmental disabilities (e.g., in Arkansas, Idaho, Oregon, Hawaii), and has studied specific facets of the field (e.g., trends in supported employment, decentralization of government responsibility for services, managed care). He directs the National Center for Family Support at HSRI, an effort funded by the Administration on Developmental Disabilities to provide technical assistance on family support to 20 states and two U.S. territories. In addition, he helped to found the national Self Advocate Leadership Network and is involved with several projects to explore design and application issues related to self-determination and participant-driven supports.

Magdalena M. Avila, Dr.P.H., M.P.H., M.S.W., is Assistant Professor of the Health Education Program in the College of Education at the University of New Mexico in Albuquerque. Dr. Avila works with communities to identify public health problems and to develop appropriate prevention and health promotion educational/research strategies. She is primarily involved in partnering with local communities to develop culturally relevant research in response to community-based needs. She has worked in the prevention field studying alcohol-related problems and their impact on Chicano/Mexican American Families and in the environmental social justice arena on issues of environmental racism. She received her doctorate from the University of California at Berkeley, School of Public Health.

Michael Barcus, M.S., has worked in the field of education and employment of individuals with disabilities for more than 25 years. Since 1983, he has worked in the Rehabilitation Research and Training Center on Workplace Supports at Virginia Commonwealth University in Richmond. Mr. Barcus earned his master's degree in education from the Johns Hopkins University with an emphasis on the education of individuals with severe disabilities. He has experience as a teacher for students with significant disabilities at the preschool, elementary, and secondary levels and as a public school special education administrator responsible for curriculum development. Mr. Barcus has served as a training specialist focused on improving competitive employment opportunities for individuals with severe disabilities. In addition, he teaches preservice courses in the areas of transition and employment and has co-authored various books, monographs, and journal articles, primarily in the areas of school-to-work transition and employment.

Robert Bogdan, Ph.D., is a professor of sociology and disability studies at Syracuse University in Syracuse, New York. In addition to teaching courses in research methods and disability studies, Dr. Bogdan directs the Interdisciplinary Doctoral Program in the Social Sciences at Syracuse University. He is also a senior researcher at the Center on Human Policy. The author of more than 10 books and close to 100 articles, Dr. Bogdan is well known for his writing about research methods and disability issues.

Valerie J. Bradley, M.A., has been President of the Human Services Research Institute since its inception in 1976. She has a master's degree from the Eagle ton Institute of Politics at Rutgers University. Ms. Bradley has directed numerous state and federal policy evaluations that have contributed to the expansion, enhancement, and responsiveness of services and supports for people with disabilities and their families. She helped to design skills standards for human services workers, conducted a study to translate the experience with decentralization in Scandinavia to an American context, is the project director of a national evaluation of self-determination, and co-directs a national project on performance measurement. She is the co-editor of *Creating Individual Supports for People with Developmental Disabilities: A Mandate for Change at Many Levels* (Paul H. Brookes Publishing Co., 1994). Ms. Bradley is the recent past chair of the President's Committee on Mental Retardation.

Valerie Brooke, M.Ed., is Associate Director of Training at the Rehabilitation Research and Training Center on Workplace Supports at Virginia Commonwealth University in Richmond. She has been a faculty member in the School of Education at Virginia Commonwealth University for approximately 20 years. Ms. Brooke has extensive background experience as a direct services provider, and since 1990 she has designed, delivered, and evaluated personnel training programs to increase the employment of people with disabilities. These training programs have been targeted to people with disabilities, teachers, rehabilitation personnel, and, most recently, employers and the business community.

Ms. Brooke consults regularly on a national basis and is a frequent contributor to journal articles, book chapters, monographs, fact sheets, and newsletters.

Vincent A. Campbell, Ph.D., is a health scientist in the Division of Birth Defects, Child Development, Disability and Health in the Disability and Health Branch of the National Center for Environmental Health at the Centers for Disease Control and Prevention (CDC) in Atlanta, Georgia. Dr. Campbell is coordinating disability surveillance activities for several of the Healthy People 2010 objectives related to quality of life for people with disabilities. Prior to his employment at CDC, he directed the client and service tracking program for the Alabama Department of Mental Health and Mental Retardation and coordinated the surveillance program for the state's CDC-sponsored mental retardation prevention program. He has extensive experience in service planning, program evaluation, and service development for people with mental retardation.

Robert B. Edgerton, Ph.D., is Professor in the departments of anthropology and psychiatry and biobehavioral sciences at the University of California–Los Angeles. Dr. Edgerton has conducted research since 1959 on the community adaptation of individuals with mental retardation. His research has focused on the life course of individuals as they cope with the various residential, vocational, and social challenges they face in the community. The research has highlighted the roles of voluntary benefactors as well as salaried social services providers in the lives of individuals with mental retardation as well as the problems of ill health and the death of loved ones in older populations. Dr. Edgerton's studies have compared African Americans with Caucasians matched on IQ scores, gender, age, and family circumstances. These studies have been based primarily on intensive ethnographic techniques calling for frequent, prolonged, and informal visits, during which conversations rather than interviews take place. By seeing participants in various environments, some sense of how they adapt to differing surroundings, individuals, and circumstances can be gained. Dr. Edgerton currently is planning additional long-term follow-up studies.

Helen Eltzeroth worked as an employer liaison for a corporate mentoring program. Her role involved assisting community employers with developing workplace supports—particularly the use of mentors as on-the-job trainers and supports for students with disabilities who were making the transition from school to work. Ms. Eltzeroth has extensive experience in business management and a keen interest in adult care services.

Holly J. Fedeyko, M.P.H., is an independent consultant in Hayward, California. Ms. Fedeyko is a graduate of Emory University's Rollins School of Public Health with a master's of public health in epidemiology and environmental and occupational health. Upon completing her master's degree, Ms. Fedeyko spent 3 years working in the Disability and Health Branch at the Centers for Disease Control and Prevention (CDC) in Atlanta, Georgia. She also has a bachelor of science degree in biology and environmental health from McGill University.

Suellen Galbraith, M.S.W., has served since 1993 as Director for Public Policy of the American Network of Community Options and Resources (ANCOR) in Annandale, Virginia. ANCOR is a national organization of nearly 700 private providers who serve more than 150,000 people with mental retardation and other developmental disabilities. At ANCOR, Ms. Galbraith tracks federal legislation and regulations that affect providers of supports to people with disabilities, with an emphasis on housing; Medicaid, Medicare, and long-term services; Social Security disability programs; and employer/employee workplace health and safety issues. Ms. Galbraith also is the co-chair of the Housing Task Force and the Long Term Supports and Services Task Force of the Consortium for Citizens with Disabilities (CCD), a Washington, D.C.–based working coalition comprised of 100 national organizations representing consumer, advocacy, provider, and professional organizations that support people with disabilities. In addition, she is the CCD representative to board of the national Coalition for Human Services. Ms. Galbraith also serves on several national advisory and work groups, including the Health Care Financing Administration's abuse and neglect and quality indicators work groups. Prior to working with ANCOR, Ms. Galbraith was Director of Residential Services, State Use, and State Associations at the National Association of Rehabilitation Facilities in Washington, D.C., from 1990 to 1993, and Executive Director of the Alabama Disabilities Advocacy Program from 1983 to 1990. Before her work in disability advocacy, she was Executive Director of a three-county Community Action Service Program in Alabama. In addition, Ms. Galbraith served in 1981 as a U.S. Congressional Fellow to the U.S. Senate Committee on the Handicapped (now the Senate Committee on Disability Policy).

William Gaventa, M.Div., is Coordinator of Community and Congregational Supports and Assistant Professor of Pediatrics (co-terminous) at the Elizabeth M. Boggs Center on Developmental Disabilities—The University Affiliated Program of New Jersey at the Robert Wood Johnson Medical School at the University of Medicine & Dentistry of New Jersey in New Brunswick. Reverend Gaventa has served in a variety of positions in services with people with developmental disabilties, including chaplain of two residential facilities and Coordinator of Family Support for the Georgia Developmental Disabilities Council. Most of his work has been in building bridges between faith communities and public advocacy and service organizations that support people with disabilties and their families. Reverend Gaventa has led projects in development of community-based respite care and, in New Jersey, serves as the Coordinator of the Training and Technical Assistance Team at the Boggs Center for the New Jersey Self Determination Initiative. He has served as volunteer Executive Secretary for the Religion Division of the American Association on Mental Retardation since 1985 and, since 1999, as co-editor of the *Journal of Religion, Disability, and Health.*

Robert M. Gettings, M.P.A., is Executive Director of the National Association of State Directors of Developmental Disabilities Services in Alexandria, Virginia. For the past 30 years, Mr. Gettings has represented the interests of the 50 state developmental disabilities agencies in Washington, D.C., and has facilitated communication among the states concerning the most effective means of serving citizens with lifelong disabilities. He has written and lectured extensively on the impact of federal legislative and administrative policy on the delivery of state and local services to individuals with mental retardation and other developmental disabilities and is widely recognized as a leading expert in this area. Mr. Gettings also has helped many states solve a variety of service delivery problems over the years and, consequently, is well-versed in program development trends across the country. Prior to joining the National Association of State Directors of Developmental Disabilities Services, Mr. Gettings was on the staff of the President's Committee on Mental Retardation and the National Association for Retarded Children.

J. Howard Green, M.S., is an instructor and business liaison in the Rehabilitation Research and Training Center on Workplace Supports at Virginia Commonwealth University in Richmond. Mr. Green has more than 25 years of experience in the rehabilitation field and tremendous experience in working with businesses on national, state, and local levels. He is a strong advocate for people with disabilities and has worked with individuals and organizations to promote full employment and active citizenship for individuals with disabilities. Mr. Green continues to provide training and technical assistance to businesses, community rehabilitation providers, and rehabilitation agencies on issues relating to disability and business. Over the past several years, Mr. Green has co-authored and contributed to several articles and book chapters relating to the employment of people with disabilities.

Mary Held, M.S., C.R.C., is a doctoral student in special education and teacher education at Indiana University in Bloomington. Prior to beginning her studies, Mary was a high school special education teacher and a rehabilitation counselor in supported employment. Her areas of interest include instruction and assessment of students with mild disabilities, transition from school-to-adult life, and self-determination.

William M. Kane, Ph.D., is a professor of health education in the College of Education at the University of New Mexico in Albuquerque. Professor Kane has extensive experience working with traditionally underserved rural and urban community members to support their development of health promotion and disease prevention programs. His experience includes working with American Indian, Hispanic, and African American communities and families. Prior to joining the faculty at the University of New Mexico, Dr. Kane served as Executive Director of the American College of Preventive Medicine and the Association for the Advancement of Health Education and was involved in the development of a health promotion disease prevention agenda. Dr. Kane is the author of many books, chapters, and journal articles on health promotion and cultural issues. He acknowledges the important role of many community members in his attempts to understand the complex issues surrounding health and culture.

Madeleine Kimmich, D.S.W., received her doctoral degree in social welfare from the University of California at Berkeley. Engaged in evaluation research and policy analysis of human services for 20 years, she has assisted decision makers at federal, state, and local levels to work collaboratively to improve the effectiveness of programs targeted to low-income children and families, adolescents, the elderly, and people with disabilities. Dr. Kimmich is currently the principal investigator for a 5-year evaluation of Ohio's Title IV-E Waiver, a child welfare system reform demonstration project that includes analysis of process implementation, participant outcomes, community impact, and cost effectiveness. She is also the project director for an evaluation of the First Step to Success Program, an evaluation funded by the Oregon Commission on Children and Families. Dr. Kimmich's work in outcome measurement, quality assurance, and system reform has included projects in South Carolina, Arizona, Connecticut, Iowa, Pennsylvania, and many other states, as well as presentations at numerous national conferences.

John Kregel, Ed.D., is a professor of special education at Virginia Commonwealth University (VCU) in Richmond. He presently serves as Director of Research and Associate Director of the VCU Rehabilitation Research and Training Center on Workplace Supports. Current research efforts are focused on evaluating the effectiveness of state and federal efforts to reform social security policy, promoting improvements in supported employment programs, and enhancing the ability of employers to provide accommodations to workers with disabilities. He is also co-editor of *Focus on Autism and Developmental Disabilities.*

Richard G. Luecking, Ed.D., is President of TransCen, Inc., in Rockville, Maryland. Dr. Luecking and his organization are dedicated to the design, implementation, and research of career development systems that benefit people with disabilities. He has extensive experience in the fields of education, rehabilitation, and workforce development. Dr. Luecking's chief area of professional interest is the promotion of interdisciplinary partnerships through his association with numerous business, professional, and community organizations, both locally and nationally. In addition to operating locally based school-to-work transition programs in Maryland and California, Dr. Luecking and his TransCen colleagues are partners in the National Center on Secondary Education and Transition.

Roger K. Peters, D. Min., is Director of Pastoral Services at the Selinsgrove Center in Selinsgrove, Pennsylvania, where he also directs the interfaith program of ministry. The Center's ministries include a large community congregational inclusion program. Dr. Peters has developed and implemented a community-building approach to ensure better access to congregational inclusion for people returning to the community from Selinsgrove Center. He has authored journal articles on ethics, spirituality, community inclusion, and sacremental inclusion.

Steven Reiss, Ph.D., is Professor of Psychology and Psychiatry and Director of the Nisonger Center for Mental Retardation and Developmental Disabilities at Ohio State University in Columbus. Dr. Reiss is the author of various books and journal articles. His most recent book, *Who Am I?: The 16 Basic Desires that Motivate Our Actions and Define Our Personalities* (Jeremy P. Tarcher, 2000), is based on his groundbreaking study about the desires that shape us as individuals. Dr. Reiss is ranked in the Social Science Citation Index as being in the top 3% of psychology professors worldwide with regard to the impact of his work.

Patricia Rogan, Ph.D., is an associate professor at the Indiana University School of Education and a research associate at the Indiana Institute on Disability and Community in Indianapolis. Dr. Rogan also is the president of the National Association for Persons in Supported Employment. She has extensive experience in the fields of special education and rehabilitation. Dr. Rogan's work focuses on secondary education, transition from school to adult life, supported employment, and organizational change from segregated to integrated services and supports. She prepares school and adult services personnel, conducts model demonstration projects, and works with multiple stakeholders toward national and statewide systems change. Dr. Rogan has published several books and numerous articles, book chapters, and monographs.

Everett M. Rogers, Ph.D., is Regent's Professor in the Department of Communication and Journalism at the University of New Mexico in Albuquerque. Dr. Rogers has been teaching in universities and conducting scholarly research for the past 45 years, including positions at Ohio State University, Michigan State University, University of Michigan, Stanford University, and the University of Southern California. A well-recognized writer of scholarly books, Dr. Rogers is widely known for his book *Diffusion of Innovations, Fourth Edition* (Free Press, 1995), which has been designated a "Citation Classic" by the Institute for Scientific Information and one of the "ten classic books in business" by *Inc. Magazine.* Dr. Rogers' international experience includes research and teaching in Colombia, India, Korea, Indonesia, Thailand, Brazil, Nigeria, Tanzania, Germany, France, Mexico, Ecuador, and Singapore. Among his many areas of expertise are cross-cultural communications, public health, agriculture, and technology transfer.

Robert Silverstein, J.D., is Director of the Center for the Study and Advancement of Disability Policy in Washington, D.C. Mr. Silverstein served for 13 years on Capitol Hill in various capacities, including Staff Director and Chief Counsel of the U.S. Senate Subcommittee on Disability Policy of the Committee on Labor and Human Resources (chaired by Tom Harkin [D. Iowa]). He holds a bachelor's degree in economics from the Wharton School, University of Pennsylvania, and a juris doctorate from the Georgetown University Law Center.

Deborah M. Spitalnik, Ph.D., is Executive Director of the Elizabeth M. Boggs Center on Developmental Disabilities—The University Affiliated Program of New Jersey at the Robert Wood Johnson Medical School at the University of Medicine & Dentistry of New Jersey in New Brunswick, where she also is Associate Professor of Pediatrics and Family Medicine. She is the chair of the President's Committee on Mental Retardation and former president of the American Association of University Affiliated Programs. Dr. Spitalnik is also the recipient of the Dybwad Humanitarian Award from the American Association on Mental Retardation. She is deeply involved in health care issues for people with developmental disabilities through the development of model service demonstrations, technical assistance to state agencies, and extensive teaching and continuing education, particularly in the area of managed health care.

Pamela Sherron Targett, M.Ed., is the director of the employment services division located at the Rehabiliation Research and Training Center on Workplace Supports at Virginia Commonwealth University in Richmond. Her direct service experiences also have included projects in special education, vocational services, and general community functioning. She has authored or co-authored journal articles and book chapters on supported employment, special education, and other disability-related issues.

Steven J. Taylor, Ph.D., is Professor of Cultural Foundations of Education, Coordinator of Disability Studies, and Director of the Center on Human Policy and the National Resource Center on Supported Living and Choice at Syracuse University in Syracuse, New York. He received his doctoral degree in sociology from Syracuse University in 1977 and held positions at the University of Minnesota and Cornell University prior to returning to the Center on Human Policy, where he served as a graduate assistant from 1972 to 1976. Dr. Taylor is the author of numerous articles and has written or edited seven books with colleagues at Syracuse University, including *Introduction to Qualitative Research Methods: A Guidebook and Resource* (John Wiley & Sons, 1998), *The Social Meaning of Mental Retardation: Two Life Stories* (Teachers College Press, 1994), *The Variety of Community Experience: Qualitative Studies of Family and Community Life* (Paul H. Brookes Publishing Co., 1995), *Life in the Community: Case Studies of Organizations Supporting People with Disabilities* (Paul H. Brookes Publishing Co., 1991), and *The Nonrestrictive Environment: On Community Integration for People with Severe Disabilities* (Human Policy Press, 1987). He was the recipient of the American Association on Mental Retardation's (AAMR) Research Award in 1997 and currently serves as editor of AAMR's journal *Mental Retardation.*

Paul Wehman, Ph.D., is Professor in the Department of Physical Medicine and Rehabilitation at the Medical College of Virginia and Director of the Rehabilitation Research and Training Center on Workplace Supports at Virginia Commonwealth University in Richmond. Internationally recognized for his service and scholarly contributions in the field of special education, psychology, and vocational rehabilitation, Dr. Wehman is the recipient of the 1990 Joseph P. Kennedy, Jr. Foundation Award in Mental Retardation and received the Distinguished Service Award from the President's Committee on Employment for Persons with Disabilities in October, 1992. He is the author or editor of more than 125 books, research monographs, journal articles, and chapters in the areas of traumatic brain injury, mental retardation, supported employment, and special education. He also is the editor of the *Journal of Vocational Rehabilitation.* Dr. Wehman's specific research interests include transition from school to work, supported employment, developmental disabilities, and brain injury.

Michael D. West, Ph.D., is Assistant Professor at Virginia Commonwealth University and is also Research Associate with the Rehabilitation Research and Training Center on Workplace Supports. Dr. West's research projects have included national surveys of supported employment policies and practices, a study of students with disabilities in higher education in Virginia, and states' use of Medicaid Home- and Community-Based Waivers to fund employment services. Dr. West also is involved in research and demonstration efforts related to Social Security disability reform at the Rehabilitation Research and Training Center on Workplace Supports at Virginia Commonwealth University.

Sheryl White-Scott, M.D., is Assistant Professor of Medicine in the Department of Internal Medicine at New York Medical College and Director of the St. Charles Developmental Disabilities Program at St. Vincent's Catholic Medical Centers of New York, located in Flushing. Dr. White-Scott previously was Director of Adult Health Services at the Westchester Institute of Human Development, the University Affiliated Program, in Valhalla, New York. Dr. White-Scott specializes in clinical services for adults with developmental disabilities. She has given numerous presentations on primary health care, prevention, and women's health and has trained medical professionals in the delivery of health services for individuals with developmental disabilities.

Acknowledgments

This book represents the work of many people. The efforts of the President's Committee on Mental Retardation—especially Jane Browning and John Pride, who were instrumental in preparing for the initial presentations of the ideas within this book—are appreciated. The forum in which the ideas were discussed was the national working-group summit cosponsored by the President's Committee on Mental Retardation and the Social Security Administration. The products of this working-group summit were initially summarized in *The Forgotten Generation: 1999 Report to the President.* Ruth Sullivan was instrumental in preparing the initial draft of the Report to the President as well as in summarizing discussion notes to guide the revisions appearing in this volume. The efforts of the individual authors first in preparing and presenting the original concept papers as part of the working groups and then in revising the chapters based on discussions are very much appreciated. We are especially grateful to the 85 initial discussants and facilitators, who contributed their weekend to the Forgotten Generation meeting, and to the Social Security Administration, which contributed generously to ensuring national representative participation.

Special recognition also is given to Shannon Sewards, who worked with the editors and the authors and prepared the chapters for publication.

Thanks also goes to Paul H. Brookes Publishing Co. acquisitions editor Jessica Allan for her commitment to the contents and quality of this book.

Dr. Tymchuk's work on this project was supported in part by grants from SHARE, Inc., the California Wellness Foundation, the Strauss Foundation, and The Entertainment Industry Foundation. This support is valued. Dr. Lakin's work on this project was supported in part by the National Institute on Disability and Rehabilitation Research.

To the memory of John F. Kennedy, Jr.

Introduction

In 1969, the President's Committee on Mental Retardation (PCMR) published a report titled, "The Six-Hour Retarded Child." This publication critiqued the status of children and youth who were identified as "educable mentally retarded (EMR)" only during the school hours and only during their school lives. Whereas this report focused on children, it recognized that people with mild cognitive limitations were expected to, and for the most part did, manage typical social roles with few or no specialized supports. However, despite the apparent overuse or misuse of the mental retardation label in schools and the inappropriate generalization of that label to other areas of life, the EMR label also assisted some students by establishing eligibility for special education services for their individual needs. Fortunately, in the years following the PCMR report, some less stigmatizing programs and educational diagnoses were created to provide students with needed assistance. Once out of school, however, these students found few such adaptations as they faced the tasks of acquiring the needed knowledge and skills for community living—work, housing, relationships, caring for their own families, health, civic participation, and dealing with the authorities—while fostering well-being. Individuals who had difficulty reading and comprehending what they read or who required additional time to grasp information were met with less patience and less help. Those who had difficulty in decision making and judgment had similar difficulty in finding and keeping jobs, pricing and choosing consumer goods, choosing people with whom to develop and maintain social relationships, and recognizing people from whom they should stay away.

Some individuals could obtain supports from developmental disability service programs by virtue of their fulfillment of eligibility criteria; others did not wish to do so. Even more individuals with mild cognitive limitations were excluded from such services because of adherence to precise and immutable service eligibility criteria. Those who then sought assistance from generic services invariably had to sink or swim with the pervasive "one type of delivery fits all" philosophy. Unfortunately, many individuals sank. Their children sank with them. Along with many others living in poverty, they were swept away by the consequences of political responses to the last economic downturn. As parts of the country began to come out of the economic downturn during the early 1990s, the cumulative impact of precipitous devolution and reduction in services and supports were being felt by low-income people who could ill afford such changes. For example, gaining access to health care, which is never easy for low-income people, had become even more difficult. People who had worked in low-paying jobs in which they might have received health benefits no longer had jobs or health benefits. Hospitals to which low-income people might go were fighting for their very existence. Low-income immigrants, too, were caught up in the political swirl of denial of services. Increasingly, alarms sounded about the rising rate of unemployment and its impact on family structures, about increased requests for welfare, and about increased numbers of people who were homeless or transient or who dropped out of school early. Additional alarms were being sounded about rising rates of teen pregnancy, substance abuse, domestic violence, crimes, and child maltreatment.

It was in this atmosphere that this project began in the fall of 1996 as a first step to find out what was really happening to the "six-hour retarded child." We were interested not only in those individuals who may have fit existing diagnostic categories but also in those who may have fallen outside the criteria. Simultaneously, change was occurring on some professional and governmental fronts. For example, the American Association on Mental Retardation (AAMR) was moving away from a strictly IQ-based classification system to a support-based system related to individual functional needs. Similarly, the World Health Organization (WHO) was moving toward a functional system of ablements and disablements, recognizing that it was possible for people to perform well in some areas while needing supports and adaptations in others. In addition, the Maternal and Child Health Bureau, recognizing that health needs of substantial numbers of children were not being met through the use of a medically based categorical system with strict either-or criteria, was moving toward a more functional inclusive system for individuals with mild cognitive limitations.

TERMINOLOGY

For the purposes of this book, the term *mild cognitive limitation* is used to facilitate discussion regarding individuals with relatively mild functional limitations across the life span for whom adaptation of interventions and supports may be required. The term *limitation* rather than *impairment* has been chosen because *limitation* suggests that the condition is not necessarily permanent, biologically accessible, or identical to current categorical disability definitions. Also, the term *limitation* includes a larger group of people than are usually included in typical calculations of disability or impairment. The term *cognitive* was chosen because this book focuses on the group of people who are marginalized by lower than average learning, communication, judgment, and understanding abilities. The term *mild* was chosen in part because the limitations of these individuals appear on the surface to be less severe than those of people with more obvious disabilities; however, it is recognized that reading difficulties or other limitations in these individuals can be just as debilitating as more severe disabilities.

Mild cognitive limitation is used in this book to describe individuals who may have fulfilled the criteria for a diagnosis of mild mental retardation at some time in their lives—typically during their school years, during which they may have received special education. Or, using the most recent classification system for mental retardation defined by the American Association on Mental Retardation (Luckasson et al., 1992), these individuals may have been labeled as having mental retardation with the need for intermittent or limited supports. Out of school, however, these individuals may or may not continue to fulfill existing criteria that are used for determining services on the basis of mental retardation. Hence, because their learning needs go unrecognized because of discontinuities between school and postschool life, these individuals are at risk. The term *mild cognitive limitations* also is being used to describe people who fell outside existing diagnostic criteria for mental retardation during school but who nonetheless displayed similar learning characteristics, living circumstances, and communities as did people who filled those diagnostic criteria. Labels such as *learning disabled, mildly disabled,* and *emotionally disturbed* may have been applied to these individuals (e.g., MacMillan, Gresham, & Bocian, 1998; Reschly, 1996; Sitlington, Frank, & Carson, 1992; Wagner, 1995). *Mild cognitive limitation* also is applied to individuals whose measured IQ score is greater than the traditional ceiling of 70–75 but for whom education and/or support *along continua* (i.e., from more to less; continuous to periodic) may be essential to their success in more complex situations (e.g., planning for and making major decisions, such as consenting to health care or other forms of treatment, participation in research, or entrance into contractual relationships; evaluating suitability of supports; coping with tragedy; accepting responsibility for self and child health care; protecting self and family from harm; responding to accusations of behavioral or criminal misconduct; defending self; initiating political self-activism) and in roles that require more complex learning, judgment, and other cognitive functions across the life span. In effect, this population arguably is the largest group of individuals who may be seen as having disabilities.

OUR PROCESS

A series of outcomes was identified. First, we put together a team of authors and experts with experience in each area and the creativity necessary to explore new ideas. Requests were made for concept papers in five key areas (income security, employment, and career development; housing and community living; health and well-being; familial, psychological, and spiritual well-being; and citizenship and civil rights). These papers then were made available to members of working groups who would meet to address each area with specific outcomes.

Second, the working groups met in Washington, D.C., on February 21 and 22, 1999. Because of the complexities of this new area, working group participants included representatives from federal agencies, professional organizations, and service provider and consumer groups in addition to the concept paper authors. Representatives from national foundations and a number of consumers also participated.

Third, the President's Committee on Mental Retardation prepared *The Forgotten Generation: 1999 Report to the President*. This report was dedicated to John F. Kennedy, Jr., and is available from the PCMR.

Fourth, this book, containing chapters based upon the original concept papers and providing recommendations for change, was written.

CHALLENGES

The following challenges were identified to direct the efforts of this process, particularly for the working groups:

1. An increasingly complex, information-based and technologically demanding society presents substantial and growing challenges, particularly in areas related to reading, arithmetic, processing abstract information, and using technology.
2. In an increasingly complex, more hurried, and less "neighborly" society, people who require support to negotiate social, commercial, and governmental settings and circumstances find access to needed supports more difficult to obtain.
3. The barriers to social, commercial, and governmental settings and circumstances caused by disability-based limitations in reading, arithmetic, use of technology, and ability to gain access to information are as significant as physical and sensory barriers but are less likely to be accommodated.
4. Changes in public policies affecting low-income, unemployed, homeless, and other disenfranchised groups have had a substantial and disproportionate effect on individuals with cognitive limitations.
5. As previously existing programs of social support are being redesigned and downsized, people with cognitive limitations are made more vulnerable by their difficulty in securing knowledge of and access to these new programs, and the time lag they experience between loss of previous supports and access to new programs is typically prolonged.
6. Most individuals with mild cognitive limitations desire that their needs be accommodated outside of service systems that bear stigma and will go to substantial lengths and disadvantage to avoid that stigma.
7. The vast majority of people with mild cognitive limitations define their needs in terms of basic income, housing, and other necessities and not in terms of their ability to gain access to a formal system of services. How-

ever, in the absence of involvement with such formal systems, few people are able to obtain access to stable and knowledgeable advocates.

8. Individuals with mild cognitive limitations are particularly vulnerable to secondary disabilities as a result of poor quality of health services, absence of preventive health care, and lack of protection from injury at work or at home or as a result of violence.

9. People with mild cognitive limitations are particularly vulnerable to secondary disabilities as a result of limited access to and quality of mental health services and as a result of the preventable effects of stress, loneliness, anxiety, and depression.

10. Individuals with mild cognitive limitations are particularly likely to be victims of crime, violence, and maltreatment because of inadequate preparation for independent living, lack of attention to their needs, tendencies toward errors of judgment, acquiescence to perceived authority, and exploitation of their vulnerabilities by others.

11. In an increasingly complex society, individuals with mild cognitive limitations are restricted in their employment opportunities by limited academic skills and higher rates of school dropout. They are restricted further by the movement toward higher performance criteria for high school graduation.

REFERENCES

Luckasson, R., Coulter, D., Polloway, E., Reiss, S., Schalock, R., Snell, M., Spitalnik, D., & Stark, J. (1992). *Mental retardation: Definition, classification, and systems of supports.* Washington, DC: American Association on Mental Retardation.

MacMillan, D., Gresham, F., & Bocian, K. (1998). Curing mental retardation and causing learning disabilities: Consequences of using various WISC–III IQs to estimate aptitude of Hispanic students. *Journal of Psychoeducational Assessment, 16,* 36–54.

Reschly, D. (1996). Identification and assessment of students with disabilities. *The Future of Children, 6,* 40–53.

Sitlington, P., Frank, A., & Carson, R. (1992). Adult adjustment among high school graduates with mild disabilities. *Exceptional Children, 59,* 221–233.

Wagner, M. (1995). Outcomes for youths with serious emotional disturbance in secondary school and early adulthood. *The Future of Children, 5,* 90–112.

Background, Challenges, and
Key Concepts in the Lives and Struggles
of Adults with Mild Cognitive Limitations

The Hidden Majority of Individuals with Mental Retardation and Developmental Disabilities

Robert B. Edgerton

As we reflect on the lives of those older adults who, many years ago, may have been called *six-hour retarded children*—"children and youth who were identified as being 'educably mentally retarded (EMR)' only during the school hours and only during their school lives" (President's Committee on Mental Retardation, 1969)—perhaps the most sobering realization is that the majority of these individuals are not cited in the research literature nor are they known to the mental retardation/developmental disabilities service delivery system. Some of these individuals may once have received such services only to drop out of sight later. Others appear never to have been served at all. Although it might be comforting to conclude that these people have no need for support services because they are doing so well in life, such a conclusion is unwarranted. Everyone needs social supports, whether from family, friends, or human services agencies, and the available research record, though incomplete, indicates that most people who might once have been considered "six-hour retarded children" are in need of a wide array of social supports. Some of these people have "disappeared" into community life as the "six-hour retarded child" concept would predict, but many others have not and continue to have unmet needs. To understand these needs, it is necessary to explore the overall life course of these individuals as well as critical transition periods in their lives.

All human societies have recognized life transitions, such as birth, puberty, marriage, and death, which usually are marked with dramatic rituals. Many societies also use rituals to reinforce the importance of other life transitions, such as adulthood, pregnancy, and old age. In 1909, Arnold van Gennep referred to such transition rituals as *rites of passage,* a term that has remained in use in social science and popular parlance ever since. The longevity of the term is not surprising once one encounters some of the vivid descriptions of rites of passage that occur so often in the ethnographic literature. Puberty rites, for example, may involve hours of singing, dancing, and drinking intoxicating beverages before initiates—males and females alike—engage in various acts or undergo

3

penile or clitoral circumcision, followed by a period in which young men are licensed to engage in violence and young women in various forms of seclusion. Soon after this ritual, both males and females display new dress and are publicly acknowledged to have attained a new status. Funerals and weddings can be equally dramatic.

Although life transitions in the contemporary United States seldom are marked by such elaborate and dramatic rituals as those used in many other parts of the world, various rituals do acknowledge births, school graduations, turning 21, marriages, deaths, and other changes involved with life achievements and aging. Some of these transition rituals are grand, whereas others, although important and stressful, pass without ceremonial recognition. Job changes, residential moves, and becoming a grandparent are transitions that seldom are marked by ritual even though they may entail significant and lasting life changes.

In the past, individuals with developmental disabilities, even those who had only minor impairments, experienced few life transitions. For those individuals who were institutionalized, and many were, there was often only one major transition—from the home to the "colony," "hospital," or "school." Most of these individuals never left these institutions, in which crowding, filth, stench, misery, and mistreatment, including surgical sterilization, were permanent features of their forgotten lives. These individuals never experienced paid employment and never married or had children; instead, they faced loneliness, deprivation, and eventually a death unmarked by ritual or remembrance.

Conditions such as these began to change in the 1960s, and today very few individuals with mental retardation and/or developmental disabilities live in large residential facilities. The few large facilities that still exist are much more humane than the majority of the earlier institutions. Since deinstitutionalization, the great majority of individuals with mild mental retardation have lived with their parents or relatives or in small group homes or supervised apartments. Others have lived independently. Many individuals undergo transitions from their parental home to a variety of other residential environments. These residential changes are among the most important experiences of their lives, in addition to transitions from school to a first job, from one job to another, from one social network to another, and from one intimate relationship to another or to none at all.

Even before deinstitutionalization created more typical life opportunities for most individuals with mild mental retardation, many such individuals were released from large state institutions because of overcrowding, regardless of whether they were thought to be capable of living successfully outside of the institutions. During World War I, Walter B. Fernald, nationally prominent superintendent of a major institution for individuals with mild mental retardation in Massachusetts, predicted that 85% of the men and women released earlier from a large residential institution would be rehospitalized or imprisoned. When his follow-up study of these people found that only 34.4% of the men and 40.8%

of the women had met either of these fates, he was so shocked that he delayed publication of his findings for 2 years (Goldstein, 1964).

Subsequent follow-up studies also found that high percentages of individuals who were released from institutions made positive adaptations to community living. This finding led one prominent author of a meta-analysis of such studies to conclude that "the most consistent and outstanding finding of all follow-up studies is the high proportion of the adult retarded who achieve satisfactory adjustments, by whatever criteria are employed" (Cobb, 1972, p. 145). Two years later, another large study found that the mean success rate—defined as no reinstitutionalization—of 9,116 formerly institutionalized individuals with mental retardation was 69% (McCarver & Craig, 1974). Despite occasional dissenting studies that found high rates of reinstitutionalization (Begab, 1978; MacMillan, 1977), including one study that found a reinstitutionalization rate of nearly 66% (Windle, 1962), and despite serious flaws in the methodology of follow-up studies, the literature came to assert that most individuals with mental retardation who were once in institutions were, in fact, capable of successful adaptation to community environments. Unfortunately, no variables that predicted success or failure were discovered, and differential long-term success of seemingly comparable cohorts went unexplained. Even today, there is no agreement among follow-up studies about why some individuals do well in their transitions from institutions to community living while others fare badly (Edgerton, 1981, 1983). Because almost all of these studies collected their data at only one point in time, they were unable to assess the often volatile life changes that individuals who had been deinstitutionalized experienced as they attempted to adapt to the new and changing demands of community living.

For most individuals who were once institutionalized, the transition from institution to community was so traumatic that there is little wonder so many of them failed to adapt to life outside the institution in which they typically had spent many years without either adequate education or vocational training. Many of these individuals were institutionalized originally because of a history of troubled community adaptation, usually involving various kinds of delinquency. When they returned to community environments after years of institutional life that offered little or no preparation for independent living, they rarely had strong support from family members, friends, or other benefactors. To make matters worse, most could only afford to live and work in deteriorated, high-crime neighborhoods. Under these conditions, it is surprising that most of these typically nonliterate, impoverished people with poor social support systems and little understanding of what was expected of them in community environments did not fail. Twenty-five percent of individuals with mild mental retardation who were released from Pacific State Hospital in Pomona, California, in the 1950s were incarcerated or reinstitutionalized within a decade; for those individuals who remained in the community, holding jobs or finding a spouse to support them were goals beyond their reach. These individuals frequently

despaired of the lives they led, and all but a few of them would have been reinstitutionalized had they not been befriended and assisted by someone in the
community who knew of their plight (Edgerton, 1967).

The second most crucial and traumatic transition, following the transition
from institution to community, became the one from school—usually special
education classes—to work. The young people making this transition had IQ
scores similar to those of individuals who had been institutionalized; however,
they had received better education, usually had more supportive families, and
often had received some vocational training. Even before the much improved
provisions of vocational training, residential placement and supervision, and
supported work programs, graduates of special classes sometimes made re-
markably positive transitions to community life. This success could be attrib-
uted in some cases to excellent social support and in others to a booming
economy. Often, the reasons were unexpected. For example, a 40-year follow-
up of individuals with mental retardation who had graduated from special
classes in San Francisco found that they had established stable marriages,
had enjoyed job success, and generally had become solid citizens living in
working-class neighborhoods. The researchers in this study suggested that this
extraordinary level of success came about in part as a result of a growing economy but also because these individuals were the children of recent immigrants
who believed in arranged marriages. The parents of these individuals arranged
to have their children marry individuals without disabilities; with this balance
of social competence and the long-term investment of family support, these
individuals prospered (Ross, Begab, Dondis, Giampiccolo, & Meyers, 1985).

Another study of the postschool adjustment of 210 graduates with mild
cognitive limitations that took place in a New England industrial city during
World War II found that 54% of the graduates were in active service in the military, 36% were employed, and only 4% had been reinstitutionalized. However,
upon further investigation it was discovered that only one of the employed individuals had been employed 100% of the time, and 25% of the sample appeared
in court to answer criminal charges. Fifty percent of these individuals were
repeat offenders (McKeon, 1946).

This latter study suggests that a more probing look at the school-to-work
transition may reveal that the apparent success of the individuals making the
transition can be illusory. Two studies conducted in the late 1970s in Los Angeles illustrated this point. One sample was drawn from Caucasian graduates with
mild cognitive limitations who lived in a middle-class suburb; the other sample
consisted of African American graduates with mild cognitive limitations from
the inner city, who were matched in age and IQ with the first sample. These
samples were studied for a 2-year period by intensive, repeated ethnographic
procedures. Preliminary studies suggested strongly that both samples had made
outstanding vocational adaptations, had achieved meaningful social lives, and
were not a danger to others in their communities. Further research told another

story. When the research concluded, it was possible to say that 18 of the 48 individuals in the Caucasian sample were, in fact, model citizens. The majority of these individuals were married and lived independently. They experienced little strife or unhappiness in their lives and enjoyed good social support from their families, friends, and agencies. However, 20 individuals from this group lived much more troubled lives. Their residential and vocational status was problematic, and their behavior often was deviant and even criminal. In addition to several psychotic episodes that attracted public attention, these men and women sometimes used drugs, drove while intoxicated (although only one was arrested), engaged in physical violence, threatened suicide, drove without licenses, used obscene language in public places, committed petty theft, and often engaged in sexually deviant and potentially troublesome sexual behavior. However, despite the numerous offenses, only three police citations were issued, and none of the 20 individuals were incarcerated (Edgerton, 1981).

The remaining 10 members of the sample were even more frequent and serious offenders who engaged in significant theft, carried knives, assaulted strangers in public places, drank to excess then drove, engaged in fraud, and threatened sexual assault on minors. Because California state policy called for the problem behavior of individuals with mental retardation to be addressed outside of the law whenever possible, only one individual served jail time (3 days), two individuals received probated sentences, and two individuals were only fined despite the seriousness of their crimes. Thus, although the entire group of 48 people remained in community environments, a superficial study of their behavior might have judged them successes when, in actuality, many of these individuals encountered numerous problems (Edgerton, 1983).

The companion study of African American special school graduates told a somewhat different story. Even though these individuals with mild mental retardation lived in deteriorated, high-crime neighborhoods, their transitions from school to work went more smoothly than did those of their Caucasian counterparts. These individuals had more marriages, closer family relationships, and more friendships. They displayed significantly less antisocial behavior and exhibited better job performance. Few of the individuals received social services, and almost all of them had strong support from networks of kin and friends (Mitchell-Kernan & Tucker, 1984).

Twelve of these African American men and women exhibited such striking social competence that it was many months before fieldworkers, themselves African American, would believe that the IQ scores of these individuals were in the 60s and that these individuals were not "controls" added to the sample for comparative purposes. After months of close company with these individuals, the fieldworkers finally learned that they were not "six-hour retarded children" at all; these people knew all too well that other people considered them "slow," and, moreover, they still suffered acutely from their own knowledge that they could not learn as quickly or as well as their siblings and friends. The psychological pain of this realization remained the dominant—yet secret—reality of their lives (Koegel & Edgerton, 1984).

Despite the implications of studies such as these that culture, race, and, gender may play a central role in the school-to-work transition, little research has focused on these factors. A study by Botuck, Levy, and Rimmerman (1996) once again has brought to our attention the need for such research. These researchers studied the outcomes of 133 youth with mental retardation and severe learning disabilities in school-to-work training for 1 year. They discovered that although 46% of the males successfully found employment for at least 30 consecutive days, only 1% of the females did so. The authors could not explain this dramatic difference; however, they believe that parents' fears that employment might leave their daughters vulnerable to unwanted sexual advances from co-workers as well as fears of employer gender discrimination might be factors. Botuck et al. also called for assertiveness and self-advocacy training for young women in such programs.

Another study, which reviewed data from the National Longitudinal Transition Study of Special Education Students, sampled 8,000 youth from 300 school districts between the ages of 15 and 21 years who were making the transition from school to work. A range of individual differences was found in what students needed to make this transition successfully. No one principle could be identified that helped all students meet their needs (Wagner & Blackorby, 1996). In 1995, Heal and Rusch used the same data set to examine the way in which the postschool employment status of adolescents with disabilities is predicted by "personal characteristics"—age, gender, ethnicity, disability type, living skills, and academic skills. Heal and Rusch's analysis suggested that these personal characteristics are the greatest predictors of employment, followed by family characteristics. They found that school programs make a small but statistically significant contribution to predicting employment. White males who were not receiving public aid and who did not require special transportation had the highest employment rates. Heal and Rusch found that vocational training did not increase employment rates; however, on-the-job training did enhance employment for youth with disabilities (Phelps & Hanley-Maxwell, 1997).

QUALITY OF LIFE

Obviously, assessing the life experiences of individuals with mild cognitive limitations during transition periods is a difficult undertaking—one that usually requires prolonged, detailed study if it is to provide useful information. The kinds of outcome measures discussed thus far—employment status, alcohol use, marriage status, antisocial behavior, and so forth—are relatively simplistic measures compared with an individual's overall quality of life. The relatively recent attempts to assess and, where possible, improve the quality of life for individuals with mental retardation are a positive development for policy planners and service providers. The field now believes that various dimensions, components, and measures indicate a person's quality of life. Briefly, these include social relationships and types of interaction, employment, self-determination and autonomy, recreation and leisure, personal competence and independent living skills, residential living conditions, community integration, social status, social acceptance, physical and material well-being, financial security, and sense of subjective well-being. Many studies have assessed a number of these measures, particularly recreational and leisure activities; however, other measures rarely have been examined. Oddly enough, the study of financial security has been neglected. Studies focused on the quality of life of individuals with mental retardation seldom are comparable to one another and are never exhaustive, but the accumulation of research on this topic has been helpful in sensitizing individuals who develop policy and deliver services to take a more holistic view of the lives of the individuals they serve.

As more and more service delivery agencies attempt to assess the changing quality of life of the individuals they serve, especially those undergoing transitions such as the shift from school to work, some cautionary remarks become necessary. First, the temptation to construct an ideal set of guidelines for an optimal quality of life should be resisted. Although a few conditions such as financial security and good health probably are valued by everyone, no single set of standards for quality living can possibly gratify all individuals with mental retardation because of their varied races, genders, cultures, family backgrounds, and individual preferences. Research has found wide variation in what individuals regard as essential to enhancing the quality of their lives. For example, for some individuals it may be independent living, for other individuals it may be a job, and for still others it may be marriage and parenthood.

Indeed, even if it could be agreed that individual choice should be the basis of any action taken to enhance the quality of individuals' lives, some individuals would not have the knowledge to choose wisely and others might be too timid to try. The cost of making individuals aware of all reasonable aspects of a choice—even a choice as obvious as visiting residential environments that might be available—would quickly become prohibitive. Therefore, although individuals with mental retardation should be involved in planning the best possible quality of life arrangements for a transition such as school to work, it is likely that many mid-course adjustments will prove desirable. The task of research will be to determine more precisely how the subjective experience of life changes during such transitions influences an individual's ability to adapt to new social roles and expectations.

My own research into the lives of young people with mental retardation who are attempting to make transitions into community environments has shown again and again that the majority of these individuals have great difficulty adapting to the demands of independent or semi-independent living. The demands of the workplace, in which a host of new social skills and forms of self-discipline are necessary, are especially difficult for these individuals. Individuals with mental retardation typically have great difficulty establishing close social relationships, especially relationships that offer them support and enhance their self-esteem. They complain of loneliness in their leisure time and frustration on the job. Transportation and health care also are recurrent problems, and few individuals are satisfied by their living arrangements. As a result, their lives are turbulent and often unhappy. As time passes, the social and vocational competence of those individuals who manage to remain in community environments tend to improve; these individuals make some friends or, at least, acquaintances and express greater satisfaction with their lives.

Because life satisfaction is what individuals ultimately seek and should be what a better quality of life provides, it is important to look more closely at the relationship between changing life circumstances and individuals' sense of well-being. First, some terminology issues need to be addressed. *Happiness* usually is used to refer to transient affective states resulting from pleasant life experiences and events. *Life satisfaction* refers to the degree to which one's life expectations are being met, whereas *well-being,* or *subjective well-being* as it is often called, refers to a person's global evaluation of the quality of his or her life (George, 1979).

In every national survey taken in the United States, a majority of the respondents have placed themselves in a *pretty happy* or *very happy* category; in fact, typically only 10% of samples consistently report unhappiness. From 1946 to 1989, Americans also have expressed a positive level of global subjective well-being. The same pattern emerges around most of the world; only people in Russia or in desperately poor countries such as India and the Dominican Republic fall below the mid-point of well-being (Keith, 1986). People with severe disabilities also typically report satisfaction with their lives (Diener & Diener, 1996). Findings such as these raise serious questions about the relationship between life events and circumstances and people's sense of well-being. Despite the fact that the loss of a job or a loved one can bring about great sadness and dissatisfaction with life, most people rebound from such trauma with remarkable resilience (Lazarus & Lannier, 1979).

Other research suggests that environmental events or circumstances predict well-being less well than do internal psychological dispositions, or *temperament,* for want of a better term. Several major longitudinal studies both in the United States and in Europe have reported that the way in which a person responds to well-being measures is primarily dependent on attributes of the individual, not on his or her environment. According to Ormel, who conducted a longitudinal study in Holland, neither improved nor worsened life circumstances seem to have any significant effects on the amount of distress or satisfaction an individual reports (Ormel, 1983).

In 1987, Costa, McCrae, and Zonderman compared the responses to a set of questions given by 4,492 American men and women early in the 1980s with their responses to the same questions given a decade earlier. The authors found that there was great similarity between the answers. The predictors of life satisfaction responses in the early 1980s study were not age, sex, race, or life events such as job loss or divorce but instead were the answers to the same questions given 10 years earlier. Other investigators also have found that people rapidly adjust to either negative events (Palmore, Cleveland, Nowlin, Ramm, & Siegler, 1979) or positive events (Brickman & Campbell, 1971; Campbell, Converse, & Rogers, 1976). This strongly suggests that temperament, not life events, affects an individual's satisfaction with life.

Previous longitudinal research with adults with mild mental retardation has produced similar findings. Although major life events, either positive or negative, brought about changes in affect and expressed well-being, these changes were short-lived. People who expressed positive affect earlier in our studies tended to do so throughout life, despite negative life events; individuals given to expressing negative affect did so even when their lives took a positive turn (Edgerton, 1990). Nevertheless, it was abundantly clear that negative life events, such as the loss of a job, a residence, or a support network, could dramatically impair a person's community adaptation, sometimes seriously lessening that person's ability to remain in community environments. It is also clear that expressions of life satisfaction can be domain-specific. Someone can express positive satisfaction with residential well-being but negative feelings about social relationships.

There is a need for longitudinal research on the interaction among various life events, individuals' backgrounds and abilities, dimensions of quality of life, and expressions of subjective well-being. This research calls for methods that allow us to observe how individuals behave in their natural environments as well as what they say about their lives.

This takes us back to the role of social support systems during the life course of individuals who may have been "six-hour retarded children." It has been argued that the transition from a large institution to community living is so challenging and so traumatic that few have succeeded without some form of support. A place to live, a job, transportation, health care—these are obvious and key needs that seldom can be managed without some assistance. However, finding friends, reading an official-looking letter, dealing with governmental agencies, or locating vocational training also are important needs. Individuals who live with relatives or residential caregivers find that not only is their present day organized, arranged, and regimented by other people, but so is their future. What is more, there is very little that individuals with mental retardation can do in most of these living arrangements to make a significant difference in their lives. As years of research in community residential facilities have made painfully clear, the lives of individuals with mental retardation are predictable. However, the individuals I have studied who live beyond the everyday control of relatives or human services delivery system personnel are largely free of such constraints. Quite literally, they can be said to have shaped the course of their own destiny, albeit sometimes a meandering, largely unpredictable one. What they become when they reach their fifties and sixties seems to be far more a product of their own internal resources, as these have been nurtured and expressed over time, than of the influence of major life events.

For the individuals I have studied, the same cognitive limitations that impaired them as children have persisted into adulthood, indeed into old age. When they were retested, these individuals did not have appreciably higher IQ scores, and they did not learn to read and write, increase their arithmetic skills, or utilize abstract concepts.

However, the *social competence* of all of the individuals in the research samples I have studied has improved as the individuals have aged. With the passage of time, communicative and interpersonal skills, in addition to the skills necessary for success in the workplace and appropriateness in public places, improve. The individuals learn how to control their emotions, use public transportation, shop more efficiently, better cope with health professionals and bureaucracies, and find the help of others when they need it. Some of these skills are evident when people with mild mental retardation are in their thirties and forties; however, as these people grow still older, they tend to become even more competent in social interactions. In fact, when they are in their sixties, they not only are more competent in absolute terms than they ever have been before, but they also seem to be relatively more competent when compared with individuals without disabilities than at any prior period in their lives. No doubt this is the result of continuing accumulation of experience and confidence, but it also appears to occur because at this age, others expect less of them. A person in his or her mid-sixties may walk and talk more slowly, appear befuddled at times, make mistakes in a market, dress shabbily, and forget things without attracting attention. In a very real sense, when individuals with mental retardation reach their sixties, they enter a niche in which their age normalizes their behavior.

Unlike the young adult African Americans we studied who often were very much involved in the everyday activities of their community, the young adult, middle-class European Americans in our research samples tended to have relationships only with other individuals with mental retardation and tended to be isolated from community activities. Now, those aging individuals who live with their parents or in community residential facilities are even more isolated. Many of these individuals never meet anyone who is not a family member, a caregiver, or a fellow resident. Those who once attended sheltered workshops may have had many friends; however, most workshops now "retire" their older workers, especially since the introduction of competitive contracts, which call for more productive workers. As a result, many of these people are quite lonely. However, aging individuals with mental retardation who have continued to live independently have become more and more involved in community life. Despite their advanced age, they walk around their neighborhoods and chat with merchants, waitresses, and acquaintances. They ride buses, sometimes using them to travel extensively. They all have acquaintances and friends and some have lovers or spouses who do not have mental retardation. Also, all of the individuals help other people with small gifts, loans of money, useful chores, or volunteer work through churches or social agencies. All in all, their lives are as varied and full as one would expect of low-income people their age.

Despite the various indications that many people with mental retardation can experience striking improvements in their life satisfaction, social competence, and quality of life as they grow older, the process of aging calls for increased social support. Years of experience help to transform individuals with cognitive limitations into satisfied "seniors," but aging also can bring ill health. Preventive health care is a major issue for service provision and policy development. Chronic illness that leads to years of suffering and dependency may be sadder still. Several of the people whose lives we have been following have suffered serious illness and physical debilitation. Others have died from preventable disorders.

All but a few seniors with mental retardation lack the financial resources to pay for health care that is not covered by Medicare or Medicaid. For example, for individuals younger than age 65 who are dependent solely on California's Medicaid program—Medi-Cal—finding adequate health care can be extremely difficult because almost all of California's Medi-Cal patients are treated by less than 4% of the state's physicians. As a result, it may be difficult for patients to determine whether a particular clinic accepts Medi-Cal or to find a nearby clinic at all. If an appropriate clinic is located, finding transportation (especially in a vast, spread-out city such as Los Angeles, where public transportation is inadequate) also can be difficult. Many of the clinics that accept Medi-Cal for low-income individuals see so many patients that histories and examinations are perfunctory; and perhaps because many of these clinics operate their own pharmacies, routine treatment often consists of the prescription of a large number of medications.

To add to the problem, for years, it has been difficult to gain access to Medi-Cal. As Romney (1990) noted, filling out a Medi-Cal application form requires the equivalent of 2 years of college. The application is 11 pages long at a minimum (there may be additional pages!), and at least 13 items of documentation must be provided. In 1986, California denied Medi-Cal to 67% of applicants for not meeting these procedural requirements. For individuals who do become eligible, Medi-Cal services are difficult to locate. In fact, less than 4% of the state's physicians are scattered throughout the neighborhoods where low-income individuals live. Even when a Medi-Cal office can be located, it is likely to be understaffed and overcrowded (Romney, 1990). The Denti-Cal program is equally limited. Individuals who are eligible for Medicare have better access to health care, but only three of the seventeen seniors in our cohort are now eligible. Several others will soon be eligible when they reach age 65, but all of the individuals will need assistance to complete the necessary forms and, of course, to deal with health care providers.

Most older adults without mental retardation have difficulties communicating with health care personnel; seniors with mental retardation are at an even greater disadvantage. Difficulties may begin even before they see a health care provider. Because many individuals with mental retardation lack an adequate vocabulary of medical terms for their symptoms, they may have difficulty explaining the nature of their complaint or understanding questions posed by a receptionist or medical aide. Most seniors with mental retardation are functionally illiterate; therefore, filling out medical history forms without help is a near impossibility. Confronted by such difficult and embarrassing problems, these older adults are likely to act as if they understand something when in fact they do not and are likely to agree with whatever may be said to avoid the embarrassment of asking for clarification. Some individuals with mental retardation are so intimidated by these challenges of communication that they avoid seeking medical care altogether.

The older adults with mental retardation whom I have followed for years typically leave their physician's offices with a number of prescriptions, instructions for their use, and various directions involving bed rest, diet, exercise, and so forth. In many cases, these instructions are either forgotten or misconstrued, and when the prescriptions are filled, few pharmacists are helpful. Now and then, a pharmacy recognizes that its customers may have cognitive limitations or may simply be illiterate. These pharmacies take care to explain how the medications should be taken. Unfortunately, most pharmacies do neither. We have seen seniors with mild mental retardation leave a pharmacy with as many as five new prescriptions and no comprehension of when or how they should be taken. The efficacy of medications that are dispensed in this manner is suspect, and the risk of unintentional overdoses or harmful drug interactions is obvious.

When funds are available, it is a relatively simple matter to provide adequate health care for older adults with mental retardation who live in community residential facilities. However, the majority of older adults with mental retardation do not live in easily identified group facilities such as these (Seltzer, Krauss, & Janicki, 1994). Like many of the older adults whose lives I have tried to document, most seniors with mental retardation live in places that are difficult to identify, where their needs for health care are far more difficult to ascertain, much less meet. More correctly, I should say that it must be *assumed* that the majority of older adults with mental retardation live like this; in reality, it is not known how many older adults with mental retardation there are in this country or where they live. Without adequate epidemiological data, we can make only the crudest of estimates about the numbers of older adults with mental retardation and their medical needs.

Even so, one way we might begin to improve health care availability is with information. If lists of health care providers located in specific neighborhoods who are willing to accept Medicare individuals could be compiled and made available in places where older people with mental retardation might run across them (e.g., bus stops, markets, pharmacies), some of these individuals who are literate might be encouraged to call. Also, if receptionists were friendly and trained to provide easy directions to the office or clinic, more older people might have access to health care. Health care providers would have to learn to speak more simply and effectively, especially concerning the importance of complying with their instructions (a concern hardly confined to seniors with mental retardation). The availability of a visiting nurse or mobile neighborhood health vans also would be of enormous help for these individuals by providing care or transporting seniors to care providers.

Even if this admittedly optimistic scenario were played out, many older people, particularly those who do not read, would not benefit. For them, the best, and perhaps only, solution would be the creation of a national network of neighborhood-based clinics (e.g., seniors' health clinics) that would become visible centers in which older individuals knew that they and people such as them could receive low-cost sympathetic care or, at least, receive information about where to find such care. Daytime care programs could serve this latter need. There is a long-established precedent in the United States for local, state, and federal funding of free clinics when there is a clear threat to public health. The polio vaccination campaign is one example; the current effort to control drug-resistant tuberculosis among new immigrants to the United States is another. The threat that untreated seniors pose is not one of infectious diseases but of the soaring cost of long-term care in nursing homes.

In addition to the obvious goals of reducing mortality and enhancing functional health, health policy should address the need to prevent chronic disability that could lead to costly long-term care and reduced quality of life (Janicki & MacEachron, 1984). The cost of long-term care varies regionally; however, 10 years ago, the national average annual cost was more than $20,000 per person (Garber, 1988), and it is surely higher now. In 1985, more than 40,000 individuals with mental retardation were in nursing homes (Lakin, Hill, & Anderson, 1991). The need to develop programs capable of preventing chronic disability has been widely recognized, both for older individuals with mental retardation and for older adults in general (Crocker, 1992; Lavizzo-Mourey & Diserens, 1990). In this regard, the need to improve Medicare and Medicaid also has been widely recognized (Feder, 1990), as has the need for lower cost, community-based, long-term care facilities (Kastner, Walsh, & Criscione, 1997; Weissert, Cready, & Pawelak, 1988). Improvements in health care education are clearly necessary, too (Gambert, Liebeskind, & Cameron, 1987), as is a greater integration of the generic network of programs and services that are available to aging individuals (Seltzer, Krause, Litchfield, & Modlish, 1989).

If greater public funding were made available, much more could be accomplished to implement the Older Americans Act Amendments of 1987 (PL 100-175) and the Developmental Disabilities Assistance and Bill of Rights Act Amendments of 1987 (PL 100-146), but greater support from the private sector also is needed. Monies from both sources are necessary to provide programs and systems, but if older individuals with mental retardation are to have success in gaining access to these systems and programs, many will require the personal assistance of advocates or benefactors. Those individuals who live with relatives or in group homes typically have advocates who assist them with their health care, but those who live more independently may not. Health problems that could be neglected safely earlier in life might now require hospitalization, and if a prolonged convalescence were necessary, the result could be a major degradation in the individual's quality of life as well as cost to the public (Pulcini & Howard, 1997).

Some older individuals with mental retardation are able to maintain relationships with advocates without assistance, but others cannot. These individuals would benefit greatly if there were organized efforts by religious or civic groups, charities, or governmental agencies to provide advocacy services (Champlin, 1991). Whether these advocates or benefactors are volunteers or salaried, their duties would involve making periodic telephone calls and visits to monitor the health status of specified older adults, transporting these individuals to health care providers when the need arises, assisting with patient–doctor communication, supervising convalescence, and so forth. Without the availability of advocate-benefactors, many older individuals with mental retardation will not be able to utilize health care systems no matter how much they may be improved.

Without thorough epidemiological research—something unlikely to happen due to its cost—it is not possible to identify or provide health care to many of the "hidden majority." However, because the available epidemiological research clearly indicates that mild mental retardation is most prevalent among low-income populations, improved health care for the poor will very likely help large numbers of individuals with mild mental retardation. Improving the quality of life for low-income populations might also reduce the number of individuals who have mental retardation.

REFERENCES

Begab, M.J. (1978, August 21). In Wyatt v. Hardin C.A., 3195-N. V. S. District Court, Middle District of Alabama, Deposition of Dr. Michael J. Begab.

Botuck, S., Levy, J.M., & Rimmerman, A. (1996). Gender-related differences in placement rates of young adults with mental retardation. *International Journal of Rehabilitation Research, 19,* 259–263.

Brickman, P., & Campbell, D.T. (1971). Hedonic relativism and planning the good society. In M.H. Appley (Ed.), *Adaptation level theory: A symposium* (pp. 287–302). New
York: Academic Press.

Campbell, A., Converse, P.E., & Rogers, W.L. (1976). *The quality of American life: Perceptions, evaluations, and satisfactions.* New York: Russell Sage Foundation.

Champlin, L. (1991). Eldercare's goal: Integrate health, social needs. *Geriatrics, 46,*
67–70.

Cobb, H. (1972). *The forecast of fulfillment: A review of research on predictive assessment of the adult retarded for social and vocational adjustment.* New York: Teachers
College Press.

Costa, P.T., McCrae, Jr., R.R., & Zonderman, A.B. (1987). Environmental and disposi-
tional influences on well-being: Longitudinal follow-up of an American national
sample. *British Journal of Psychology, 78,* 299–306.

Crocker, A.C. (1992). Expansion of the health-care delivery system. In, L. Rowitz (Ed.),
Mental retardation in the year 2000 (pp. 163–182). New York: Springer-Verlag.

Developmental Disabilities Assistance and Bill of Rights Act Amendments of 1987, PL
100-146, 42 U.S.C. §§ 6000 *et seq.*

Diener, E., & Diener, C. (1996). Most people are happy. *Psychological Science, 7,*
181–185.

Edgerton, R.B. (1981). Crime, deviance and normalization: Reconsidered. In R.H. Bruininks, C.E. Meyers, B.B. Sigford, & K.C. Lakin (Eds.), *Deinstitutionalization and
community adjustment of mentally retarded people* (Monograph No. 4, pp. 145–166).
Washington, DC: American Association on Mental Deficiency.

Edgerton, R.B. (1983). Failure in community adaptation: The relativity of assessment.
In K. Kernan, M. Begab, & R.B. Edgerton (Eds.), *Environments and behavior: The
adaptation of mentally retarded persons* (pp. 123–143). Baltimore: University Park
Press.

Edgerton, R.B. (1990). Quality of life from a longitudinal research perspective. In R.L.
Schalock (Ed.), *Quality of life: Perspectives and issues* (pp. 149–160). Washington,
DC: American Association on Mental Retardation.

Edgerton, R.B. (1992). *The cloak of competence: Stigma in the lives of the mentally retarded* (Rev. ed.). Berkeley: University of California Press.

Feder, J. (1990). Health care of the disadvantaged: The elderly. *Journal of Health Politics, Policy and Law, 15,* 259–269.

Gambert, S.R., Liebeskind, S., & Cameron, D. (1987). Lifelong preventative health care
for elderly persons with disabilities. *Journal of The Association for Persons with
Severe Handicaps, 12,* 292–296.

Garber, A.M. (1988). Cost-containment and financing the long-term care of the elderly.
Journal of the American Geriatric Society, 36, 355–361.

George, L.K. (1979). The Happiness syndrome: Methodological and substantive issues
in the study of social psychological well-being in adulthood. *The Gerontologist, 19,*
210–216.

Goldstein, H. (1964). Social and occupational adjustment. In H.A. Stevens & R. Heber
(Eds.), *Mental retardation: A review of research* (pp. 214–258). Chicago: University
of Chicago Press.

Heal, L.W., & Rusch, F.R. (1995). Predicting employment for students who leave special education high school programs. *Exceptional Children, 61,* 472–487.

Janicki, M.P., & MacEachron, A.E. (1984). Residential, health, and social service needs of elderly developmentally disabled persons. *The Gerontologist, 24*,128–137.

Kastner, T.A., Walsh, K.K., & Criscione, T. (1997). Overview and implications of Medicaid managed cared for people with developmental disabilities. *Mental Retardation, 35*, 257–269.

Keith, K.D. (1986). Measuring quality of life across cultures: Issues and challenges. In R.L. Schalock (Ed.), *Quality of life: Vol. 1. Conceptualization and measurement* (pp. 73–82). Washington, DC: American Association on Mental Retardation.

Kiernan, W.E., & Stark, J.A. (Eds.). (1986). *Pathways to employment for adults with developmental disabilities.* Baltimore: Paul H. Brookes Publishing Co.

Koegel, P., & Edgerton, R.B. (1984). Black "'six-hour retarded' children" as young adults. In R.B. Edgerton (Ed.), *Lives in process: Mildly retarded adults in a large city* (pp. 60–69). Washington, DC: American Association on Mental Retardation.

Lakin, K.C., Hill, B.K., & Anderson, D.J. (1991). Persons with mental retardation in nursing homes in 1977 and 1985. *Mental Retardation, 29*, 25–33.

Lavizzo-Mourey, R., & Diserens, D. (1990). Preventative care for the elderly. *Occupational Medicine, 5*, 827–835.

Lazarus, R., & Lannier, R. (1979). Stress related transactions between person and environment. In L. Pervin & M. Lewis (Eds.), *Perspectives in international psychology* (pp. 142–156). New York: Plenum.

MacMillan, D.L. (1977). *Mental retardation in school and society.* Boston: Little, Brown.

McCarver, R.B., & Craig, E.M. (1974). Placement of the retarded in the community: Prognosis and outcome. In N.R. Ellis (Ed.), *International review of research in mental retardation* (pp. 146–159). New York: Academic Press.

McKeon, R.M. (1946). Mentally retarded boys in wartime. *Mental Hygiene, 30*, 47–55.

Mitchell-Kernan, C., & Tucker, M.B. (1984). The social structures of mildly mentally retarded Afro-Americans: Gender comparisons. In R.B. Edgerton (Ed.), *Lives in process: Mildly retarded adults in a large city* (pp. 150–166). Washington, DC: American Association on Mental Retardation.

Older Americans Act Amendments of 1987, PL 100-175, 42 U.S.C. §§ 6000 *et seq.*

Ormel, J. (1983). Neuroticism and well-being inventories: Measuring traits or states? *Psychological Medicine, 72*, 165–176.

Palmore, E.B., Cleveland, Jr., W.P., Nowlin, J.B., Ramm, D., & Siegler, I.D. (1979). Stress and adaptation in later life. *Journal of Gerontology, 34*, 841–851.

Phelps, L.A. & Hanley-Maxwell, C. (1997). School-to-work transitions for youth with disabilities: A review of outcomes and practices. *Review of Educational Research, 67*(2), 197–226.

President's Committee on Mental Retardation. (1969). *The six hour retarded child.* Washington, DC: U.S. Government Printing Office.

Pulcini, J., & Howard, A.M. (1997). Framework for analyzing health care models serving adults with mental retardation and other developmental disabilities. *Mental Retardation, 35*, 209–217.

Romney, B. (1990). *Code blue: The Medi-Cal emergency.* San Francisco: The West Coast Regional Office of Consumers Union.

Ross, R.T., Begab, M.J., Dondis, E.H., Giampiccolo, Jr., J.S., & Meyers, C.E. (1985). *Lives of the mentally retarded: A forty year follow-up study.* Stanford, CT: Stanford University Press.

Seltzer, M.M., Krauss, M.W., & Janicki, M.P. (Eds.). (1994). *Life course perspectives on adulthood and aging.* Washington, DC: American Association on Mental Retardation.

Seltzer, M.M., Krauss, M.W., Litchfield, L.C., & Modlish, N.J.K. (1989). Utilization of aging network services by elderly persons with mental retardation. *The Gerontologist, 29,* 234–238.

Wagner, M.M., & Blackorby, J. (1996). Transition from high school to work or college: How special education students fare. *The Future of Children, 6*(1), 103–120.

Weissert, W.G., Cready, C.M., & Pawelak, J.E. (1988). The past and future of home- and community-based long-term care. *The Milbank Quarterly, 66,* 309–388.

Windle, C.D. (1962). Prognosis of mental subnormals. Monograph Supplement to *American Journal of Mental Retardation, 66*(5) 213–217.

2

Life at the Margins

Intellectual, Demographic, Economic, and Social Circumstances of Adults with Mild Cognitive Limitations

Alexander J. Tymchuk, K. Charlie Lakin, and Ruth Luckasson

Despite increased recognition that adults with mild cognitive limitations are at heightened societal risk because of an absence of supports, there has been no systematic effort to examine and address the issues that confront them. Some critical issues that should be considered to develop a systematic approach are presented in this chapter. This chapter also presents background information regarding what is known about the lives of individuals with mild cognitive limitations and suggests a number of strategies to facilitate the development of support systems for individuals with mild cognitive limitations and ways to implement these strategies.

SIGNIFICANT STRIDES HAVE BEEN MADE IN THE DISABILITIES FIELD

Since 1975, significant developments have occurred within the disabilities field. In addition to the progress that has been made within the education system (e.g., Education for All Handicapped Children Act [PL 94-142]; Individuals with Disabilities Education Act of 1990 [IDEA; PL 101-476]; IDEA Amendments of 1991 [PL 102-119]; IDEA Amendments of 1997 [PL 105-17]), progress includes the passage and continuing implementation of the Americans with Disabilities Act (ADA) of 1990 (PL 101-336) and an increased emphasis on self-actualization, individual autonomy, and self-determination (Tymchuk, 1997; Wehmeyer & Metzler, 1995) by attempts to ensure full participatory citizenship and application of protections (Conley, Luckasson, & Bouthilet, 1992; Lyall, Holland, & Collins, 1995) and through continuing evolution of the self-advocacy

The writing of this chapter was supported in part by grants from SHARE, Inc., The California Wellness Foundation, and the Strauss Foundation and from The Entertainment Industry Foundation to the first author. This support is appreciated. The authors wish to thank Shannon Sewards for her assistance in the preparation of this chapter.

movement (Hayden, Lakin, Braddock, & Smith, 1995; Miller & Keys, 1996). An increase in new explanatory models and in theoretical perspectives (Hickson, Golden, Khemka, Urv, & Yamusah, 1998) as well as an expansion of approaches to supports and living (Luckasson et al., 1992; Schalock, 1990) also have occurred. Many of these efforts, however, largely have focused on the substantial needs of individuals with severe disabilities, including individuals with moderate or severe mental retardation and the individuals' families of origin. Conversely, little attention has been given to what has been perceived as the fewer and less poignant needs of individuals with less apparent disabilities and to these individuals' families of origin as well as their own families.

OTHER STRIDES THAT HAVE POTENTIAL
TO POSITIVELY IMPACT INDIVIDUALS WITH DISABILITIES

Other developments also have occurred that have significant potential to positively impact individuals with disabilities, including individuals with less apparent disabilities and their families. Within health care, for example, these developments include advocacy for a shift from a model that emphasizes palliative care to one that increases self-health care responsibility with an emphasis on preparation, prevention, and well-being (U.S. Department of Health & Human Services, 1990, 1995, 2000); the passage and initial implementation of the Patient Self-Determination Act of 1990; and the introduction of the concept of Advanced Healthcare Directives and Durable Power of Attorney for Healthcare (Daar, Nelson, & Pone, 1995). However, none of these initiatives directly addresses the needs of people with less apparent disabilities, thus creating an oversight within these developments based on fulfillment of criteria rather than actual need. For example, whereas Healthy People 2010, a set of health promotion goals and objectives to increase the health status and life expectancy of the U.S. population, contains an entire chapter devoted to disabilities, like its predecessor, Healthy People 2000, it still does not address the needs of individuals with less apparent disabilities, particularly individuals with mild cognitive limitations (Campbell & Fedeyko, in press; U.S. Department of Health and Human Services, 2000).

SIGNIFICANT ISSUES STILL UNADDRESSED

Despite the significant progress that has been made in the disabilities and mental retardation fields, limited attention has been given to adults with mild cognitive limitations, which has placed these individuals in an increasingly vulnerable position within society. This lack of attention is not a recent phenomenon. For generations, young people with mild cognitive limitations have left school and entered the job market, participated in relationships, cared for their children, and been involved in their communities. However, the dramatic changes in the sociopolitical climate, particularly since 1990, coupled with the increased complexity and number of demands placed on people by society have emphasized the lack of preparedness of young people with mild cognitive limitations to satisfactorily respond to society's demands and to lead satisfactory lives. For these individuals and their predecessors, the longer suitable programs to address their needs are unavailable, the greater the deleterious intergenerational effects and the greater the cumulative impact on society. Also, any effort to overcome cumulative needs becomes more expensive than if the needs were properly addressed when they first arose. Therefore, it is necessary to examine alternatives to identify and provide preparatory supports for this population. Such action is required to ensure stability in the lives of these individuals by helping to prevent disruptions that have occurred in the past.

DEFINITIONS AND DESCRIPTIONS: A CONTINUING DILEMMA

A number of issues[1] exist that have contributed to the lack of attention given to adults with mild cognitive limitations. These issues relate to the rationale for and use of classification systems and associated nomenclature within the general area of disabilities (including mental retardation). The continued reliance on categorical classification systems masks the true nature of the functional needs of people. In addition, the availability of so many systems that can be used, in effect, to describe the same person over his or her life encourages discontinuity.

In order to properly address continuities in abilities over life's stages and particularly from school to adulthood, a functional approach is used[2]. Adoles-

---

[1]These confounding issues include the heavy reliance on a medical/disease model used to describe behavioral phenomena; differences in classification systems across disciplines (e.g., American Psychiatric Association), organizations (e.g., American Association on Mental Deficiency/Mental Retardation; World Health Organization), and/or service sectors (e.g., early intervention or early education, health care, education, child/adult protection, legal); historical changes in classification systems and associated nomenclature and the significant delay between those changes and their complete, consistent use within various societal groups; the variety of terms used to describe a disability as well as the criteria used for application of the term; and the variability in intervention with the people to whom the terms have been applied. Other confounding issues include the reliance on one or two dimensions taken to portray the multidimensional phenomena of living; the use of either/or and all-or-none decision rules for categorical inclusion or exclusion, thereby excluding people with similar attributes; the lack of concordance between category and life attainment; the lack of utility of current categories to describe people of all ages from infancy to old age; and most importantly, the lack of utility of categorical classifications for the development of successful functional interventions.

[2]A functional perspective has been adopted within this chapter in order to facilitate examination of the complexities of life as they pertain to individuals with mild cognitive limitations. The use of a functional approach, as opposed to a categorical approach or description, allows for an emphasis on the determination of a person's current knowledge and skills, of their learning abilities, and of the circumstances under which the person successfully learns or applies what is learned. The advantages of the functional approach are its focus on abilities rather than inabilities and its examination of the circumstances that either encourage or hamper learning. It also allows for the presentation of phenomena as continuous. These considerations allow for tailored educational

cents who had difficulty recognizing words they viewed; comprehending, re-membering, and following complicated directions; or quickly manipulating numbers and who required larger print, discrete ideas, repetition, additional time, or other adaptations to succeed academically while in school will have similar needs when they face comparable demands outside of school. Once they are out of school, some individuals with mild cognitive limitations may voluntarily shed any special education or other diagnostic label because they no longer wish to carry one. Others may no longer fulfill categorical eligibility criteria for exist-ing community-based services. In either instance, however, the learning needs of these individuals remain the same; therefore, the absence of recognition of and adaptations for the individuals' needs within the employment, health care, judicial, financial, or social services sectors or within any of the other multiple sectors of life places adults with mild cognitive limitations in jeopardy.

INCREASED VULNERABILITY

The health and welfare of individuals with mild cognitive limitations is depen-dent on the current status of public policy, economic stability, and provision of services and supports. Any change in one of these areas has a direct impact on individuals with mild cognitive limitations. Unfortunately, changes in these areas are most likely to be to the disadvantage of these individuals. This sus-ceptibility and socioecological change places individuals with mild cognitive limitations in a vulnerable and often deleterious position in life.

Shifts in Public Policies

A number of significant shifts within society have contributed substantially to the vulnerability of adults with mild cognitive limitations and their families. In response to the most immediate economic downturn, federal devolution cou-pled with changes in private enterprise have translated directly into disruption, reduction, and substantial changes in health care, education, social services, and other services for low-income groups (e.g., Breslow, 1997; Jorgensen, 1994). Significant disruption and diminution in research funding in areas of impor-tance to low-income people also have occurred. Individuals of minority status, particularly those who have recently immigrated to the United States, have been disproportionately negatively affected.

---

methods or strategies, for tailored supports, or for tailored services that fit the person's specific needs and circumstances. Other advantages to the functional approach include its applicability across all ages, all realms of living, and all performance levels. Furthermore, a functional approach diminishes the probability of occurrence of stigma often associated with being included in cate-gorical definitions.

In the continuing disengagement from a government increasingly being seen as lacking a coherent view of full citizenship, known for fragmented decision making both within and across levels, and often influenced by special interest groups, these changes have reinforced this view among many (Zigler, Kagan, & Hall, 1996). People with histories of limited social supports who live at the economic fringes of society usually are the first to have any limited existing services reduced during economic downturns and are the last to receive services or to have services reinstated, if they ever are. Invariably, the time lag between service reduction and service restitution is substantial; the effects become cumulative and intergenerational (Hollomon, Dobbins, & Scott, 1998).

Although private foundations and other organizations have begun to pool resources in order to thoughtfully mitigate the adverse consequences of the changing roles of government on people in poverty, it is unclear whether the needs of people with mild cognitive limitations have been included in these efforts. Even if they have been included, these individuals continue to struggle during the time required for these efforts to evolve. Although the total funds available from foundations are a small fraction of what were provided in the past, the role holding the greatest promise for foundations is one of catalyst.

Although limited data are available, adults with mild cognitive limitations and their families have been disproportionately adversely impacted (Tymchuk, 1999). Already faced with limited supports and services, these adults face even more limited and fragmented services, improvements in the economy notwithstanding. With a limited base of planning, decision making, coping, self-health care, or other knowledge and experiences from which to draw; with difficulty understanding and utilizing information in the formats commonly used within society; and with fewer information and acquisition skills, these adults are significantly less likely to successfully adapt to changing circumstances (Koegel & Edgerton, 1984). These adults, too, are less likely to lobby for supports on their own behalf or to have others do so for them.

Faced with the substantial demands of survival, they also are less likely to be aware of, participate in, and enjoy activities that enhance their well-being, resiliency, and satisfaction with life and that might help to mitigate future difficulties and to inoculate them against poor health or the effects of an uncertain life (e.g., Pack, Wallander, & Browne, 1998).

Significant Gaps in Resources and Services

As the nation continues to redefine its "social–contractual relationships," significant gaps in resources and services available to individuals of low socioeconomic status have emerged (DiSimone, 1996; Zigler et al., 1996). Devolution from federal to state to local governments and the time lag between transfer and implementation have led to significant and negative impacts on a broad array of service providers who have struggled to assist and ensure an evenness of supports to people of low socioeconomic class. These negative impacts have ranged from outright closure of agencies to privatization, downsizing, and reconfiguring of responsibilities across sectors to reduction in type and extent of services with modification of criteria for service inclusion or exclusion. Seeking and effectively using services under these circumstances is cumbersome and exhausting and stretches the personal resources of everyone; adults with mild cognitive limitations are affected even more than the average person (Tymchuk, 1999).

As a result of shifting public policies, gaps in resources and services, and a lack of educational preparedness, adults with mild cognitive limitations and their families have fallen even further down the economic ladder and have become increasingly at risk for homelessness (Teesson & Buhrich, 1993), inadequate physical health status, and inadequate long-term health outcomes (Bassuk et al., 1997) due to preventable diseases and disorders (Tymchuk, 1992), unintentional home injury (LaGreca & Varni, 1993), and injury from violence (Browne, 1993). They also are at an even greater risk for mental illness due to untreated or preventable behavior or psychological disorders including stress, depression, loneliness, anxiety, and substance use and abuse (Wagner, 1995). If left untreated, the presence of each of these disorders can act as a gateway to exacerbated difficulties. Individuals with mild cognitive limitations also are at heightened risk of victimization, maltreatment, and acts of violence against them (Conley et al., 1992; Lyall et al., 1995), lowered life satisfaction and living standards (Edgerton, 1984), and child removal, family disintegration, and placement of children within foster care (Glaun & Brown, 1999; Miller, 1994; Taylor et al., 1991; Tymchuk, 1996). It is unknown whether these individuals are at increased risk for committing crimes. It is known, however, that they are at increased risk for failures in the judicial system, including inadequate representation, unfair prosecution, and lack of suitable disposition. Similarly, legal doctrines such as competence and culpability are confused, misapplied, and unrecognized.

Women with mild cognitive limitations appear to be at even greater risk for inadequate physical and mental health and well-being, for being seen as incompetent as a parent (Hayman, 1990; Tymchuk & Andron, 1990) in the absence of effective supports (Carter, 1996), for lowered educational achievement (Kirby, 1997; Levine & Edgar, 1994; U.S. Department of Education, 1997), for lowered income and employment opportunities, and for lowered life satisfaction due to inadequate care, injury from violence, and powerlessness (Cruz, Price-Williams, & Andron, 1988; Doren, Bullis, & Benz, 1996; Hickson et al., 1998; Miller, 1994). In treatment, both men and women may be seen as recalcitrant or even untreatable; consequently, they are at a heightened risk for treatment being withdrawn or limited, thus increasing their difficulties as well as their risk for being seen as incompetent. In reality, difficulties in understanding and lowered facility in communication are unrecognized. All of this has resulted in *de facto* disenfranchisement.

POPULATION AND PARAMETERS

Clearly, there is a need for an encapsulation of what is meant by *mild cognitive limitation* within the *new federalism* and within the new economy (Geen, Zimmerman, Douglas, Zedlewski, & Waters, 1997). Although any estimates must utilize a functional definition, there also is a need for accurate descriptive information. At present, there are limitations to estimating the numbers and complexity of needs of adults with mild cognitive limitations of any age or within any sector of society. These limitations stem from the lack of a systematic approach that is used to describe this population, from the varieties of approaches used across governmental and service sectors in describing disabilities in general, from shifts in definitions and processes that have occurred over time, and from the delays that occur in the application of new definitions to data collection.

At present there is no single database that addresses the complexities of life for this population of individuals across their life spans. Inferences can be drawn from tangentially related databases meant for other purposes; however, this has not occurred. These databases include the Behavioral Risk Surveillance System (Centers for Disease Control, 1995a); the National Child Abuse and Neglect Data System (National Center on Child Abuse and Neglect, 1996); the National Crime Victimization Survey (U.S. Department of Justice, 1995); the National Health Interview Survey (Centers for Disease Control, 1991); the National Health Interview Survey on Disability (Centers for Disease Control, 1994); the National Longitudinal Transition Study of Special Education Students (U.S. Department of Education, 1991); the National Maternal and Infant Health Survey (U.S. Public Health Service, 1988a); the National Maternal and Infant Health Survey—Field Follow-up (U.S. Public Health Service, 1988b); the National Pediatric Trauma Registry (The Research and Training Center in Rehabilitation and Childhood Trauma, 1994); and the Youth Risk Behavior Survey (Centers for Disease Control, 1995b).

There have been several opportunities to collect more direct information, such as including a special education category on the National Maternal and Infant Health Survey; however, this has not occurred. Although databases that are more diverse are now being explored, these require cooperation and collaboration among agencies charged with these responsibilities and among groups interested in this population from the governmental and public and private professional, consumer, and entrepreneurial sectors.

Despite these limitations, however, estimates can be made regarding how many individuals actually have mild cognitive limitations and what their needs are across the life span, and descriptions can be made regarding research, programs, and policies (Baugh, Rotwein, Hakim, & Boschert, 1998; Boyle,

Decoufle, & Yeargin-Allsopp, 1994; Dunne, Asher, & Rivara, 1993). One follow-up study of youth who participated in the Metropolitan Atlanta Developmental Disabilities Study (Yeargin-Allsopp, Murphy, Oakley, & Sikes, 1992) offered an opportunity to examine a number of issues related to people with mild cognitive limitations. Recognizing issues related to the use of a normal distribution of IQ scores, population estimates can be made regarding the expected percentage of individuals who may have IQ scores that are in the mild cognitive limitation range. Examination of Figure 2.1 shows that, according to the Wechsler scales, almost 16% of IQ scores would be expected to be between 55 and 85. Although not all individuals who would score in this IQ range would require supports, this figure nonetheless can be used for projections. Viewing cognitive abilities along a range also emphasizes the continuity of abilities.

Schools

Estimates also can be made based on individuals' receipt of special education while in school. During the 1997/1998 academic year, nearly 6 million children ranging in age from 3 to 21 received special education in the United States (U.S. Department of Education, 1998). This number has increased by 60% (3.5 million) since the 1976/1977 academic year (the first year following full implementation of PL 94-142), largely because of the number of children who now are diagnosed with specific learning disabilities. In 1976/1977, 2.16% of all school-age students were served in programs for children with mental retardation, and 1.8% of students were served in programs for children with learning disabilities. By 1992/1993, however, the number of students served in programs for children with mental retardation had decreased to 1.23% of the total school population, whereas the number of students served in programs for children with learning disabilities had increased to 5.85%. This change appears to be due to the recognition that learning abilities occur on a continuum. Figure 2.2 depicts the continuum among common diagnostic categories with associated IQ ranges in juxtaposition with educational placement.

The figure of 5.85% can be used to estimate the number of children with mild cognitive disabilities (Reschly, 1996) who might be expected to exit schools with specific learning needs and to enter the job, housing, or other markets. This figure also can be used to estimate the number of individuals with mild disabilities who might appear in judicial, child protective, welfare, or other systems (Mellard, 1999; Wagner, 1995). Therefore, processes in all of these systems need to be tailored to ensure that the rights of these individuals are respected and that they understand what is expected of them in a particular situation (e.g., when accused of a crime, when reported for suspected child maltreatment, when applying for social assistance). Schools then could help their students interact with each sector while public sectors prepare to accept individual differences.

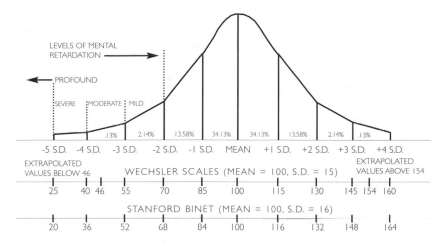

Figure 2.1.   Normal distribution of IQ scores. (Reprinted from Tymchuk, A. (1976). Intelligence: Its nature and measurement. In J. Das & D. Baine (Eds.), *Mental Retardation: A handbook for special educators.* Courtesy of Charles C Thomas, Publisher, Ltd., Springfield, Illinois)

To the present, this has been "catch as catch can," with adolescents falling through the cracks.

Dropout Rate   Youth with disabilities are reported to drop out of school at higher rates than youth without disabilities. In 1995, young adults with reported disabilities accounted for 6.9% of the population but 8.5% of the dropouts in the 16–24 age group. Youth with mental illnesses or with mental retardation were at the highest risk for dropping out. Although there was no difference between male and female students, African American students with disabilities are more likely to drop out than European American students with disabilities (U.S. Department of Education, National Center for Education Statistics, 1997).

Below Grade Expectations   Based on the National Longitudinal Survey of Youth (NLSY; *youth* being defined as students in secondary school between 1979 and 1983 between the ages of 15 and 20), students who were labeled as having mental retardation scored almost six grade levels behind grade expectations in reading and mathematics, whereas the lag across all disabilities was three grades behind expectations (Wagner, 1995). Again these data provide valuable information regarding the learning needs of at least some people exiting school. Graphically displayed in Figure 2.3, these data are startling.

Therefore, based on the NLSY, when a person with a mild disability, as defined by the school system, exits school, he or she can be expected, on average, to read between three and six grades behind his or her grade expectancy. For example, if he or she has exited school early, perhaps at ninth grade, he or she may read at a fourth-grade level. Analyses of health care, medication, consent, contractual, and financial documents as well as other public use materials

30

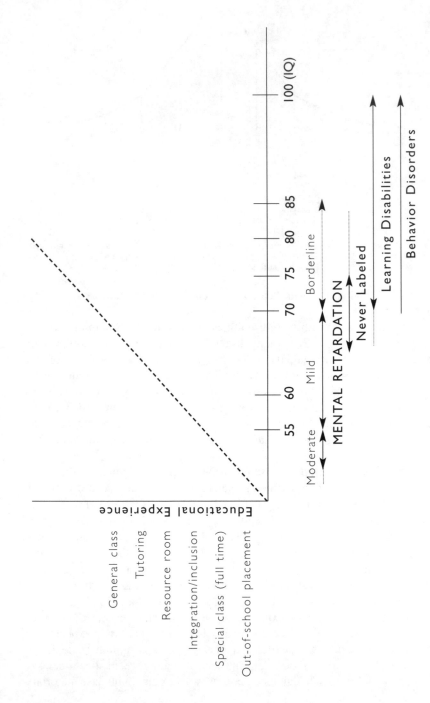

Figure 2.2.   Common diagnostic categories and associated IQ score ranges.

Reading Grade Achieved

Actual Grade Completed		12	11	10	9	8	7	6	5	4
	12				█	█	█			
	11					█	█	█		
	10							█	█	█
	9								█	█

Figure 2.3.   Reading grade obtained compared with school grade completed by students with disabilities.

have shown that these materials are written at a twelfth-grade level and are densely presented, thereby being of limited use to individuals with mild cognitive limitations (Doak, Doak, & Root, 1996).

These data tell us that a substantial number of people exit school with skills in reading recognition, reading or listening comprehension, or communication and cognitive areas that are significantly lower than those needed to use information presented across various sectors of life. For example, below average reading ability has been shown to be related to below average health status and below average use of health services (Baker et al., 1997).

At present, it is unknown whether these skills improve, remain the same, or deteriorate over an individual's life span. However, specific studies show that the impairments in reading are very real. For example, minor or expectant parents who live in poverty and are referred by child protection, disability, education, health, or other social services agencies for self- and child-health care, injury prevention, and well-being education show significantly lower than expected average reading recognition and comprehension skills based on either age or grade completed (Tymchuk, Groen, & Dolyniuk, in press). These below average reading scores correlated with below average maternal knowledge and skills and with heightened child injury risk status.

Available health information is written at complexity levels much greater than what individuals with mild cognitive limitations can effectively utilize (Davis et al., 1994). Although Healthy People 2000 and Healthy People 2010 emphasize increased self-health care responsibility with the recognition that in order to be effective, materials and processes for delivery must be matched to individual abilities, effective strategies have not yet been developed. It also is unclear to what extent managed care has attempted to develop effective strategies (McManus & Fox, 1995). When materials and processes for delivery are matched to individual abilities, the individual not only experiences increased understanding and utilization but also increased satisfaction and improved self-esteem. Presumably, these individuals also will experience improved health status and outcomes resulting in reductions in costs.

IMPLEMENTATION STRATEGIES AND OPTIONS

A number of strategies can be implemented in response to the growing recognition that the support needs of a substantial number of people with mild cognitive limitations are not being addressed.

Development of Models Mirroring the Lives of Individuals with Mild Cognitive Limitations

A need exists for the development of models of living that realistically portray the lives of people with mild cognitive limitations during these evolving and increasingly complex times. These models must consider the educational, experiential, economic, community, and cultural heterogeneity of people with mild cognitive limitations and their families and must more closely approximate their lives; continuity of stages over these individuals' life spans must be examined rather than focusing on discrete often artificial age groups. Although most of the attention within this chapter and this book relates to younger adults with mild cognitive limitations, a significant gap exists in our understanding of what happens to these adults as they get older. Based on the study of cognitive processes in older individuals in long-term care, mild cognitive limitation appears to be related to lower than average educational attainment (Tymchuk, Ouslander, Rahbar, & Fitten, 1988). Although older adults with developmental disabilities have been studied, the research has been conducted on cross-sectional and nonrepresentative samples, and none of the studies have examined people with mild cognitive limitations. Although the life spans of people with mild cognitive limitations have not been studied, it may be that without suitable supports, these individuals may become impaired earlier as they age and suffer from more and severe health disorders. Figure 2.4 displays a hypothetical accomplishment curve over the life span across certain developmental milestones. Prospective studies are needed, then, to examine whether education could prevent impairments. For the present, however, retrospective studies of long-term care facility residents might show that people who received special education are among those individuals who show the greatest impairments.

Use of Models to Examine Continuities

The previously mentioned models can be used to examine continuities among service sectors with which people with mild cognitive limitations are in contact, even when these sectors appear to be disparate. Not only are adults with

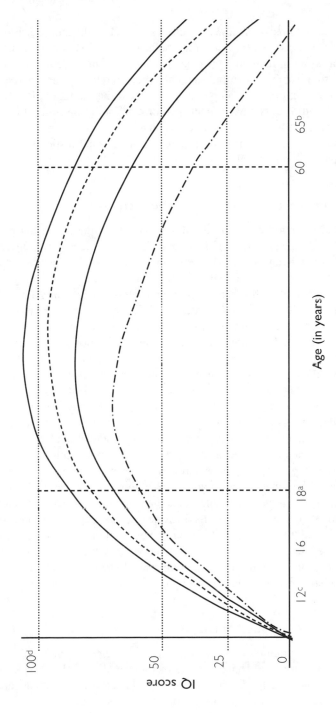

Figure 2.4. Hypothetical accomplishment curve over the life span ([a]legal age of competency; [b]age of retirement; [c]decision making as one element of legal competency seen as adequate; [d]presumed attainment of typical development; ----- average attained with typical cognition; ——— range of developmental abilities considered typical; —·—·— attainment of people with mild mental retardation.

33

mild cognitive limitations involved with sectors such as health care, education, and welfare, for example, but they also may be involved with child protection and the judicial system, including criminal justice. Although seemingly disparate, each sector must recognize and adequately respond to the needs of these adults. In child protection, for example, it is estimated that between 30% and 70% of the reported parents have a functional or categorical disability (Tymchuk, 1999). Despite this estimate, no attention has been given to the personal needs of these parents within the child protection or criminal justice systems (National Research Council, 1993).

Development of Functional and Prescriptive Systems

These models also could be used in the development of functional and prescriptive systems of assessment, classification, and direct services provision that are more inclusive and nonvaluative, that emphasize strengths and potential for growth rather than perpetuate a belief of static immutability, and that emphasize individual autonomy, self-determination, and self-actualization. Although perhaps not without difficulties, coordinated service systems can be developed. For example, the existence of a number of discontinuities between the experiences of people with mild cognitive limitations while in school and their experiences once they exit school impedes a full examination of their needs as adults. These discontinuities include the absence of approaches for follow-along services as these individuals exit school, the lack of suitable transition assistance upon exiting school, the lack of timely feedback mechanisms to show that the services provided in school in fact are or are not working up to expectations, the absence of education in school regarding new key areas of adult life (e.g., developing and maintaining financial lives; starting and maintaining a family or other relationship; participating in civic life; ensuring one's own physical and mental health as well as that of one's family; protecting oneself and one's family and responding to external events such as being involved in an accident, having a serious illness, being attacked, or having one's competence questioned; or ensuring stability in one's life), and the discrepancies between school nomenclature and those used by community-based services. A logical first step to developing such a functional prescriptive system would be to expand the study of transitions of students who receive special education into community life.

Coordination and Integration of Efforts

Coordination and integration of efforts is needed to develop a successful system. Ideally, each sector would have in place methods and trained personnel to implement the methods, help identify the functional needs of individuals, and ensure the use of effective strategies to respond to those needs.

Implementation Strategies

In the short term, a number of implementation strategies would be beneficial. These include the identification of program, research, and policy initiatives being considered both within the public and private domains in any service sectors, consideration of including the interests of adults with mild cognitive limitations into these initiatives, and development of a broad-based plan to examine the needs of these individuals. Task forces may be established to accomplish these efforts. Multilevel, cross-sector collaboration and coordination, then, may not be only political watchwords unless we wish to continue to sacrifice the well-being of individuals with mild cognitive limitations.

REFERENCES

Americans with Disabilities Act (ADA) of 1990, PL 101-336, 42 U.S.C. §§ 12101 *et seq.*

Baker, D., Parker, R., Williams, M., Scott Clark, W., & Nurss, J. (1997). The relationship of patient reading ability to self-reported health and use of health services. *American Journal of Public Health, 87,* 1027–1030.

Bassuk, E., Weinreb, L., Buckner, J., Browne, A., Salomon, A. & Bassuk, S. (1997). The characteristics and needs of sheltered homeless and low-income housed mothers. *Journal of the American Medical Association, 276,* 640–646.

Baugh, D., Rotwein, S., Hakim, R., & Boschert, R. (1998). Hospitalizations for injury among Medicaid children: California, 1992. *Health Care Financing Review, 19,* 129–147.

Boyle, C., Decoufle, P., & Yeargin-Allsopp, M. (1994). Prevalence and health impact of developmental disabilities in U.S. children. *Pediatrics, 93,* 399–403.

Breslow, L. (1997). *Report of review of public health programs and services in Los Angeles County, Department of Health Services.* Los Angeles: University of California–Los Angeles, School of Public Health.

Browne, A. (1993). Violence against women by male partners: Prevalence, outcomes, and policy implications. *American Psychologist, 48,* 1077–1087.

Carter, N. (1996). *See how we grow: A report on the status of parenting education in the U.S.* Philadelphia: The Pew Charitable Trusts.

Centers for Disease Control. (1991). *National health interview survey.* Atlanta, GA: Author.

Centers for Disease Control. (1994). *National health interview survey on disability.* Atlanta, GA: Author.

Centers for Disease Control. (1995a). *Behavioral risk surveillance system.* Atlanta, GA: Author.

Centers for Disease Control. (1995b). *National youth risk behavior survey.* Atlanta, GA: Author.

Conley, R.W., Luckasson, R., & Bouthilet, G.N. (Eds.). (1992). *The criminal justice system and mental retardation: Defendants and victims.* Baltimore: Paul H. Brookes Publishing Co.

Cruz, V., Price-Williams, D., & Andron, L. (1988). Developmentally disabled women who were molested as children. *Social Casework, 69*(7), 411–419.

Daar, M., Nelson, T., & Pone, D. (1995). *Durable powers of attorney for health care manual: An advocacy tool for mental health consumer empowerment and patient choice.* Sacramento, CA: Protection & Advocacy, Inc.

Davis, T., Mayeaux, E., Fredrikson, D., Bocchini, J., Jackson, R., & Murphy, P. (1994). Reading ability of parents compared with reading level of pediatric patient education materials. *Pediatrics, 93,* 460–468.

DiSimone, R. (1996). Major welfare reforms enacted in 1996. *Social Security Bulletin, 59,* 56–63.

Doak, C., Doak, L., & Root, J. (1996). *Teaching patients with low literacy skills* (2nd ed.). Philadelphia: J.B. Lippincott Company.

Doren, B., Bullis, M., & Benz, M. (1996). Predictors of victimization experiences of adolescents with disabilities in transition. *Exceptional Children, 63,* 7–18.

Dunne, R., Asher, K., & Rivara, F. (1993). Injuries in young people with developmental disabilities: Comparative investigation from the 1988 National Health Interview Survey. *Mental Retardation, 31,* 83–88.

Edgerton, R. (Ed.). (1984). *Lives in process: Mildly retarded adults in a large city.* Washington, DC: American Association on Mental Retardation.

Geen, R., Zimmerman, W., Douglas, T., Zedlewski, S., & Waters, S. (1997). *Income support and social services for low-income people in California.* Washington, DC: Urban Institute.

Glaun, D., & Brown, P. (1999). Motherhood, intellectual disability, and child protection: Characteristics of a court sample. *Journal of Intellectual and Developmental Disabilities, 24,* 95–105.

Hayden, M., Lakin, K., Braddock, D., & Smith, G. (1995). Growth in self-advocacy organizations. *Mental Retardation, 33,* 342.

Hayman, R. (1990). Presumptions of justice: Law, politics, and the mentally retarded parent. *Harvard Law Review, 103,* 1202–1271.

Hickson, L., Golden, H., Khemka, I., Urv, T., & Yamusah, S. (1998). A closer look at interpersonal decision-making in adults with and without mental retardation. *American Journal on Mental Retardation, 103*(3), 209–224.

Hollomon, H., Dobbins, D., & Scott, K. (1998). The effect of biological and social risk factors on special education placement: Birth weight and maternal education as an example. *Research in Developmental Disabilities, 19,* 281–294.

Jorgensen, C. (1994). Health education: What can it look like after health care reform? *Health Education Quarterly, 21,* 11–26.

Kirby, D. (1997). *No easy answers. Research findings on programs to reduce teen pregnancy.* Washington, DC: The National Campaign to Prevent Teen Pregnancy.

Koegel, P., & Edgerton, R. (1984). Black "six-hour retarded children" as young adults. In R. Edgerton (Ed.), *Lives in progress: Mildly retarded adults in a large city.* Washington, DC: American Association on Mental Retardation.

LaGreca, A., & Varni, J. (1993). Editorial: Interventions in pediatric psychology: A look toward the future. *Journal of Pediatric Psychology, 18,* 667–679.

Levine, P., & Edgar, E. (1994). An analysis by gender of long-term postschool outcomes for youth with and without disabilities. *Exceptional Children, 61,* 282–300.

Luckasson, R., Coulter, D., Polloway, E., Reiss, S., Schalock, R., Snell, M., Spitalnik, D., & Stark, J. (1992). *Mental retardation: Definition, classification, and systems of supports* (9th ed.). Washington, DC: American Association on Mental Retardation.

Lyall, I., Holland, A., & Collins, S. (1995). Offending by adults with learning disabilities: Identifying need in one health district. *Mental Handicap Research, 8,* 99–109.

MacMillan, D., Gresham, F., & Bocian, K. (1998). Curing mental retardation and causing learning disabilities: Consequences of using various WISC-III IQs to estimate aptitude of Hispanic students. *Journal of Psychoeducational Assessment, 16,* 36–54.

McManus, M., & Fox, H. (1995). *Strategies to enhance preventive and primary care services for high-risk children in health maintenance organizations.* Washington, DC: Fox Health Policy Consultants.

Mellard, D. (1999). *The adult learning disabilities screening.* Lawrence: University of Kansas.

Miller, A., & Keys, C. (1996). Awareness, action, and collaboration: How the self-advocacy movement is empowering for persons with developmental disabilities. *Mental Retardation, 34,* 312–319.

Miller, W. (1994, April 10, 11, 12). State of neglect: Judged unfit before they try. Mentally retarded rarely allowed to raise their babies. *The Spokesman Review,* pp. H1, H4.

National Center on Abuse and Neglect. (1996). *National child abuse and neglect data system.* Washington, DC: Author.

National Research Council. (1993). *Understanding child abuse and neglect.* Washington, DC: National Academy Press.

Pack, R., Wallander, J., & Browne, D. (1998). Health risk behaviors of African American adolescents with mild mental retardation: Prevalence depends on measurement method. *American Journal on Mental Retardation, 102,* 409–420.

Patient Self-Determination Act of 1990, PL 101-508, 42 U.S.C. §§ 1395cc(f)(1), 1396a(w)(1).

Reschly, D. (1996). Identification and assessment of students with disabilities. *The Future of Children, 6,* 40–53.

The Research and Training Center in Rehabilitation and Childhood Trauma. (1994). *National Pediatric Trauma Registry (1988–1994).* Boston: Author.

Schalock, R. (Ed.). (1990). *Quality of life: Perspectives and issues.* Washington, DC: American Association on Mental Retardation.

Sitlington, P., Frank, A., & Carson, R. (1992). Adult adjustment among high school graduates with mild disabilities. *Exceptional Children, 59,* 221–233.

Taylor, C., Norman, D., Murphy, M., Jellinek, M., Quinn, D., Poitrast, F., & Goshko, M. (1991). Diagnosed intellectual and emotional impairment among parents who seriously mistreat their children: Prevalence, type, and outcome in a court sample. *Child Abuse and Neglect, 15,* 389–401.

Teesson, M., & Buhrich, N. (1993). Prevalence of cognitive impairment among homeless men in a shelter in Australia. *Hospital and Community Psychiatry, 44,* 1187–1189.

Tymchuk, A. (1992). Predicting adequacy and inadequacy of parenting by persons with mental retardation. *Child Abuse and Neglect, 16,* 165–178.

Tymchuk, A. (1996). *Parents with "functional or categorical" disabilities: Risk assessment, case management, and techniques for improving parenting skills. A training manual for caseworkers.* Los Angeles: Center on Child Welfare, University of Southern California.

Tymchuk, A. (1997). Informing for consent: Concepts and methods. *Canadian Psychology, 38,* 55–76.

Tymchuk, A. (1999). Moving towards integration of services for parents with intellectual disabilities. *Journal of Intellectual and Developmental Disabilities, 24,* 59–74.

Tymchuk, A., & Andron, L. (1990). Mothers with mental retardation who do or do not abuse or neglect their children. *Child Abuse and Neglect, 14,* 313–323.

Tymchuk, A., Groen, A., & Dolyniuk, C. (in press). Health, safety, and well-being reading recognition abilities of young parents with disabilities: Construction and preliminary validation. *Journal of Physical and Developmental Disabilities.*

Tymchuk, A., Ouslander, J., Rahbar, B., & Fitten, J. (1988). Medical decision making among elderly people in long term care. *The Gerontologist, 28*(Suppl.), 59–63.

U.S. Department of Education. (1991). *National longitudinal transition study of special education students (1987–1993).* Washington, DC: Author.

U.S. Department of Education, National Center for Education Statistics. (1997). *Dropout rates in the United States: 1995.* Washington, D.C.: Superintendent of Documents.

U.S. Department of Education, Office of Special Education and Rehabilitative Services. (1998). *21st annual report to Congress on the implementation of the Individuals with Disabilities Education Act.* Washington, DC: Author.

U.S. Department of Health and Human Services. (1990). *Healthy People 2000: National health promotion and disease prevention objectives.* Washington, DC: Author.

U.S. Department of Health and Human Services. (1995). *Healthy People 2000: An update.* Washington, DC: Author.

U.S. Department of Health and Human Services. (2000). *Healthy People 2010.* Washington, DC: Author.

U.S. Department of Justice. (1995). *National crime victimization survey.* Washington, DC: Author.

U.S. Public Health Service. (1988a). *National maternal and infant health survey.* Washington, DC: Author.

U.S. Public Health Service. (1988b). *National maternal and infant health survey—Field follow-up.* Washington, DC: Author.

Wagner, M. (1995). Outcomes for youths with serious emotional disturbance in secondary school and early adulthood. *The Future of Children, 5,* 90–112.

Wehmeyer, M., & Metzler, C. (1995). How self-determined are people with mental retardation?: The National Consumer Survey. *Mental Retardation, 33,* 111–119.

Yeargin-Allsopp, M., Murphy, C., Oakley, G., Sikes, R. (1992). A multiple-source method for studying the prevalence of developmental disabilities in children: The Metropolitan Atlanta Developmental Disabilities Study. *Pediatrics, 89*(4, Pt. 1), 624–630.

Zigler, E., Kagan, S., & Hall, N. (1996). *Children, families, and government: Preparing for the twenty-first century.* New York: Cambridge University Press.

Renegotiating the Social Contract

Rights, Responsibilities, and Risks for Individuals with Mild Cognitive Limitations

Robert M. Gettings

Since the founding of the United States of America, people with mild cognitive limitations have lived in the shadows of American society, often ignored except as targets of ridicule by their fellow citizens. Sporadic attempts have been made to call attention to the plight of this overlooked segment of the population. However, these efforts usually have been short-lived and have had limited impact.

The purpose of this chapter is to examine societal responsibilities to and expectations of individuals with mild cognitive limitations. Is the American public more supportive and accepting of people with intellectual disabilities today than they were in the 1970s? And, if so, how are these changes reflected in law, social programs, and public attitudes? As we enter the 21st century, what barriers do people with mild cognitive limitations face to becoming valued, participating members of American society? And, how can those of us who are committed to breaking down such barriers mobilize the forces that will be required to achieve essential changes in public policies?

Before examining the changes that have occurred since the 1970s and attempting to map out possible future strategies, it is important to understand the broader social context within which public policies that affect individuals with mild cognitive limitations have evolved during this turbulent period. What are the historical origins of current policies, and how have they been shaped by the public's general views regarding the role of government versus the responsibilities of individuals and families? And, are there key lessons to be drawn from our experiences over the past 30 years that should be taken into account in developing future public policies toward individuals with mild cognitive limitations?

THE SIX-HOUR RETARDED CHILD AND WINNING THE WAR ON POVERTY

The Six-Hour Retarded Child (President's Committee on Mental Retardation [PCMR], 1969) was issued during a rare and short-lived period of optimism concerning the government's capacity to eliminate poverty and address the health, education, training, income maintenance, and employment assistance needs of individuals with mild cognitive limitations in American society. President Lyndon Baines Johnson captured this spirit of national optimism in a 1964 commencement address at the University of Michigan–Ann Arbor, during which he said, "The challenge of the next century is whether we have the wisdom to use [the nation's vast] wealth to enrich and elevate our national life to prevent the old values from being buried under unbridled growth" (Lyndon B. Johnson, May 22, 1964). In the months following this "Great Society" speech, Johnson deluged Congress with a blizzard of special messages—an astonishing 63 documents in 1965 alone—requesting action on a bewildering array of legislation. "No longer," he said in one message, "should older Americans be denied the healing miracles of modern medicine." In another message, he declared "a national war on poverty," making it clear that "total victory" was the only acceptable outcome (as cited in Kearns, 1976, p. 219).

In response to Johnson's call to arms, Congress proceeded in the mid-1960s to enact the most extraordinary array of landmark domestic legislation that had been added to the federal statutory code since the early days of the New Deal. Among the most important new programs authorized under this legislation were

- The Medicare program, which guaranteed health care coverage for all individuals older than 65 years as well as for Social Security beneficiaries younger than the age of 65 who had qualifying disabilities
- The federal-state Medicaid program, which consolidated and vastly expanded financial assistance to help states ensure that low-income individuals and families gained access to medical, health, and long-term services
- The U.S. Civil Rights Commission and other mechanisms to enforce the requirements of the Civil Rights Act of 1964 (PL 88-352)—the first major civil rights law to be enacted since the Civil War era
- Grants-in-aid to improve elementary and secondary education programs— the first broad-based program of federal assistance to local public schools
- The Manpower Development and Training Act of 1962, the first major federal job training program
- The Housing Act of 1964 (PL 93-383), which for the first time authorized rent subsidies for low-income families living in privately owned and managed housing units
- The Food Stamp Act of 1964 (PL 91-671), which permanently authorized food coupons for impoverished families

Collectively, these and other less prominent federal laws enacted during the early years of the Johnson administration fundamentally redefined the federal government's role in the social policy arena and raised the prospect that government, indeed, could conquer poverty and create a more caring, egalitarian society.

By the time *The Six-Hour Retarded Child* was released, the Head Start program had been launched, and the wide-ranging programs of the White House Office of Economic Opportunity (OEO) were in full swing.[1] The fiscal and societal consequences of the military quagmire in Vietnam were becoming evident; but, still there was considerable optimism in Washington and across the country that the pervasive effects of poverty could and should be addressed through a coordinated, sustained series of government programs and initiatives.

A number of the members of the President's Committee on Mental Retardation at the time were liberals with close political ties at the highest levels of the Johnson administration. Passionately committed to the President's domestic policy agenda, they believed that ending poverty and racial discrimination, and subsequently the social pathology they spawned, was the most effective means of combating the incidence of mental retardation. As a result, the interrelationship between poverty and mental retardation was a major focus of the Committee's work during the late 1960s. For example, in its 1968 report to President Johnson, the Committee called attention to the following facts:

- Three fourths of those with mental retardation in the United States are to be found in the isolated and impoverished urban and rural slums.
- Conservative estimates of the incidence of mental retardation in inner-city neighborhoods *begin* at 7%.
- A child in a low-income rural or urban family is 15 times more likely to be diagnosed as having mental retardation than a child from a higher income family.
- Forty-five percent of all women who have babies in public hospitals have received no prenatal care. Avoidable complications of pregnancy, which are often the harbingers of crippling conditions in children, soar in this group.
- [The] [i]ncidence of premature births (among whom neurological and physical disorders are 75% more frequent than in full-term babies) is almost three times as great among low-income women as among other groups of women.
- The mortality rate of infants born to low-income mothers is nearly double that of infants born to mothers in other income brackets.
- The children of low-income families often arrive at school with neither the experience nor the skills necessary for systematic learning.
- Students in the public schools of inner-city, low-income areas have been found in numerous studies to be from 6 months to 3 years behind the national norm of achievement for their age and grade.

---

[1]OEO was an independent agency created by President Johnson to oversee the War on Poverty. It operated the Head Start program, the Foster Grand Parents program, and a variety of other anti-poverty initiatives, large and small.

• The rate of Selective Service System rejections for intellectual under-achievement is 23% nationally and soars to 60% and more among groups whose members are largely from low-income areas. (p. 19)

Taking all of this evidence into account, the Committee concluded that "the condition of life in poverty—whether in an urban ghetto, the hollows of Appalachia, a prairie shack-town or an Indian reservation—cause and nurture mental retardation" (PCMR, 1968, p. 19).

The contents of *The Six-Hour Retarded Child* also were influenced by the early studies of Mercer and her colleagues at the University of California–Riverside. These studies revealed the close linkages between race and low socioeconomic status and the likelihood that a child would be placed in a special education class. Based on her findings, Mercer warned against labeling children as "mentally retarded," pointing out the devastating consequences that such labels carried—particularly for children with mild cognitive limitations—not only with respect to the child's educational attainment but also with respect to his or her adjustment to adult life (Mercer, 1973). The term *six-hour retarded child* was coined during the preparation of the PCMR report to characterize physically typical but academically challenged minority children from economically disadvantaged backgrounds.

The conventional wisdom is that the Great Society programs fell victim to the increasing budgetary demands of the Vietnam War.[2] But, the real explanation is far more complicated. Even without the fiscal burdens and the political divisiveness of the war in Southeast Asia, it seems, in retrospect, highly unlikely that the deep-seated, historic inequalities in American society would have yielded to the hodge-podge of government initiatives launched during the late 1960s. Indeed, read more than 30 years later, the official pronouncements of the time seem almost breathtakingly naïve, given the enormity of the problem and the narrowly focused, uncoordinated solutions that were offered. As Kearns pointed out, the objective of the Johnson administration was to "make laws," not to figure out "how programs could actually be made to work" (1976).

The vision of a more egalitarian and caring nation faded with the Great Society programs. Even though most of the federal programs enacted during that brief, frenetic period of our legislative history remain (in greatly expanded form) today, the United States is still a society deeply divided along racial, class, and economic lines. This reality has a direct, compelling impact on societal supports for people with mental retardation and their families. Based on an analysis of data obtained through the Bureau of the Census's 1991 Survey of Income and Program Participation (SIPP), Fujiura (1998) pointed out that

---

[2]Looking back on his White House experiences, former president Johnson put this argument best when he said, "[T]he sound of the bugle put an immediate end to the hopes and dreams of the best reformers: The Spanish-American War drowned the populist spirit; World War I ended Woodrow Wilson's New Freedom; World War II brought the New Deal to a close" (Kearns, 1976).

1) the vast majority of the estimated 2.97 million individuals with mental retardation and related developmental disabilities lived with their families and received little if any assistance from the formal mental retardation/developmental disabilities service delivery system, and 2) households of all types—but particularly single-parent–headed households—that provide support to a member with a lifelong disability had less income and received means-tested benefits more frequently than the average U.S. household. Furthermore, the effects of poverty were accentuated among minority groups, especially in terms of their reliance on means-tested benefits (Fujiura & Yamaki, 1997).

The fact that access to specialized mental retardation/developmental disabilities services remains so very inadequate for individuals with lifelong disabilities who live in lower socioeconomic households—particularly those individuals with mild cognitive limitations who are from racial and ethnic minorities—can be traced to Great Society assumptions about conquering the social ills of poverty. The belief at the time was that familial mental retardation was largely the consequence of economic deprivation, and, therefore, the only enduring solution to the problem was to mount a broad-based attack on the root causes of poverty, lack of education, and discrimination. According to this theory, individuals with mild cognitive limitations would benefit from the rising tide of improvements in generic health care, housing, job training, employment, and public assistance programs. Furthermore, by remaining outside the formal mental retardation service system, such individuals would avoid being labeled and, thereby, enhance their prospects of blending into the mainstream of American society. Meanwhile, it was thought that specialized services should be reserved primarily for individuals with moderate to profound mental retardation, who, after all, were most likely to require a sustained array of professionally tailored supports throughout their life spans.

The promised improvements in the basic social infrastructure, of course, never materialized. Roughly the same percentage of the American population is mired in poverty today as was the case in the 1970s (Dalaker & Naifeh, 1998). People with mild cognitive limitations remain overrepresented among low-income Americans. Therefore, the basic public policy issue that needs to be discussed is whether specialized mental retardation/developmental disabilities services systems should assume broader responsibilities for assisting individuals with mild cognitive limitations with gaining access to needed services and supports or, conversely, whether the future of such individuals should continue to rest on the uncertain prospects of broader social reforms.

RELEVANT TRENDS IN HEALTH AND SOCIAL WELFARE SYSTEMS

As mentioned previously, families play a crucial role in supporting and caring for individuals with mental retardation; and such families, particularly families of individuals with mild cognitive limitations, tend to be highly reliant on means-tested benefits—Temporary Assistance to Needy Families (TANF) payments, Supplemental Security Income (SSI) benefits, Medicaid coverage, food stamps, and so forth. It is particularly important, therefore, to assess the current status and future prospects of these social safety net programs.

Broadly speaking, two interrelated forces are likely to influence the availability and accessibility of safety net benefits in the years ahead: 1) the devolution of control to state and local jurisdictions and 2) the aging of the American population. At times, these forces may interact in strange, unpredictable ways, and the pathway to the future could take some seemingly contradictory twists and turns. But, for better or worse, public policy will be shaped to a considerable extent by these demographic and political/organizational imperatives.

Devolution

The recent changes in the federal-state public assistance program are the prime example to date of the devolution of responsibility to the states. The 1996 welfare reform legislation (PL 104-193) ended the 60-year-old Aid to Families with Dependent Children (AFDC) program and created in its place a block grant program to assist the states in returning able-bodied adults to the labor force. Under the TANF program, which replaced AFDC, states are delegated broad authority to determine the most effective approaches to reducing their welfare caseloads. Meanwhile, by shifting from open-ended entitlement funding to fixed block grant allocations, the federal government has placed its fiscal obligations on a far more predictable and sustainable course (Katz, 1997).

Thus far, welfare caseloads have declined at a much faster rate than originally anticipated in most states. Whether these results are attributable to the success of the welfare-to-work programs that states have initiated over the past few years or are due mainly to the strict time limits imposed under state welfare reform laws is still unclear. Studies analyzing the factors that have contributed to the decline in welfare caseloads have yielded conflicting results. But one fact is clear: The booming national economy and the resulting low unemployment rate and high tax revenues have cushioned the impact of welfare reform. Blessed with huge surpluses, many states have been able to offer welfare recipients intensive job training and placement services, subsidized child care, and other social supports to facilitate their return to economic self-sufficiency.

However, even during the longest sustained period of economic prosperity in the nation's history, many low-income families continue to struggle. A 1999 national survey of 44,461 randomly selected households, commissioned by the Urban Institute as part of its multiyear "Assessing the New Federalism" project, found the following:

*   Dramatic variations in the economic well-being of families by state and income level. The number of adults, not including older adults, who were

living in families with incomes under the poverty level in 1996 was 9% in New Jersey and Wisconsin, compared with 20% in Alabama and California and 25% in Mississippi.

- More than half of low-income families were worried about or had difficulty affording food, compared with one out of seven high-income families.
- Nearly three of ten low-income families told the project surveyors they could not pay mortgage, rent, or utility bills at some point during the previous year.
- Twelve percent of low-income children and twenty-one percent of low-income adults reported that they had no health insurance coverage at the time of the survey.

If the social safety net is inadequate under present circumstances, what will happen to low-income families during the next economic recession? With history as a guide, we can predict that the poverty rate will rise, social benefits will be trimmed to meet state budgetary constraints, and underprivileged individuals will bear a disproportionate share of the burden.

As the experience with welfare reform tends to demonstrate, states and localities are better able to tailor their policies and programs to real human needs and use dollars more efficiently when they have broad discretion over the deployment of all related public resources (i.e., federal, state, and local). However, local control is not a substitute for a social ethic that tolerates economic deprivation; nor will it assure interstate parity with regard to access to needed social benefits. In this sense, the American public and its political leaders have yet to step up to the enormous challenges of creating a Great Society.

For the foreseeable future, however, the shift of authority from the federal government to the states (and, in turn, from the states to localities) is likely to continue along an uneven path.[3] At the moment, the odds are slim that Congress will delegate additional major health and human services responsibilities to the states. The more likely scenario is a gradual realignment of intergovernmental responsibilities as a result of incremental changes in statutory and administrative policies. The transformation that is occurring within state Medicaid programs as more and more Title XIX recipients are enrolled in managed care plans illustrates the point. Because these changes are taking place gradually, state by state, outside the context of any sweeping revisions in federal statutory or regulatory policy, their devolutionary effects are not as immediately apparent as they are in the case of welfare reform. But, their impacts on the relationships among program recipients, service providers, and the states, as well as between the states and the federal government, are no less profound.

---

[3]It is important to note, for example, that while transferring control over public assistance programs to the states in 1996, Congress ultimately rejected legislative proposals to delegate similar responsibilities to the states for child nutrition and Medicaid services following several presidential vetoes.

The Graying of America

Between 1996 and 2025, the U.S. Bureau of the Census projects that there will be an 83% increase in the 65 and older segment of the population. By the year 2030, nearly 20% of the nation's population will be older than 65, compared with 12.8% today (Bectel & Tucker, 1998). The aging of the huge baby boom generation carries with it enormous ramifications for federal social benefit programs. By 2025, the growing number of senior citizens not only will exhaust existing surpluses in the Social Security trust funds but also will cause a steep rise in Medicare and Medicaid outlays. The average health care costs of senior citizens run about three times as much as those of adults younger than 65.

The political consequences of this demographic tidal wave are just beginning to be felt in Washington. In his 1999 State of the Union address, former president Clinton called on Congress to set aside three quarters of the surplus that is expected to accumulate over the next 15 years ($2.8 trillion) to shore up the Medicare Trust Fund and stabilize Social Security financing through the middle of the 21st century (Taylor, 1999). Since then, the two major political parties have vied for the mantle of reformer, each presenting its own, quite different, version of a reform plan. But the truth is that neither political party has been willing to address the tough policy choices that inevitably will have to be made to secure the long-range financial stability of the Social Security and Medicare trust funds beyond the first two or three decades of the 21st century.

The unsettling reality is that even if the projected federal budget surplus were to materialize and be earmarked exclusively to pay the medical bills and retirement benefits of older Americans—a highly uncertain prospect at best—the underlying fiscal dilemma would be postponed only for about 25–30 years. Federal spending represented about 20% of the gross domestic product (GDP) in 1997. More than a third of these expenditures (8% of the GDP) were used to cover Social Security, Medicare, and Medicaid payments. Outlays for all other federal programs (e.g., education, medical research, agricultural subsidies, food stamps, national defense, veterans benefits) made up about 9% of the GDP, and interest payments on the national debt equaled 3% of the GDP (Samuelson, 1999).

By 2020, the Congressional Budget Office projects that Social Security, Medicare, and Medicaid payments will consume 13% of the GDP, or five percentage points more than in 1997. Assuming that no changes occur in the benefit structure during the intervening years, federal policymakers would have to reduce spending on all other programs by more than 50% or increase federal taxes by about 25% in order to achieve a balanced budget (Samuelson, 1999).

Given the enormous—and growing—political clout of the senior citizens lobby, any attempt to reduce Medicare, Social Security, and Medicaid benefits will produce a grueling, no-holds-barred struggle that will generate strong pressures to contain the growth in all other areas of federal spending. The outcome is difficult to predict at this point. Nonetheless, it is clear that the fiscal realities associated with addressing the needs of the nation's aging population will be a major force shaping federal policy over the next few decades. The policy trade-offs involved in "saving Social Security and Medicare" may subject other parts of the low-income safety net to extraordinary pressures, as is already evident in selected program areas (Weinstein, 1999).

For example, in 1996 Congress enacted legislation tightening childhood eligibility for SSI benefits following a sharp increase over the preceding 5 years in the number of beneficiaries younger than 19 years of age. The Social Security Administration has estimated that by the time the legislation is fully implemented, approximately 100,000 children—the vast majority of whom have cognitive disabilities—will be dropped from the SSI rolls (Social Security Administration, 1997).

The rapid growth in the number of working-age recipients of SSI and Old-Age, Survivors, and Disability Insurance (OASDI) disability benefits also has drawn increased attention in Washington. The federal disability rolls have more than doubled since the 1990s, and the aggregate cost of federal cash assistance payments to SSI and Social Security Disability Insurance (SSDI) beneficiaries almost tripled over the same period (exceeding $75 billion by 1998) (Kirchhoff, 1998). There is little likelihood in the near term that Congress will tighten the eligibility criteria for adult disability benefits. However, should the recent pattern of growth continue, it is certain to be an issue on the table as Congress and the White House attempt to fashion an acceptable Social Security reform plan. If so, people with mild to moderate cognitive limitations will have a large stake in the outcome because they will be at the end of the queue in any efforts to trim the benefit rolls. In 1998, approximately 1.25 million adults with mental retardation were receiving SSI and/or OASDI Disabled Adult Child benefits (once the figures are adjusted to account for dual eligibility) (Social Security Administration, 1998).[4] The termination of benefits could mean not only the loss of vital cash assistance but, for most recipients, automatic eligibility to receive health and long-term care services paid for through the federal-state Medicaid program.

The hopeful news from the perspective of people with mild cognitive disabilities and their advocates is that they will have powerful allies in the strug-

---

[4]As of December 1997, 27.7% of the 4,441,420 SSI beneficiaries who were blind or had other disabilities had a primary diagnosis of mental retardation. Not included in this figure were about 400,000 children younger than age 19 with a primary diagnosis of mental retardation who were receiving SSI benefits. In addition, roughly 700,000 adults between the ages of 18 and 64 were receiving Social Security "adult disabled children's" benefits. Within the latter group, approximately two thirds have a primary diagnosis of mental retardation. These statistics underscore, once again, the important role Social Security and SSI benefits play in furnishing basic income supports for individuals with mental retardation. Readers should note that these figures do not take into account individuals assigned to an alternative diagnostic category who, nonetheless, have mental retardation.

gle to preserve the social safety net. But, a cautionary note also seems to be in order. The battle is likely to consist of a fiscally driven, rearguard action to maintain the existing benefit structure. Even if these efforts succeed, closing existing gaps in the safety net will remain an uphill struggle in the budgetary environment the nation will face over the coming decades.

TRENDS IN SPECIALIZED SERVICES AND SUPPORTS

State and local service systems for people with developmental disabilities, meanwhile, are in the early stages of a transformation that challenges many of the basic precepts of the past. Largely as a result of improved access to federal Medicaid funding, most states have substantially downsized the number of individuals served in large, multipurpose public institutions over the past 30 years and have aggressively expanded community living arrangements. The number of individuals residing in large, state-run facilities for individuals with mental retardation declined from 194,650 in 1977 to 51,485 in 1998, whereas the number of people living in small community living arrangements (with six or fewer residents) skyrocketed from 19,700 to 199,851 over the same period. By June, 1998, more than two thirds of the states (37 states) were serving a majority of individuals with developmental disabilities in residential settings with six or fewer individuals (Prouty & Lakin, 1999).

The resulting transformation from an institutionally dominated to a community-centered system of services, however, may be only a prelude to even more fundamental changes that lie ahead. Unable to keep pace with current service demands and facing a new generation of consumers and family members with much different expectations, more and more states are exploring alternative strategies for financing and delivering services that are better attuned to present realities.

Between 1977 and 1996, the total number of individuals receiving residential services increased by 36% (from 290,220 to 394,284), or at an average annual rate of 2%. Meanwhile, total public funding for specialized developmental disabilities services of all types grew over this 19-year period by 167%, after adjusting for the effects of inflation (from $3.5 billion to $22.8 billion) (Braddock et al., 1998). Most of the growth in residential capacity has occurred over the past decade. The total number of individuals receiving residential services increased by 27% between 1987 and 1996, or at an average annual rate of 3%. But, as Lakin points out, the demand for residential placements grew at an even faster pace (approximately 4% per year) during the same period. As a result, by June 30, 1996, an estimated 87,000 individuals were waiting for a residential placement. Lakin estimated that the states' aggregate residential capacity would have to be expanded by 27% simply to meet the current demand (Lakin, 1998).

Present waiting list data, however, probably understate the true dimensions of the problems facing state and local service systems. The societal impacts of the graying of America that were discussed previously—longer life expectancies and the population boom of individuals born between 1946 and 1964—are accentuated among individuals with mental retardation and other developmental disabilities. Janicki (1996) pointed out that, as a result of improved access to modern health care, the average life span of individuals with mental retardation is approaching that of the general population. The average age at death of individuals with Down syndrome, he reported, rose from 9 years in the 1920s, to 30.5 years in the 1960s, to 55.8 years in 1993 (Janicki, 1996). As a result, baby boomers with developmental disabilities, now in their mid-thirties to mid-fifties, are having and will continue to have an exaggerated impact on state and local service systems for several more decades.

In addition to a much larger cohort of aging individuals with disabilities, society will have to cope with the growing phenomenon of senior citizens serving as primary caregivers for their middle-age sons and daughters with developmental disabilities. In his analysis of the Survey of Income and Program Participation (SIPP) data, Fujiura (1998) found that 25% of primary family caregivers were 60 years of age or older, and an additional 35% were between the ages of 41 and 59. Extrapolating from these data, Braddock has estimated that in 1996 more than 1.1 million individuals with developmental disabilities were living in the household of an older adult or middle-age family caregiver (Braddock, 1999). In other words, developmental disabilities service systems are experiencing the impact of the baby boom generation several decades before its full, general effects will wash across American society.

Having seen service waiting lists climb steadily despite healthy rates of growth in public outlays, officials in many states have concluded that it is time to redefine the public's obligation in ways that make more effective use of available resources and that are more responsive to the expressed needs and desires of consumers and families. The basic precepts underlying this new approach can be encapsulated as follows:

- Making a strong commitment to individually tailoring supports to the needs and aspirations of each individual, rather than "slotting" individuals into a limited range of program and facility models
- Placing an emphasis on assisting each individual to live a meaningful, productive life in the community, rather than "treating" his or her disability
- Giving the individual with the disability, in consultation with friends and family, a decisive voice in establishing his or her own personal goals and determining the most effective deployment of available public dollars to help achieve these goals

- Fostering the development and use of informal support networks as well as strong ties to the local community
- Limiting paid supports to those aspects of an individual's service plan that 1) are deemed essential to achieving his or her life goals and 2) cannot be accomplished by the individual's informal support network

These precepts are evident in the waiting list reduction initiatives that a number of states launched in 1998 and 1999 (Smith, 1999). In keeping with the principle of personalizing support strategies, a number of states have elected to focus their efforts broadly on meeting current service demands rather than concentrating solely on expanding the capacity of specialized residential settings. Progress is to be measured in terms of the number of additional individuals and families receiving services and support of their own choosing rather than on the number of additional residential beds that are brought on line or the number of new day service slots that are filled. The underlying aim is to influence the demand curve for out-of-home placements by offering a wide range of alternative in-home, daytime, and crisis supports of varying types and intensities, thereby expanding the number of individuals and families that can be served with a given resource base. The end goal is a publicly financed system of services that is more accessible and responsive to consumer expectations as well as one that operates within tolerable levels of public expenditures.

EMBRACING A NEW POLICY FRAMEWORK

But what do waiting list reduction strategies and systemic reforms have to do with addressing the needs of individuals with mild cognitive limitations? To begin, historically, little attention has been given to this population in designing state and local mental retardation/developmental disabilities long-term support systems. As noted earlier, since the 1960s one key operating premise has been that the vulnerabilities of individuals with mild cognitive limitations are best addressed through generic health, education, income maintenance, housing, and social services programs. It followed, therefore, that specialized long-term supports should be targeted primarily to individuals with more substantial disabilities. The reality, however, is that too often people with mild cognitive impairments, lacking the intellectual capacity to deal with the byzantine rules that frequently regulate access to government aid, fall through the huge cracks in the nation's generic safety net programs. Evidence of this fact can be found in the overrepresentation of people with mild cognitive limitations in foster homes for neglected and abused children, adult board and care facilities, state prisons and local jails, and community mental health service systems.

For decades, mental retardation has been defined in terms of the interaction between limited general intelligence and adaptive behavior (Luckasson et al., 1992). Among individuals classified as having mental retardation, the influence of general intelligence on adaptive behavior is most apparent among individuals with mild cognitive limitations (McGrew, Bruininks, & Johnson, 1996). One need look no further than existing human services systems (both specialized and generic) for verification of this reality. For example, within state and local mental retardation/developmental disabilities service systems, the most challenging and expensive individuals to serve frequently are individuals who have mild cognitive limitations coupled with dangerous antisocial or self-destructive behaviors.

The field of mental retardation must face up to the reality that the nation's generic safety net programs are ill-equipped to meet the needs of a relatively small but significant number of individuals with mild cognitive limitations. Advocates for individuals with mental retardation should continue to press for improved and expanded access to low-income housing, income maintenance, and health and social services benefits; but, in doing so, they should recognize, based both on past experience and likely future realities, that the basic scope of the nation's social safety net is not likely to improve appreciably in the foreseeable future. As a result, specialized mental retardation/developmental disabilities service systems must be prepared to play a supportive, back-up safety net role as well as have an explicit strategy for carrying out such responsibilities. This strategy must include the following elements:

- *Stronger linkages with the generic human services systems that also serve children and adults with developmental disabilities:* The purpose of creating such cross-system linkages is to assure that each person with a disability has access to services and supports appropriate to his or her individual needs. It does not mean that a specialized mental retardation/developmental disabilities service system will assume responsibility for serving individuals who are part of juvenile or adult correction systems, enrolled in (or eligible for) vocational rehabilitation or manpower development programs, or part of the target population for other generic social benefits. In the vast majority of cases, the role of the mental retardation/developmental disabilities service system in assisting individuals with mild cognitive limitations will be restricted to the provision of technical assistance and consultation on disability-specific issues. At the same time, it is important to recognize that maintaining such cross-system ties must be viewed as a critical part of the 21st century role of state and local mental retardation/developmental disabilities systems; therefore, sufficient resources have to be allocated and the organization must be structured appropriately to carry out related functions.
- *Improved management information capabilities that permit public officials to track the status of children and adults with mental retardation across generic and specialized service systems:* One of the major reasons for the existing gaps and discontinuities in disability services is the proliferation of

separate, single-purpose data systems within the human services arena. As a result, it is very difficult to track the interactions individuals with mental retardation have with various components of the human services system across their life spans (e.g., the early intervention system, the public school system, the foster care system, the mental retardation/developmental disabilities service system, the Social Security/public welfare systems, the mental health system, the vocational rehabilitation and manpower training systems, the juvenile and adult corrections systems). Given the incredible advances that have occurred in information technology in the 1980s and 1990s, it now is feasible to design and construct a human services information system in which data on an individual's interactions with a variety of human services systems across time can be accessed instantaneously. Although such systems have to address the thorny issues of individual privacy and access to confidential information, there is no question that the capability of obtaining comprehensive, cross-system data will be a key to improving interagency planning and monitoring the individual progress of people with mental retardation.

- *A stronger commitment to prevention, early intervention, and advanced long-range planning:* One common indictment of public disability service systems is that they tend to operate in a reactive and insular manner. Too often, the individual's needs are ignored until they provoke a crisis, at which point the costs of intervening escalate considerably. Furthermore, the solutions prescribed rarely reach beyond the confines of the service system in which the individual is currently enrolled. To improve overall performance, the mental retardation/developmental disabilities service system must do the following:

  1. *Begin with a strong, sustained emphasis on primary and secondary prevention and early intervention in order to minimize the incidence of developmental disabilities within American society.* Despite the enormous strides that have been made in these areas over the past 30 years, the United States still has a higher incidence of mental retardation than most other advanced industrialized nations around the globe.
  2. *Stress collaborative planning and problem solving across human services systems.* Unless we are able to mobilize the resources and expertise of all affected service systems, the solutions that are concocted will continue to be fragmented and plagued by the inefficient use of available resources.
  3. *Emphasize advanced planning aimed at facilitating the transition of individuals between human services systems.* Joint intersystem planning is particularly important during critical stages in the life of an individual with a disability, such as the period of initial identification (i.e., diagnosis, evaluation, family counseling and support, and enrollment in

early intervention services), entry into the school system, the transition from school to adult life, and preparation for retirement.

None of the above proposals are new. Indeed, the concept of collaborative, interagency, cross-system planning has been at the heart of most disability reform proposals for at least four decades. The main difference here is the proposition that for individuals with mild cognitive limitations, specialized state and local mental retardation/developmental disabilities systems have an important bridge-building role to play in assuring access to appropriate services over the life span of the population. Yes, it is important to avoid the use of stigmatizing labels. But, the avoidance of labels should not be used as a rationale for ignoring the plight of individuals with mild cognitive limitations who fall through the cracks in society's porous social safety net. The unfortunate reality is that we live in a society with an inadequate general social safety net, which triggers the need for specialized safety nets.

Building such a secondary safety net for individuals with mild cognitive limitations will be a difficult task. Bureaucratic turf issues create and sustain deep rifts between human services systems that erode trust and undermine cooperation. Collaborative gestures, furthermore, can and often are interpreted as an open invitation to shift responsibilities to an alternative service system with "real expertise" in serving the population. These barriers to interagency and intersystem cooperation and collaboration will be no easier to surmount than they have been in the past. But, the alternative—continuing to embrace the premise that the vulnerabilities of individuals with mild cognitive limitations can be adequately addressed within the context of generic social safety net programs— flies in the face of the accumulated evidence of the past three decades. As difficult as it may be to formulate and implement, a new policy construct is long overdue.

REFERENCES

Bectel, R.W., & Tucker, N.G. (Eds.). (1998). *Across the states: 1998—Profiles of long-term care systems* (3rd ed.). Washington, DC: American Association of Retired Persons, Public Policy Institute.

Braddock, D. (1999, April). Aging and developmental disabilities: Demographic and policy issues affecting American families. *Mental Retardation,* 155–161.

Braddock, D., Hemp, R., Parish, S., & Westrich, J. (1998). *The state of the states in developmental disabilities.* Washington, DC: American Association on Mental Retardation.

Civil Rights Act of 1964, PL 88-352, 20 U.S.C. §§ 241 *et seq.*

Dalaker, J., & Naifeh, M. (1998). *Poverty in the United States: 1997.* Washington, DC: U.S. Department of Commerce, Bureau of the Census.

Fujiura, G.T. (1998). Demography of family households. *American Journal on Mental Retardation, 103*(2), 225–235.

Fujiura, G.T., & Yamaki, K. (1997). An analysis of ethnic variations in developmental disability: Prevalence and household economic status. *Mental Retardation, 35,* 286–294.

Janicki, M.P. (1996). Longevity increasing among older adults with intellectual disabilities. *Aging, Health and Society, 2*(2).

Katz, J.L. (1997, August 3). After 60 years, more control is passing to the states. *Congressional Quarterly Weekly Report.*

Kearns, D. (1976). *Lyndon Johnson and the American dream.* New York: Harper & Row.

Kirchhoff, S. (1998, November 28). Breaking down barriers for the working disabled. *Congressional Quarterly Weekly Report, 3209-3212.*

Lakin, K.C. (1998, April). On the outside looking in: Attending to waiting lists in systems of services for people with developmental disabilities. *Mental Retardation,* 157–162.

Luckasson, R., Coulter, D.L., Polloway, E.A., Reiss, S., Schalock, R.L., Snell, M.E., Spitalnik, D.M., & Stark, J.A. (1992). *Mental retardation: Definition, classification, and systems of supports* (9th ed.). Washington, DC: American Association on Mental Retardation.

McGrew, K.S., Bruininks, R.H., & Johnson, D.R. (1996). Confirmatory factor analytic investigation of Greenspan's model of personal competence. *American Journal of Mental Retardation, 100,* 533–545.

Mercer, J.R. (1973). *Labeling the mentally retarded.* Berkeley: University of California Press.

President's Committee on Mental Retardation (PCMR). (1968). *MR 68: The edge of change.* Washington, DC: U.S. Government Printing Office.

President's Committee on Mental Retardation (PCMR). (1969). *The six hour retarded child.* Washington, DC: U.S. Government Printing Office.

Prouty, R.W., & Lakin, K.C. (Eds.). (1999). *Residential services for persons with developmental disabilities: Status and trends through 1998.* Minneapolis: University of Minnesota, Research and Training Center on Community Living, Institute on Community Integration.

Samuelson, R.J. (1999, January 27). Surpluses in the sky. *The Washington Post,* p. A21.

Smith, G. (1999). *Closing the gap: Addressing the needs of people with developmental disabilities waiting for supports.* Alexandria, VA: National Association of State Directors of Developmental Disabilities Services.

Social Security Administration. (1998). *SSI annual statistical report: 1997.* Washington, DC: SSA Office of Research, Evaluation and Statistics, Division of SSI Statistics and Analysis.

Social Security Administration (1997, December 17). *SSA to review 45,000 cases of children who had SSI disability benefits ceased; offer second chance for appeal to all* [News release]. Washington, DC: Author.

Taylor, A. (1999, February 6). Clinton's strength portends a tough season for the GOP. *Congressional Quarterly Weekly Report, 290–295.*

Urban Institute. (1999, March). NSAF shows strength of, and challenges facing, low-income families. *New Federalism Policy Research and Resources, 5.*

Weinstein, M.M. (1999, April 1). Economic scene: No comfort in new solvency figures. *The New York Times.*

4

Community and Culture

World Views and Natural Affiliations as the Basis of Understanding, Trust, Assistance, and Support

William M. Kane, Magdalena M. Avila, and Everett M. Rogers

This chapter examines the role of community and culture in supporting adults with mild cognitive limitations, the interpretations of cognitive limitations within various communities and cultures, and the identity/role that communities and cultures assign to adults with mild cognitive limitations. This chapter also relates the decisions faced by people with cognitive limitations in affirming membership in a particular community and culture and in rejecting membership in the "developmental disabilities" culture. Further, alternative roles for community and cultural institutions in supporting adults with mild cognitive limitations are investigated.

The assumptions guiding this chapter are that all adults have unique strengths and assets and, therefore, can and should be contributing and valued members of their communities. Wise families and communities recognize, utilize, and celebrate individuals' strengths and, as a result, reap the unique benefits each person has to offer.

This chapter also provides the professional community with recommendations that build on an understanding of communities and cultures to enhance the quality of life of adults with mild cognitive limitations and the contribution they can make to their families and communities.

COMMUNITIES AND CULTURE AND ADULTS WITH MILD COGNITIVE LIMITATIONS

A multitude of perceptions of developmental disabilities exist within each community and across cultures. Literature that examines the role of community and culture in supporting and shaping the identities of adults with mild cognitive limitations is scarce. Issues of perceptions as influenced and affected by language, terminology, and communication may reveal multiparadigms for understanding and explaining the differences and similarities in which communities and cultures engage in a process that ascribes meaning to individuals with mild cognitive limitations.

Mackelprang and Salsgiver (1996) provided a historical context and perspective in discussing how people with disabilities have been ostracized, rejected, and discriminated against in society, illustrating the importance of addressing these issues and their role in shaping the lens by which disabilities are defined and ascribed meaning.

Bollini and Siem (1995) concluded that ethnic minorities and other groups (e.g., immigrants) often have reduced entitlements in receiving societies. They discussed their belief that members of these groups, many exposed to poor working and living conditions—often determinants of poor health—have decreased access to health care. If adults with mild cognitive impairments encounter societal challenges and setbacks, then adults with cognitive impairments from ethnic minority communities (e.g., African American, Latino, Native American, Asian American) could be expected to encounter even greater social inequities.

Susman (1994) argued for the importance of new conceptual frameworks as greater numbers of people with disabilities resist stigma/deviance imputations. Stigma/deviance imputations for adults with mild cognitive impairments need to be better understood relative to the community and cultural context in which individuals reside to further illuminate the influence of negative and/or positive perceptions.

Majumjdar, Browne, and Roberts (1995) identified the importance of a system of ethno-cultural data collection as well as provision of cultural sensitivity training programs to enhance staff knowledge and skills. Meeting the needs and challenges of adults with mild cognitive limitations requires a better understanding of how to serve the community/culture in which the individual lives; this includes the individual, his or her family, and the residents who create, shape, maintain, and have an impact on the community environment. Information regarding culture and community needs to be integrated more fully into the professional training curriculum of academics and providers in order to provide increased understanding of the importance of the community and culture of adults with mild cognitive impairments. Classification, prevalence, prevention, and rehabilitation of mild cognitive limitations require more exhaustive approaches, stemming from a community approach that supplements a professional top-down approach.

The health needs of vulnerable populations continue to require our renewed attention. Aday (1997) described how those at especially high risk for disease, injury, and disability often lack the resources to cope with their problems. According to Aday, vulnerable populations include older adults, minority communities that are poverty-based, undocumented immigrants, seasonal laborers, children, individuals with mental illness, substance abusers, and homeless individuals. Aday discussed how the defeat of national health care reform and reduced benefits of Medicare, Medicaid, and other welfare programs increase the importance of new approaches to providing services to vulnerable populations.

MILD COGNITIVE LIMITATIONS: IN SEARCH OF A DEFINITION

Because there is not presently a consensus definition of the term *mild cognitive limitations,* the opportunity exists to shape the thinking regarding this issue from the perspectives of functionality in communities and cultures. In the absence of a consensus definition, it is important to consider the appropriateness of the definition of mental retardation provided by the American Association on Mental Retardation (AAMR) in *Mental Retardation: Definition, Classification and Systems of Support* (Luckasson et al., 1992) for describing adults with mild cognitive limitations. Luckasson and her colleagues defined mental retardation as "substantial limitations in present functioning . . . characterized by significantly subaverage intellectual functioning, existing concurrently with related limitations in two or more of the following applicable adaptive skill areas: communication, self-care, home living, social skills, community use, self-direction, health and safety, functional academics, leisure and work" (1992, pp. 5–7). The definition was further refined with the application of four assumptions:

1. Valid assessment considers cultural and linguistic diversity as well as differences in communication and behavioral factors. . . .
2. The existence of limitations in adaptive skills occurs within the context of community environments typical of the individual's age peers and is indexed by the person's individualized needs for support. . . .
3. Specific adaptive limitations often coexist with strengths in other adaptive skills or other personal capabilities. . . .
4. With appropriate supports over a sustained period, the life functioning of the person with mental retardation will generally improve. (Luckasson et al., 1992, pp. 6–7)

The authors of these recommendations leave open the spectrum of approaches that can be incorporated into the process to integrate these assumptions.

Mental retardation has been described as a "particular state of functioning that begins in childhood and in which limitations in intelligence coexist with related limitations in adaptive skills [functioning]" (Luckasson et al., 1992, p. 9). Edgerton described mental retardation as a "relative concept, the limits of which have meaning only in terms of social condition" (1967, p. 3). When using the American Association on Mental Retardation (AAMR) definition to guide thinking about individuals with mild cognitive limitations, it is important to recognize that the concept of functionality—a specific individual's ability to successfully negotiate the environment in which he or she lives—is greatly affected by culture. Edgerton concluded that mild mental retardation was a social phenomenon with its roots in society and culture.

The concept of functionality coexisting with limitations in intelligence is problematic when used to define adults with mild cognitive limitations. Documenting mild limitations in intelligence requires confirmation of below average intellectual functioning with a thorough, valid psychological examination. One dimension of *valid* assumes that standardized measures are available to assess individuals whose social, linguistic, and cultural backgrounds vary greatly (Luckasson et al., 1992). This validity issue is further complicated by the use of IQ scores as a normative means for establishing limitations in intelligence. Many researchers have challenged the validity of IQ tests as a measure of intelligence for individuals living in or from cultures other than European American cultures (Condon, 1979; de la Cruz, 1996; Heller, 1982; *Larry P. v. Riles*, 1972; Lipsky & Gartner, 1995; Rose & Huefner, 1984). In addition, the IQ test mean of 100 and the standard deviation of 15 presents issues concerning measurement and definition when attempting to diagnose individuals with mild cognitive limitations.

Luckasson and her colleagues suggested that

> If appropriate standardized measures of conceptual intelligence are not available (as, for example . . . when persons are observed in cultural settings different from their home countries), the general guideline for consideration of intellectual functioning performance as determined by clinical judgment is that it must be below the level attained by approximately 97 percent of persons of comparable age and cultural backgrounds. (1992, pp. 35–36)

The concept of using "clinical judgment" appears to be made in the spirit of strengthening standard measurement techniques of intelligence in cultural communities where specific techniques are not available. Using clinical judgment to strengthen validity seems appropriate if the clinician has an extensive and thorough understanding of the culture. However, in the absence of in-depth understanding of the culture, clinical judgment would be viewed through an ethnocentric lens (which will be discussed later) and could be expected to be less than accurate. It appears that the suggestion of "level attained by approximately 97 percent of persons of comparable age and cultural backgrounds" is an attempt to accommodate the "error" in clinicians' cross-cultural judgment. Personal lessons learned in working across cultures lead the chapter authors to suggest that the ability of professionals to interpret other cultures accurately renders "clinical judgment" an invalid tool in assessment.

Compounding these problems are concerns regarding the effects of labeling and the potential stigma that can result, as expressed by Luckasson et al. (1992) as well as others (Edgerton, 1967; Susman, 1994). This concern is particularly troublesome when working with adults whose cognitive limitations are mild. If diagnosed, these individuals may encounter stigma and labeling that may be more compromising than the cognitive limitation.

Tajfel and Fraser (1979) suggested that self-esteem was a function of one's identity as a member of a group, with relative status being defined as either "in-group" or "out-group" by other groups and society. According to Phinney (1990), ethnic identity is comprised of several elements, including self-identification and a sense of belonging. Ogbu (1992) distinguished between voluntary and involuntary minorities and described involuntary minorities as those who have been denied true assimilation into mainstream society. The potential exists that adults with mild cognitive limitations who are not European Americans are doubly seen as involuntary minorities, denied access based on both cognitive limitations and cultural heritage.

Edgerton (1967) described adults with mild cognitive limitations as individuals in society who attempt to cover themselves with a "cloak of competence" (p. 217). He described this cloak as "at best, a tattered and transparent garment that is held together only with the help of others" (p. 218). He also acknowledged that the stigma attached to individuals with mild cognitive limitations is even more critical than the problem of incompetence. The stigma of being defined as "mentally inferior" led the individuals he studied to devote their lives to "passing" (as typical) and denying to themselves that they were "mentally retarded." Edgerton's work has never been more applicable than now. Professionals, institutions, and communities have not yet learned to deal with the problem of stigma.

Lipsky and Gartner (1995) adopted the position that special education policy constitutes a double segregation of ethnic minority students. They concluded that special education services sort out minority students, limit their educational achievements, and then provide justification for their failure. This inability to deal successfully with the issue of stigma is a major barrier to the development of a rubric that addresses the issue of adults with mild cognitive limitations. Most adults who can be identified as having mild cognitive limitations prefer not to be; they walk a tightrope of marginality so as to avoid being labeled, which leads to stigmatization. How can we address a segment of the population that does not wish to be addressed under a stigmatizing label? How do we move people and communities forward and assist, train, and provide resources in an area in which there is great need but insufficient means of documenting and measuring the degree of need? What mechanisms can we develop and provide to communities to help them move forward in meeting the needs of adults with mild cognitive limitations? Should the profession harness its resources to forcibly create mechanisms for labeling; or, does the profession have the will, understanding, and ability to invoke more creative, open, and reciprocal ways to work with individuals, their families, and communities in diagnosing and meeting the needs of adults with mild cognitive impairments? The authors of this chapter urge the latter approach. Learning and working within communities and cultures is an essential part of a broad strategic approach to successfully uncloak the stigmatization and move toward a productive system of support for and integration of adults with mild cognitive limitations.

The concept of "adaptive skills" identified by Luckasson et al. (1992) appears to be useful in guiding the thinking of professionals about adults with mild cognitive limitations. As mentioned previously, adaptive skills include communication, self-care, home living, social skills, community use, self-direction, health and safety, functional academics, leisure, and work. The value or weighing of importance that each culture places on "adaptive skills" differs greatly. Some communities and cultures recognize other important adaptive skills that are not reflected in the profession's definition. Assessment and provision of services utilizing the adaptive skill criteria may be problematic and even, at times, inappropriate in some communities.

Professionals working to serve adults with mild cognitive limitations must address the complex scientific and social issues of definition and identification. An alternative to identifying and working with adults with mild cognitive limitations is to develop public policy and programs that support all adults, consequently reaching unidentified adults with mild cognitive limitations. The notion of Americans establishing policies and programs and adapting behaviors, resulting in a "kinder and gentler" society, is appealing. The interaction among professionals and communities and cultures, the understanding of functionality, and individuals' ability to successfully negotiate the environment is at the heart of efforts to shape programs that support adults with mild cognitive limitations.

DEMOGRAPHICS AND EPIDEMIOLOGY

A natural starting point for public health professionals exploring the topic of adults with mild cognitive limitations is to review the demographics and epidemiology of the condition. A literature review produced little information regarding the demographics and epidemiology of adults with mild cognitive limitations. Obvious reasons for this dearth of demographic information include the absence of consensus regarding a definition of mild cognitive limitations and a lack of valid instrumentation to identify and classify adults with mild cognitive limitations. From the point of view of a public health professional, this is problematic. The inability to identify the population may mean that those who would benefit from interventions may not receive them. For example, living independently is difficult for some adults with mild cognitive limitations. Evidence from longitudinal studies shows that programs for individuals with developmental disabilities can increase the likelihood of independence (Lozano, 1993). Establishing this understanding enables the profession to better serve adults with mild cognitive limitations. However, the issue of stigma associated with identification, as described by Edgerton (1967), provides a compelling argument against proceeding down the path of diagnosis.

The United States is a diverse society, as is the subgroup of adults with mild cognitive impairments. African Americans represent 12.7% of the total population of the United States. Latinos represent 10.9%, Asian and Pacific Islanders 3.7%, and American Indians and Alaskan Natives 0.9% of the population (Bureau of Census, 1990). People of other ethnicities, immigrants, and children of mixed ethnicity are a growing population in the United States. Cultural diversity is greater in large U.S. cities.

The general trend is for a breakdown in the process of assimilation, as the American "melting pot" gives way to the concept of a cultural "tossed salad." A decreased rate of assimilation and a corresponding increase in diversity are the result of a dramatic increase in the number of immigrants to the United States—peaking at 1.8 million people in 1991—and a change in the composition of these immigrants. Prior to the 1990s, the majority of immigrants to the United States came from Europe, and their assimilation was relatively easy. In 1990, only 15% of immigrants to the United States came from Europe, 44% came from Latin America and the Caribbean, and 37% came from Asia (Rogers & Steinfatt, 1999).

Each community's interpretation of health and approaches to health care are influenced by various elements of culture, religion, spirituality, psychosocial relationships among members, kinship patterns, group compositions, social roles, language, values and beliefs, and attitudes about health, suffering, and death (Molina & Aguirre-Molina, 1994; Wright & Santa Cruz, 1983). The degree to which these and other factors affect the cultural interpretation and perceptions of ethnic/racial groups with regard to individuals with cognitive limitations is relatively unknown. It is important to recognize the desirability of investigating the extent to which the needs of individuals with cognitive limitations constitute an interest to people of different cultures and communities. No group lacks an explanation of the conditions that must be fulfilled or maintained for an individual to enjoy good health. In addition, no group lacks explanations for the causes of illness or physical and mental disabilities.

The actual prevalence rates of adults with mild cognitive limitations have not been established. Based on household interviews of the civilian noninstitutionalized population, an estimated 1,562,000 individuals with mental retardation who have conditions that cause limitation of activity live in communities throughout the United States. Annually, approximately 10 per 1,000 individuals experience limited activity because of their disabilities. The annual number of adults receiving federal Social Security payments for impairments as a result of mental retardation differs also depending on the family's socioeconomic status. Almost three times as many individuals experience limited activity annually as a result of mental retardation in families with incomes less than $20,000 than in families with incomes in excess of $35,000. Limited activity by geographical region differs little (U.S. Bureau of Census, 1990). Individuals with mental retardation accounted for 27.7% of people receiving federal Social Security income payments during December 1997. This percentage amounted to a total of 712,916 adults between the ages of 18 and 64 who received Social Security income payments during that month (U.S. Social Security Index, 1998).

Using data from 1990 to 1991, Fujiura and Yamaki (1997) provided prevalence estimates of developmental disabilities by ethnic groups for individuals older than 3 years of age. They estimated that 1 in 100, or 1%, of the population in the United States has developmental disabilities. Estimated prevalence rates by ethnic group were as follows: Caucasian, 0.90%; African American, 1.36%; and Latino/Hispanic, 0.82%. Sample sizes for Native and Asian American populations were too small to construct valid estimates. An analysis of monthly household income found income differences among households that had a family member who had developmental disabilities. Households with a family member who had developmental disabilities had significantly lower monthly incomes than households with no family members with developmental disabilities. These differences held true across ethnic groups. The researchers were careful to point out that the relationship of race and ethnicity is complex. "Race and ethnicity are not 'causes' of disability and not presented as explanatory variables" (Fujiura & Yamaki, 1997, p. 290). The findings of Fujiura and Yamaki (1997), Asbury (1991), and Asian Human Services of Chicago (1996) support the complex relationships among ethnicity, disabilities, poverty, access to services and social institutions, and general circumstances of health and well-being described by Ficke (1992). For example, estimates of the prevalence of mental retardation among Asian Americans in Chicago were set at 2,277 individuals. This number was almost 20 times the number (117 people) actually receiving services for the disability (Asian Human Services of Chicago, 1996). These complex relationships have long been issues of concern in public circles.

Fujiura and Yamaki (1997) identified three conceptual and methodological challenges that must be overcome in establishing demographic descriptions of individuals with disabilities in America. They included "defining developmental disability using survey data, determining the validity of the identification, and establishing relatively stable low-prevalence population estimates" (p. 291). Individuals representing the culture of the community need to be partners in efforts to address these challenges.

Issues of ethnicity and culture are complex and sometimes confused. Ethnicity is based in family genetics. Culture, on the other hand, is based in the beliefs, norms, and practices of the family and community in which one lives. Because culture is difficult to quantify, data regarding the demographics and health status of cultural groups are not readily available. The federal government and most states do collect and classify demographic and health information by ethnicity. However, this approach has contributed to confusion about ethnicity and culture in demographic and epidemiological issues.

COMMUNITY

The term *community* is broad and has been used to refer to a group of people who share 1) a common locality or common government, 2) common values, or 3) common characteristics. Within the context of this chapter, the term *community* is used interchangeably with the word *culture*.

The public is the product of many communities of diverse people whose interests and needs usually overlap (Reagan & Brookins-Fisher, 1997). The public includes sub-groups self-defined by religion, race, politics, sexual orientation, gender, geography, and socioeconomics. Individuals are dispersed in socially differentiated communities, each with its own unique health risks and needs (Reagan & Brookins-Fisher, 1997). However, each community is part of the public concern and welfare.

A community is a "dynamic whole that emerges when a group of people participate in common practices, depend on one another, make decisions together, identify themselves as part of something larger than the sum of their individual relationships, and commit themselves for the long term to their own, one another's, and the group's well-being" (Schaffer & Anundsen, 1993, pp. 7–8). A community, in itself, is not static; it is a viable, changing entity that is continuously being redefined by internal and external factors, with complex processes leading to further change.

The community context is critical and must be addressed in order to meet future challenges for providing service and assistance to adults with mild cognitive limitations. In working with communities to identify and provide assistance to adults with mild cognitive limitations in the new millennium, community and community health must include advocacy, empowerment, asset mapping, and capital (i.e., resources) building. Community-based approaches must include open-mindedness toward social issues and culturally unique issues, including the manner in which these issues shape perceptions. This is particularly critical when addressing issues of mild cognitive limitations among the poor and communities of color. In the past as well as the present, communities of color and low-income communities have had to deal with a multiplicity of factors that account for a disproportionate representation of minorities being misclassified and misdiagnosed in the field of special education (Asbury, 1991; Chan, 1979; Condon et al., 1979; Heller, 1982; Manni, 1980; Rueda, 1993). Overrepresentation of many minority groups in areas such as mental retardation and special education have led to mistrust and unease when addressing this very topic with institutional and professional culture. As a result, developing understanding, trust, assistance, and support among different communities may involve reopening dialogue with a community in addition to just addressing the needs of an overlooked, if not forgotten, segment of American society.

CULTURE

No consensus exists on the definition of *culture* or the interpretation of the ways that culture affects human behavior. There are as many definitions and conceptions of culture as there are disciplines and fields of study. Culture can be seen as a socially inherited "lens" through which an individual perceives and understands the world he or she inhabits (Helman, 1995). This cultural lens provides a framework for transmitting guidelines (implicit and explicit) about individual behavior and beliefs in relation to other people, social forces, and the environment. Individuals or group members slowly acquire the cultural lens of the society of which they are a part, a process known as enculturation. Additional divisions within the cultural framework, such as family configuration, gender, age, and geographic region (sometimes known as subcultures), provide the dimensions and domains of culture.

One of the oldest debates in anthropology has been over the term *culture*. Some problems arise from how the term refers to both a process (i.e., the "passing on" of what has been learned before to succeeding generations) and a particular class (e.g., "shared knowledge"). The term *culture* first appeared in an English dictionary in the 1930s. The first use in an anthropological work was traced to Tylor, who defined culture as "that complex whole which includes knowledge, belief, art, moral, laws, customs and any other capabilities and habits acquired by man as a member of society" (Kroeber, 1949, p. 123). In addition, two widely used definitions were proposed later. Linton suggested that culture means "the total social heredity of mankind" (1936, p. 78), and Herskovitz described culture as "the manmade part of the human environment" (1948, p. 17). Hall described culture as "those deep, common, unstated experiences which members of a given culture share, which they communicate without knowing, and which form the backdrop against which all other events are judged" (1966, p. 121). These concise definitions contrast with lengthy listings of what is included in culture. Wissler (1923) included speech, material traits, art, knowledge, religion, society, property, government, and war. Kroeber and Kluckhohn also provided a definition of culture:

> Culture consists of patterns, explicit (customs and behaviors) and implicit (ideas and meanings), of and for behavior acquired and transmitted by groups, including their embodiments in artifacts. The essential core of culture consists of traditional (i.e., historically derived and selected) ideas and especially their attached values. Cultural systems may on the one hand be considered as products of action, on the other as conditioning elements of future action. (1952, p. 181)

Culture, broadly defined, provides the blueprint for the way that individuals and groups perceive, believe, evaluate, and behave (Giroux, 1988; Goodenough, 1987). LeVine described culture as "a shared organization of ideas that include the intellectual, moral and aesthetic standards present in a community" (1984, p. 80). Culture imposes order and meaning on all experiences and provides clues to help predict how people will react in certain situations. Culture is learned, beginning at birth. Cultural customs bind individuals together and provide guidelines that make it possible for them to function as a community. Culture is continually changing and adapting to environmental conditions, natural resources, technological resources, and power structures (Gollnick & Chinn, 1990). "No events, reactions or habits of a group of people can be understood without understanding the context of the culture of which they are a part" (Gollnick & Chinn, 1990, p. 7). Within the U.S. macroculture, based primarily on European customs and practices, many microcultures and subcultures exhibit distinct patterns that are not common to the macroculture. For example, professionals working in the field share a common bond that could be considered a subculture.

In every society, there is a spectrum between what people regard as normal and abnormal social behavior. This spectrum affects the ways that health is recognized, determined, labeled, explained, and treated. Definitions of normality, similar to definitions of health, vary widely throughout the world; in many cultures, these two concepts overlap. Definitions are based on shared beliefs within a group of people as to what constitutes the ideal, "proper" way for individuals to conduct their lives in relation to others (Helman, 1995). There is no recipe to determine cultural behavior, beliefs, and perceptions among any one cultural group; to provide one is to assume that cultures, like communities, are static entities with set outcomes. At best, what one can provide is a set of general guidelines that serve to inform about, not dictate, health-related behavior and action among an identified community/cultural group.

HEALTH BELIEFS AND PRACTICES IN AMERICA

Cultural factors are an important determinant of health-related behaviors and beliefs. They play an essential role in terms of health (Helman, 1995; Molina & Aguirre-Molina, 1994). No medical system (i.e., a network of ideas about causes and cures of disease) is either entirely rational or entirely irrational. Because curing and healing practices are a function of the beliefs about the nature of health and the causes of illness, most curative procedures are understandable and logical in light of those beliefs. Health beliefs in all cultures are among those held to most tenaciously. The stress of illness and the everpresent fear or acceptance of death are not conducive to "rational actions," if by "rationality" one means abandonment of traditional procedures for new and little-understood approaches.

Within the study of culture, social scientists have delineated specialized subfields. Medical anthropology specifically addresses health and illnesses in different cultural contexts. Its focus includes the way that different social groups explain the causes of ill health, the types of treatment in which they believe, and the various structures of access to health care. Margaret Clark's (1959) seminal work, *Health in the Mexican-American Culture: A Community Study*, illustrates the integration of anthropological and public health approaches to show how medical systems are affected by major categories of culture (e.g., economics, family structure, education, language, social relationships). The work of Helman serves as an excellent example of the different theoretical frameworks that exist in medical anthropology for examining culture and health. In *Culture, Health and Illness: An Introduction for Health Professionals*, Helman (1995) focuses on how a consideration of sociocultural context uncovers crucial relationships among modes of living, behavior, and health. He examines cultural and social meanings and symbols and the extent to which aspects of health and illness are culture-bound.

Asad (1973) claimed that "the concept of culture can be used to subordinate as well as to liberate" (p. 12). In developing emerging frameworks that address culture as part of a strategic approach to better understand the status and challenges of adults with mild cognitive impairments, professionals working in this field must avoid a serious danger—the overemphasis of culture in interpreting how people behave and believe. Although examining a person's culture is of key importance, the emphasis on cultural factors must not preclude examination of other significant and contributing factors.

The growing diversity of society has emphasized the importance of understanding that all ethnic/racial groups have some similarities but also set differences in perceptions and explanations concerning health and illness. Given the changing nature of society and the communities of which society is comprised, this emphasis must be expanded to include the status, roles, and challenges of adults with mild cognitive impairments. Just as with illness and disease, ethnic/racial groups can and do differ in their perceptions and interpretation of individuals with mild cognitive impairments, although this area of study rarely has been addressed. The growing number of children and adults with special health care needs as a result of mild and serious cognitive impairments point to a growing need to understand more about cultural group variations in this area.

ISSUES OF PROFESSIONAL CULTURE

For most professionals, a disparity exists between their culture and the culture of the communities they serve. Individuals working with adults with mild cognitive limitations are not unique. Professionals working in the field of mental retardation have been the recipients of aggressive advocacy from families, friends, and citizens with mental retardation. As a result, the culture of professionals has to some degree been positively influenced by the culture of the community. This influence has contributed to a recent change in the way professionals view mental retardation.

Members of the macroculture, surrounded by others whose understandings are defined by the macroculture, struggle to overcome ethnocentrism. Even well-intentioned professionals working in the field of mental retardation are not exempt from this struggle. Ethnocentrism is the inability to view other cultures as providing equally viable alternatives in explaining reality as one's own culture. It is common to view one's own culture as natural, correct, and superior and to perceive other cultures as odd, amusing, inferior, or even immoral (Gollnick & Chinn, 1990). Individuals who share the macroculture and who have received their professional preparation in academic settings that reflect the macrocultural values face lifelong struggles to avoid interpreting the acts of others through their own cultural screens. Ethnocentrism is also reflected in public policy. Braddock and Fujiura (1991) found that the strength of consumer groups and historical orientations toward adoption of policies promoting racial equality were highly significant predictors of state spending patterns for community mental retardation services. The inability to view cultures through a lens other than one's own is a barrier to understanding; it can negatively affect the services those in other cultures receive.

LESSONS LEARNED FROM PUBLIC HEALTH

During the 1990s, professionals working in the disabilities field began to explore preventive and early interventions in an effort to prevent, delay the onset of, or minimize developmental delays (Adams & Hollowell, 1992; Ager, 1990; Berlin, 1990; DeMoor, Van Waesberghe, Hosman, Jaeken, & Miedems, 1993; Fiene & Taylor, 1991; Koenning et al., 1995; Majnemer, 1998; Shonkoff, Hauser-Cram, Krauss, & Upshur, 1992; Simeonsson, 1991; Simeonsson, Bailey, Huntington, & Brandon, 1991). In a review of early intervention and prevention programs to minimize developmental delays, Majnemer (1998) found a growing consensus that preventive efforts can produce moderate effects. Simeonsson (1991) identified goals of prevention interventions in the context of community-based rehabilitation: to enhance development and minimize delay to reduce the future need for special services and the likelihood of institutionalization and other restrictive outcomes. Professionals serving adults with mild cognitive limitations should carefully consider the lessons that public health leaders learned as they shaped the disease prevention and health promotion movement during the 1970s, 1980s, and 1990s.

Emerging Models of Prevention

The rapid development of computer-based technologies in the early 1970s made it possible to identify risk factors for chronic disease. As a result, a model of prevention is emerging from the "disease model" that has dominated health care in the 20th century. The beginning point in the disease model was when an individual presented to the physician with symptoms of illness. A *diagnosis* was made, *treatment* was applied, and, when necessary, *rehabilitation* was provided. Treatment to prevent future complications and limitations caused by illness was labeled *tertiary prevention.* The ability to identify risk factors that increased the likelihood of future disease provided an opportunity to intervene to eliminate or reduce those risk factors prior to the development of the disease—*secondary prevention.* Interventions designed to prevent risk factors from developing or to delay the onset of risk factors in healthy populations were labeled *primary prevention* efforts. The development of the prevention model and preventive interventions were clearly anchored in the disease model. Currently, health professionals are reassessing their view of primary prevention and asking the question: What do children need to grow up healthy? The answer has begun to shape a component of primary prevention built on a model of family and community strengths, personal and social skills, opportunity, and support. Primary preventive interventions constructed from this perspective are very different from those anchored in the disease model. Professionals serving adults with mild cognitive limitations should consider the implications of this development.

Vulnerable and Target Populations

Majnemer (1998) identified two groups of children with developmental delays that might be "targeted" for early interventions: children who were biologically vulnerable and children who were environmentally vulnerable. Although the criteria and process of identifying biologically vulnerable children seems fairly straightforward, public health professionals have found the idea of identifying environmentally vulnerable populations is full of cultural pitfalls and bias. The concept of environmental vulnerability assumes judgments based on cultural perspectives. For example, early in the prevention movement, environmental risk factors were identified through the ethnocentric lens of public health leaders. These risk factors invariably included elements of the micro- or subculture that were perceived as risky by the macroculture because of the macroculture's inability to view the world in terms other than its own. As a result, individuals, families, and communities were targeted for interventions designed to bring them in line with the macroculture's health beliefs and practices. Today, community-based approaches have reported success using a community health advocate who is familiar with the culture, traditions, and languages of the families he or she serves to identify the family's needs and to interpret issues (Ardito, Botuck, Freeman, & Levy, 1997; Bauer, 1993). Such an approach would be advisable for those providing services to adults with mild cognitive limitations.

Lessons learned in public health lead us to advise professionals serving adults with mild cognitive limitations to proceed cautiously in efforts to identify those at "environmental risk." The definition of environmental risk is unique to each community and culture. We would also urge professionals to discard the concept of targeted populations and replace it with a concept that sounds less like the computerized dropping of a Scud missile.

Models for Working in Communities

The profession's conceptualization of a model that uses capabilities, environments, and functioning to define those individuals with mental retardation is similar to a paradigm called the *Public Health Model,* which emerged in the first half of the 20th century as a model to prevent infectious diseases. In recent years, public health professionals have modified this model and developed other models that reflect increased understanding of the importance of environmental factors and new ways of working with communities and cultures. This is consistent with the work of Edgerton (1988), Garber (1988), and Landesman and Vietz (1987), which identified the importance of the environment in supporting and fostering development. "For individuals with [cognitive limitations] these positive environments constitute settings that are . . . appropriate for the individuals' sociocultural background" (Luckasson et al., 1992, p. 12). Schalock and Kiernan (1990) described desirable environments as those that provide individuals with opportunities to fulfill their needs; foster physical, social, cognitive, and material well-being; and promote stability, predictability, and control. From the occupational therapy profession, Kalscheur (1992) recommended moving away from the deficit model traditionally used to serve individuals with disabilities to an environmentally centered model that emphasizes education and consultation with businesses and individuals for the purposes of altering the environments to be accessible and accommodating. Hahn (1995) was critical of the individual deficit model used in special education and argued for a sociopolitical definition that views disability as a consequence of the interactions between individuals and the environment. Gelberg and Andersen (1997) suggested that professionals providing services to vulnerable populations use a modified *behavioral model of health services utilization,* which incorporates the concept of social support to enable a person to gain better access to services. Aday (1997) discussed the importance of applying models of health service utilization, which can be especially helpful in identifying the particular challenges each specific community faces in obtaining needed services.

Community Organizing

Professionals interested in the interactive relationship between communities and adults with cognitive limitations should consider the lessons learned in public health. Minkler (1990) described two opposing models of community organizing. The "paternalistic" model grew out of the American social worker movement and attempted to serve the needs of newly arrived immigrant populations near the end of the 19th century. Needed social services were identified and brokered by professional social workers who perceived themselves to be acting in the best interests of the individuals they served (paternalism). In this well-intended process, social workers identified the needs of their clients, developed and delivered interventions, and evaluated the consequences. The clients were either passive or not-so-passive recipients. Clients who objected or resisted services were ignored or discounted. The remnants of this paternalistic model still can be found today in social services, public health, and educational institutions. In some institutions, the paternalistic model dominates. Knoll (1992) cited strong elements of paternalism in testimonies of families describing the experience of raising a child with a disability or a chronic disease. Knoll cited many examples in which the families described social services professionals, including special educators, who implied that the family was out to "milk the system." Families were treated as beneficiaries of benevolent charity. The paternalistic model is problematic and especially inappropriate when service providers from one culture attempt to determine the needs of clients from another culture.

The second community organizing model grew out of the labor and political activist movement of the 1950s. Political activists and trade unionists developed an approach to working with communities in collaborative ways to identify issues and problems and to initiate change. These movements illustrate that adults with mild cognitive limitations are not alone in their recent and increasing demands for participation and inclusion in community decisions and in the way that services and supports are provided (Bollini & Siem, 1995; Braddock & Fujiura, 1991; DeMoor et al. 1993; Mackelprang & Salsgiver, 1996; Susman, 1994). These issues of equity, autonomy, empowerment, and control over destiny have been organizing forces for other historically excluded groups, including laborers, migrant farm workers, and individuals and families living in poverty in barrios and ghettos across the nation. Individuals and groups who wish to construct policies and programs to support adults with mild cognitive limitations should consider the successes in these arenas.

Empowerment

Fiene and Taylor (1991) suggested that the empowerment of parents should be the goal of family-oriented, community-based case management for all children with developmental disabilities. Although *empowerment* has become a widely used term, it is a difficult concept to define. Rappaport suggested that the absence of empowerment, that is, "powerlessness, helplessness, and alienation," is easier to define than the presence of empowerment (1987, p. 2). Rappaport pointed out that the presence of empowerment "takes on a different form in different people and contexts" (1987, p. 2). Wallerstein added to the definition of empowerment by describing it as a "multilevel construct that involves people assuming control and mastery over their lives . . . gaining a sense of control and purposefulness . . . as they participate" (1992, p. 189).

Zimmerman (1990) described the empowerment of individuals as including participatory behavior, motivation to exert control, and feelings of efficacy and control. Fetterman, Kaftarian, and Wandersman (1996) described the purpose of empowerment as to help people help themselves and to improve their situations by using self-reflection, action, and self-evaluation. Wallerstein (1992) has suggested that the indicators of empowerment include self-efficacy, or perceived ability to be successful in accomplishing a specific task; perceived control; critical thinking ability; and the presence of social support.

The empowerment approach to working with families and communities in ways that are consistent with the culture has been emerging slowly within social services and community health professions. Health professionals' support for the empowerment approach is reflected in the proceedings of the World Health Organization (WHO) Conference on Health Promotion held in Ottawa, Canada, in 1986. The definition of *health promotion* emerging from that conference reflected a shift in thinking regarding the relationships among professionals and their clients, communities, and cultures. Health promotion was defined as "the process of enabling people to increase control over, and improve their health." Conference attendees further concluded that, "To reach a state of complete physical, mental and social well-being an individual or group must be able to identify and to realize aspirations, to satisfy needs, and to change or cope with the environment." Health was defined as a "positive concept emphasizing social and personal resources, as well as physical capacities" (WHO, 1986, p. 1). Cultural heritage is at the core of personal and social resources.

"Health promotion works through concrete and effective community action in setting priorities, making decisions, planning strategies and implementing them to achieve better health. At the heart of this process is the empowerment of communities [and individuals], their ownership and control of their own endeavors and destinies" (WHO, 1986, p. 3). This focus signaled the end of an era in public health dominated by the medical model in which clients were identified by their "problems" (as viewed by the culture of the professional), and interventions were designed to target the clients and their problems. Emerging from the 1986 conference was the view of the professional as a specialist and consultant whose responsibility is to work with individuals, families, and communities to enable them to achieve their fullest health potential. The social and personal resources and physical capacities of each individual, family, and community subsequently became the building blocks for achieving good health. One of the greatest assets of most individuals, families, and communities is their cultural heritage.

Freire's (1970, 1993) philosophies and theories related to empowerment were originally developed for and applied to adult literacy and education in Brazil. He believed that the ability of critical reflection differentiates human beings from animals and that oppression denies humans the right to reflect critically on and direct their relationship with the world. When people are given the opportunity to reflect critically on their world, they develop what Freire considered the first stage of emergent consciousness. From transitive consciousness, people progress to critical consciousness, a stage that includes an apprehension and analysis of reality as a problem and challenge.

The application of empowerment has focused primarily on groups of people and communities. These strategies often have included community organizing and have used the power of numbers for change (Hanna & Robinson, 1994). Community empowerment strategies take into account the context of the participants and are built on the traditions, cultures, and strengths of the participants.

Wallerstein (1992) described the following model for professionals working to empower communities. The first stage involves community members in a thorough investigation of the culture and customs that shape their lives. In the second stage, professionals work with community members to help identify themes that may better enable the community to analyze the root causes of a situation. The third and final stage involves planning, implementing, and evaluating a course of action to overcome the situation in which the community finds itself.

Working with Clients

The role and responsibilities of the professional as an expert consultant serving individuals, families, and communities require skills and knowledge not necessarily acquired in professional preparation programs. Briskin and Liptak (1995) described the importance of physicians in helping families to understand the emotional effects of disabilities; providing information about diagnosis, prognosis, and associated issues; providing nonjudgmental listening; providing information about community resources, including parent support groups; and ensuring adequate communication among those involved in the care of family members. Rosenbaum (1998) identified useful issues that the professional should consider in interpreting and sharing results of screening tests and standardized assessments with individuals and their families. Abrams and Goodman (1998) concluded that the diagnoses of developmental disabilities are constructed jointly through informal negotiations between parents and professionals. Understanding the culture and health beliefs of the family is essential to successful negotiations.

Sustainability

Sustainability of programs has long been a concern of professionals and funding agencies working across cultures; but during the 1980s and 1990s, sustainability has been recognized as the key quality of health and other development programs, especially in Latin America, Africa, and Asia. For instance, the World Bank refuses to initiate development programs unless they have a high likelihood of continuing after the original technical and financial assistance ends. Ager (1990) expressed the opinion that to be truly effective and sustainable, programs serving individuals with disabilities need to consider the culture of the communities in which they operate. The concept of sustainability is an important consideration for professionals as they work with families and communities to shape programs that support adults with mild cognitive limitations.

Mapping and Building on Strengths

The notion of "strengths," or social and personal competence (Greenspan, 1979, 1981, 1990; McGrew & Bruininks, 1990), was used to guide the development of the capacity concept, one of the three key elements in the definition of mental retardation in Luckasson et al. (1992). Although language used to describe the element of capacity presents the view that all individuals have social and personal competence or strengths, the primary focus appears to be on the absence of such strengths or competencies (Luckasson et al., 1992). This perspective on deficiency has been a barrier to public health professionals' attempts to develop prevention efforts. The public health concept of "good health" has been overshadowed by the definition imposed by the medical model, which defines health as the absence of sickness. Public health professionals have found this deficit thinking detrimental to their efforts to support healthy development within individuals, families, and communities.

McKnight and Kretzmann (1990), working out of the Center for Urban Development at Northwestern University, introduced public health professionals to a concept they had originally used to guide thinking related to the redevelopment of urban centers. This approach was capacity focused, with policies and activities built on the capacities, skills, and assets of the community. The capacities, skills, and assets become the building blocks of the development of the community.

This thinking has helped many public health professionals clarify the concept that assets and resources, not problems and deficiencies, are the basis of healthy development. In the mid- to late 1990s, public health and social services leaders have begun to apply this conceptual thinking to the health and development of individuals, families, and communities, which traditionally had been "mapped" and provided social services based on their deficiencies. Individuals, families, and communities are now viewed in terms of their strengths.

This approach makes good sense when applied personally. None of us have achieved our personal or professional goals by focusing on our shortcomings. Our achievements have been built on our strengths. When viewed in terms of their strengths, adults with mild cognitive limitations have great potential. This concept of assets is not new or unknown to families, friends, and communities who have supported adults with mild cognitive limitations.

QUALITY OF LIFE: LIVING WITH MILD COGNITIVE LIMITATIONS

Schalock and Kiernan (1990) identified the important contribution of community environment to quality of life. Edgerton (1967) provided rich descriptions of the quality of life of 48 adults with mild mental retardation who were attempting to live successfully in communities. Edgerton's descriptions indicated that the lives of individuals with mild mental retardation are filled with abuse, manipulation, despair, and isolation. Dossa (1992) presented a framework for use in assessing quality of life of individuals based on ethnographic analysis. The quality of life for individuals with disabilities is a function of their own personal behavior and the support available and accommodations made within their families and communities. Community-based instruments to assess quality of life for adults living with mild cognitive limitations may get at the heart of issues faced by these adults.

ADVOCATES AND BENEFACTORS

Many university-based programs preparing professionals to work in social services fields have identified advocacy as one of their stated outcomes. The literature clearly supports the notion that professionals have an important role in advocating for policy and legislation and in connecting individuals with needed services. Edgerton (1967) devoted an entire chapter to identifying the individuals who acted as "benefactors" for adults he studied. He found that almost all of the more than 40 adults studied were successful in acquiring one or more benefactors who supported them in their efforts to live successfully within the community. These benefactors (in order of most commonly identified) included 1) partners or spouses, 2) employers, 3) neighbors or community members, 4) family members, and 5) professionals. From the rich descriptions provided by Edgerton, it appears that benefactors contributed greatly to the quality of life for these adults. The importance of advocates and benefactors has implications beyond professional preparation programs. Policies and programs that support employers' and community members' efforts to act as advocates and benefactors need to be considered.

OTHER ISSUES OF COMMUNITIES AND CULTURE

The experiences of the authors have resulted in the identification of additional issues of communities and culture that might be considered in supporting people with mild cognitive limitations.

Differing Cultural Priorities

Definitions within the field of mental retardation have argued that intelligence and adaptive behavior should have equal weight in diagnosis and follow-up services and programs (Luckasson et al., 1992). Several references were cited by Luckasson et al., who noted that "in practice, IQ has typically dominated and thus, has been overemphasized both in terms of professional decision-making and classification (e.g., Furlong & LeDrew, 1985; Harrison, 1987; Reschly & Ward, 1991) and research (e.g., Hawkins & Cooper, 1990; Smith & Polloway, 1978)" (p. 39). Reviewing the 10 adaptive skill areas identified by the expert panel (Luckasson et al., 1992) from a community and cultural perspective raises important issues. It appears that these skill areas are defined by the culture of the professional. Do they accurately represent the perceptions of any community or culture? Are they appropriate reflections of the multiple communities and cultures of America in which professionals work with families to serve adults with mild cognitive impairments?

Different weighting and criteria reflecting values exist in all communities and cultures. For example, although individuals are viewed in terms of all 10 of the adaptive skills areas, in rural Iowa the criteria is defined by working-class, European descendants who place a high value on hard work. Midwest farmers often describe an individual as a "good worker," reflecting their community's value for work. Individuals are not judged primarily on their intellectual capacity, as they might be in academic settings, but on their work capacity. In the same vein, adults with highly defined work skills are not viewed in terms of their mild cognitive limitations or perceived as a burden in midwestern culture. Adults who do not work hard, regardless of their intellectual capacity, may be viewed as a burden.

In many indigenous cultures, qualities of "goodness" and "intentions" are highly valued. An elder American Indian described a primary value of his culture: "We have seen you people come and go for generations. We are able to assess your intentions. It is like a sense. In addition to being able to see, hear, touch and smell something, we have the ability to see inside people. We can see whether your intentions are good" (personal communication, 1995). Fijians reflect similar cultural values in describing individuals as "good" or "not good." In many cultures, individuals with selfless intentions are valued highly. Adults with selfless intentions and mild cognitive limitations are not viewed as a problem. Adults with unclear or selfish intentions, regardless of intellectual capacity, are problematic.

It is interesting to note that "work," but not "goodness," is considered an adaptive skill. Adaptive skills appear to be limited to ten areas that academicians have the ability to conceive and measure—personal and professional culture. The profession needs to ask the question, "Do the medical model, cultural ethnocentrism, and principles of scientific inquiry limit professionals' ability to adequately assess the strengths of an individual?"

Families and Communities Supporting Development

Traditionally, families, friends, and communities have shouldered the responsibility and invested large amounts of time in supporting the development of individuals with mild cognitive limitations. Family businesses and farms and subsistence living provide adults with mild cognitive limitations opportunities to be successful and to contribute in meaningful ways. This approach continues today in many cultures in the United States. In many extended families, several generations contribute to the family business. For example, grandmothers make tamales or kimchee. Children do dishes, clean, and wait tables. Mothers, aunts, and uncles cook. Grandfathers and uncles arrive early at the market to purchase fresh fish and vegetables, and college-bound children handle the finances. The wide range of duties and responsibilities in small businesses allows the owner to accommodate adults with mild cognitive limitations. Edgerton (1967) found that nonfamily employers often became the benefactors or advocates for adults with cognitive limitations who were integrated into the community. In a small business, strong loyalty and trustworthiness are often more valuable commodities than high intellectual capacity. The sense of responsibility and the concept of valuing the assets of individuals—"She's a good worker"—are alive and well among small business owners.

The sense of responsibility for family and community members differs among cultures. Informal support can come from extended family members and even community members (Spicer, 1981). Tennstedt and Chang (1998) found that cultural factors accounted for differences in need for and receipt of informal care among African American, Puerto Rican, and non-Hispanic white adults. Even when controlling for disability, older African American and Puerto Rican adults received more informal care than did older Caucasians. Mary (1990) found that Hispanic mothers showed greater attitudes of self-sacrifice toward children with mental retardation than did Caucasian or African American mothers. The needs of individuals with disabilities also appear to be a factor in the amount of time families invest in support activities. Crowe (1993) found that mothers of children with multiple disabilities spent significantly more time on child-related activities than did mothers of children with Down syndrome and mothers in a control group. The support that family and community provides to individuals with mild cognitive limitations is an important element in their ability to successfully integrate and contribute to that community. As a nation, we must build on the concepts of family and community support. We must consider public policies that support and enable small family and community businesses to be successful. Such infrastructure is an essential element contributing to the success of adults with mild cognitive limitations.

Individual, Family, and Community Rights

Students in public health often ask professors, "What do I need to know and what skills do I need to work with individuals and families from other cultures?" The answer is not found in the *Framework for Development of Competency-Base Curriculum for Entry Level Health Educators* (National Commission for Health Education Credentialing, 1985), as defined by the profession. Our experience is that the decision as to whether a professional should work with a particular individual, family, or community is rightfully made by the individual, family, or community and not by the professional. Individuals, families, and communities routinely exercise this decision-making power. An assessment of the professional's "intentions" is often one criteria that is used when service providers of the macroculture seek to work in communities of another culture. The decision to allow or not allow the professional to work in the community is not always communicated directly. In some instances, such as on American Indian reservations, the decision may be directly communicated, and professionals perceived as inappropriate may not be given permission to work or may even be asked to leave the reservation. In other instances, the individual, family, or community may only indirectly communicate the decision through noncooperation. In these cases, professionals sometimes label the client as noncompliant.

Competition, Individualism, and Cooperation

During the 16th, 17th, and 18th centuries, a new American culture emerged from European roots, overpowering the native cultures that had existed in North America for thousands of years. Europeans brought with them cultural mores that placed a high value on the concept of competition. The social value for competition was bolstered by the concept of survival-of-the-fittest and the establishment of the Constitution of the United States, which emphasized the power of the individual. Concepts of competition and individualism have served some Americans well and have enabled them to achieve great power and wealth. However, adults with mild cognitive limitations often are unable to compete successfully and find only isolation in a society dominated by these social values.

Many cultures, including those of indigenous people around the world, embrace and value a contrasting concept—cooperation. Prior to the arrival of Europeans in the Americas, life in indigenous families and communities was based on cooperation and willingness to produce food, provide support and assistance, and aid development that enhanced the community. Success was celebrated collectively by all community members. Failure was shared by all. Today many families and communities in which adults with mild cognitive limitations live share these values. Many Americans and some professionals serving these adults fail to understand cultures that value cooperation and collective good. While living on the Fijian Island of Taveuni, one of the authors of this chapter met an American who, shaking his head, concluded, "No wonder these Fijians are so poor. They can't even make money running the only store. If a relative or friend needs something and has no money, the store-keeper just gives it away. . . . No wonder they never get ahead." The American was referring to the Fijian concept of *kari-kari,* which means that all goods belong to the society and that it is the social norm and expectation that those who have excess will share with relatives and friends. It is culturally appropriate and expected that the owner of the store would share his goods. Such behavior serves all Fijians well, including adults with mild cognitive limitations.

Professionals working in communities that value cooperation can build on that cultural strength to better serve adults with mild cognitive limitations. In cultures that place high value on competition, professionals working with adults with mild cognitive limitations might pursue research, program development, evaluation, and policies that introduce the concept of cooperation. This ability to use perspectives and strengths from other cultures is a true reflection of the achievement of multiculturalism—the recognition that several different cultures can exist in the same environment and benefit each other (Rogers & Steinfatt, 1999).

Striving Toward Multiculturalism and Cultural Pluralism

Despite the historical dominance of the macroculture, life in America today is influenced by hundreds of micro- and subcultures. In the year 2000, Americans of non-European descent constitute more than 28% of the population (Bureau of Census, 1995). Although America is a multicultural society, many Americans are not multicultural. Hoopes defined multiculturalism as "states in which one has mastered the knowledge and developed the skills necessary to feel comfortable and communicate effectively 1) with people of the culture encountered and 2) in any situation involving groups of people of diverse cultural backgrounds" (1979, p.21). Some professionals (most of them from micro- or subcultures) have competencies in and can operate successfully in two or more cultures. The concept of multiple cultures co-existing on an equal basis, referred to as cultural pluralism (Kallen, 1915), has not yet been achieved in the United States. Kallen challenged Americans to recognize that each culture has something to contribute to American society. He believed that the ideas of democracy and equality carry an implicit assumption that there are differences among groups of people and that individuals from different cultures are equal. Services for adults with mild cognitive limitations embedded within cultural pluralism and multiculturalism are the appropriate response and the goal for the future. Rogers and Steinfatt (1999) provided guidelines for professionals for developing intercultural competence; overcoming ethnocentrism, stereotyping, prejudice, and discrimination; and moving toward multiculturalism.

REFERENCES

Abrams, E.Z., & Goodman, J.F. (1998). Diagnosing developmental problems in children: Parents and professionals negotiate bad news. *Journal of Pediatric Psychology, 23*(2), 87–98.

Adams, M.J., Jr., & Hollowell, J.G. (1992). Community-based projects for the prevention of developmental disabilities. *Mental Retardation, 30*(6), 331–336.

Aday, A. (1997). Expanding the behavioral model of health services to explore the health status and health services use of homeless and other vulnerable populations. In L. Gelberg & R.M. Andersen, *Association Health Services Research, 14,* 63–64.

Ager, A. (1990). The importance of sustainability in design of culturally appropriate programmes of early intervention. *International Disability Studies, 12*(2), 89–92.

Ardito, M., Botuck, S., Freeman, S.E., & Levy, J.M. (1997). Delivering home-based case management to families with children with mental retardation and developmental disabilities. *Journal of Case Management, 6*(2), 56–61.

Asad, T. (Ed.). (1973). *Anthropology and colonial encounter.* New York: Humanitics Press.

Asbury, C.A. (1991). *Disability prevalence and demographic association among race/ethnic minority populations in the United States: Implications for the 21st century* (No. 2) Monograph Series Number Two. Washington, DC: Research and Training Center for Access to Rehabilitation and Economic Opportunity, Howard University.

Asian Human Services of Chicago. (1996, June). *A study of the special needs of Asian-Americans with developmental disabilities in the Chicago metropolitan area.* Chicago: Author.

Bauer, S. (1993). Community clinic offers access to care: A system and city collaborate to care for an immigrant population. *Health Progress, 74*(8), 42–44, 65.

Bauwens, E. (1981). Medical beliefs among low income Anglos. In E.H. Spicer (Ed.), *Ethnic medicine in the southwest,* (pp. 241–258). Tucson: The University of Arizona Press.

Berlin, I.N. (1990). The role of the community mental health center in prevention of infant, child and adolescent disorders: Retrospective and prospective. *Community Mental Health Journal, 26*(1), 89–106.

Bollini, P., & Siem, H. (1995). No real progress toward equity: Health of migrants and ethnic minorities on the eve of the year 2000. *Social Science and Medicine, 41*(6), 819–828.

Braddock, D., & Fujiura, G. (1991). Politics, public policy, and the development of community mental retardation services in the United States. *American Journal on Mental Retardation, 95*(4), 369–387.

Briskin, H., & Liptak, G.S. (1995). Helping families with children with developmental disabilities. *Pediatric Annals, 24*(5), 262–265.

Bureau of Census. (1990). *Statistical Abstract of the United States.* Washington, DC: U.S. Department of Commerce.

Bureau of Census. (1995). *Statistical Abstract of the United States* (116th ed.). Washington, DC, U.S. Department of Commerce.

Bureau of Census. (1997). *Statistical Abstract of the United States* (117th ed.). Washington, DC: U.S. Department of Commerce.

Chan, K.S., & Rueda, R. (1979). Poverty and culture in education: Separate but equal. *Exceptional Children, 45*(6), 422–428.

Chan, S.Q. (1979). *Services for the developmentally disabled: A study of Asian families.* Unpublished dissertation, Los Angeles: University of California.

Clark, M. (1959). *Health in the Mexican-American culture: A community study.* Berkeley: University of California Press.

Condon, E.C. (1979). *Special education and the Hispanic child: Cultural perspectives.* New Brunswick, NJ: Rutgers, The State University, Johnson and Johnson Institute for Intercultural Relations and Ethnic Studies.

Crowe, T.K. (1993). Time use of mothers with young children: The impact of a child's disability. *Developmental Medicine and Child Neurology, 35*(7), 621–630.

de la Cruz, R.E. (1996). *Assessment-bias issues in special education: A review of literature.* Washington, DC: ERIC Document Reproduction Service No. ED 390 246.

DeMoor, J.M., Van Waesberghe, B.T., Hosman, J.B., Jaeken, D., & Miedems, S. (1993). Early intervention for children with developmental disabilities: Manifesto of the Eurlyaid working party. *International Journal of Rehabilitation Research, 16*(1), 23–31.

Dossa, P.A. (1992). Ethnography as narrative discourse: Community integration of people with developmental disabilities. *International Journal of Rehabilitation Research, 15*(1), 1–14.

Edgerton, R.B. (1967). *The cloak of competence: Stigma in the lives of the mentally retarded.* Berkeley: University of California Press.

Edgerton, R.B. (1988). Community adoption of people with mental retardation. In J.F. Kavanagh (Ed.), *Understanding mental retardation: Researcher accomplishment and new frontiers* (pp. 311–318). Baltimore: Paul H. Brookes Publishing Co.

Fetterman, D.M., Kaftarian, S.J., & Wandersman, A. (Eds.). (1996). *Empowerment evaluation: Knowledge and tools for self-assessment and accountability.* Thousand Oaks, CA: Sage Publications.

Ficke, R. (1992). *Digest of data on persons with disabilities.* Washington, DC: National Institute on Disability and Rehabilitation Research.

Fiene, J.L., & Taylor, P.A. (1991). Serving rural families of developmentally disabled children: A case management model. *Social Work, 36*(4), 323–327.

Freire, P. (1993). Translated by Myra Bergman Ramos. *Pedagogy of the oppressed.* New York: Continuum.

Fujiura, G.T., & Yamaki, K. (1997). Analysis of ethnic variations in developmental disability prevalence and household economic status. *Mental Retardation, 35*(4), 286–284.

Furlong, V.J., & LeDrew, L. (1985). IQ=68=mildly retarded? Factors influencing multidisciplinary team recommendations on children with FS IQs between 63 and 75. *Psychology in the Schools, 22,* 5–9.

Garber, H.L. (1988). *The Milwaukee Project: Preventing mental retardation in children at risk.* Washington, DC: American Association on Mental Retardation.

Gelberg, L., & Andersen, R.M. (1997). Expanding the behavioral model of health services to explore the health status and health services use of homeless and other vulnerable populations. *Associated Health Services Research (14)*2, 62–63.

Giroux, H.A. (1988). *Teachers as intellectuals: Toward a critical pedagogy of learning.* Granby, MA: Bergin & Garvey.

Gollnick, D.M., & Chinn, P.C. (1990). *Multicultural education in a pluralistic society.* Columbus, OH: Merrill.

Goodenough, W. (1987). Multiculturalism as the normal human experience. In E.M. Eddy & W.L. Partridge (Eds.), *Applied anthropology in America* (pp. 89–96). New York: Columbia University Press.

Greenspan, S. (1979). Social intelligence in the retarded. In N.R. Ellis (Ed.), *Handbook of mental deficiency: Psychological theory and research* (2nd ed., pp. 1–89). Hillsdale, NJ: Lawrence Erlbaum Associates.

Greenspan, S. (1981). Defining childhood social competence: A proposed working model. In B.K. Keogh (Ed.), *Advances in special education* (Vol. 3, pp. 1–39). Greenwich, CT: JAI Press.

Greenspan, S. (1990). *A redefinition of mental retardation based on a revised model of social competence.* A paper presented at the annual meeting of the American Association on Mental Retardation, Atlanta.

Hahn, H. (1995). Challenges to the current special education system: Two analyses. *NCERI Bulletin, 2*(1).

Hall, E.T. (1966). *The hidden dimension.* New York: Doubleday.

Hanna, M., & Robinson, B. (1994). *Strategies for community empowerment.* New York: Mellen.

Harrison, P.L. (1987). Research with adaptive behavior scales. *Journal of Special Education, 21*, 255–262.

Hawkins, G.D., & Cooper, D.H. (1990). Adaptive behavior measures in mental retardation research: Subject description in AJMD/AJMR (1979–1987). *American Journal on Mental Retardation, 94*, 654–660.

Heller, K.A. (Ed.). (1982). *Placing children in special education: Equity through valid educational practices: Final report.* Washington, DC: Institute of Medicine, National Research Council.

Helman, C. (1995). *Culture, health, and illness: An introduction for health professionals.* Boston: Wright Publishing.

Herskovitz, M.J. (1948). *Man and his works. The science of cultural anthropology.* New York: Knopf.

Hoopes, D.S. (1979). Intracultural communication concepts and the psychology of intercultural experience. In M.D. Pusch (Ed.), *Multicultural education: A cross cultural training approach* (pp. 9–38). LaGrange, IL: Intercultural Network.

Kallen, H.M. (1915). *William James and Henri Bergson: A study in contrasting theories of life.* Chicago: University of Chicago Press.

Kalscheur, J.A. (1992). Benefits of the Americans with Disabilities Act of 1990 for children and adolescents with disabilities. *American Journal of Occupational Therapy, 46*(5), 419–26.

Knoll, J. (1992). Being a family: The experience of raising a child with a disability or chronic illness. *Monographs of the American Association on Mental Retardation, 18,* 1–56.

Koenning, G.M., Todaro, A.W., Benjamin, J.E., Curry, M.R., Spraul, G.E., & Mayer, M.C. (1995). Health services delivery to students with special health care needs in Texas public schools. *Journal of School Health, 65*(4), 119–124.

Kroeber, A.L. (1949).The concept of culture in science. In A.L. Kroeber (Ed.), *The nature of culture* (pp. 118–135). Chicago: Chicago University Press.

Kroeber, A.L. & Kluckhohn, C. (1952). *Culture: A critical review of concepts and definitions.* Cambridge, MA: Peabody Museum

Landesman, S., & Vietz, P. (Eds.). (1987). *Living environments and mental retardation.* Washington, DC: American Association of Mental Retardation.

Larry P. v. Riles. Civil No. C-71-2270, 343 F. Supp. 1306 (N.D. Cal., 1972).

Levine, R.A. (1984). Properties of culture: An ethnographic view. In R.A. Shweder & R.A. Levine (Eds.), *Culture theory: Essays on mind, self, and emotions* (pp. 67–87). New York: Cambridge University Press.

Linton, R. (1936). *The study of man.* New York: Appleton-Century-Crofts.

Lipsky, D.K., & Gartner, A. (1995). The evaluation of inclusive educational programs. *NCERI Bulletin, 2*(2), 2–11.

Lozano, B. (1993). Independent living: Relation among training, skills, and success. *American Journal on Mental Retardation, 98*(2), 249–262.

Luckasson, R., Coulter, D.L., Polloway, E.A., Reiss, S., Schalock, R.L., Snell, M.E., Spitalnak, D.M., & Stark, J.A. (1992). *Mental retardation: Definition, classification and systems of supports.* Washington, DC: American Association on Mental Retardation.

Mackelprang, R.W., & Salsgiver, R.O. (1996). People with disabilities and social work: Historical and contemporary issues. *Social Work, 41*(1), 7–14.

Majnemer, A. (1998, March). Benefits of early intervention for children with developmental disabilities. *Seminars in Pediatric Neurology, 5*(1), 62–69.

Majumjdar, B., Browne, G., & Roberts, J. (1995). The prevalence of multicultural groups serving in-home service from three community agencies in southern Ontario: Implications for cultural sensitivity training. *Canadian Journal of Public Health/Revue Canadienne de Santé Publique, 86*(3), 206–211.

Manni, J.L. (1980). *The status of minority group representation in special education programs in the state of New Jersey: A summary report.* Trenton: New Jersey State Department of Education, Bureau of Pupil Personnel Services.

Mary, N.L. (1990). Reactions of black, hispanic, and white mothers to having a child with handicaps. *Mental Retardation, 28*(1), 1–5.

McGrew, K., & Bruininks, R. (1990). Defining adaptive and maladaptive behavior within a model of personal competence. *Social Psychology Review, 19,* 53–57.

McKnight, J., & Kretzmann, J. (1990). *Program on community development: Mapping community capacity.* Chicago: Center for Urban Affairs and Policy Research, Northwestern University.

Minkler, M. (1990). Improving health through community organization. In K. Glanz, F.M. Lewis, & B.K. Rimer (Eds.), *Health behavior and health education: Theory, research and practice* (pp. 236–257). San Francisco: Jossey-Bass.

Molina, C., & Aguirre-Molina, M. (1994). Latino populations: Who are they? In C. Molina & M. Aguirre-Molina, *Latino health in the US: A growing challenge* (pp. 3–22). Washington, DC: American Public Health Association.

National Commission for Health Education Credentialing. (1985). *Framework for development of competency-base curriculum for entry level health educators.* New York: National Commission for Health Education Credentialing.

Ogbu, J.U. (1992, November). Understanding cultural diversity and learning. *Educational Researcher,* 5–24.

Phinney, J.S. (1990). Ethnic identity in adolescence and adulthood: A review of research. *Psychological Bulletin, 108,* 499–514.

Rappaport (1987). Terms of empowerment—exemplars of prevention: Toward a theory of community psychology. *American Journal of Community Psychology, 23*(5), 569–579.

Reagan, P.A., & Brookins-Fisher, J. (1997). *Community health in the 21st century.* Needham Heights, MA: Allyn & Bacon.

Reschly, D.J., & Ward, S.M. (1991). Use of adaptive behavior and overrepresentation of black students in programs for students with mild mental retardation. *American Journal on Mental Retardation, 96,* 257–268.

Rogers, E.M., & Steinfatt, T.M. (1999). *Intercultural communications.* Prospect Heights, IL: Waveland Press.

Rose, E., & Huefner, D.S. (1984). Cultural bias in special education assessment and placement. In T.N. Jones & D.P. Semler (Eds.), *School law update: Preventive school law* (pp. 179–188). Kansas State Department of Education.

Rosenbaum, P. (1998). Screening tests and standardized assessments used to identify and characterize developmental delays. *Seminars in Pediatric Neurology, 5*(1), 27–32.

Rueda, R. (1993). An analysis of special education as a response to the diminished academic achievement of Chicano students. In R. Valencia (Ed.), *Chicano school failure and success: Research and policy agendas for the 1990s* (pp. 252–271). New York: Falmer Press.

Schaffer, C., & Anundsen, K. (l993). *Creating community anywhere: Finding support and connection in a fragmented world.* New York: Putnam.

Schalock, R.L., & Kiernan, W.E. (1990). *Habilitation planning for adults with developmental disabilities.* New York: Springer-Verlag.

Shonkoff, J.P., Hauser-Cram, P., Krauss, M.W., & Upshur, C.C. (1992). Development of infants with disabilities and their families: Implications for theory and service delivery. *Monographs of the Society for Research in Child Development, 57*(6), 1–153.

Simeonsson, R.J. (1991). Early prevention of childhood disability in developing countries. *International Journal of Rehabilitation Research, 14*(1), 1–2.

Simeonsson, R.J., Bailey, D.B., Jr., Huntington, G.S., & Brandon, L. (1992). Scaling and attainment of goals in family-focused early interventions. *Community Mental Health Journal, 27*(1), 77–83

Smith, J.D., & Polloway, E.A. (1978). The dimension of adaptive behavior in mental retardation research: An analysis of recent practices. *American Journal on Mental Retardation, 84*, 203–206.

Spicer, E.H. (1981). *Ethnic Medicine in the Southwest.* Tucson: The University of Arizona Press.

Susman, J. (1994). Disability, stigma and deviance. *Social Science and Medicine, 38*(1), 15–22.

Tajfel, H. & Fraser, C. (1978). Introducing social psychology. New York: Penguin.

Tennstedt, S., & Chang, B.H. (1998). The relative contribution of ethnicity versus socio economic status in explaining differences in disability and receipt of informal care. *Journal of Gerontology, Series B, Psychology Sciences and Social Sciences, 53*(2), S61–70.

Turner, J.C., Brown, R.J., & Rajfel, H. (1979). Social-comparison and group interest in group favoritism. *European Journal of Social Psychology, 9*(2), 187–204.

Tylor, E.B. (1871). *Primitive culture.* London: Murray.

U.S. Social Security Index. (1998). *SSI annual statistical report 1997.* Washington, DC: Social Security Administration, Office of Research, Evaluation and Statistics.

Wallerstein, N. (1992). Powerlessness, empowerment, and health: Implications for health promotion programs. *American Journal of Health Promotion, 6*(3), 197–205.

Wissler, C. (1923). *Man and culture.* New York: Thomas Y. Crowell Co.

World Health Organization. (1986). *Ottawa charter for health promotion.* Ottawa: Author.

Wright, P., & Santa Cruz, R. (1983, Fall). Ethnic composition of special education programs in California. *Learning Disability Quarterly, (6)*4, 387–394.

Zimmerman, M. (1990). Taking aim on empowerment research: On the distinction between individual and psychological conceptions. *American Journal of Community Psychology, 23*(5), 581–597.

II

Income Security, Employment, and Career Development

5

Promoting Employment Opportunities for Individuals with Mild Cognitive Limitations

A Time for Reform

John Kregel

The chronic unemployment of individuals with mild cognitive disabilities continues to frustrate self-advocates and their families, as well as the service providers and policy makers who work with these individuals. The unemployment rate for individuals with mild cognitive disabilities remains between 70% and 80% (Wehman & Kregel, 1998) and seems immune to federal and state policy efforts designed to address the problem. Negative and stereotypical attitudes held by some employers continue to discriminate against qualified workers with cognitive disabilities. Many individuals, particularly adolescents and young adults exiting special education systems, remain unable to access the services or supports they need to successfully enter the work force. Still others continue to be isolated in nonintegrated employment settings that hold little hope for long-term career advancement.

The seeming intractability of the employment problems of individuals with mild cognitive disabilities is particularly vexing because substantial efforts have been made to alleviate many of the underlying causes of this dilemma. Federal legislative initiatives, structural changes in the American economy, advancements in rehabilitation technology, changes in societal attitudes, improvements in high school preparation programs, and substantial increases in public expenditures for employment services have combined to raise employment expectations for a generation of individuals with mild cognitive disabilities. For example,

- The Americans with Disabilities Act (ADA) of 1990 (PL 101-336) was passed in 1990 to eliminate employment discrimination and promote career opportunities for qualified individuals with cognitive and other disabilities.

- The rise of the contingent workforce—self-employed, temporary, contracted, and part-time workers—and our booming economy have provided new and exciting alternatives to many individuals who previously had faced restricted job opportunities or had been channeled into stereotypical, dead-end career choices.
- Supported employment has proven to be a highly successful rehabilitation alternative that has allowed tens of thousands of individuals with cognitive disabilities to escape the "black hole" of nonintegrated employment settings (Blanck, 1998) and to participate in the economic life of their local communities.
- A generation of adolescents and young adults with mild cognitive disabilities has benefited from improvements in our nation's special education programs, particularly the recent emphasis on efforts to improve the transition of adolescents with cognitive disabilities from public schools to adult services and employment settings.
- Business and industry have increasingly recognized the value of employees with disabilities and are developing innovative programs to recruit, train, accommodate, and retain workers with cognitive disabilities.
- The national strategy of using Medicaid monies as the primary funding mechanism for residential and employment services for individuals with cognitive disabilities has led to a rapid rise in program expenditures and expansion of program capacity in many states.

Many of the causes of the chronic unemployment of individuals with mild cognitive disabilities are well known. Ongoing myths and misconceptions that lead to employment discrimination, our antiquated and ineffective service delivery system, the irrational disincentives to employment found in the Social Security disability programs, the lack of access by individuals with cognitive disabilities to employment programs funded through the Department of Labor, and school-to-work transition programs that fail to enable adolescents and young adults to enter the workforce upon graduation from secondary school all have been identified as key obstacles to employment.

In many instances, the solutions to these problems are equally well known. Consumers and advocates have long called for major changes to our service system that would both expand the capacity and improve the quality of service provision. Successful strategies used by employers to include individuals with cognitive disabilities in the workforce as well as models used by local communities to implement effective school-to-work transition programs can easily be replicated in many communities across the country. Shortcomings in the Social Security disability programs have been the target of reforms for many years, and efforts are under way to make changes in these programs.

This chapter identifies and describes four major obstacles to employment faced by individuals with cognitive disabilities including

- The need to develop new partnerships with business and industry
- The need to reform our nation's system of sheltered workshops and activity centers
- The need to remove disincentives in the Social Security disability programs
- The need to increase access to programs operated through the Workforce Investment Act of 1998 (PL 105-220)

For each obstacle, recommendations are offered that specify actions that can be taken by federal, state, and local governments as well as employers and community rehabilitation programs to address and overcome the identified barriers.

FORGING NEW PARTNERSHIPS WITH EMPLOYERS

When the ADA was passed in 1990, it was hailed as a watershed event that would change the nature of the relationship between potential employers and individuals with disabilities. The law has done much to promote awareness of the employment potential of individuals with disabilities, including individuals with cognitive disabilities. However, critics have argued that after nearly a decade of implementation, the law has not fulfilled its original promise and has in fact resulted in an attitudinal backlash that has prolonged discrimination against individuals with cognitive disabilities.

Individuals with cognitive disabilities rarely have been involved in litigation under the ADA. Available data collected from 1992 to 1997 indicate that of 82,000 Title I complaints, only 320 (less than 1%) involved individuals with cognitive disabilities. Of the 320 reported charges, 67% involved discharge from employment, 17% involved workplace accommodations, and 21% involved workplace harassment. It is interesting that very few, if any, of the complaints are related to hiring discrimination, illustrating the complexities involved in determining whether an individual with cognitive disabilities 1) is considered a person with a disability under the ADA and 2) is a "qualified worker" as defined by the law.

A careful review of the recent employment experiences of individuals with mild cognitive disabilities makes clear that the ADA will not solve or overcome all of the employment obstacles faced by these individuals. In some instances, individuals with mild cognitive disabilities may not even be covered by the employment protections of the ADA. In other instances, the legally required accommodations prescribed in the law may be insufficient to allow an individual to successfully maintain employment for an extended period of time. In other words, an employer may be in full compliance with the ADA yet still fail to provide the accommodations needed to enable an individual to succeed on the job.

THE NEED FOR A NEW PARADIGM

A new strategy is required. Ensuring that employers comply with the requirements of the ADA is a necessary, but insufficient, approach to employment policy for individuals with cognitive disabilities. New policies must be forged that enlist employers as key partners in the employment process and encourage them to move beyond simple compliance with the law. *Emphasis must be placed on identifying employers who value workforce diversity and realize the contribution that individuals with cognitive disabilities can make to the long-term profitability of the business or industry.*

Blanck (1998) has found that the presence of a positive and proactive corporate culture may have a greater influence on ADA compliance, employer attitudes, and business strategies than the actual provisions of the law and its regulations. Those companies that have implemented the law proactively as a component of an overall diversity management strategy have experienced indirect benefits to the business and its customers. Across the nation, employers of all types are implementing innovative strategies that increase the number of individuals with mild cognitive disabilities who are participating in their labor force and are providing individuals with mild cognitive disabilities with the accommodations necessary to ensure long-term employment success (President's Committee on Mental Retardation [PCMR], 1998). Consider the following examples:

- Employers are incorporating individuals with cognitive disabilities into their human resource and disability management programs. Services are coordinated to allow individuals with cognitive disabilities, as well as all other employees with special needs, to make a significant contribution to the company.
- Large and small businesses are successfully organizing and implementing mentorship programs in which workers with cognitive disabilities are paired with co-workers who have expressed an interest in serving as a mentor.
- Employer–human services agency partnerships have been developed in a number of communities across the country. In these partnerships, employers are responsible for conducting initial training and for providing employee accommodations; human services agencies are responsible for identifying qualified potential applicants and assisting in the design of accommodations as necessary.

The Drive for an Integrated Service System

The supported employment movement has forever changed our nation's view of the employment potential of individuals with cognitive disabilities. As recently as 1986, fewer than 10,000 individuals were served through supported employment programs. In 1999, more than 100,000 individuals with cognitive disabilities were employed in integrated jobs in their local communities through participation in supported employment.

Individuals with cognitive disabilities have consistently comprised approximately 70% of all supported employment participants (Kregel & Wehman, 1997). Individuals with mild cognitive disabilities make up about 45% of all participants with cognitive disabilities. Those individuals who are able to participate in supported employment experience outcomes vastly superior to their counterparts, who continue to be served in segregated employment settings.

Individuals increase their average annual earnings by at least 500% through participation in supported employment (Wehman, Revell, & Kregel, 1998). Supported employment participants earn twice as much as individuals served in sheltered employment settings (Murphy & Rogan, 1995). More than two thirds of individuals participating in supported employment maintain their initial jobs for more than 1 year, and approximately half maintain employment for more than 3 years. In addition, supported employment participants report being more fully integrated into their community and are more satisfied with their jobs than those individuals served in nonintegrated settings. Furthermore, individuals working through supported employment programs are accepted by their co-workers and are rated highly by their supervisors for their work performance.

Supported employment programs generate employment outcomes far superior to those experienced by individuals who continue to be served in sheltered employment situations (Wehman, West, & Kane-Johnston, 1997). In addition, the costs of providing supported employment services are generally similar to, or less than, the costs of nonintegrated employment alternatives. In light of these clear advantages for both consumers and taxpayers, it is difficult to understand why the vast majority of individuals with cognitive disabilities, including those with mild cognitive disabilities, continue to be served in segregated employment alternatives.

A Segregated System

In 1996, state mental retardation/developmental disabilities agencies spent $409 million to provide supported employment services to more than 90,000 individuals with cognitive disabilities (Braddock, Hemp, Parish, & Westrich, 1998). However, four of five adults served by mental retardation/developmental disabilities agencies continue to be served in sheltered workshops, day habilitation, or adult activity centers (Braddock et al., 1998). It is becoming increasingly clear that after a decade of movement toward a more integrated service system, progress is stagnant. Our nation's day service programs seem "capped" in a system in which 80% of all adults continue to be served in segregated settings.

Time for Bold Solutions

The reasons for the continuation of our predominantly segregated service system are well known (Mank, 1994; Murphy & Rogan, 1995). Community rehabilitation programs are often fearful of the staffing, budgetary, and programmatic changes that are necessary when converting traditional day services to integrated employment alternatives. Inequitable reimbursement rates and funding mechanisms create powerful disincentives that severely restrict opportunities for change. Lack of accurate and timely information has made it difficult for consumers and their family members to make informed choices or influence policy.

In 1998, PCMR convened an employment summit to develop policy recommendations regarding community employment of individuals with cognitive disabilities. A group of experts was assembled to discuss the obstacles that presently stifle movement toward a more integrated services system and to design strategies to address the obstacles. The major recommendations of the summit work group on conversion of traditional day services are summarized in the following sections.

Initiate Federal Leadership   Strong federal leadership is required to establish a national policy of expanding integrated community services for individuals with cognitive disabilities. Congress and the federal government should clearly and unequivocally state their commitment to the expansion of community integrated employment alternatives for individuals with disabilities and express their simultaneous intent to reduce expenditures and support for existing segregated employment options. Existing federal employment programs should be reviewed to ensure that current practices are consistent with this stated goal.

Address the Imbalance in Federal Funding   Congress and the federal government should work to ensure that federal monies appropriated through the Rehabilitation Act of 1973 (PL 93-112), Titles XIX and XX of the Social Security Act of 1935 (PL 74-271), and the Individuals with Disabilities Education Act (IDEA) of 1990 (PL 101-476) are used exclusively to support integrated employment alternatives. The Rehabilitation Act should be amended so that placement into segregated employment alternatives no longer represents a successful rehabilitation closure.

Provide Incentives to States   Simultaneously, federal agencies should encourage and promote the efforts of individual states to expand community integrated employment opportunities. States should be allowed to use federal funds to stimulate and support conversion of segregated day services to community integrated employment. Federal reimbursement mechanisms should include clear financial incentives for provision of integrated services. States and local communities attempting to convert to integrated employment services should not be financially penalized.

Provide Assistance to Local Programs   State and local agencies attempting to convert their segregated settings into community-integrated employment options should have access to resources and assistance to guide them through this difficult and complex process. For example, state and federal funds should be used to support people, not service agencies. If an individual who is receiving services in a segregated setting enters a community-integrated employment option, monies used to support the individual's participation in the segregated setting should follow the person into the integrated employment setting. If an individual moves from one community to another within a state, funding for that individual should be "transferred" from one provider agency to another.

Promote Consumer Involvement   State and local agencies must recognize that consumers and their families may be concerned or skeptical about dismantling segregated employment settings that they or their sons and daughters have attended for many years. Service providers must understand that these concerns are quite natural. The attitudes and preferences of consumers and their families should be acknowledged and addressed throughout the conversion process.

Eliminate Disincentives to Employment   Since the mid-1970s, federal expenditures for education, income support, health, and rehabilitation have grown steadily in size, approaching $200 billion annually (Berkowitz, 1996). In no area has this growth in expenditures been more dramatic than in the area of the Social Security disability programs—Social Security Disability Insurance (SSDI) and Supplemental Security Income (SSI) (Stapleton & Dietrich, 1995). The SSDI and SSI programs are designed to rectify the effects of work disability (loss of earnings income) by providing partial earnings replacement. The SSDI program protects workers from financial hardship when significant illness or injury temporarily or permanently interrupts their earning ability. In most instances, the SSDI benefit amounts to less than half of the individual's prior income. In contrast, the SSI program is needs based. It is designed to provide a basic level of income support for individuals with severe work disabilities. Presently, the federal benefit rate has been established at approximately 70% of the federal poverty level (Mashaw & Reno, 1996).

The disincentives in the current Social Security system are very real and extremely damaging to individuals with cognitive disabilities. For example, many individuals who attempt to return to or obtain employment do not experience increases in their net income (Burkhauser & Wittenburg, 1996). The structure of our disability benefit programs threatens many individuals with loss of income supports and health care coverage if they attempt to work. Entering the work force should enable individuals to increase their earnings while lessening the need for income support. However, in many instances, individuals actually are penalized for going to work rather than remaining on benefits.

Reform SSI and SSDI   Participants at the 1998 PCMR Employment Summit felt quite strongly that consumers who choose to obtain employment and pursue a long-term career should not be penalized financially. Individuals should not have to choose between having a job and maintaining access to the health care and other support services they vitally need. A number of specific recommendations were made to reform the SSI and SSDI programs in a way that would allow consumers to attempt to work while not jeopardizing their basic needs for food, clothing, shelter, and medical care. The recommendations included the following:

- Entering the work force should enable individuals to increase their earnings while lessening the need for income support. The current "earnings cliff" in the SSDI should be replaced by a gradual ramp from benefits to work consisting of a $1 SSDI cash reduction for each $2 of earned income after a $500 earned income exclusion.
- Individuals whose benefits have stopped due to increased earnings but who have not medically recovered from their disability should remain eligible for future benefits should they lose their jobs or be unable to work in the future. Continued eligibility should be based solely on medical recovery, not on earnings, to encourage individuals with significant disabilities to enter or return to work.
- In 1999, the monthly earnings level for Substantial Gainful Activity (SGA) was raised from its previous level of $500 (which had been in effect since 1990) to a new level of $700 per month. Even with this raise, the present restrictions on individuals' earning resulting from the current SGA does not provide individuals the ability to earn a living wage and maintain even a modest standard of living. The SGA level should be increased to the $1,000 level in place for individuals who are blind and subsequently indexed to adjust for inflation.

   Maintain Health Coverage   Unfortunately, current beneficiaries who desire to obtain employment face many disincentives that restrict their ability to pursue a career. Individuals with cognitive disabilities and other disabilities generally report that the potential loss of health insurance (physical and mental) is the greatest disincentive to employment. Employer-based insurance frequently is not available, and private insurance generally is unaffordable (Government Accounting Office, 1996).

   The potential loss of medical benefits or lack of access to adequate health insurance is perhaps the greatest single obstacle preventing large numbers of individuals from leaving the beneficiary rolls and entering employment. Individuals should not have to choose between obtaining a job and maintaining their medical coverage. The recently passed Ticket to Work and Work Incentives Improvement Act of 1999 establish new health coverage provisions that allow individuals with disabilities to maintain or procure Medicaid coverage while remaining employed.

States should participate in the Medicaid buy-in program, established in 1997, which ensures that individuals will have access to comprehensive, affordable health care coverage that remains available even after individuals enter the workforce.

States also should participate in the Medicaid buy-in program targeted to meet the needs of individuals who would be eligible for the SSDI program except for earnings above SGA.

Ongoing access to medical services, assistive technology, personal assistant services, and transportation should be made available to people with disabilities through establishment of Medicaid/Medicare buy-in options and expansion of impairment-related work expense incentives.

Co-payment requirements for individuals served through the Medicaid Home and Community-Based Waiver program should be reduced to allow individuals to keep more of their salary as their earnings increase over time.

The Workforce Investment Act of 1998

Congress passed the WIA of 1998 (PL 105-220) as an attempt to consolidate and improve the efficiency of a myriad of employment programs. The WIA represents the first major reform of the nation's job training system in more than 15 years, replacing the previous Job Training Partnership Act of 1982 (PL 97-300) and its system of Private Industry Councils. The purpose of the WIA is to establish a nationwide system of coordinated and consolidated employment services that provides information, advice, job search assistance, and training to workers, while meeting the needs of employers for skilled labor.

The WIA is intended to overcome many of the weaknesses of our current, splintered system of federal employment programs for individuals with disabilities and other groups in need of employment services, such as welfare recipients, veterans, displaced workers, and homeless individuals. It is based on the following principles:

- Allowing individuals to choose among providers and select job training that best meets their needs
- Providing accurate and complete information regarding available jobs, the skills required by those jobs, and the training institutions that most effectively prepare people for those jobs
- Eliminating duplication of services and promoting the coordination of federal, state, and local employment activities
- Increasing accountability to ensure that financial rewards are targeted to the most effective and efficient local programs

The foundation of the new workforce investment system is a national system of One-Stop Career Centers that will concentrate a wide range of training, education, and employment programs into a single, user-friendly system. The

WIA requires that a One-Stop system be established in each local area. A local board, in collaboration with the local elected official, will be allowed considerable flexibility in the design and operation of the One-Stop system in their local area.

Coordination can be achieved through strategies such as the use of common intake and case management systems. Core services, intensive services, and training will be available to meet the needs of a variety of customers, including individuals with cognitive disabilities. Core services include such things as determination of eligibility for services, intake, orientation to the One-Stop system, initial assessment, job search and placement assistance, career counseling, and provision of labor market information. Intensive services are defined as including diagnostic testing, development of an individual employment plan, individual counseling and career planning, case management, and short-term prevocational services. Training services also are provided to some individuals who are unable to obtain or retain employment through intensive services.

Accommodate Individuals with Cognitive Disabilities in One-Stop Centers

The system of One-Stop Career Centers is designed as the cornerstone of our nation's effort to provide effective and comprehensive employment services to all citizens, including individuals with disabilities. But does "all" in this case really mean *all* citizens, or will individuals with cognitive disabilities be frustrated when attempting to access needed support services through the system? After all, few individuals with cognitive disabilities were able to easily and effectively gain access to services through the Job Training Partnership Act, the precursor to the present program (Wehman, 2001).

WIA specifically requires that individuals with disabilities, individuals whose primary language is not English, and other individuals be accommodated within One-Stop Career Centers. However, efforts to date have focused almost exclusively on eliminating architectural barriers and physical accessibility. Little if any emphasis has been placed on ensuring that personnel in the One-Stop Career Centers will be knowledgeable of the needs of individuals with mild cognitive disabilities and able to work with these individuals in the development of person-centered employment plans. Furthermore, the types of training and support services needed by many individuals with cognitive disabilities, such as supported or transitional employment, have not traditionally been provided by One-Stop Career Centers.

It is imperative that these potential shortcomings not be viewed as insurmountable obstacles that preclude the participation of individuals with cognitive disabilities in programs provided through the WIA. The vast array of resources available through the act and its key role in long-term employment policy make it essential that individuals with cognitive disabilities be included and fully benefit from the program.

CONCLUSION

A little more than a decade ago, Burton Blatt, when reflecting on the history of our field, described what he termed the "special amnesia" of mental retardation professionals: "There are more cornerstones than remembrances of why the buildings were built, what the vision promised, if there had even been a vision at the dedication. In our field, there are more heroes than victories" (1987, p. 362). As we enter the new millennium, Blatt's words continue to ring true. There are still many heroes in our world:

- The individuals with cognitive disabilities who overcome stereotypes and limited expectations each day as they contribute to the economic vitality of their communities
- The personnel managers who ignore the skepticism of their colleagues and supervisors to incorporate individuals with cognitive disabilities into the labor force
- The job coaches and other direct services personnel who allow individuals with cognitive disabilities to direct their own careers and choose the services and supports they need
- The advocates who continue to fight for needed services and reforms while political and economic forces attempt to overwhelm

The contributions of our heroes must not be underestimated or ignored. Yet, for all of our efforts, our victories have been few. The Americans with Disabilities Act has not resulted in the dramatic changes we hoped it would make. The powerful momentum toward integrated community services has not been sustained. Waiting lists for employment services continue to expand, and we cannot promise our current generation of high school students with cognitive disabilities that they will be able to exit school and immediately begin to pursue their career goals.

We know what to do! We know which policies are senseless, which components of the service system are antiquated, and which of many new and effective innovations must be made available to all individuals with cognitive disabilities who desire employment. We must summon the personal and collective courage to address these issues. We must turn the achievements of our heroes into victories for our field.

REFERENCES

Americans with Disabilities Act (ADA) of 1990, PL 101-336, 42 U.S.C. §§ 12101 *et seq.*

Berkowitz, M. (1996, October 31). *Federal programs for persons with disabilities: To what extent is employment supported?* Employment and Return to Work for People with Disabilities. Washington, DC: National Press Club.

Blanck, P.D. (1998). *The Americans with Disabilities Act and the emerging workforce: Employment of people with mental retardation.* Washington, DC: American Association on Mental Retardation.

Blatt, B. (1987). *The conquest of mental retardation.* Austin, TX: PRO-ED.

Braddock, D., Hemp, R., Parish, L., & Westrich, J. (1998*). The state of the states in developmental disabilities* (5th ed.). Washington, DC: American Association on Mental Retardation.

Burkhauser, R.V., & Wittenburg, D.C. (1996). How current disability policies discourage work: Analysis of the 1990 SIPP (Panel IV). In S. Daniels, *Employment and return to work for people with disabilities* (pp. 1–44). Washington, DC: National Press Club.

Government Accounting Office. (1996). *People with disabilities: Federal programs could work together more efficiently to promote employment.* Washington, DC: Author.

Job Training Partnership Act of 1982, PL 47-300, 29 U.S.C. §§ 1501 *et seq.*

Kregel, J., & Wehman, P. (1997). Supported employment: A decade of employment outcomes for individuals with significant disabilities. In W.E. Kiernan & R.L. Schalock (Eds.), *Integrated employment: Current status and future directions* (pp. 31–48). Washington, DC: American Association on Mental Retardation.

Mank, D. (1994). The underachivement of supported employment: A call for reinvestment. *Journal of Disability Policy Studies, 5(2)*, 1–24.

Mashaw, J. & Reno, V. (1996*). Balancing security and opportunity: The challenge of disability income policy: Findings and recommendations of the Disability Policy Panel.* Washington, DC: National Academy on Social Insurance.

Murphy, S.T., & Rogan, P.M. (1995). *Closing the shop: Conversion from sheltered to integrated work.* Baltimore: Paul H. Brookes Publishing Co.

President's Committee on Mental Retardation [PCMR]. (1998). *A better place: The contribution of Americans with mental retardation to our nation's workforce.* Washington, DC: Author.

Stapleton, D., & Dietrich, K. (1995, July 20–21). *Long-term trends and cycles in application and growth in awards.* Paper presented at the SSA/ASPE conference on the Social Security Administration's Disability Programs, Washington, DC.

Wehman, P. (2001). *Life beyond the classroom: Transition strategies for young people with disabilities* (3rd ed.). Baltimore: Paul H. Brookes Publishing Co.

Wehman, P., & Kregel, J. (Eds.). (1998). *More than a job: Securing satisfying careers for people with disabilities.* Baltimore: Paul H. Brookes Publishing Co.

Wehman, P., Revell, G., & Kregel, J. (1998, Spring). Supported employment: A decade of rapid growth and development. *American Rehabilitation, 24*(1), 31–43

Wehman, P., West, M., & Kane-Johnston, K. (1997). Improving access to competitive employment for persons with disabilities as a means of reducing social security expenditures. *Focus on Autism and Other Developmental Disabilities, 12*(1), 23–30.

Workforce Investment Act of 1998, PL 105-220, 29 U.S.C. §§ 794d.

6

Corporate-Initiated Workplace Supports

Paul Wehman, Pamela Sherron Targett, Michael D. West,
Helen Eltzeroth, J. Howard Green, and Valerie Brooke

Individuals with cognitive limitations represent one of the greatest untapped human resources for the nation's labor force. Yet, thousands of these individuals remain situated in day treatment programs, adult activity centers, sheltered workshops, nursing homes, and even state institutions despite numerous written and videotaped reports showing the obvious employment capabilities and potential of these individuals. The reasons for the unemployment of individuals with cognitive limitations, as well as individuals with other significant disabilities, were well chronicled in the 1990s (Wehman, 1996; Wehman & Kregel, 1998). Health care and social security disincentives, transportation barriers, employer and parent attitudes, and funding problems each contribute to the limited participation of individuals with cognitive limitations in competitive employment.

Clearly, the U.S. economy cannot be blamed for a lack of jobs; throughout the 1990s and into the new millennium, the economy has been in the best shape that it has been in in decades. More jobs have been created since 1992 than in any other time period in the 20th century. The inflation rate in the year 2000 was lower than it was during the early 1950s. Consumer inflation in particular was at an 11-year low in 1997 (Wilson, 1998). The unemployment rate in the United States was at or below 5% from April 1997 to July 1999 (Bureau of Labor Statistics, 1998a). The September 1998 unemployment rate of 4.6% has not been lower since March 1970 with the exception of the rates for April and May 1998, which dipped to a low of 4.3% (Bureau of Labor Statistics, 1998a). Interest rates have been moderate and have not interfered with the growth of the economy, which was anticipated to expand at an average rate of approximately 2.6% annually from 1993 to 1999 (Reynolds, 1998). Fourteen million new jobs were created between 1991 and 1997 (Melzer, 1997). In April 1998 alone, about 250,000 new jobs were created in the national economy ("Unemployment Plunges Further," 1998).

As a result of outsourcing and a wave of corporate mergers, more and more economic activity is being shifted out of inefficient firms—or those parts of firms that are inefficient—and into the hands of large, specialized companies that have determined the most economical way to accomplish particular tasks and that can take advantage of the economies of scale. Furthermore, innovations such as telecommuting, employee leasing, temporary work agencies, the Internet, computer technology, mobile telecommunication devices, part-time work, and self-employment have helped companies utilize existing personnel in a more efficient way (Bureau of Labor Statistics, 1997, 1998b). Technological advances undergird a number of these new innovations and probably will play an important role in making the new workplace accessible to individuals with disabilities (McCormick, 1994). Companies also are increasingly using training and education as a means of developing human capital and meeting strategic goals (Franzis, Gittleman, Horrigan, & Joyce, 1998). Significantly, participation in employment-related training appears to occur more frequently for young workers with more formal education (Hight, 1998). Individuals with disabilities also may benefit from this new emphasis on training and education.

Increasingly, the questions become, "What must happen in the workplace to help individuals with disabilities capitalize on the extraordinary changes that are transpiring and enjoy the fruits of well-paying jobs in competitive employment?" and, "What role will people with disabilities play, especially as the demand for labor becomes incredibly tight?" In 1998, the vice chairman of the Federal Reserve was quoted as saying, "At the rate businesses are hiring, the U.S. economy will soon run out of workers"; based on this statement, there is something terribly wrong, or at least highly inefficient, with a labor market in which large numbers of individuals with disabilities remain unemployed. In a 1998 poll of 15,600 employers, Manpower, Inc. ("Labor Shortage," 1998), found that 32% of these employers planned to hire more people in the next 3 months than they hired in the previous quarter. Manpower, Inc., indicated that there are huge gaps at the entry level and that employers have the strongest hiring intentions since 1978.

WORKPLACE SUPPORTS

Both the public and private sectors have recognized support as a key variable in promoting job retention. For example, *ongoing supports,* as defined in the amended regulations of the Rehabilitation Act of 1973, PL 93-112 (*Federal Register*, June 24, 1992, p. 28438), are those "needed to support and maintain an individual with severe disabilities in supported employment." They are the activities and relationships that help a person maintain a job in the community. Supports differ for each individual and can vary widely in type and intensity for the duration of employment; they are initiated from a variety of sources. Supports can be provided by the employer, co-workers, rehabilitation professionals, and/or family members. The trend in recent years has been to move toward the most natural support or to support provided by the workplace (Trach, Beatty, &

Shelden, 1998). Table 6.1 classifies a few of the types of workplace supports that have been developed and utilized successfully since 1985.

Supports play a critical role in helping to determine whether a person with a disability is truly task "competent" or "incompetent." For example, a worker who is slow but who brings with him a tax credit policy to offset the company's bottom line may be viewed as sufficiently productive to retain. Or, a person with a mental illness who has excellent family/medical support may be a very valuable worker, as opposed to one who does not have this type of support.

It is clear, however, that all businesses—not only external not-for-profit community agencies—should advocate and be involved with supported employment. Therefore, we are proposing a model of intervention that reflects a much greater emphasis on business-initiated supports than has been conducted using the more traditional job coach model (Wehman, 1981). We believe that developing lasting relations with businesses provides a number of advantages to all stakeholders, as illustrated in Table 6.2.

One approach to improving the likelihood of the occurrence of business-initiated supports is to use more of a corporate-initiated workplace support approach, which can provide a framework for forging lasting relationships with employers. However, in order for this type of approach to exist, providers and individuals with disabilities need to make a firm commitment to support the concept. Policy makers also must recognize the value of this approach and agree that the advantages outweigh those of existing practices. This chapter presents a model that focuses primarily on a business approach to helping individuals with disabilities. Included is a discussion of how to implement the model, especially with individuals with mild cognitive limitations.

THE CORPORATE-INITIATED WORKPLACE SUPPORT MODEL

The Corporate-Initiated Workplace Support model serves as a catalyst for creating a corporate culture supportive of job seekers, employees, and customers with disabilities. This model utilizes employer knowledge to build on existing workplace supports to develop solutions to both current and future business needs and to the needs of workers with disabilities. Changes in the corporate culture to better support individuals with disabilities can improve the work environment for all employees. Two major categories of supports can be conducted in the workplace: *environmental* and *procedural*. Environmental supports are defined as physical structures, surroundings, and/or objects present in the business that make the site more accessible or acceptable to future or current employees. Procedural supports are actions and/or activities that employers provide to assist both potential and current employees with their job and job-related functions. Either existing practices are expanded or new practices are created to reach all workers. Accommodations are defined as modifications or adjustments to a work environment, employment policy, practice, or job that

Table 6.1. Workplace supports to enhance job retention

Business accommodations	Rehabilitation interventions	Treatments	Public policy protections and supports
Early Return-to-Work programs	Job coaching	Medication	Americans with Disabilities Act of 1990 (PL 101-336)
Co-worker mentoring	Assistive technology	Behavioral/cognitive therapy	Social Security Act (PL 74-271)
Employer Assistance Programs	Compensatory strategies	Psychotherapy	U.S. Treasury tax credits

are not generally available to all applicants or employees but that are specifically tailored to enable an individual with a disability to participate in employment practices and perform his or her job effectively.

The Corporate-Initiated Workplace Support model is responsive to employers in the business community as well as to individuals with disabilities who want to gain and maintain a place in the labor force or return to work after a period of absence due to disabilities. The model, which endorses a collaborative effort among the business, job seekers and employees with disabilities, and vocational rehabilitation professionals, is founded on three basic premises: 1) business knows best how to support its work force; 2) job seekers as well as employees with disabilities should be provided with services that maximize their independence and should receive as much workplace support as possible to obtain, maintain, or return to employment; and 3) access to a corporate-oriented vocational rehabilitation professional, such as a corporate liaison who specializes in workplace supports, is an effective way to assist businesses and workers with disabilities.

With the implementation of the Americans with Disabilities Act (ADA) of 1990 (PL 101-336) and as more workers with disabilities attempt to enter the work force, businesses may desire assistance in modifying or developing ways to help facilitate successful employment outcomes for individuals with disabilities. This might involve identifying ways to expand the business's existing capacity to support people with disabilities in accessing the workplace and tools and/or participating in the areas of employee recruitment, application and screening, interviewing, new employee orientation, job skills training, job performance, company-sponsored social events, or career advancement. Because all businesses are unique and may desire varying degrees of assistance, services always must be tailored to the organization's preferences.

Job seekers with disabilities also may desire and require supports to assist them with employment. Preemployment supports may be associated with locating work opportunities or participating in hiring practices. These activities may include identifying vocational strengths, potential accommodation needs, and work opportunities; completing applications; participating in the prescreening or interview process; and analyzing job tasks in order to identify accommodations or a "job match."

Once employed, efforts might involve using existing workplace supports and further identifying and implementing individualized accommodations. Accommodations may be related to participating in the new employee orientation or job skills training program. Other workplace support services may relate

Table 6.2. Advantages of developing long-term business partnerships

For businesses

Provides a source of labor

Supports training of a future work force

Reduces costs and time involved with recruitment

Provides an opportunity to tap into the talent of potential workers by considering job restructuring

Consistent responsiveness from corporate liaison to provide assistance with developing in-house programs

Assistance with establishing policy statements to define company culture

Ongoing education and technical assistance on disability- and employment-related issues

Teaches the work force that people with disabilities make great workers

Provides resources on accommodations and individualizing job skills training

Promotes a positive community image reflective of the community served and in which it operates

For individuals with disabilities

Immediate access to a pool of employers who may have a suitable job opportunity

Provides updated information on future career opportunities and hiring trends to guide vocational assessment and training activities

Information on workplace supports is available for review

Teaches job seekers to openly inquire about workplace supports and speak about personal strengths and accommodation needs

Applications are submitted to employers who have made a commitment to diversity

Employment opportunities are at businesses that value diversity

For vocational rehabilitation providers

Assigns staff with exceptional strengths in the area of business and disability to give adequate time to establishing and nurturing business relationships

Provides ongoing information on the business and its priorities

Reduces employer fears related to hiring individuals through education and training

Reduces cost associated with individualized job placement activities

Provides job placement assistance in a timely manner

Allows an ongoing opportunity to explore job creations and restructuring

Provides instruction on how to gain access to employer supports rather than doing an activity for the job seeker or employee

Potentially reduces transportation barriers by encouraging employers to develop ride sharing programs, van purchase, etc.

Allows the chance to review existing workplace supports

to gaining access to and participating in employer-based social activities, employee development programs, and promotions. It is important for businesses to keep in mind that no two individuals with disabilities are alike, and although the employer may have a general idea of the type of support or accommodation that a prospective employee may need, the support usually will require some fine tuning once the individual starts work and begins to participate in the various employment practices.

Once a company assumes responsibility for supporting workers with disabilities or once a person with a disability leaves vocational services, professional involvement continues to be important. However, decision making and service delivery shift from the vocational rehabilitation professionals to company representatives and the individuals with disabilities. As previously stated, the intent is to help businesses build on existing practices and develop new work force strategies that successfully incorporate people with disabilities into or back into the work force while promoting greater participation among people with disabilities in gaining and maintaining their careers. This collaborative effort brings together private companies, individuals with disabilities, and vocational rehabilitation professionals to create a win-win situation for everyone. It is believed that employers and employees who work together to move beyond the letter of the law outlined in the ADA will pave the way for unforeseen long-term benefits.

THE ROLE OF CORPORATE LIAISON

A vocational rehabilitation professional known as the *corporate liaison,* who specializes in workplace supports and accommodations, may introduce businesses to the concept of adopting a program that facilitates hiring workers with disabilities as an ongoing practice. If the business is interested, the corporate liaison offers to assist the employer in performing an analysis of the company's employment policies and procedures. The assistance offered to the business is tailored and timed to coincide with the organization's long-term plans. The business is the driver in the change process, and the corporate liaison is the facilitator and the resource for education, training, and technical expertise. As a result of these and future efforts, it is hoped that the organization will adopt a philosophy and ongoing practice of employing workers with disabilities and will modify its policies and procedures to reflect this attitude.

The corporate liaison also serves individuals with disabilities who are interested in locating jobs or returning to work after being out on disability. The assistance provided to the person focuses on identifying whether support is needed, the types of support that are needed, and ways to maximize the individual's personal independence in the process.

THE CORPORATE CUSTOMER

Experience suggests that many employers are aware of the benefits of hiring workers with disabilities and are willing to provide supports (Roessler & Sumner, 1997). Employers also may assist job seekers in matching their talents to the workplace, provide skills training to new employees, and develop ways to help employees enhance their performance and advance their careers. However, employers remain concerned about the extent to which accommodations for people with disabilities will increase costs and/or necessitate changes in company policies and procedures (Roessler & Sumner, 1997; Schall, 1998). In addition, expanding on the existing capacity to support workers with disabilities is a new frontier for many organizations (Gates, Akabas, & Oran-Sabia, 1998). Some businesses have established innovative approaches for assisting workers with disabilities and those who acquire disabilities with re-entering the work force (Mills, 1997; Owens, 1997). In-house vocational rehabilitation services and disability management programs have proven to be beneficial and cost effective for companies. Other corporations are interested in these concepts but desire assistance with the process.

The Corporate-Initiated Workplace Support model can work with any employer, but certain characteristics may be viewed as indicative of success. These characteristics may include all or some of the following:

- Management has demonstrated its community support and/or awareness of disability issues through its actions.
- Future growth plans are anticipated.
- Economic stability has been demonstrated.
- Entry-level positions exist.
- A broad range of positions exist.
- Locations are accessible to a broad segment of the population.

THE JOB SEEKER OR THE EMPLOYEE CUSTOMER

The corporate liaison plays a key role in promoting employment opportunities for people with disabilities. Newcomers to employment may receive assistance with identifying, choosing, and gaining access to existing workplace supports, as well as with arranging or providing "individual" supports or accommodations if necessary.

The type and intensity of support provided is contingent on the individual's abilities, the presence of workplace supports, and/or the employer's willingness to create new supports and/or provide accommodations. For example, one job seeker may be able to complete an application using in-house assistance, or, once employed, an individual may be able to learn how to do the job through existing internal supports (e.g., the business's job training program).

However, another person may need assistance with the hiring process and individualized skills training through the use of an external support, such as job coaching services. Although a general understanding of an individual's potential support needs can be determined prior to his or her hire or return to work, the complete picture of what may be necessary to facilitate success cannot be ascertained fully until the workplace supports are understood. The following vignette provides Justine's viewpoint about her employment support program. Justine is a 19-year-old African American woman who currently lives with her sister, three nieces, and two nephews. Justine dropped out of high school in the tenth grade. She has had two other jobs in the past but was unable to keep them because of her inability to meet the employers' standards.

> *What I like best is a lot of things. The man that is helping me had already talked to the company, and this was nice because he and I met before the interview and talked about how I could do the application. You see, I do not read too good, because I never learned it in school. That is why I dropped out. It makes me feel scared and nervous to read and write stuff. The company had someone there, and I just asked if I could get some help, and they gave it to me. I also got a mentor named Mary. She is one of my co-workers but also my friend. She tells me how good I am at doing my job, and if I ever have a problem I can talk to her about it, even if it does not have anything to do with work. One day my car was broke down, and she helped me figure some different ways to get it to the shop and still be on time for work. Having a mentor means a lot to me.*

BUSINESS SERVICES

The primary emphasis of the Corporate-Initiated Workplace Support model is on identifying and expanding corporate supports while strengthening linkages between businesses and individuals with disabilities. Following are guidelines on how the corporate liaison can help facilitate this process.

1. *Conduct a labor market screening.* The corporate liaison conducts a community labor market screening to identify a cross-section of industries in the business community to contact regarding potential career opportunities for individuals with cognitive limitations. During the screening, the corporate liaison should be provided with answers to the following questions: What types of employers are common in the area? Which businesses anticipate future growth? What new employers have surfaced in the area? And, what transportation is available to get to area businesses?

It is very important for the corporate liaison to keep an open mind when conducting a labor market analysis to avoid limiting the work options for individuals with disabilities. For example, the liaison should not only consider positions available in the service industry, such as pot scrubbing or bussing dirty tables. The reality is that job options for people with disabilities reach well beyond the service industry. The corporate approach encourages identification of nontraditional places of employment, such as financial institutions, health care facilities, and computer-related industries, to name a few. A list of potential businesses for the corporate liaison to contact is generated from the labor market screening.

2. *Conduct a survey of the desires and strengths of future job seekers.* After conducting a labor market analysis but prior to contacting businesses, it is necessary to gather some information about the individuals who are seeking employment. Because employment must reflect the desires of the job seekers, the corporate liaison should become familiar with the expectations of the individuals who are seeking work as well as with the different types of industries and potential work opportunities in the area. One way to gain input is to share the list of potential business contacts derived from the job market analysis with the individuals seeking jobs and their family members, teachers, and vocational rehabilitation personnel. This information can be prioritized to indicate the job seekers' preferences and to provide the corporate liaison with direction.

3. *Contact businesses.* Some corporate customers may have previously employed individuals who were involved in some type of formal employment support program, such as supported employment, whereas other customers may not have been traditional targets of vocational rehabilitation professionals and, therefore, may not have had any experience with employment support programs. The Corporate-Initiated Workplace Support model targets traditional and nontraditional corporate entities. The type of organization and the size of the work force are not limiting factors; instead, they highlight the need for individuality and flexibility in designing strategies in partnership with the companies that match the job seekers' goals. Formal approaches may be appropriate for large corporations, whereas informal tactics may suit the needs of smaller businesses. The goal for all of the establishments, however, is to tailor the approach so that it is compatible with the businesses' objectives.

The method for making initial contacts with the businesses, as well as the types of interventions decided upon, will vary. Meeting with professional and community groups may be an appropriate first contact for large enterprises, whereas scheduling a face-to-face meeting with an owner or manager may be the best approach for small businesses. Reaching the decision maker at the business is important in both cases because a change in the corporate culture is best initiated from the top down. Many rehabilitation professionals target the human resources department as their initial contact; however, although this may be the first step in the process, it is important to keep in mind that getting upper management to accept the method is the key to creating a corporate philosophy that supports the idea that workers with disabilities can make an important contribution to the work force.

4. Gain the corporate commitment. The corporate liaison should state clearly what type of commitment is being sought from the company and must be prepared to present workplace support options for the business to consider. Although all business customers should adopt the philosophy that facilitates the hiring of workers with disabilities, the extent to which the business will want or be able to undertake the ongoing responsibility for ensuring that the work environment is responsive to the employee's needs may vary. For example, the business may have the resources to develop its own training programs for workers with disabilities instead of relying on the corporate liaison to facilitate the training. The extent to which the employer will undertake tasks in creating a diverse work force may vary based on a number of factors, such as the type of business and the number of people it employs. The company's turnover rate may also be a consideration. The business may choose to design a program around its existing staff and utilize its supervisors or other key employees as primary supports. Again, flexibility is the key in helping the business find a level of support that adheres to the business's bottom line and with which the business is comfortable.

In helping a business reach a decision regarding the extent of its participation, it is important to emphasize the benefits of the Corporate-Initiated Workplace Support model to all of the employees. Certainly, one of the most compelling reasons for businesses to provide supports or to make accommodations is economic in nature. Through the creative use of internal supports and by maximizing external resources, a Corporate-Initiated Workplace Support program can be implemented to provide a range of services. It can reduce the cost incurred if an employee acquires a disability by encouraging the employee to return to work and can thereby protect profits while meeting the expectations of the community. Furthermore, it enables businesses to tap into an underutilized pool of labor and reduces recruitment costs. The fact that accommodations for workers with disabilities can be simple and inexpensive is highlighted, and employers are reminded that accommodation is a good business practice and that it can be cost effective. In the same way that businesses establish routines for workers without disabilities to increase their productivity and to utilize the employees' best skills, employers can support individuals with disabilities. Building and expanding existing supports for workers with disabilities translate to increased support for all employees and sends a message to the work force that all employees are valued. In an economic environment of corporate consolidation and downsizing, employees may feel that their employer does not value them. Creating a more supportive environment for all employees can help offset this opinion. This same message can be sent to the community in which the business operates, resulting in the business being recognized as "a good place to work." Businesses also are prompted to take actions to receive positive press and media coverage from the local community through the publication of articles, press releases, and televised news stories. All of the suggested activities are designed to enhance the corporate image and the business's competitive edge. By demonstrating that it is a leader in developing a diverse work force reflective of the community it serves, a business can serve as a role model for other businesses.

The employer or corporate liaison also may request a long-term educational and training program specifically designed to reduce the effects of prejudice while creating an awareness of the abilities of workers with disabilities Some examples of topics for an employer educational program are provided in Table 6.3.

5. Analyze workplace supports. Most organizations provide their employees with a wealth of resources; some of these resources are generic to most businesses, and others are unique to a particular company. Evaluating these workplace supports is a fundamental step in the Corporate-Initiated Workplace Support model.

First, to evaluate these supports, workplace supports that already exist within a company and that are available to all employees need to be identified.

Table 6.3. Employer education topics

Accommodations are Good Business Sense

Accommodations are developed on an individual basis between the person with a disability and the employer. This session is designed to develop a general knowledge of the different types and reasonableness of accommodations. Topics include identifying the need for accommodations, high- and low-technology accommodations, the selection process, and funding resources. Emphasis also is placed on reducing the cost of disability by accommodating workers who acquire disability with a return to work.

New Waves in Employment Practices

Business leaders are expanding upon their existing resources to better support workers with disabilities. This session discusses the newest trends related to tapping into this underutilized source of people power through an expansion of workplace supports. New practices in disability management also are reviewed.

The Americans with Disabilities Act (ADA) of 1990

This session offers an overview of the ADA as it relates to employment practices.

Evaluating Accessibility in the Workplace

This session gives a step-by-step process for evaluating workplace accessibility. Participants actually perform an assessment to see how accessible the workplace is for individuals who may have sensory, physical, and/or cognitive disabilities. Ideas on how to make improvements also are provided.

Effective Communications with Workers with Disabilities

Communication is the key to understanding, and this session helps prepare employers to interact comfortably with a person with a disability. A number of communication strategies and aids are reviewed. No one likes to be stereotyped based on one aspect of his or her life, including people who have a disability. The session also reviews how person-first language can bring people together.

Disability Etiquette

Some people may feel a bit uncomfortable being around a person who has a disability. This training will put personnel at ease by getting them up to speed on the latest in disability etiquette.

Second, after identifying current supports, the effectiveness of each support should be rated for job seekers and employees with disabilities. Simultaneously, ideas for new supports should be generated, discussions should be held, and viable options should be implemented. Third, the company, with the assistance of the corporate liaison, should determine how to approach the process. A formal approach involves a review of both the physical setting as well as employment policies and practices. One business may decide to form a small task force for the purpose of reviewing and/or generating ideas on new supports. Another business may want to hold focus groups with various personnel or may want the human resources officers to work exclusively with the corporate liaison initially, then include other personnel in the process.

The environmental review generally involves a survey of the physical surroundings to ensure that the environment is accessible to individuals with a variety of accommodation needs—sensory, physical, communication, or cognitive disabilities. Oftentimes, accessibility surveys are geared toward mobility impairments and fail to recognize some simple yet important changes that could be made to accommodate other types of disabilities and, in some instances, business customers with disabilities.

Another task involves recognizing how employment practices currently are being handled within the company. This task should be followed by a discussion of the effectiveness of the existing methods for job seekers and/or workers with disabilities. Next, ideas for modifications or new supports should be discussed. Afterward, a decision can be made regarding changes and whether the changes should be made available to all workers or should only be viewed as an accommodation for a job seeker or an employee with a disability.

Some businesses may desire to take a less formal approach and go about change at a slower pace, evaluating supports specific to workers with disabilities who have been hired or who are returning to work after an injury or illness. This approach may seem to have the drawback of taking a long time to implement, but that is not necessarily true. First, this approach is still a step in the right direction, and second, some businesses may be required to go through rigorous approval procedures to make changes. Once a business has committed to providing supports for individuals with disabilities, the corporate liaison must take full advantage of this opportunity.

   6. *Modify or expand workplace supports.* Workplace supports and accommodations are provided to facilitate successful employment outcomes for individuals with disabilities and the businesses that hire them. If a formal approach is being used, after a careful review and discussion of existing employment practices and modifications, expansion can begin. The corporate liaison presents suggestions regarding alternatives that the business should consider; however, it is important, ultimately, for the business to decide on the appropriate changes that it will need to succeed. Change takes time, and there are a number of factors that will influence the time line, such as the stability of the business's existing work force. If the business is experiencing a high turnover

of employees, the type of supports selected may include both short-term and long-term options. This also may be true for corporations in the process of a merger in which procedures will change once all merger activities are completed.

CORPORATE MENTOR PROGRAM

The development of a corporate mentor program is one innovative approach that some businesses are adding to their workplace support repertoire. A corporate mentor program can be implemented quite easily. First, a survey with members of management or all personnel should be conducted to identify potential mentors and mentoring activities. After the mentors have been identified, a "mentor training" session should be held. The topics covered during the session may include, "What is Mentoring," "How to Understand the Mentee's Needs," or "Successful Mentoring." As the mentors are being trained, job seekers will be submitting their applications and interviewing for jobs. Once a new employee is hired, he or she will be paired with a trained mentor. Some companies prefer a less formal approach, and the mentoring activities are selected by the mentor and new employee (mentee) on the first day of work. In this case, the corporate liaison provides individualized mentor training with the designated employee.

Whether a formal or informal method is used, it is extremely important that on the first day of work the mentor and new employee meet to review each other's roles and expectations. At this time, the pair should also establish times to meet. In the following vignette, Roberto talks about some of the activities he shares with his mentor.

> My mentor works in the same department as me. We get together every week and kind of talk about how everything is going. He has been here a long time and has some good advice. He can show me the ropes. We take breaks together, and he introduces me to other guys, so I am already part of the gang. I think it is good to have a mentor.

Orientation

New employees with disabilities always should participate in the standard orientation provided by a company. However, depending on the sophistication of a particular program and the new employee's skill level, the mentor might help the new employee complete necessary personnel forms, tour the workplace, and/or learn the procedures to use when he or she is not able to report to work.

Training the New Employee

If possible, the mentor may provide job skills training, and the corporate liaison can provide insight into how to teach the new employee and promote independence. A number of reliable methods exist for training a person on a new skill. For example, the mentor could facilitate the occurrence of the task using naturally occurring cues, modify the method by which the task is performed to match the workers abilities, provide systematic instruction, or teach in mass trials. Training the new employee may require that the mentor become familiar with new methods of instruction delivery.

The involvement of co-workers is essential to the long-term maintenance of employment for many individuals with disabilities, and these relations should be fostered. However, it is equally important that the mentor and the co-workers understand and respect the worker by allowing him or her to perform tasks independently. Other employees must understand that doing a job for the employee is not beneficial, and their co-worker deserves the chance to perform to the best of his or her ability. The new worker needs supports that facilitate independence. The mentor can help by reminding those who become "too helpful" that the worker is learning and that he or she should eventually be able to do the job independently.

It is critical that the mentor understand the importance of determining the need for additional supports or accommodations. Sometimes, because of the nature of the job, the new employee's abilities, and the mentor's time constraints, a "job coach" may be needed to provide individualized skills training to the new employee. Furthermore, adaptations such as the use of compensatory strategy (e.g., memory aids) or arranging for assistive technology may also be required.

Building Relationships

Mentors play a vital role in building relationships between the new worker and the other employees. Positive relationships can be fostered in a number of ways. For example, the mentor can help the new employee establish favorable relationships by teaching the new employee the names of his or her co-workers, encouraging the employee to ask co-workers for advice and to take breaks with them, and ensuring that the new employee is involved in company-sponsored activities. Mentors also can keep a pulse on the worker's level of job satisfaction. If necessary, a referral to appropriate resources to help the individual work through dissatisfaction or other employment-related issues, such as a need for transportation or help arranging child care, can be offered. The following vignette illustrates how Charles's mentor helped him handle a difficult situation.

> My mentor is Rick. He is the manager of the hotel. He teaches me a lot of new things, so I don't think I am in a dead-end job. It is up to me; I can go places if I want to. He helps me with my problems, like one time I was upset because I was doing a lot of work and my co-workers were goofing off. Actually, I caught them drinking beer outside of the kitchen, so I told Rick. He told me not to worry. He would take care of it, and they

would never know that I was the snitch. Rick and I sometimes do some-
thing outside of work. Like once we went fishing at a pond over by his
father's house. It was a lot of fun, and I caught an 8-pound bass. No fish
tale!

SUPPORTS FOR INDIVIDUALS WITH COGNITIVE LIMITATIONS

This section describes some ways to make the Corporate-Initiated Workplace Support model work for individuals with cognitive impairments. The development of employer accommodations and rehabilitation interventions plays a large role in the implementation of work supports for employees with cognitive limitations. These supports can assist workers with cognitive limitations to become independent and valued employees. Table 6.4 illustrates types of workplace supports that have been used successfully to assist workers with cognitive impairments. A brief description of each follows.

Natural Employer Workplace Supports

The use of the word *natural* in *natural employer workplace supports* implies that the supports being used typically are available to all workers in the workplace. These supports are not artificial or used solely for workers with cognitive limitations. Natural supports for a worker may include such things as a co-worker mentor who assists the worker with learning the job or a supervisor who monitors an employee's work performance and provides reinforcement. Work that involves interdependence among co-workers may be an ideal match for some workers with cognitive limitations; this natural "cueing system" helps the employee determine what he or she should be doing at a given moment.

Job Coach/Employment Specialist

Supported employment is a concept that includes career planning, job development, on-the-job support, and ongoing supports. An employment specialist, or job coach, is a professional who provides or arranges these supports. Typically, the employment specialist assists with identifying strengths and supports, locates work opportunities, and, once an employee is hired, assists with job skills training and/or arranging accommodations. The employment specialist fades assistance once the employee becomes independent but is available to provide additional help if needed.

Workplace Modifications/Accommodations

In some instances, modifications to a work environment are needed, such as locating a quiet and commotion-free work space or rearranging a work area. Some workers may have trouble filtering out irrelevant information, which may

Table 6.4. Work supports

Natural employer workplace supports	Co-worker teaches the worker the job
	Supervisor monitors work performance
	Mentor assists with social interactions
Job coach/employment specialist	Helps identify and choose support options
	Trains employer to provide support
	Provides job skills training
	Provides extended support
Workplace modifications/accommodations	Post directional signs
	Rearrange work station
	Create quiet work area
Individualized work skills training	Least prompts
	Positive reinforcement
	Mass practice
Compensatory strategies	Written list of job duties
	Picture book of job task sequences
	Reference manual
Assistive technology	Electronic stapler
	Colored file divider
	Electronic communication device
Community supports	Arranges or trains to use public transportation
	Refers to legal assistance
	Assists with housing application
Long-term supports	Retrains previously learned skills
	Trains new skills
	Refers to community resources

include noise created by people or machines. An abundance of visual activity can be disturbing, too. Discovering ways to eliminate and minimize the various distractions in the workplace can help the employee's performance. Learning to locate a quiet and commotion-free workplace or to create one by closing a door, turning off a telephone, or turning on a sound machine to mask noise may help.

Individualized Work Skills Training

The use of instructional strategies for training workers with cognitive impairments has been well documented. Prompt sequences, positive reinforcement, and task modification are a few examples of effective strategies. The trainer needs to know not only how to use specific procedures but also when, under what conditions, and in what combination to use them.

Compensatory Strategies

A number of memory aids exist that can be used at work to enhance new learning and cue performance and, later, serve as a source of reference. These aids include using a checklist, flow chart, or written guidelines that delineate how to perform specific duties and using electronic memory devices, such as tape recorders, or electronic cueing devices, such as an organizer.

Memory aids may also promote self-management—the worker's ability to oversee his or her own performance. For example, a worker may learn to pre-set an alarm on his or her wrist watch to signal when it is time to take a break or to make a checklist to monitor his or her production by placing a check mark on a data recording sheet as he or she completes a task. Compensatory strategies must be designed with input from the worker and employer.

Assistive Technology

The use of assistive equipment and devices is one of the most important strategies for increasing a worker's independence and performance. Assistive technology ranges from high- to low-tech. High-technology devices include voice-activated dictation machines, talking calculators, and voice synthesizers. Low-technology devices are simpler and may have few or no moving parts, such as the use of an oversized handle on a tool or pole to extend an individual's reach, a Dycem nonskid mat to stabilize work materials, or a jig to hold a stapler steady. Assistive equipment may be newly purchased, or something the employer owns may be modified to make an accommodation. Again, it is always important to include the employer and worker in the identification and selection of these devices.

Community Supports

Community supports may be arranged to assist with independent living, transportation, and financial management. Frequently, the worker may need help beyond signing up for community services. For example, an individual may need instruction regarding how to arrange an appointment for specialized transportation or how to use the bus to get to and from work. Therefore, a skills trainer may be needed; if so, the skills trainer should train and support the individuals in learning how to gain access to services rather than gain access to the services for them.

Long-Term Supports

Many factors can affect the stability of a worker's support network. Changes in supervision, co-workers, the work environment, or a job description may necessitate support for the employee. The provision of long-term supports is a defining characteristic of supported employment. A job coach monitors how the employee is doing both on and off the job and is available to provide assistance if community- or work-based supports become ineffective.

SUMMARY

As individuals with disabilities are integrated into the work force, a more productive and understanding society is created. This chapter has described a process for enhancing or expanding existing corporate workplace supports to create an environment more conducive to potential and current employees with disabilities. A corporate mentor program and effective supports for workers with cognitive disabilities also have been presented.

REFERENCES

Bureau of Labor Statistics. (1997, February). Contingent and alternative employment arrangements. *United States Department of Labor, USDL 97-422.* (Available: http://stats.bls.gov/newsrels.htm)

Bureau of Labor Statistics. (1998a). Economy at a glance. *United States Department of Labor.* (Available: http://stats.bls.gov/eag.table.htm)

Bureau of Labor Statistics. (1998b). Work at home in 1997. *United States Department of Labor, USDL 98-93.* (Available: http://stats.bls.gov/newsrels.htm)

Federal Register (1992, June 24). 57 (122), 28432–28442 Washington, DC: U.S. Government Printing Office.

Franzis, H., Gittleman, M., Horrigan, M., & Joyce, M. (1998). Results from the 1995 survey of employer-provided training. *Monthly Labor Review Online, 121*(6), 3–13.

Gates, L.B., Akabas, S.H., & Oran-Sabia, V. (1998). Relationship accommodations involving the work group: Improving work group prognosis for persons with mental health conditions. *Psychiatric Rehabilitation Journal, 21*(3), 264–272.

Hight, J.E. (1998). Young worker participation in post-school education and training. *Monthly Labor Review Online, 121*(6), 14–21.

Labor shortage. (1998, May 22). The Wall Street Journal, p. 1.

McCormick, J.A. (1994). *Computers and the Americans with Disabilities Act: A manager's guide.* New York: McGraw-Hill.

Melzer, T.C. (1997). To conclude: Keep inflation low and, in principle, eliminate it. *Federal Reserve Bank of St. Louis Review, 79*(6), 3–7.

Mills, D.L. (1997). Building joint labor-management initiatives for worksite disability management. In D.E. Shrey & M. Lacerte (Eds.), *Principles and practices of disability in management in industry* (pp. 225–248). Boca Raton, FL: CRC Press.

Owens, P.M. (1997). Integrated health and disability management in the workplace. *Compensation & Benefits Management, 13*(3), 31–36.

Reynolds, A. (1998). Grading the 1993–1997 economy. *The Public Perspective, 9*(2), 73–75.

Rivlin, A. (1998, May 12). *USA Today,* Business section, p. 1.

Roessler, R., & Sumner, G. (1997). Employer opinions about accommodating employees with chronic illnesses. *Journal of Applied Rehabilitation Counseling, 28*(3), 29–34.

Schall, C.M. (1998). The Americans with a Disability Act: Are we keeping our promise? An analysis of the effect of the ADA on the employment of persons with disabilities. *Journal of Vocational Rehabilitation, 10*(3), 191–203.

Trach, J.S., Beatty, S.E., & Shelden, D.L. (1998). Employers' and service providers' perspectives regarding natural supports in the work environment. *Rehabilitation Counseling Bulletin, 41*(4), 293–311.

Unemployment plunges further: Practitioners keep wage costs under control (1998). *Security Letter, 28*(10), 15.

Wehman, P. (1981). *Competitive employment: New horizons for severely disabled individuals.* Baltimore: Paul H. Brookes Publishing Co.

Wehman, P. (2001). *Life beyond the classroom: Transition strategies for young people with disabilities* (3rd ed.). Baltimore: Paul H. Brookes Publishing Co.

Wehman, P., & Kregel, J. (1998). *More than a job: Securing satisfying careers for people with disabilities.* Baltimore: Paul H. Brookes Publishing Co.

Wilson, T. (1998). Consumer inflation in 1997 at 11-year low. *Monthly Labor Review Online, 121*(5), 36 39.

7

Career Development

Helping Youth with Mild Cognitive Limitations Achieve Successful Careers

Patricia Rogan, Richard G. Luecking, and Mary Held

Despite years of federal legislation and policy to promote the employment of people with disabilities, there has been and continues to be a host of barriers and challenges to achieving higher rates of successful employment. Federal legislation, including the Rehabilitation Act of 1973 (PL 93-112), the Individuals with Disabilities Education Act (IDEA) of 1990 (PL 101-476), and the Americans with Disabilities Act (ADA) of 1990 (PL 101-336), has addressed this problem both directly and indirectly. The Rehabilitation Act of 1973 and subsequent reauthorizations allow the allocation of money to states for services extended to job seekers with disabilities. IDEA and its reauthorization, the IDEA Amendments of 1997 (PL 105-17), mandate that schools develop a yearly plan for the transition from school to work and adult life of each student age 14 and older who receives special education services. The ADA prohibits the discrimination of people with disabilities in employment and other areas of life and requires employers to make reasonable accommodations so that their facilities and jobs are more accessible. Each of these significant federal legislative acts is designed to increase the likelihood that people with disabilities receive an education and live and work within their communities. The Carl D. Perkins Vocational and Applied Technology Education Act Amendments of 1990 (PL 101-392), the School-to-Work Opportunities Act of 1994 (PL 103-239), and the Workforce Investment Act of 1998 (PL 105-220) have enhanced further the support system for youth and adults in the employment arena.

According to a 1998 Louis Harris and Associates national survey of people with disabilities, more than 71% of working age adults with disabilities are unemployed, despite the fact that two thirds of these individuals want to work. Moreover, in 1992, an extensive national longitudinal study of students with disabilities who had exited schools found that the employment rates of individuals with disabilities lagged significantly behind those of their peers without disabilities (Wagner, D'Amico, Marder, Newman, & Blackorby, 1992).

Individuals with disabilities also received lower wages and fewer benefits when they did find employment. Other studies confirm a continuing troublesome trend toward high rates of unemployment or underemployment for former recipients of special education services (Colley & Jamison, 1998; Rogan, 1997). These results suggest that educational and career development approaches still need to be identified and implemented for individuals with disabilities to receive reasonable opportunities to obtain employment and lead satisfying lifestyles.

The good news is that research and practice have confirmed many of the curricular interventions and career development activities that result in positive postschool employment outcomes. The purposes of this chapter are to 1) discuss characteristics of effective career exploration and development approaches, 2) provide examples of such innovative efforts that include youth and adults considered to have mild cognitive limitations, and 3) make recommendations for future direction.

THE EVOLUTION OF VOCATIONAL EDUCATION AND CAREER DEVELOPMENT OPPORTUNITIES

Vocational education options for students with mild cognitive disabilities have steadily evolved since the 1970s. The term *special vocational needs* (now *vocational special needs*) was first widely used with the passage of the Vocational Education Act Amendments of 1968 (PL 90-576), and funding was targeted for youth who were considered "disadvantaged and disabled." With the passage of the Education for All Handicapped Children Act of 1975 (PL 94-142), students with disabilities were increasingly deinstitutionalized and mainstreamed; however, relatively little attention was given to vocational skills. A high percentage of youth with mild disabilities "flunked out," were expelled, or dropped out of high school. They floundered in an educational arena that struggled to understand their characteristics and needs (Gajar, Goodman, & McAfee, 1993; Gerber & Brown, 1997). Strategies for preparing and supporting individuals with mild cognitive limitations for and in the workplace were continuing to be developed (Meers & Towne, 1997).

During the 1980s vocational education programs became commonplace in schools. Some form of work-study program, community-based vocational experiences, or career-related classes was offered in most high schools. In 1984 the Carl D. Perkins Vocational and Technical Education Act (PL 98-524) was passed, which mandated vocational assessment, counseling, support, and transition services for adolescents who were identified as being disabled and disadvantaged. Vocational goals were to be included in each student's individualized education program (IEP), and training was to be provided in the least restrictive environment (Stodden, 1998). According to the Perkins Act, the interests and abilities of students with disabilities were to be assessed upon the students' enrollment in vocational education, and the students were to be provided with appropriate training. However, because schools often have excluded students with disabilities from vocational education, the Perkins Act fell short of its original legislative intent (Sarkees, 1995). Unfortunately, the pervasive assumption seems to have been that students with disabilities either were incapable of working, too difficult to accommodate, or better served in "special" programs. The incentives in the Perkins Act to include students with disabilities were insufficient to ensure widespread access to vocational education programs.

In the early 1980s the Office of Special Education and Rehabilitative Services (OSERS) made transition a national priority. Overall, students with disabilities were involved in separate education and vocational tracks than students without disabilities. Despite participation in vocational programs, many students with disabilities exited school unemployed or with part-time, entry-level positions (Halpern, 1993) and with minimal access to postsecondary education.

In the late 1980s the National Occupational Information Coordinating Committee (NOICC), made up of federal, state, and local leaders in the field of career development, formulated guidelines for career development that now guide most programs involving both students and adults. According to this group, career development may be considered a lifelong process and one that is developmental and sequential in nature. That is, activities for young children need to be different than activities for adults. Career development opportunities and experiences should focus on the areas of self-knowledge, educational and occupational exploration, and career planning (NOICC, 1989).

Today a complex array of vocational education and career development opportunities exists for students with disabilities, including cooperative vocational education, youth apprenticeships, work-study, school-based enterprises, career academies, and tech prep. The School-to-Work Opportunities Act of 1994 (PL 103-239) provides a framework for states to develop school-to-work transition systems. This legislation has set into motion the most significant reform agenda for vocational education programs in 3 decades (Cobb & Neubert, 1998), emphasizing the involvement of *all* students, including those with disabilities, in school- and work-based learning as well as connecting activities.

Although great strides have been made to provide career development opportunities for adolescents with mild disabilities, issues and challenges remain. Students with mild disabilities typically follow schedules and curricula very similar to those of other students. However, students with mild cognitive limitations are not always given individualized support services to promote their success. As a result, students often fall behind academically. The lack of functional academic and vocational services directly impacts the dropout rate of students. Wagner (1991) reported that the dropout rate for 15- to 20-year-old students with disabilities was 42.9%, compared to 31.6% for the general population. Negative consequences of dropping out include unemployment, lack of postsecondary education opportunities, and diminished involvement in productive activities (Wehman, 1996). MacMillan (1991) found higher dropout rates for students with mild disabilities, particularly for students with emotional disorders and learning disabilities.

Because their disabilities are not visible, challenges exist for youth with mild cognitive limitations. They may experience problems with employment, independent living, and community access (Wehman, 2001). If they do get hired, they often lose jobs as a result of a lack of accommodations and supports both inside and outside of the workplace. These youth often reject stigmatizing disability services, and other types of support services (if available) are not always utilized.

The growing movement to elevate the standards of achievement for all youth represents another critical and complex barrier to youth with disabilities. Many schools are now under pressure to raise student achievement, which is measured primarily by test scores. Already such tests drive the curriculum in the direction of the "3 Rs" and further divide the student population into academic "haves" and "have nots" (Oakes & Wells, 1992). Youth with disabilities often are excluded from these tests, or their scores are omitted from reports to state agencies. This practice appears to reflect a concern by many educators that test revisions or accommodations will undermine the validity of these tests. Thus, excluding students with disabilities from standards-based reform initiatives not only suggests that they cannot achieve high standards, but it also effectively reduces the critical need to use alternative (authentic) means of measuring student performance, such as the use of portfolios, curriculum-based assessment, criterion-referenced tests, or other performance-based measures.

CHARACTERISTICS OF EFFECTIVE CAREER PREPARATION AND DEVELOPMENT

A growing emphasis in the education field is on the preparation of students to problem-solve, think critically, and work cooperatively—all skills that contribute to employment success. An additional goal is to assist youth to acquire knowledge, skills, and attitudes to pursue career pathways (Lynch & Reimer, 1997). Based on research (e.g., Halpern, Benz, & Lindstrom, 1992; Kohler, 1993, 1996) and the experiences of innovative programs, this section presents key characteristics of effective career development approaches.

Student-Centered Planning, Self-Determination, and Family Involvement

Effective career preparation and development approaches involve students and family members as the central driving agents of vocational and career education decisions. Self-awareness and self-determination are supported from a young age as students learn about themselves and the relationship between school and work. Students are taught to identify their interests, strengths, and aspirations; make choices and informed decisions about various options and opportunities; utilize support systems; and evaluate their achievements. This process of career maturity and overall self-determination continues throughout life.

Family members (including extended family members) are typically the primary source of long-term support and advocacy for individuals with disabilities. Family members often influence career values as well as job or career choices and assist individuals to find and keep jobs (Morningstar, 1997). Effective career development approaches keep parents informed and involved according to their needs and wishes.

Early and Longitudinal Career Development

Effective career exploration and development approaches should begin in elementary school and continue to build through high school and beyond in a coordinated and comprehensive fashion. Smooth transitions occur between each grade level and each school change. Current teachers and staff members communicate with future teachers and staff to ensure programmatic continuity. Students benefit from ongoing opportunities to learn about possible careers, explore personal strengths and interests, pursue relevant courses of study, and obtain experiences that will lead to desired outcomes. Through early planning and involvement, parents may develop typical future career and lifestyle visions and high expectations for their sons and daughters who have disabilities.

School–Family–Community Partnerships

School–family–community partnerships ensure coordination among stakeholders and help secure community resources to meet the needs of individual students, as well as improve the capacity of schools and communities to deliver effective transition services for all students (Benz & Lindstrom, 1997). Successful partnerships among schools, students, families, businesses, and other key community constituents ensure authentic work experiences and mentoring relationships for students, inform educators of priority skill areas, and meet local workforce needs. Collaborative partnerships build effective, responsive, and comprehensive services that lead to better outcomes for students.

Real-World Experiences

Direct, hands-on experiences in actual business environments allow students to apply the academic and occupational knowledge acquired in school while learning the workplace competencies valued by employers. These experiences help all youth understand themselves, the working world, and the relationship between education and earning power (Benz & Lindstrom, 1997).

Quality-of-Life Dimensions

Recently, quality of life has emerged as an essential concept when referenced to postschool outcomes. Common elements of various quality-of-life definitions include physical and material well-being (e.g., food, clothing, housing), performance of adult roles (e.g., employment, educational attainment, citizenship), and personal fulfillment (e.g., happiness, satisfaction) (Rusch & Millar, 1998). Effective career development approaches address the full range of quality-of-life dimensions that affect work performance. In addition to employment, adult roles include postsecondary education, home maintenance, community involvement, and personal and social relationships. For individuals with special needs to succeed as adults in the employment arena, issues that are affecting other areas of their lives must be addressed.

Follow-Up Services and Outcomes

Follow-up services provided by school personnel, adult services agencies, or generic community services assist young adults who may falter after exiting high school in addition to young adults who wish to improve already positive situations. Such services may be minimal—mentoring or advocacy on behalf of the young adult—or significant—requiring support services that may not be in place.

Follow-up data provide information regarding former students' postschool status and needs and are necessary to determine factors that promote or impede successful outcomes. Follow-up information addresses not only employment status but other quality-of-life dimensions as well.

CAREER DEVELOPMENT TRENDS AND EDUCATION REFORM

Various approaches to career development that involve a developmental, lifespan approach to career and vocational education have been espoused (Szymanski, 1994). These models typically include three stages: career awareness, career exploration, and career experiences that involve school-based and work-based learning. Recently, education and workforce development initiatives (e.g., Carl D. Perkins Vocational and Applied Technology Education Act Amendments of 1990 & 1998; the Workforce Investment Act of 1998; and the School-to-Work Opportunities Act of 1994) have put renewed and more focused attention on career development as a critical component of education and lifelong workforce development initiatives. These initiatives likely will have far-reaching and long-lasting effects on how youth enter into and advance in their chosen career paths. Many of these trends are emerging as a result of an increasing disparity between what students are taught in school and what skills they will need to get good jobs in an increasingly complex, fast-paced work environment. Therefore, more and more educators and policy makers believe it is imperative that schools embed into the curricula the so-called "soft skills," including the ability to solve problems, work in teams, get along with customers and co-workers, and respond to supervision (SCANS, 1991). Many believe that schools also need to link their curricula with industry-referenced skill standards (Murnane & Levy, 1996).

For students with mild disabilities, it is also critical that they have opportunities to develop these higher-level skills. But, as previously discussed, these students frequently are excluded from educational initiatives that promote vocational skill development and higher achievement. Therefore, students with disabilities need increased access to such educational programs. In addition, upon access, appropriate accommodations and supports are essential to ensuring student success in such activities. The next few paragraphs discuss ways in which career development trends and education reform initiatives can benefit all youth, including and especially those with mild disabilities.

Three related initiatives are particularly illustrative of how trends in career development can affect youth with disabilities: the school-to-work movement, tech prep, and career academies. These three, while having different and specific focuses, represent educational reform efforts that have at their core the notion that most students learn best when they can relate subject matter to their own lives and can understand how the material can be used functionally. These initiatives also represent educational reforms that share a common belief that career development activities are most effective when students have opportunities to experience them in real-life environments and that students can build skills of value to future employers when employers are involved actively in the educational process. These trends offer glimpses of what is possible but are by no means widespread practices.

School-to-Work Opportunities

Since the passage of the School-to-Work Opportunities Act of 1994, all 50 states plus the District of Columbia and Puerto Rico have received federal seed money to promote the development of local systemic efforts in which educators, businesses, students, and other stakeholders work together to promote the connection between classroom learning and work-based learning. The School-to-Work Opportunities Act contains no mandates as such but rather is designed to be a catalyst for the planning, development, and integration of activities that will contribute to educational reform, making learning more relevant to the workplace while at the same time maintaining academic rigor. The School-to-Work Opportunities Act is designed to include all students, including those with disabilities, in these activities. Unlike in IDEA, participation by students with disabilities is not an entitlement. However, in order to ensure that students with disabilities are included in school-to-work initiatives, state and local governance structures have taken a number of proactive steps.

For example, in San Francisco, the city's Unified School District has merged its recently formed school-to-work unit with the special education transition unit. This was done in order to unify and coordinate efforts to recruit employers and to provide work-based learning experiences for all secondary students who have chosen to augment their classroom work with relevant work opportunities.

In Seattle, Washington, a program called Career Ladders offers progressively longer supervised work experiences called Community Classrooms, paid employment in jobs targeted for postschool employment, and ongoing postschool follow-up. Career Ladders originally was designed for youth with mild disabilities, but because of its effectiveness, it now includes a range of students with and without disabilities and is operated out of the school system's school-to-work office.

In rural Wayne, West Virginia, the local high school made two specific changes in its curriculum as a result of a local school-to-work grant. First, it developed a ninth-grade career exploration class that features multiple job shadowing experiences with local employers. All students, including those receiving special education services, participate in this class together. A second shift occurred in the roles of its work-study coordinators. Where they previously had one coordinator for vocational education students, one for special education, and one for cooperative education—all working separately—their assignments were reorganized so they all work in concert to develop work-based experiences for all students. From ninth through twelfth grades, all students receive career exploration and work-based learning experiences embedded into their course of study.

Finally, in Maryland there is a deliberate focus on avoiding duplicate efforts and minimizing categorical approaches to career development through its school-to-work initiative and its transition systems change project (Unger & Luecking, 1998). For example, the city of Baltimore has two vocational education high schools that actively include students with disabilities in work-based experiences in their occupational offerings. General and special educators work together to ensure that effective accommodations are provided for students as needed.

As more efforts such as these are implemented throughout the country, it is possible that traditional educational structures will begin to transform. The hope is that fewer students will be forced to choose between traditional academic programs that are not likely to provide the skills necessary for success in the workplace and alternative programs outside of the educational mainstream that fail to provide opportunities for academic achievement.

Tech Prep

Tech-prep programs involve 2 years of high school and 2 years of higher education or an apprenticeship program designed to lead to an associate degree or certificate in a specific career field. Tech-prep curricula usually are designed to build student competency in academic subjects and to provide technical preparation in a career domain. These programs feature formal articulation agreements between secondary schools and postsecondary institutions detailing the content and sequence of curricula and the experiences and area of career emphasis to be provided at each institution. The components of tech prep include career paths for technical occupations, direct entry into the workplace that complements classroom instruction, and local consortia that govern partnerships involving secondary schools, postsecondary schools, employers, labor unions, and community-based organizations. Many regard tech prep as a key strategy for building school-to-work systems (Hull & Grevelle, 1998). Its value as an educational reform initiative was reiterated in the 1998 passage of the Carl D. Perkins Vocational Education Act Amendments that renewed the federal allocation for maintaining and expanding local tech-prep consortia in the country.

The National Assessment of Vocational Education (NAVE) reported "special population students are not usually a priority in the development of tech-prep programs, although the majority of programs are making an effort to assure that they are included" (Boesel, Rahn, & Deich, 1994b, p. 128). There are, however, examples of effective inclusion of students with disabilities in tech-prep programs. Gugerty (1996) reported that in Wisconsin the use of Designated Vocational Instruction (DVI) has been successful for including students with disabilities in tech-prep programs. DVI involves a special educator who provides direct support for students with IEPs who are enrolled in academic and vocational classes. These teachers are trained in collaboration and consultation skills and help academic and vocational instructors accommodate the learning needs of students with disabilities. Community work experiences also are supported by DVI instructors. Approximately 200 Wisconsin school districts have implemented the DVI model.

In Washington State, access to and participation in tech-prep programs for special populations is achieved in some measure by providing a number of support services, including career counseling, child care, transportation, and close monitoring of students following enrollment.

Career Academies

Typically structured as schools within schools, career academies offer students academic programs organized around broad career themes (National School-to-Work Office, 1997). Work-based learning is integrated into classroom experiences, with local business partners playing a major role in the process.

Businesses may provide classroom speakers, host field trips, and may even offer assistance in determining program and curricula structure. Business partners also provide internships and individual mentors for the students.

The National School-to-Work Office (1997) cites the Academy of Law, Criminal Justice and Public Administration in Philadelphia as an example of a place where academic coursework is integrated with year-long projects that explore legal issues. For example, students may study DNA for trial purposes but also analyze its composition for chemistry and write a research paper for English.

In Montgomery County, Maryland, students in the finance academy receive internships and participate in field trips in area banking institutions. Their coursework integrates these experiences into major subject classes such as English and mathematics.

Reform Implications

It is not a coincidence that the practices engendered by these three reform initiatives bear a striking familiarity to what most special educators consider to be effective practice for preparing students with disabilities for the transition from school to work. Educational practices associated with positive postschool employment outcomes for youth with disabilities align with key components of these reform initiatives: integrating academic and vocational learning, providing expanded opportunities for work-based experiences, and supporting students throughout the process. It also is worth noting that many school-to-work systems also have adapted Individual Career Plans for use by all students for the transition from school to work (Hershey, Siverberg, Haimson, Hudis, & Jackson, 1998). Many school systems have decided that all students, regardless of whether they have a disability label, could benefit from the same individual transition planning that, when it drives instruction and career development, has been effective for youth receiving special education services. The challenge for all of these initiatives will be to meld these efforts with special education services so that more students with disabilities can take advantage of their promise.

GROWING CAREERS AFTER EXIT FROM SCHOOL: WORKFORCE DEVELOPMENT INITIATIVES

According to Super's theory (1990), individuals do not fully develop career maturity or select a specific career and occupation until their late twenties or early thirties. Career development continues long past students' exit from high school. Furthermore, in our society today, it is not uncommon for people to change jobs and careers throughout their adult lives. Thus, employment-related services that assist job seekers are vital for those individuals who are unemployed or underemployed.

The Workforce Investment Act of 1998 (PL 105-220) consolidated more than 60 federal training programs into three block grants to states: adult employment and training, disadvantaged youth employment and training, and adult education and family literacy programs. The intent of the law is to streamline job-training systems and give localities more decision-making authority. It also granted a 5-year reauthorization of the Rehabilitation Act Amendments of 1992 (PL 102-569). The Workforce Investment Act attempts to further welfare reform initiatives and address the labor shortage of skilled workers.

The Workforce Investment Act creates "individual training accounts" that essentially provide vouchers to individuals seeking employment training and establishes more individual, consumer control over choice of services. The new voucher system is based on increased access to employment services and information through a "one-stop shopping" approach. State and local "workforce investment boards" must plan for services that include special needs populations. The promise of the Workforce Investment Act is the potential to move from a disability-focused employment system to a generic, natural approach (Callahan, 1999). Given the relatively recent passage of the act, it remains to be seen how one-stop shops and vocational rehabilitation will collaborate and coordinate services to individuals with disabilities.

RECOMMENDATIONS FOR FUTURE DIRECTIONS

Educators, policy makers, and researchers have submitted various models of career education and transition planning. To date, most of the models omitted or minimized the role of students and families as the focal point of service delivery and planning (Wehman, 1992). As we move ahead in this new millennium, it is imperative that any approach to career development be student- and family-centered, lifelong, comprehensive, and closely involve businesses and communities in the process. In the following section, recommendations are offered for what students and families, schools, agencies, and employers can do to support career development.

What Students and Families Can Do

1. *Stay informed.* The education and adult services systems can be overwhelming and complex. It is important that students with disabilities and their families obtain sufficient information about their rights, available (and unavailable) options, and how to secure those options. Being involved and informed also helps students and families achieve equal status and influence with professionals.
2. *Understand the impact of one's disability on daily life.* Each individual is unique in the way his or her disability impacts day-to-day functioning. Self-

awareness about strengths, interests, support needs, and how one learns best helps each person direct his or her own life.

3. *Advocate for desired experiences, services, and supports (even if they do not yet exist).* The voices of students and parents can be very powerful in shaping existing school and adult services, as well as in obtaining new or previously unavailable services. Through self-advocacy, individuals can articulate their desires and help design services to meet their needs.

4. *Direct the development of individualized education programs and individualized transition programs.* The popular phrase among those with disabilities "Nothing about me without me" aptly describes the need for students to be active participants in the development of their educational and career plans. Students can participate in planning in multiple ways but may need information, preparation, and support to do so.

5. *Practice problem-solving, decision-making, social, and communication skills.* As stated previously, "soft" skills such as problem solving and social skills are required in employment and life situations and often determine success or failure for individuals with disabilities. Each skill should be embedded throughout students' educational experiences and reinforced in adulthood.

6. *Explore job and career opportunities that match personal strengths, interests, and aspirations.* It is through actual exploration of career opportunities and experiences in real workplaces that individuals come to understand what they like, want, and need. Job matching based on strengths, interests, and aspirations is essential to success.

7. *Gain multiple work- and community-based experiences during high school.* The adage "one learns best by doing" applies to most people. If students acquire multiple work and life experiences during high school (similar to their same-age peers), it is likely they will be in a better position to make choices and decisions about their future aspirations. Employers also will be more likely to look favorably on their resumes.

8. *Participate fully in integrated and relevant school classes and activities.* Caution must be taken not to pull students out of general environments to provide career exploration and development activities. It is helpful to continually reference the typical activities in which same age peers without disabilities are engaged and to promote maximal integration in the life of the school.

9. *Participate in performance-based, authentic assessment processes.* Although students with mild cognitive limitations should be required to participate in statewide testing with appropriate accommodations, opportunities for these students should exist to demonstrate competence via performance-based, authentic assessment options in addition, or as an alternative, to paper and pencil tests.

What Educators Can Do

1. *Work together to develop a more inclusive education system.* Special educators and general education personnel no longer can operate in isolation from, or parallel to, each other. For students to be fully included, educators must also integrate themselves to develop equitable opportunities for all students.
2. *Foster collaboration with students, parents, administrators, businesses, postsecondary education professionals, and the community at large.* Education and transition services require a coordinated team approach involving interagency collaboration and cooperation. Although challenging for education environments, this situation provides a wealth of opportunities to develop mutually satisfying partnerships, maximize resources and supports, and ensure seamless transitions.
3. *Utilize student-centered planning approaches to drive the IEP process, and develop an outcome-oriented IEP that integrates transition goals into the curriculum.* Student-centered planning requires the involvement of students in their life planning, as well as the involvement of other individuals who know the student best. Transition plans and IEPs that are outcome-oriented continually focus on a vision of desired lifestyles during and after high school.
4. *Advocate for inclusion of students in general education courses and activities with necessary supports.* Working together, educators can differentiate instruction in inclusive environments to accommodate learners with various abilities and interests. Individualized supports further promote student success.
5. *Integrate school-based and work-based learning; offer nonschool learning experiences for all students.* Referencing school-based learning to real life contexts, including employment, increases the relevance of school for secondary age students. Other nonschool learning experiences such as service learning are becoming more common for all students as a way to link curriculum to community contexts and to develop meaningful attitudes and skills.
6. *Assist businesses and other generic community services to accommodate individuals with disabilities.* Employers may be willing to hire individuals with disabilities but may need support to determine how best to make reasonable accommodations. School vocational personnel and adult employment service providers can be a valuable resource for employers in this area.
7. *Maintain high expectations for all students' capacity for achievement; increase opportunities and support for postsecondary education, self-employment, high-tech jobs, and other challenging career options.* If

schools maintain a "zero exclusion" policy, then all students, regardless of their support needs, should be given access to job training and other experiences that will prepare them for adulthood. Students with disabilities have proven repeatedly that adult expectations for them are too low. School personnel must hold high expectations to invest in preparing all students for typical adult lifestyles.

8. *Engage in ongoing professional development activities; keep abreast of current trends and best practices.* Because the education and human services fields continually evolve and change, educators must keep abreast of positive practices through ongoing professional development. Professional development activities may include attending conferences and workshops, reading current journals and other literature, visiting exemplary programs, corresponding with leaders in the field, and taking university courses.

9. *Conduct research and disseminate findings; track student outcomes through follow-up studies.* Educators continually need to evaluate the success of their efforts as evidenced by graduate outcomes. Graduate follow-up studies can provide valuable data for assessing the effectiveness of particular practices and for making informed changes in policies and programs.

What Adult Services and Funding Agencies Can Do

1. *Connect with students, families, and educators as early as possible prior to students' last year in high school.* For most students, families, and educators, the adult service world and funding mechanisms are a complex, confusing, and often frustrating maze. Through early involvement and ongoing collaboration, adult service providers and related funding representatives (e.g., Departments of Vocational Rehabilitation) can provide information and assist with seamless transitions.

2. *Listen to and support the preferences and needs of each service recipient.* Self-determination and informed choice are central tenets of the Rehabilitation Act and its amendments, but true choice is limited due to the control professionals hold within the system. Choice and control of services and supports should be in the hands of those whose lives are most directly affected: individuals with disabilities. Professionals from funding and provider agencies need to relinquish control of decisions and shift their roles to honor choices and assist individuals in achieving their goals.

3. *Promote easy entry into the service system using the One-Stop approach.* One-Stop career centers are charged with providing access to a set of core employment-related services. It is critical that disability-related services actively participate in the early stages of developing implementation plans and operating One-Stop centers to ensure that people with disabilities can have full access to these generic services.

4. *Utilize flexible funding structures that support choice and individual needs.*
   Money drives programs and services. To be maximally individualized,
   funding must be flexible and responsive to the needs of individuals.
5. *Keep abreast of innovations in the field, and invest in professional devel-*
   opment to implement best practices. As exciting local, state, and national initiatives unfold (e.g., choice vouchers/personal budgets, self-determination,
   self-employment), it is imperative that service providers and funding agencies keep abreast of positive practices. To do so, there must be ongoing investment in professional development activities as well as training and
   technical assistance as needed to implement effective innovations.

What Employers Can Do

1. *Provide a variety of work-related experiences for students and adults with*
   disabilities. Providing opportunities such as job shadowing, information
   interviews, internships, apprenticeships, and paid work for youth with disabilities typically results in a win-win situation. Individuals with disabilities acquire valuable skills and experiences while businesses can screen,
   train, and hire competent employees. During this period of low unemployment, individuals with disabilities represent an untapped labor pool.
2. *Identify the return when investing resources in career development part-*
   nerships. Many companies have found that participation in these partnerships is sustained when they directly contribute to their economic
   self-interest, rather than merely represent "corporate good citizenship."
   Lowered recruitment costs, improved employee productivity, reduced
   training and supervision costs, and closer association with the larger community market are the key benefits that are reported by companies that are
   engaged with schools to provide work-based learning opportunities to students (National Employer Leadership Council, 1998).
3. *Assist educators to understand the demands of the business world and to*
   integrate priority skills into the curriculum. The nature of school culture is
   such that there are typically few opportunities for educators to understand
   and embrace business practice and values, such as prompt and efficient
   customer service and "time is money" orientation. These practices, as well
   as the industry-specific skill needs, can be communicated to educators
   through involvement in business advisory groups and by offering extern-
   ships to teachers so they can directly experience the business world.
4. *Support job accommodations and other employee support mechanisms that*
   promote productivity and job satisfaction. Employers have become more
   adept at supporting a diverse workforce. However, employers may need to
   seek outside expertise if they feel uninformed or ill equipped to meet the
   needs of employees with disabilities for workplace accommodations and

supports. The key is attitudinal: Employers must be willing to provide reasonable adaptations and modifications for all workers.

5. *Share positive experiences about the capacity of employees with disabilities with other employers and community members.* Satisfied employers who have hired people with disabilities can be powerful spokespersons among their business colleagues and other community members. By sharing their experiences, employers can spur others to provide similar opportunities and reduce anxieties about doing so. Presentations to local service clubs and Chambers of Commerce help shape community attitudes and perceptions about the abilities of people with disabilities.

6. *Promote diversity training and support within the company culture.* Businesses that provide diversity training are likely to support a company culture that accepts and promotes individual differences. In such a climate, people with disabilities are more likely to find support and develop relationships among co-workers.

CONCLUSION

Educators and policy makers are suggesting that the future of learning for all students will be student-centered, experiential and contextual, and technology savvy. Student-centered and experiential learning has been a hallmark of special education best practice for years. General, special, and vocational education professionals, counselors, and others who formerly operated in parallel modes must continue to forge partnerships and share their expertise to work together on behalf of all students. Changing the way we prepare all students in school likely will result in a new generation of self-advocates who succeed in the workplace, direct their own lives, and gain access to community resources to meet their needs.

The workplace of the future will be constantly changing. Technological advances continue to change the ways and speed with which we work. Downsizing, rightsizing, mergers, home-based employment, outplacement, and other variables impact jobs and careers (Meers & Towne, 1997). Lifespan development with a consistent pattern of education and training must become part of career planning, and career pursuits for all people must be flexible. Employers must continue to invest in their future workforce, including people with disabilities. Through partnerships with schools and other community entities, businesses will continue to build the capacity for supporting a diverse workforce.

As our larger communities come to know people who experience disability, and as people with disabilities are given opportunities to make meaningful contributions at work and in their communities, community members may realize that we are better and stronger for our diversity. As this societal transformation occurs, the impact of anyone's disability will be minimized, and a focus on relationships and supports as essential quality-of-life ingredients will take hold.

REFERENCES

Americans with Disabilities Act (ADA) of 1990, PL 101-336, 42 U.S.C. §§ 12101 *et seq.*

Benz, M., & Lindstrom, L. (1997). *Building school-to-work programs: Strategies for youth with special needs.* Austin, TX: PRO-ED.

Boesel, D., Rahn, M., & Deich, S. (1994). *National assessment of vocational education final report to Congress*: Vol. 3. *Participation and quality of vocational education.* Washington, DC: U.S. Department of Education, Office of Educational Research and Improvement.

Callahan, M. (May/June 1999). The promise and pitfalls of the Workforce Investment Act. *TASH Newsletter*, 15–18.

Carl D. Perkins Vocational and Applied Technology Education Act Amendments of 1990, PL 101-392, 104 Statutes at Large 753–804, 806–834.

Carl D. Perkins Vocational and Applied Technology Education Act of 1984, PL 98-524.

Cobb, B., & Neubert, D. (1998). Vocational education: Emerging vocationalism. In F. Rusch & J. Chadsey (Eds.), *Beyond high school: Transition from school to work* (pp. 101–126). Belmont, CA: Wadsworth Publishing Company.

Colley, D.A., & Jamison, D. (1998). Post school results for youth with disabilities: Key indicators and policy implications. *Career Development for Exceptional Individuals*, *21*, 145–160.

Gajar, A., Goodman, L., & McAfee, J. (1993). *Secondary schools and beyond: Transition of individuals with mild disabilities.* New York: Macmillan Publishing Company.

Gerber, P., & Brown, D. (1997). *Learning disabilities and employment.* Austin, TX: PRO-ED.

Gugerty, J. (1996). *A guidebook for serving students with disabilities in tech prep.* Madison: University of Wisconsin, Center on Education and Work.

Halpern, A. (1993). Quality of life as a conceptual framework for evaluating transition outcomes. *Exceptional Children*, *59*, 486–498.

Halpern, A., Benz, M., & Lindstrom, L. (1992). A systems change approach to improving secondary special education and transition programs at the community level. *Career Development for Exceptional Individuals*, *12*, 167–177.

Hershey, A., Siverberg, M., Haimson, J., Hudis, P., & Jackson, R. (1998, October). *Expanding options for students: Report to Congress on the national evaluation of school-to-work implementation.* Princeton, NJ: Mathematica Policy Research, Inc.

Hull, D., & Grevelle, J. (1998). *Tech prep: The next generation.* Waco, TX: CORD Communications.

Individuals with Disabilities Education Act Amendments of 1997, PL 105-17, 20 U.S.C. §§ 1400 *et seq.*

Individuals with Disabilities Education Act (IDEA) of 1990, PL 101-476, Title 20, U.S.C., 1400 et seq.

Kohler, P. (1993). Best practices in transition: Substantiated or implied? *Career Development for Exceptional Individuals*, *16*, 107–121.

Kohler, P. (1996). Preparing youth with disabilities for future challenges: A taxonomy for transition programming. In P.D. Kohler (Ed.), *Taxonomy for transition programming: Linking research and practice* (pp. 1–62). Champaign-Urbana: University of Illinois Transition Research Institute.

Louis Harris and Associates. (1998). *The ICD Survey III: Employing Disabled Americans.* Washington, DC: National Organization on Disability.

Lynch, P., & Reimer, J. (1997). Meeting the needs of special populations in the 21st century: The role of vocational special needs personnel. *The Journal for Vocational Special Needs Education, 19*(3), 99–102.

MacMillan, D. (1991). *Hidden youth: Dropouts from special education.* Reston, VA: The Council for Exceptional Children.

Meers, G., & Towne, V. (1997). Missions and milestones: Yesterday, today and tomorrow in vocational special needs education. *The Journal for Vocational Special Needs Education, 19*(3), 94–98.

Morningstar, M. (1997). Critical issues in career development and employment preparation for adolescents with disabilities. *Remedial and Special Education, 18*(5), 307–320.

Murnane, R.J., & Levy, F. (1996). *Teaching the new basic skills: Principles for educating children to thrive in a changing economy.* New York: The Free Press.

National Employer Leadership Council. (1998). *Intuitions confirmed: The bottom-line return on school-to-work investment for students and employers.* Washington, DC: Author.

National Occupational Information Coordinating Committee. (1989). *National Career Development Guidelines.* Washington, DC: Author.

National School-to-Work Office. (1997). *School-to-work: Glossary of terms.* Washington, DC: Author.

Oakes, J., & Wells, A.S. (1992). Detracking: The social construction of ability, cultural politics, and resistance to reform. *Teachers College Record, 98*(3), 483–512.

Rehabilitation Act of 1973, PL 93-112, 29 U.S.C. §§ *et seq.*

Rogan, P. (1997). *Review and analysis of post-school follow-up results: 1996-1997 Indiana post-school follow-up study.* Indianapolis: Indiana Department of Education. Division of Special Education.

Rusch, F., & Millar, D. (1998). Emerging transition best practices. In F. Rusch & J. Chadsey (Eds.), *Beyond high school: Transition from school to work* (pp. 36–59). Belmont, CA: Wadsworth Publishing Company.

Sarkees, M. (1995). *Vocational special needs.* Homewood. IL: American Technical Publishers, Inc.

School-to-Work Opportunities Act of 1994, PL 103-239, 20 U.S.C. §§ 6101 *et seq.*

Secretary's Commission on Achieving Necessary Skills (SCANS). (1991). *What work requires of schools: A SCANS report for America 2000.* Washington, DC: U.S. Department of Labor.

Stodden, R. (1998). School-to-work transition: Overview of disability legislation. In F. Rusch & J. Chadsey (Eds.), *Beyond high school: Transition from school-to-work* (pp. 60–76). Belmont, CA: Wadsworth Publishing Company.

Super, D. (1990). A life span, life-space approach to career development. In D. Brown, L. Brooks, & Associates (Eds.), *Career choice and development: Applying contemporary theories to practice* (2nd ed., pp. 197–261). San Francisco: Jossey-Bass.

Szymanski, E. (1994). Transition: Life span and life-space considerations for employment. *Exceptional Children, 60,* 402–410.

Unger, D., & Luecking, R. (1998). Work in progress: Including students with disabilities in school-to-work initiatives. *Focus on Autism and Other Developmental Disabilities, 13,* 94–100.

Wagner, M. (1991). *Dropouts with disabilities: What do we know? What can we do? A Report from the National Longitudinal Transition Study of Special Education Students.* Menlo Park, CA: SRI International.

Wagner, M., D'Amico, R., Marder, C., Newman, L., & Blackorby, J. (1992). *What happens next? Trends in post school outcomes of youth with disabilities*. Menlo Park, CA: SRI International.

Wehman, P. (2001). *Life beyond the classroom: Transition strategies for young people with disabilities* (3rd ed.). Baltimore: Paul H. Brookes Publishing Co.

Workforce Investment Act of 1998, PL 105-220, 29 U.S.C. §§ 794d.

III

Housing and Community Living

8

A Home of One's Own

The Role of Housing and Social Services Agencies

Suellen Galbraith

Public opinion and public policies regarding housing for people with disabilities have changed dramatically through the years. Increasingly, consumers, family members, advocates, and service providers have cast aside the failed and expensive facility-based models of the past and have created a new person-centered, person-controlled approach—accompanied by service and support technologies—to support people with disabilities in living in homes of their own. Access to decent, safe, and affordable housing has fostered greater community inclusion for people with disabilities and has increased their access to natural supports (e.g., family, friends, co-workers) as well as social and recreational opportunities routinely enjoyed by all Americans. Another transformation is taking place—one based on the economic empowerment of people with disabilities. With access to mainstream education, job training, and employment, people with disabilities can achieve greater financial self-sufficiency and select mainstream housing options.

A natural outcome of these shifts in disability policy is a significant increase in the number of people with disabilities, many of whom are of low socioeconomic status, who are seeking access to affordable housing in the community utilizing the federally subsidized housing delivery system. Because federal housing policy is affected by federal, state, and local laws, policies, and practices, it is imperative that people with disabilities and their families, service providers, and other advocates become active and informed participants in the legislative and political processes at every level. Without their involvement,

Portions of this chapter are from various issues of Opening Doors, a publication of the Technical Assistance Collaborative, Inc. (TAC), and the Consortium for Citizens with Disabilities (CCD) Housing Task Force. The author of this chapter gratefully acknowledges the work of Ann O'Hara, Associate Director of TAC in Boston, Massachusetts, and funding from the Melville Charitable Trust that enables TAC to collaborate on housing issues with the CCD Housing Task Force in Washington, D.C. Appreciation also is extended to fellow CCD Housing Task Force co-chairs Kathy McGinley of The Arc and Andrew Sperling of the National Alliance for the Mentally Ill for their tireless advocacy and background information used in the preparation of this chapter.

communities tend to develop housing strategies that ignore the needs of people with mental retardation and other disabilities.

Historically, people with developmental disabilities have endured discrimination. Unfortunately, American society continues to reject certain segments of the population—particularly those with low incomes and cultural and ethnic differences—in typical mainstream neighborhoods. Whether because of the rise of gated communities or less visible, informal local policy, low-income individuals face growing restrictions regarding inner-city and suburban living.

Finding ways to accept and live together with individuals who have historically been rejected and exploited is now becoming more than an expression of humanitarian concern—it is becoming a matter of economic and social survival. The challenge is to develop housing reforms for all people—including those with low incomes and those with disabilities—within a broad context of including all people in the community. The challenge is not just to help *them* reach fulfillment but to find ways in which *all* of us can gain.

However, without the informed involvement of people with disabilities and their advocates, the needs of these individuals will continue to go unnoticed and unmet when communities develop their housing strategies. Involvement of individuals with disabilities, advocates, and service providers in housing-related decisions at local and state levels is one of the most critical components to the success of people with mild cognitive limitations in realizing their potential in the 21st century.

INELIGIBLE OR INVISIBLE FOR MANY BENEFITS AND SERVICES

People with mental retardation are among the most vulnerable individuals in our nation and, unfortunately, among the poorest. They also may be invisible to many of the social, educational, and employment services systems. Although prevalence rates may provide aggregate estimates of people with mild cognitive limitations and the extent to which it affects the U.S. population, it is far more difficult to identify individuals. When examining some of the typical points of entry into social programs, it becomes apparent that individuals with mild cognitive limitations—the forgotten generation—are likely to slip through the cracks.

Historically, people with developmental disabilities have been assumed to be unable to work and have been identified with the Social Security disability programs—in particular, with the Supplemental Security Income (SSI) program, which does not require a work history. To be eligible for SSI benefits, an individual must be 1) age 65 or older, blind, or disabled and 2) a United States citizen or an eligible noncitizen who resides in the United States. An individual also must meet income and resource limits to ensure continued eligibility for SSI benefits. In addition to the nonmedical criteria, eligibility for SSI disability benefits requires that an individual must be unable to engage in substantial gainful activity (SGA) because of an impairment that is expected to last at least 12 months or to result in death.

The Social Security Administration reports that 6.5 million individuals who are blind or have a disability rely on SSI for the basic necessities of food, clothing, and shelter (SSA, 1999). Of the 5.7 million adults with disabilities who receive SSI

- More than half (58.6%) were female.
- The average age is about 45 years old.
- The average monthly SSI benefit in 1999 was $359.45. Only about 30% also received Social Security benefits, and those benefits averaged $367 a month.
- His or her income is—on average nationally—18.5% of the typical one-person income in the community.
- Almost three out of five have some form of cognitive impairment.

The Personal Responsibility and Work Opportunity Reconciliation Act of 1996 (PL 104-193) changed the definition for children under the SSI program, requiring a child to have a physical or mental impairment that can be proven medically and that results in *marked* and *severe* functional limitations. The 1996 changes in law make it more difficult for children with mild cognitive limitations to become eligible for SSI.

In addition to changing SSI eligibility in 1996, Congress transformed the Aid to Families with Dependent Children (AFDC) program into the Temporary Assistance to Needy Families (TANF) block grant. Although the new periods of eligibility for cash assistance, mandatory work requirements, and individual state practices have yet to fully demonstrate the effectiveness of the TANF program, states are only just beginning to identify TANF populations with chronic employment problems and disabilities, such as mild cognitive limitations.

Although the federal SSI program provides critical financial support to individuals in society whose needs are greatest, it is unlikely that a child or adult who has mild cognitive limitations—without a secondary disability—is eligible for this cash assistance. Furthermore, SSI funding is inadequate to affordably rent even a one-room studio apartment in any county or city in the United States (Edgar, O'Hara, et al., 1999).

POVERTY, UNDEREMPLOYMENT, AND THE LINK TO THE HOUSING CRISIS

First and foremost, many people of low socioeconomic status lack decent, affordable, and safe housing, often spending years on waiting lists to secure quality housing. The President's Committee on Mental Retardation (PCMR; 1969) reported a substantial association between mental retardation and low socioeconomic status. Unfortunately, communities increasingly do not direct substantial housing resources to address the needs of any low-income individuals (Consortium for Citizens with Disabilities Housing Task Force and The Technical Assistance Collaborative, 1996). It is critical to underscore the link between mental retardation and poverty for other reasons. Poverty is associated with reduced access to services and supports, compromised by lack of transportation, lack of resources for educational and home supports, lack of information regarding what supports are available, and unmet health and mental health needs.

Underemployment

Individuals with mental retardation and other disabilities represent an employment resource that has been largely overlooked, contributing to their low socioeconomic status. How fully are people with mental retardation and other disabilities participating in the American work force? According to the 1999 National Organization on Disability (NOD)/Louis Harris and Associates survey, "Americans with disabilities still face gaps in securing jobs, education, accessible public transportation and in many areas of daily life including recreation and worship" (National Organization on Disability, 2000).

Among the most startling findings about the workforce, the NOD/Louis Harris and Associates survey exposed significant gaps between the employment rates of individuals with and without disabilities. Only 32% of individuals with disabilities of working age (18–64) work full or part time, compared with 81% of individuals without disabilities. Of those individuals with disabilities of working age who are not working, more than two thirds stated that they would prefer to work. Other findings are also striking:

- 30% of Americans with disabilities live below the poverty line versus only 21% of all Americans.
- 29% of adults with disabilities live in households in which the total income is $15,000 or less versus only 10% of Americans without disabilities.
- 68% of people with disabilities are unemployed and out of the work force versus less than 10% of all Americans.
- 22% of people with disabilities did not complete high school, versus only 19% of all Americans.
- 62% of people with disabilities are registered to vote versus 78% of all Americans.
- 30% of adults with disabilities identified inadequate transportation as a problem versus 10% of adults without disabilities.
- 70% of adults with disabilities socialize with close friends, relatives, or neighbors at least once a week versus 85% of adults without disabilities. (National Organization on Disabilities, 2000)

Negative attitudes and low expectations by professionals, employers, families, and people with disabilities themselves continue to restrict job opportunities. People with mental retardation continue to be underrepresented in employment and workforce development programs.

Inadequate Health Coverage

Low wages and part-time employment reduce opportunities for self-sufficiency. For example, individuals with disabilities frequently have no or limited access to health insurance. Without SSI eligibility, people with mild cognitive limitations lack the automatic linkage to Medicaid benefits. If working, all too often they are in jobs in which they do not have access to employer health coverage and cannot afford private health insurance. Most private health care coverage does not provide important long-term supports that are needed for some people to live and work independently in the community.

AMONG THOSE WITH THE WORST CASE HOUSING NEEDS

As discussed previously, individuals with mild cognitive limitations are unlikely to meet eligibility for guaranteed disability income under the SSI program; often fall through the social services cracks, either by accident or due to ineligibility through design of public policy; are more likely to be unemployed or underemployed than adults without disabilities; and are highly likely to have very low incomes. In fact, they face the same problems in obtaining adequate housing options as anyone who is poor and not well educated.

In its 1999 *Report to Congress on Worst Case Housing Needs,* the U.S. Department of Housing and Urban Development (HUD) identified nine major findings (HUD, 2000). This and subsequent reports point out a mismatch between available extremely low-rent housing units and extremely low-income renters and that the gap is large and getting larger throughout the nation. HUD defined "worst case housing needs" as unassisted renters with incomes below 50% of the local median, who pay more than half of their income for rent or live in severely substandard housing.

Among the key findings, HUD found that the most serious housing needs are concentrated among households with the lowest incomes. Almost 4.2 million of the 5.4 million households with worst case needs have extremely low incomes—below 30% of the median. Almost 7 of every 10 such households pay more than one half of their income for rent or live in severely inadequate housing when they are not receiving assistance.

Of the 12.3 million individuals with worst case housing needs, HUD found that between 1.1 million and 1.4 million were adults with disabilities, 1.5 million were older adults, and 4.3 million were children. It is clear that both individuals with disabilities who live alone and households in which an individual with disabilities lives face substantial and growing housing problems.

Despite robust economic growth throughout the 1990s, the number of very low-income American households with worst case housing needs reached an all-time high—5.4 million. In addition, the availability of affordable rental properties declined. Despite these facts, Congress eliminated funding for new rental assistance in the mid-1990s.

HUD found that between 1991 and 1997, the number of rental units affordable to families with incomes below 30% of median income dropped by 5%, a decline of more than 370,000 units. By 1997, the number of households with worst case housing problems increased by 4%, twice the rate of growth in the number of all U.S. households (HUD, 2000).

Perhaps most startling in HUD's findings is that worst case housing needs increased most rapidly among the working poor during this time period. Although full-time work should provide sufficient income to afford a decent place to live, a disturbing trend existed in the opposite direction during the economic recovery of the 1990s. Research with SSI program data suggests that housing needs among people with disabilities increased slightly. Although working-age people with disabilities represent less than 13% of total households that receive federal housing assistance, they make up more than 25% of the households with worst case housing needs (Miller & O'Hara, 2001).

Unfortunately, HUD has never assessed how many people with disabilities who receive SSI or have other forms of income (Social Security Disability Insurance [SSDI], Workman's Compensation, earned income) are in need of federal housing assistance. Nor does the American Housing Survey accurately estimate the housing needs of people with mental retardation and other disabilities. Even when the housing needs of people with disabilities are estimated through a federally mandated community consolidated planning process, the affordable housing delivery system has been resistant to expanding housing opportunities for people with various disabilities.

Neither HUD, the National Housing Survey, nor community consolidated planning processes have published data on the housing needs of people with disabilities by cognitive impairment. Although a community's plan may address vulnerable populations, such as older adults and people with disabilities, it usually reflects a need for project-based supportive housing.

Among the many reasons for this lack of response at federal, state, and local levels is a lack of information and understanding of the housing needs of people with disabilities, the stigma associated with having a disability, and continuing discrimination within the affordable housing delivery system.

SEVERITY OF HOUSING PROBLEM

A groundbreaking 1998 report by The Technical Assistance Collaborative, Inc. (TAC), working in collaboration with the Washington-based Consortium for

Citizens with Disabilities (CCD) Housing Task Force, documented the severity of the housing affordability problem for people with disabilities.

> Simply put, the millions of people with disabilities who receive SSI bene-fits are too poor to obtain decent and affordable housing in virtually any community in the United States. Unfortunately, we see the effects of this housing crisis every day—in people with disabilities living at home with aging parents, living in substandard housing or crowded homeless shel-ters, or paying 75%–80% or more of their monthly income for rent. (Edgar, O'Hara, et al., 1999, p. 3)

Unfortunately, at a time when public policy promotes people with dis-abilities living in typical housing in the community rather than in costly insti-tutions or congregate facilities, changes to federal housing policies have reduced the supply of affordable housing available to people with disabilities younger than age 62.

Because of laws passed in the 1990s, owners of federally subsidized hous-ing are permitted to restrict or exclude access by people with disabilities to sub-sidized housing units that previously were available to them. TAC and the CCD Housing Task Force estimated that approximately 275,000 apartments in fed-erally subsidized older adult/disabled housing buildings would no longer be open to people with disabilities younger than age 62 in the year 2000. Thus far, Congress has approved funds to replace only approximately 25,000 apartments for tenant-based assistance over the past several years.

The average SSI income in 2000 of 18.5% of the national median income is well below the level required to receive housing assistance (Miller & O'Hara, 2001). HUD considers a person to have a very low income if he or she is at 50% of the national median income—more than twice as much income as the aver-age SSI recipient.

There is not a single city or urban county in the United States where a per-son with a disability receiving SSI benefits can afford to rent a modest effi-ciency apartment. This finding is based on current federal housing affordability standards for very low-income households, which suggest that no more than 30% of one's monthly income should be spent on housing costs. In the 39 cities or counties in the United States with the highest rental housing costs, the rent for an efficiency apartment is more than a person's *entire* SSI monthly benefit (Edgar, O'Hara, et al., 1999).

The TAC and the CCD Housing Task Force estimate that it takes 98% of a monthly SSI check to pay the rent for a one-bedroom apartment (Miller & O'Hara, 2001). Nationally, the average cost for a one-bedroom apartment is 69% of SSI income and more than the entire SSI monthly income in 143 coun-ties in the United States.

Using the HUD Fair Market Rents as the standard for modest rental hous-ing, nowhere in the United States can an SSI recipient rent a one-bedroom apartment for less than 50% of his or her income. This is a critical finding because responsible landlords and housing management companies usually deny rental applications when the rent would cost more than half of the person's income.

In every state across the country, people with disabilities are in the midst of an acute and increasing affordable housing crisis—one that is getting worse. In 1998, 4,375,650 people with severe disabilities (adult SSI recipients younger than age 65 reported in June 1997 by SSA) saw their purchasing power in the rental market continue to erode (Edgar, O'Hara, et al., 1999).

OBSTACLES

Considerable obstacles face the disability community in trying to convince housing officials to address the housing needs of people with mental retardation and other disabilities and to recruit affordable housing providers.

Cost

It costs much more to make housing affordable for an extremely low-income household than it does to make housing affordable for a low- to moderate-income household (i.e., a household with an income of $25,000 per year). Therefore, for financial and political reasons, it often is easier for local housing officials to use federal affordable housing funds for homeownership initiatives targeted to working households with low to moderate incomes rather than for rental assistance targeted to people with disabilities with extremely low incomes.

Stigma and Resistance

The stigma experienced by people with mental retardation and other disabilities persists in many communities and, too often, makes gaining access to or developing affordable housing difficult. Often local public housing authorities, housing developers, and city officials would rather avoid serving people with disabilities than face the possible controversy. In the worst cases, these housing providers and officials share the prejudices and fears of the community at large.

Lack of Information or Advocacy

Finally, effective advocacy can greatly influence who receives housing assistance. Strongly organized housing constituencies, such as homeless coalitions or homebuilders associations, already exist in many communities. These groups often receive affordable housing assistance because they are active and known players in the affordable housing system. Other housing advocates may not readily accept the disability community as a player, particularly if it is advocating for a change in the way that scarce federal affordable housing funds are distributed by local housing officials.

Despite these obstacles, coordination and advocacy can and does have an impact on local, state, and federal housing decisions. Effective advocacy begins with a clear message. To develop a powerful and effective message, the disability community should begin with a strong statement regarding affordable housing needs.

KEY FEDERAL HOUSING ASSISTANCE

Given the obstacles of poverty, low rates of employment, and discrimination, what housing resources and advocacy strategies are available to afford individuals with mild cognitive limitations and other disabilities the dignity of and support for personal housing? Though often referred to as an affordable housing delivery system, a multitude of agencies responsible for administering affordable housing programs exist in any one community. The trend in affordable housing programs today is toward greater local discretion regarding the use and targeting of federal housing assistance.

The federal government funds most housing assistance. HUD is the federal agency responsible for the administration and oversight of most affordable housing programs throughout the country. In addition to its headquarters in Washington, D.C., HUD maintains at least one local field office in each state. These local HUD field offices are responsible for program oversight and technical assistance in their regions. For a listing of HUD field offices, refer to the agency's web site at http://www.hud.gov/local.html.

HUD contracts with public and private agencies and governments (city, county, and state) to administer housing assistance programs on its behalf. The primary agencies with whom HUD contracts include the following:

- *Public Housing Authorities (PHAs):* These public agencies are overseen by a Board of Commissioners that is either elected or appointed by the city or town. PHAs were created with the passage of the first Housing Act in 1937 to develop, own, and mange public housing under contract with HUD. PHAs administer conventional public housing and Section 8 tenant-based vouchers. Historically, PHAs have been highly regulated by HUD.
- *City, county, and state governments:* Since 1974, Congress has created several housing and community development programs (generally known as block grants or formula grants) that are allocated through HUD to cities,

counties, and states using criteria that consider populations, poverty indices, and housing market conditions. States receive *balance of state* funding for those cities and towns that are not large enough to receive funding directly from HUD. These block grants have income targeting requirements and specify eligible housing activities, but affordable housing program design and administration is largely left to the responsible city, county, or state government agencies.

- *Housing developers:* Housing developers are private nonprofit or for-profit entities that develop affordable housing (either through acquisition, rehabilitation, or new construction) using federal housing assistance. In the 1960s and 1970s, many housing developers contracted directly with HUD for housing assistance to build or rehabilitate affordable housing. These housing developments (many of which have Section 8 project-based units) make up the privately owned, federally assisted housing inventory affected by *elderly only* tenant selection policies.

Most communities have an existing supply of affordable housing that has been developed over the course of many years. This inventory generally includes the following:

- *Public housing projects* developed and owned by the PHA
- *Section 8 vouchers administered by the PHA:* Individuals who have vouchers use them to secure decent, moderately priced rental housing in the private market. They can also be reused when someone leaves the program and, therefore, represent an ongoing supply of housing assistance in the community. On average, approximately 10% of vouchers will turn over in a year.
- *Privately owned rental housing* in which all—or a portion of—the units have affordable rents because the owners have received some form of housing assistance.

In addition to the existing supply of affordable housing in a community, Congress provides new funding each year to increase the number of households that will receive housing assistance across the country. Currently, this housing assistance includes the following:

- Block grant funding from HUD to cities, counties, and states for affordable housing activities to assist additional low-income households: The key programs include the HOME Investment Partnership Program, Community Development Block Grant (CDBG) Program, Housing Opportunities for Individuals with AIDS (HOPWA) program, and the Emergency Shelter Grant (ESG) Program. To find out what funding a particular city, county, or state receives, consult the HUD web site at http://www.hud.gov/community/.

- A limited number of Section 8 vouchers for which PHAs may apply
- A limited number of *Mainstream* Section 8 vouchers open to application by both nonprofit organizations and public housing authorities
- Funding to rehabilitate deteriorated public housing projects

Not all of the previously listed housing assistance is available in every community. For example, a small PHA may own and manage several public housing buildings but may not administer any Section 8 certificates and vouchers. A small or rural town may not receive housing block grant funding directly from HUD. However, town governments or local housing developers can apply to the state—or perhaps counties—for federal affordable housing funding.

SECTION 8 RENTAL ASSISTANCE OFFERS CHOICE AND CONTROL

The Section 8 voucher programs funded by HUD provide the greatest flexibility in housing assistance available to individuals with low incomes, including people with mild cognitive limitations and other disabilities. Vouchers are commonly referred to as tenant-based rental subsidies because they are given to individuals and to families to use in rental housing of their choice as long as the housing meets the Section 8 program requirements. Once a rental unit is selected and approved, the Section 8 program participant (who then becomes a Section 8 tenant) pays a limited percentage of his or her income (usually around 30%) as rent. The balance of the rent is then paid to the owner through the voucher program.

In addition, Section 8 vouchers are portable, making them available for use on a rental unit anywhere in the country—not just in the location of the PHA through which the application was approved (CCD Housing Task Force & TAC, 1998, April). However, a few specific restrictions exist regarding when a voucher becomes portable. This ability to move to another community, or to another state, provides people with disabilities with many more housing options and the opportunity to relocate.

The Section 8 program is a very effective way to help people with disabilities obtain decent, safe, and affordable housing. Unfortunately, too often people with disabilities and their advocates become frustrated in their efforts to obtain Section 8 vouchers because of long waiting lists and cumbersome rules and regulations that must be followed. Although no federal government housing program is perfect, a Section 8 certificate or voucher enables a person with a disability to gain access to affordable housing in the private market and to exercise some choice regarding the apartment and the neighborhood in which he or she wants to live.

Because Section 8 is an appropriate housing strategy for each community, there has never been a better time to engage local PHAs or your state housing agencies in obtaining more Section 8 resources. In 1996, Representative Rodney Frelinghuysen (R-NJ) and Senator Kit Bond (R-MO), working closely with the CCD Housing Task Force, led the way in Congress in authorizing new Section 8 vouchers targeted to people with disabilities and in authorizing HUD, in 1999, to allow application by nonprofit organizations for certain mainstream Section 8 resources (CCD Housing Task Force & TAC, 1998, April). The disability community must press their PHAs to apply for additional Section 8 assistance or work with nonprofit organizations to submit their own application.

ConPlan AS A LINK TO AFFORDABLE HOUSING

Because the need for affordable housing among low-income families and individuals far exceeds the supply of housing assistance in almost all communities, cities and counties must decide among competing demands for affordable housing. Local governments and housing providers generally are required by HUD to justify any affordable housing decisions in their communities through the use of affordable housing needs data.

Without the involvement of the disability community, local housing officials may completely overlook the housing needs of people with mental retardation and other disabilities. Most housing officials, housing developers, and PHAs do not recognize or understand the acute housing needs experienced by people with mental retardation and other disabilities.

As people with mental retardation and their families, advocates, and service providers look to gain access to and expand affordable housing opportunities in their communities, they must be prepared to collect housing needs data and to use it to inform the affordable housing community of the housing needs of people with disabilities. They must also be ready to educate housing providers, housing officials, and the community at large about the preference and capacity of people with mental retardation to live in the community.

One way to educate local housing officials about the affordable housing needs of people with mental retardation and other disabilities is to get involved in the process of preparing your community's *Consolidated Plan* (commonly referred to as the *ConPlan*). The ConPlan is not just a bureaucratic requirement. It is intended to be a comprehensive, long-range (5-year) planning document that describes housing needs, market conditions, and housing strategies and outlines an action plan for the investment of federal housing funds (TAC, 1999).

Cities and counties that receive federal housing assistance (typically cities and counties with populations of more than 50,000 and 250,000 respectively) are required by law to submit a ConPlan to HUD. In this plan, HUD requires the city or county to quantify and prioritize the affordable housing needs of low- and very low-income people in its community—including individuals with mental retardation and other disabilities. The ConPlan also must describe how the city or county plans to use the block grant funding it receives to best meet the community's priorities.

The ConPlan usually is prepared by the city or county community development or planning department. Two public hearings are required to collect accurate data on the community housing needs for the ConPlan. In addition, local officials who are preparing for the plan must consider any written comments they receive regarding the ConPlan and respond to these comments in the plan.

Before states and communities can receive federal funds, they must prepare or update their ConPlan. Because of these annual updates to the ConPlan, it is never too late to influence the development of the next ConPlan in a particular city or state. The disability community should take advantage of this opportunity to influence local officials to both identify people with mental retardation and other disabilities as among the other low-income households in their community and to describe their housing needs. In addition, the disability community can use the ConPlan process to request federal block grant or formula grant funding to expand affordable housing opportunities for people with disabilities.

The ConPlan is likely to be even more important in the future than it is right now. Since 1990, the federal government has been slowly devolving (shifting) responsibility and decision-making for federal housing programs to state and local governments. In the future, virtually all decisions regarding how federal housing funding is spent in a community will be based on the ConPlan. To ensure that people with mental retardation and other disabilities receive their fair share of the more than $26 billion in federal funds spent on housing and community development each year across the country, the disability community must become more involved in the preparation of the ConPlan at both state and local levels.

DOCUMENTING AFFORDABLE HOUSING NEED AND A COMMUNITY'S TRACK RECORD

Disability advocates should help local officials quantify the number of people with disabilities who currently benefit from housing assistance in the community. This means estimating the number of people with disabilities who live in public housing, have received a Section 8 voucher, or are living in federally (or otherwise publicly) assisted affordable housing. This information is important because in most communities, people with disabilities traditionally have not received their fair share of available affordable housing. PHAs and federally assisted housing management companies should be able to provide information regarding the number of people with disabilities who live in housing made available by their programs or who have a Section 8 voucher.

Begin first by contacting the person responsible for administering the Section 8 program and the person responsible for managing the public housing projects. They are required to report information regarding the number of people with disabilities that they house to HUD, though they do not distinguish among types of disability. If the PHA or property manager refuses to report this information, case managers may be an alternate source for this information. A last resort may be filing a request with the HUD Field Office for this information under the Freedom of Information Act.

Other valuable information can be located in a city, county, or state ConPlan that is available upon request from the government agency responsible for preparing it. The ConPlan is a valuable resource on current and past efforts, if any, to meet the affordable housing needs of people with disabilities.

In most communities, people with disabilities have not received a fair share of the affordable housing assistance available relative to their affordable housing needs. Keep in mind that it has only been since 1988, with the passage of the Fair Housing Amendments Act, that people with disabilities even had fair housing protections. When advocating for affordable housing, it is very useful to know the community's track record of providing housing for people with disabilities.

In the absence of good information from public and assisted housing waiting lists, or in addition to this waiting list information, the disability community should look to alternative sources of information within their systems to document affordable housing needs. Examples of these sources include studies of the following:

• The number of individuals on service provider waiting lists for community housing options
• The number of individuals living at home with aging parents
• The number of young adults graduating from public and private schools without housing
• The number of individuals residing in state-operated facilities without affordable housing options in the community
• The number of individuals residing in intermediate care facilities (ICFs), group homes, board and care homes, nursing homes, or other residential settings because of a lack of affordable housing options in the community
• The number of individuals who are homeless
• The number of individuals who are paying more than 50% of their income for housing or who are living in seriously substandard housing (CCD Housing Task Force & TAC, 1999)

DISCRIMINATION

HUD regulations specify activities that are prohibited by agencies that receive federal housing funding, such as a Public Housing Authority (PHA) that administers the Section 8 program or a city that receives CDBG funding. The regulations also outline the proactive steps that these agencies must take to comply with the law and to ensure nondiscrimination of people with disabilities. Under Section 504 of the Federal Rehabilitation Act, agencies administering or receiving federal housing dollars must ensure the following:

* *Discrimination against people with disabilities does not take place.* People with disabilities cannot be denied access to a housing program or service based on their disability. Services generally must be provided in an integrated manner and must not be provided separately for people with disabilities. The same types and quality of services must be provided to people with disabilities as are provided to people without disabilities.
* *Programs are accessible to people with disabilities.* Recipients of federal funds must operate housing programs and activities so that the program—when viewed in its entirety—is readily accessible to and usable by people with disabilities.
* *Housing policies and practices are modified to ensure nondiscrimination.* Housing policies and practices must be reasonably modified as needed on an ongoing basis to ensure that people with disabilities are not discriminated against.
* *Facilities that are newly constructed or substantially rehabilitated are made accessible.* This includes a requirement that a minimum of 5% of housing units be made accessible for people with mobility impairments and a minimum of 2% of housing units be made accessible to people with hearing or vision impairments.
* *Alterations to existing facilities are accessible to individuals with disabilities.* When making alterations to existing housing facilities that do not constitute substantial rehabilitation as described above, the alterations shall, to the maximum extent feasible, be made readily accessible and usable by people with disabilities.
* *Communication is effective.* The recipient must provide auxiliary aids and services as needed to ensure equal participation by individuals with disabilities. These might include TTYs, sign language interpreters, or the provision of materials in layperson terms—aimed at a third- or fourth-grade reading level. (CCD Housing Task Force & TAC, 1998, September)

Five Steps To Ensure Nondiscrimination

Any agencies administering or receiving federal housing dollars must take five steps to ensure nondiscrimination against people with disabilities:

1. Conduct a self-evaluation or review of all of their program and practices.
2. Conduct an assessment of the need for wheelchair accessible units in the community.
3. Develop a transition plan if needed to provide the required number of accessible units.
4. Designate a Section 504 coordinator.
5. Adopt grievance procedures, and inform program participants, the public, and others about discrimination.

HOMEOWNERSHIP FOR PEOPLE WITH DISABILITIES

The 1998 *State of the Nation's Housing Report* prepared by the Joint Center for Housing Studies at Harvard University describes not only an increase in home-ownership rates for all Americans but a prosperous economy that has propelled homeownership rates to an all-time high (CCD Housing Task Force & TAC, 1998, December). Although the report paints an optimistic picture, what does it mean for people with mental retardation and other disabilities? The National Home of Your Own Alliance (HOYA), a program funded by the Administration on Developmental Disabilities to help individuals with disabilities find oppor-tunities to purchase and take care of their own homes, estimates that only 1% of all people with developmental disabilities are homeowners and less than 5% of the 6.5 million people with disabilities living on SSI or SSDI are homeown-ers (CCD Housing Task Force & TAC, 1998, December).

Unfortunately, many people with mental retardation live on limited or fixed incomes and are not considered for homeownership. Because of SSI and Medicaid resource and asset restrictions, many people with mental retardation and other disabilities are prohibited from accumulating enough savings to enable them to afford down payments, closing costs, and long-term repair expenses associated with homeownership. These limitations, in combination with other institutional barriers and long-term stigma, have precluded tradi-tional financial institutions and government housing programs from viewing homeownership as a viable option for people with disabilities.

However, after years of advocacy by individuals with disabilities, their family members, service providers, and advocates, there are increasing efforts underway across the country that are beginning to make homeownership a real-ity for more and more people with disabilities. Homeownership for people with mental retardation and other disabilities has evolved from home purchases made by parents on behalf of their children to local, state, and federal home-ownership initiatives that are helping individuals with disabilities buy their own homes in communities across the country. This homeownership movement is an outgrowth of the desire of people with mental retardation and other disabil-ities to have a say in where and how they live—to exercise control over their lives—and to enjoy the long-term security that homeownership can provide.

GOALS AND BENEFITS OF HOMEOWNERSHIP

Some of the goals and benefits of homeownership include the following:

- Personal control over housing decisions
- Separation of housing from decisions regarding level of services and supports
- Long-term housing stability
- Community integration
- Long-term financial stability and an opportunity to build equity
- Empowerment
- Institutional change and cost savings to state and federal systems

Like Section 8 rental assistance and other models of rental housing that do not have a service requirement, homeownership provides individuals with mental retardation and other disabilities more choice and control over support relationships, such as case managers, live-in personal assistants, or paid support staff.

Homeownership also promotes the goal of community integration for people with mental retardation and other disabilities. The increased visibility of individuals with disabilities as homeowners and good neighbors is helping to change public attitudes and is challenging historical perceptions about the *abilities* of people with disabilities. Expanding homeownership by individuals with disabilities in typical neighborhoods across the country helps break down the stereotypes and stigma that frequently prevent people with mental retardation and other disabilities from gaining access to rental housing and homeownership options in communities of their choice.

When discussing homeownership for people with mental retardation and other disabilities, it is important to remember that not all people want to own their own home. Buying and maintaining a home is a challenging prospect for any homeowner. These challenges may be compounded for people with disabilities when confronted with stigma and the limitations of living on a fixed or very low income.

Homeownership is a serious responsibility involving a long-term financial commitment and should not be entered into lightly. Not only does the cost of homeownership include the mortgage, home insurance, and tax payments, but it also includes the financial obligations of long-term maintenance and repairs of the home. Although homeownership should be an option for all Americans, it is not an option that everyone wants or can afford.

Although homeownership efforts throughout the country each combine their own set of financial, organizational, and advocacy resources, they all have key ingredients for success in common. These principles for success include buyer motivation and decision making, pre-and postpurchase homeownership education and counseling, down payment assistance and flexible mortgage lending practices, coalition-building, agency coordination, and community education and marketing. Other factors also play an important role in home-ownership:

- Successful homeownership programs for people with mental retardation and other disabilities are designed specifically to maximize the individuals' involvement, decision-making, control in all aspects of homeownership program planning, design, and oversight.
- People with mental retardation and other disabilities should be included on program steering committees, hired as staff, and made a part of any effort to evaluate program outcomes and customer satisfaction.
- Homeownership advocates as well as homeownership program staff must be mindful not to substitute their own advocacy and enthusiasm for the motivation of the prospective homebuyer (CCD Housing Task Force & TAC, 1998, December).

Homebuyer Counseling

Homebuyer and homeownership counseling also are key ingredients to successful homeownership for people with mental retardation and other disabilities. Counseling helps the individual understand the long-term implications of homeownership and prepares him or her for the long and complicated process of purchasing a home. Effective homebuyer and homeownership counseling activities are tailored to meet the specific needs of individuals with a variety of disabilities. For example, people with cognitive impairments may need brief homebuyer training sessions spread out over a period of time. Homeownership counseling programs cover all the aspects of home purchase, including

- Budgeting and credit
- Working with realtors
- Fair housing laws
- The mortgage process
- Accessing down payment assistance
- Legal aspects of the purchase, sale, and closing
- Appraisals and home inspections
- Long-term responsibilities of maintenance, repair, and record keeping
- Homeowner's insurance
- Neighborhood or condo rules

Too often, the emphasis of homeownership programs is focused exclusively on getting the person into the home rather than on helping the homeowner with problems that may occur following his or her purchase of a home. Unfortunately, postpurchase programs are not as common or readily available as programs designed to help with the home-buying process (O'Hara & Miller, 2000). Table 8.1 provides a list of challenges to homeownership and strategies for overcoming those challenges.

Table 8.1. Challenges to home ownership and strategies for overcoming the challenges

Challenges to home ownerhsip	Strategies in overcoming challenges
Stigma	Educate community
Affordability	Find flexible mortgage applications and approval criteria
	Establish savings accounts up-front to allowable limits
	Look at low-cost housing areas for purchase
Down payment and closing costs	Look for lower down payment requirements
	Set aside in traditional homeownership programs
	Family gifts or loans
Poor or no credit history	Establish credit
	Request credit report and begin credit history clean-up
	Look for lenders who will accept nontraditional credit histories
Property maintenance	Set up an escrow account
	Establish relationship with neighbor or non-profit to provide maintenance, such as lawn service and painting
Long-term repairs	Set up escrow account held by nonprofit
	Look into state and city funds
	Look into service agency funds
Limited postpurchase	Set up up-front training for homebuyer to address possible problems
	Look for support and establish where to go for assistance

From CCD Housing Task Force & TAC. (1998, December). Homeownership for people with disabilities: A movement in the making. *Opening Doors 6.*

Homeownership Programs and Financial Assistance

Many people with disabilities have low incomes, and their ability to accumulate savings often is limited. To overcome this barrier, low down payment requirements are usually incorporated into homeownership programs for people with disabilities. For example, Fannie Mae's HomeChoice mortgage assistance program for people with disabilities provides a fixed rate mortgage and requires a reduced down payment ($250 or 2% of the sales price) to accommodate the often limited means of people with disabilities (CCD Housing Task Force & TAC, 1998, December). Fannie Mae's program also factors in the costs of rehabilitation of the home, if necessary, in order to make the property accessible.

Banks throughout the country are slowly adopting more flexible downpayment requirements to address the particular circumstances of people with disabilities and to allow them greater access to mortgage financing. For example, some lenders now allow the down payment for a home to come from a gift, a trust, or the value of work contributed by or on behalf of the homebuyer (so-called sweat equity). Lenders also have increased the maximum amount that can be borrowed through a mortgage by taking into consideration nontraditional sources of income (e.g., food stamps, supports available through the Medicaid home and community-based waiver services) a homeowner uses in order to cover his or her monthly living expenses.

Although these changes have allowed greater access to homeownership, it is still necessary for most people with disabilities to acquire significant down payment assistance in order to qualify for mortgages and successfully manage the responsibilities of homeownership over the long term. A higher down payment results in smaller monthly mortgage payments, leaving more disposable income for ongoing maintenance. Table 8.2 provides a list of individuals and organizations from which a potential homeowner may obtain financial assistance for down payment and closing costs.

Recent changes in mortgage lending practices and more flexible mortgage products, such as Fannie Mae's HomeChoice mortgage, are beginning to remedy this situation by minimizing down payment requirements and closing costs. Many state and local housing and community development agencies offer first time home buyer programs that allow individuals with very low incomes the ability to purchase homes below market interest rates with smaller than standard down payment contributions.

It is important to note that government-funded homeownership assistance (e.g., reduced interest rates on loans or grants for down payment assistance) usually includes *recapture* provisions. These provisions may require the repayment of the down payment assistance upon resale and/or limit how much the homeowner can benefit from any increase in the value of the property; however, these requirements often are phased out after the home has been owned for a specified period of time (CCD Housing Task Force & TAC, 1998, December).

If building equity is a primary goal for the homebuyer, then other nontraditional sources of down payment assistance may be preferred. Nontraditional sources include gifts or loans from family or friends, money from a special needs trust, and grants from foundations.

Table 8.2.   Sources of down payment and closing cost assistance

Type	Source
Gifts	Family, friends, special needs trust, religious organizations, community groups, fraternal organizations
Grants and soft second loans[a]	Independent living centers, developmental disabilities councils, state human services agency, federal home loan bank, state and local HOME funds, state and local development CDBG funds, state and local housing trusts, state housing finance agencies, Community Housing Development organizations (CHDOs), rural community development programs, sweat equity, contribution from the seller, private foundations, local housing funds, corporations

Adapted from Klein & Black, 1995.

[a]Loans may be 1.0% loans that are forgiven at the end of the loan term.

Although these changes have enabled more people with disabilities who have limited incomes to purchase homes, other long-term costs associated with homeownership also need to be considered before a home is purchased. A home is an *asset* that will age over time and require periodic repairs, some of which may be costly. The long-term costs that need to be factored into the decision to purchase beyond the standard monthly mortgage payment, private mortgage insurance, and taxes include the following:

- Homeowner's insurance
- Furniture and appliances
- Maintenance (e.g., lawn, paint, snow removal, weatherization)
- Repairs (e.g., new roof, boiler, siding)

When working with homebuyer counseling agencies and lenders, it is important that people with mental retardation address up front 1) how much they can realistically afford for housing costs, 2) how much down payment assistance they have available to them, and 3) the condition and location of homes on the market that they can afford.

INDIVIDUAL DEVELOPMENT ACCOUNTS

Because people with mild mental retardation face the same problems encountered by any individuals who do not have enough money to afford a decent place to live, Individual Development Accounts (IDAs) may be one way to build assets to buy a home, further education, or even start a small business. IDAs were first included as part of the federal welfare reform law, the Personal Responsibility and Work Opportunity Reconciliation Act of 1996 (PL 104 193). IDAs are dedicated savings accounts, similar in structure to individual retirement accounts (IRAs) that can be used only for buying a first home, for education or job training expenses, or for starting a small business.

IDAs are managed by community organizations, with the accounts held at local financial institutions. Contributions from participants with low incomes are matched using both private and public resources. The IDAs included in the welfare law are limited to use by people who are recipients of Temporary Assistance for Needy Families (TANF).

IDAs are necessary because low-income families need productive assets if they want to get out of poverty and achieve economic self-sufficiency. The federal government helps individuals who have average to high incomes acquire assets (through the home mortgage interest deduction and tax breaks for saving for college), but does not have a way to help individuals with low incomes acquire assets. IDAs—through the use of matching deposits and supportive nonprofit organizations—can help individuals with low incomes acquire both the capital and skills they need to jumpstart their lives, set goals for their future, and integrate into America's mainstream.

The Assets for Independence Act (AFIA; PL 105-285), signed into law in 1998, builds significantly on the IDAs authorized in the changes in the welfare law of 1996. The AFIA authorized a 5-year demonstration beginning in fiscal year 1999.

The three uses of IDAs are the same under the TANF program and the AFIA. However, AFIA-authorized IDAs are different in that they

- Are not restricted to individuals eligible for the TANF program
- Allow for emergency withdrawals
- Are available (on a competitive basis) to nonprofit entities throughout the country—regardless of whether the state includes IDAs in its TANF plan
- Provide federal matching funds and related program costs
- Exclude only matching deposits in determining eligibility for federal means-tested programs (that is, unlike TANF IDAs, participant savings in IDA authorized accounts under the AFIA may be considered)
- Are monitored and formally evaluated

Nonprofit organizations that wish to participate in AFIA accounts must raise matching funds from either public or private sources. Another important difference between the two types of IDAs is that under TANF-authorized IDAs, all funds—including matches and the individual's deposits—are disregarded in determining eligibility for other means-tested programs.

To be eligible for AFIA-authorized IDAs, a person must qualify for the Earned Income Tax Credit (EITC) and meet a net worth test. Household net worth cannot exceed $10,000, excluding the value of the primary dwelling unit and one motor vehicle owned by the household. Other factors to be considered with AFIA-authorized IDAs include

- IDAs can be transferred to eligible family members (spouse or dependent child)
- Federal funds in any one IDA cannot exceed $2,000 per individual (and $4,000 per household) over the course of the demonstration
- Only savings generated from *earned income* can be deposited into an IDA
- The nonprofit organization will set the match rate
- The federal deposit will then equal the nonfederal deposit

For example, assuming the nonprofit organization adopts a 2 to 1 matching rate, if a participant deposits a total of $100 over 3 months, then the nonfederal match will be $200, and the federal match will be $200, for a total balance in the IDA of $500 (plus accrued interest).

Nonprofit organizations may submit their applications in conjunction with a state, local, or tribal entity and may collaborate with financial institutions and for-profit community development corporations to conduct the demonstration. For a copy of the legislative text and information on the demonstrations, visit http://www.idanetwork.org/.

COALITION BUILDING AND A COORDINATING ENTITY

Most successful homeownership initiatives involve a formal coalition or collaboration that pulls key stakeholders together to coordinate and simplify the homeownership process for people with disabilities. A homebuyer coalition organized for people with disabilities should include organizations and stakeholders from both the disability community, the housing industry, and financial institutions. This approach helps identify and overcome potential barriers, such as stigma and institutional and regulatory barriers, and helps leverage public and private resources for down payment assistance and other program costs.

Coalitions also foster the education of the housing industry (i.e., lenders and local housing officials) as well as the individuals with disabilities. Housing organizations have the opportunity to learn about needed reasonable accommodations and to make adjustments in their practices. Service providers have a chance to meet important members of the housing community and to learn about other affordable housing resources.

In most cases, successful collaborations or homeownership coalitions are coordinated by a lead agency. Table 8.3 lists some of the successes of these collaborations and coalitions. Lead agencies can provide a single point of contact and the administrative capacity critical in reaching the goal of homeownership. Lead agencies can be nonprofits agencies that are working on affordable housing or disability issues or local, county, or state housing or human services agencies.

Ideally, lead agencies identify and incorporate all of the interested and necessary parties (e.g., lenders, realtors, housing developers, service providers, advocates, people with disabilities, appraisers, state housing and human services agencies, and home-buying counseling agencies) into the program's design and implementation strategies. Lead agencies play a key role in aggregating the government and private funding (e.g., Federal Home Loan Bank funds, HOME and CDBG block grant funds, IDAs, foundation grants) that are needed for down payment assistance and other program costs

POOR OR NONEXISTENT CREDIT HISTORIES

Unfortunately, a limited income may have adversely affected a person's credit history or prohibited someone from establishing any credit history at all. Because financial institutions are relying more heavily on credit scoring than in the past, the lack of credit may pose a serious impediment to people with disabilities. Fortunately, many new mortgage programs designed for people with disabilities consider nontraditional credit histories. Service providers, advocates, and state homeownership programs also are working with people with disabilities to clear up bad credit histories and to help establish traditional credit, while also cautioning against the accumulation of debt.

Table 8.3.   Successes reaped by collaborations and home ownership coalitions

Funding for down payment and closing cost assistance from federal, state, and local
    housing programs.

Pro bono (free) legal services for closings

Access to rehabilitation programs to make necessary home modifications

In kind or donated appraisals and home inspection services

New government funding for loans or grants to make homes accessible

Flexible mortgage financing aimed at increasing participation and access by people with
    mental retardation and other disabilities

Specialized home buyer counseling programs

American Homeownership and Economic Opportunity Act of 2000 (PL 106-569) allows
    Section 8 assistance to be used for home purchase

From CCD Housing Task Force & TAC. (1998, December). Homeownership for people with disabilities:
A movement in the making. *Opening Doors 6.*

Overall, it is important to remember that the traditional mortgage process has not worked well for people with disabilities and that reasonable accommodations should be made when appropriate. People with disabilities may require more time between the mortgage approval and the actual closing—when the mortgage payments become their responsibility. In some instances, personal assistance or more flexible support services must be arranged before an individual can move into his or her new home, or the home may require modifications that must be approved and funded by another agency. Despite these and other challenges, the benefits of homeownership for people with disabilities who can afford it are worth the planning and bureaucratic steps required to achieve it.

Successful homeownership initiatives usually involve organized outreach and marketing and community education efforts that target financial institutions, state human services agencies, service providers, realtors, families, housing specialists, and people with disabilities. Effective homeownership initiatives have included

- Workshops, training, and conferences on homeownership
- Newsletters detailing successful examples of home purchases by people with disabilities
- Meetings with legislators and policy makers on the option of homeownership
- Articles in local newspapers
- Presentation of information to case managers regarding homeownership and solicitation of support in presenting homeownership as an option to people with disabilities
- Education of people with disabilities regarding their housing options and promotion of their hopes and expectations.

The September 1998 National Home of Your Own Alliance newsletter reported that more than 500 people with disabilities had recently become home-owners. For these individuals, the benefits of homeownership—increased quality of life, control, and housing stability—have become realities (CCD Housing Task Force & TAC, 1998, December). In addition, these recent homeowners help in the ongoing battle against stigma. As homeowners, these households are now neighbors and stakeholders in a community and a neighborhood. Community members are able to see that people with disabilities are productive members of the community: They maintain their properties, pay taxes, vote, and patronize local businesses.

Increasing all housing options for people with disabilities is critical as more and more resources (e.g., rental assistance, affordable housing development resources) grow scarce, exacerbating the acute shortage of affordable housing available for low- and very low-income people with disabilities. It is important to look toward all housing options that promote choice and independence. Although challenges will continue to arise, the concerted efforts of people with disabilities, their family members, and advocates is making homeownership a reality for a growing numbers of people with disabilities.

COLLABORATION WITH OTHER ORGANIZATIONS

Advocates must work with other low income housing and service organizations to scan the environment and develop their community's housing track record. Actions to take include the following:

- Review a copy of the ConPlan currently in effect. Obtain it from the city/county or state community development department.
- Go to HUD's web site (http://www.hud.gov/progdesc/conplan.cfm) to learn more about the ConPlan.
- Meet with the officials responsible for developing the ConPlan to learn more about the local, county, or state ConPlan process and how the officials will facilitate required public participation. Advocates should determine how to help in the process.
- Share this study and any needs estimates/data with public officials.
- Attend public advisory group meetings, if they occur, and testify at public hearings.
- Work with the media on stories that demonstrate the locale's affordable housing needs and that highlight the accomplishments of people with disabilities who are living in the community.
- Inquire about the lead ConPlan agency's working relationship with mental health officials. Ask for suggestions to strengthen collaboration.
- Advocate that a fair share of housing resources from specific block grant programs (HOME and CDBG) benefit people with disabilities.

CONCLUSION

The time is right for the disability community—armed with the Fair Housing
Amendments Act of 1988, Section 504 of the Rehabilitation Act of 1973, the
Americans with Disabilities Act of 1990, and other federal protections—together with federal rental assistance programs that are controlled at local levels and local, state, and federal homeownership programs to help people with
mild mental retardation gain decent affordable housing in typical neighborhoods in all communities throughout the nation. It is time for individuals with
disabilities to be welcomed in every community and for the doors to be opened
to them to all of the housing options that are available to other Americans.

REFERENCES

Americans with Disabilities Act (ADA) of 1990, PL 101-336, 42 U.S.C. §§ 12101 *et
    seq.*
Consortium for Citizens with Disabilities Housing Task Force and The Technical Assis-
    tance Collaborative. (1996, September). Recommendations for a federal policy to
    address the housing needs of people with disabilities. *Opening Doors.* (Available:
    http://thearc.org/ga/opendoor.html)
Consortium for Citizens with Disabilities Housing Task Force and The Technical Assis-
    tance Collaborative. (1998, April). The Section 8 certificate and voucher programs.
    Opening Doors 4. (Available: http://www.c-c-d.org/odoors.html)
Consortium for Citizens with Disabilities Housing Task Force and The Technical Assis-
    tance Collaborative. (1998, September). The ten year anniversary of the Fair Housing
    Amendments Act: Celebration or Vigil. *Opening Doors 5.* (Available: http://www
    .c-c-d.org/od-sept98.htm)
Consortium for Citizens with Disabilities Housing Task Force and The Technical Assis-
    tance Collaborative. (1998, December). Homeownership for people with disabilities:
    A movement in the making. *Opening Doors 6.* (Available: http://www.c-c-d.org/
    od-dec98.htm)
Consortium for Citizens with Disabilities Housing Task Force and The Technical Assis-
    tance Collaborative. (1999, September). Affordable housing in your community.
    What you need to know! What you need to do! *Opening Doors 8.* (Available: http://
    www.c-c-d.org/od-sept99.htm)
Edgar, E., O'Hara, A., et al. (1999). *Priced out in 1998: The housing crisis for people
    with disabilities* (2nd ed.). Boston: The Technical Assistance Collaborative. (Avail-
    able: http://www.c-c-d.org/priced_out_in_1998.htm)
Klein, J., & Black, M. (1995). *Extending the American dream.* Durham, NH: National
    Home of Your Own Alliance, Institute on Disability. (Available: http://alliance.unh
    .edu)
Miller, E., & O'Hara, A. (2001). *Priced out in 2000: The crisis continues* (3rd ed.).
    Boston: The Technical Assistance Collaborative.
National Organization on Disability. (2000). *Harris survey of Americans with disabili-
    ties, 2000.* Washington, DC: Author.
O'Hara, A., & Miller, E. (2000). *Going it alone: The struggle to expand housing oppor-
    tunities for people with disabilities.* Boston: The Technical Assistance Collaborative.
    (Available: http://www.c-c-d.org/going_alone.htm)

Social Security Administration, Office of Research, Evaluation, and Statistics, Division of SSI Statistices and Analysis. (1999, June). *SSI annual statistical report, 1998.* Washington, DC: Author.

Technical Assistance Collaborative. (1999). *Piecing it all together in your community: Playing the housing game. Learning to use HUD's Consolidated Plan to expand housingopportunities for people with disabilities.* Boston: Author.

U.S. Department of Housing and Urban Development, Office of Public Development and Research. (2000). *A report on worst case housing needs: Rental housing assistance—The worsening crisis.* Washington, DC: Author.

9

Social and Community Participation

How to Enhance Supports for
People with Mild Cognitive Limitations

Valerie J. Bradley, John M. Agosta, and Madeleine Kimmich

This chapter addresses issues of community inclusion for people with mild cognitive limitations. Although a good deal has been written about inclusion for people with complex and significant disabilities (e.g., Bradley, Ashbaugh, & Blaney, 1994; Heal, Haney, & Novak Amado, 1988; Nisbet, 1992; Taylor, Bogdan, & Racino, 1991; Towell & Beardshaw, 1991), very little has been written about the particular dilemmas faced by those with mild cognitive limitations. This chapter examines the lessons learned from the experiences in formal mental retardation systems of support, to identify those areas that have resonance for people with mild disabilities and to note approaches that may be unique to this group of individuals.

INCLUSION AS A TRANSFORMATIVE GOAL

The notion of inclusion was, in one form or another, a motivating force for reform in the field of mental retardation during the last quarter of the 20th century. Conceptually, inclusion has evolved from an aspiration linked to place to one tied to participation, choice, and relationships. Probably the earliest expression of the idea, at least as a concept with specific entailments, was in Wolfensberger's (1972) *The Principle of Normalization in Human Services.* As Wolfensberger's compelling yet deceptively simple notion began to invade public mental retardation service systems, it was used to criticize a variety of practices and settings, including institutional surroundings, the infantalization of decorations and language, and inadequate day activities. As the concept was refined and honed, it spawned more encompassing aspirations such as community integration and community membership (Bradley et al., 1994). The notion of community integration was directly related to the movement of people out of institutions and implied a reentry by those who had been excluded. Likewise, community membership implied joining a fellowship from which one had been alienated.

Conceptions that stressed integration and community-based services also influenced public policy, which in turn influenced practice. Phrases such as *least restrictive environment* and *mainstreaming* emerged as part of the landmark right-to-education legislation. Class action lawsuits brought during the 1970s, including the *Pennhurst State School & Hospital v. Halderman* litigation, which found habilitation in the community to be a right, also echoed these notions. These powerful legal ideals had a transformative impact on the delivery of educational as well as residential and day services for people with mental retardation.

As fewer and fewer children and adults left their communities to receive services and as institutional populations began a precipitous decline, the ideals that emerged to goad the system had less to do with opposition to a dominant norm (e.g., exclusion, extrusion, institutionalization, alienation) and more to do with affirmative notions of equality and accommodation of differences. No longer was the system exhorted to provide better surroundings and opportunities than those available in the institution but, instead, was prompted to facilitate supports that would allow people with mental retardation to lead lives more like those available to their peers without mental retardation. Now, the basis for judgment is whether people with mental retardation are able to enjoy shared "goods," such as relationships, friendships, home ownership, real jobs, spiritual fulfillment, and exercise of personal choice. These assumptions about what constitutes satisfying life have come to be known as *inclusion*. The outlines of this vision were offered by Knoll and Peterson in 1992:

> In inclusive communities, we move from focusing on services provided exclusively by agencies to support for involvement in typical community activities, based on the needs and choices of the individual. Disability service agencies work in partnership with community services, support networks (friends, family, peers), and the person with a disability. The primary role is to help connect and support the individual in school, home, community, and work. (p. 1)

Implications of Inclusion Values

The attributes that have come to characterize inclusive services and supports clearly have meaning for people with varying degrees of disability. However, the challenges faced by people with mild cognitive limitations in achieving full participation are different in character from those encountered by individuals with more severe disabilities. For the most part, people with mild cognitive limitations have not been institutionalized—they have lived in communities. Furthermore, the services and supports they have received from the formal service system, if they have received any at all, have been minimal, implying that the public has less responsibility to enhance their life choices. Individuals with mild cognitive limitations also are less likely to request formal services because such requests might be stigmatizing.

People with mild cognitive limitations have a sporadic rather than a constant need for supports—a contingency that most formal systems cannot as of yet accommodate. Also, the nature of the supports that they require may be very different in substance from the supports required by individuals with more severe disabilities. For example, providing supports for a person with severe disabilities to enable him or her to participate on a board of directors may involve explaining the broad outline of the agenda and assisting the individual during the meeting to make predetermined points. For an individual with a mild cognitive limitation, the support task may be much more intense; it may involve interpreting the written materials, discussing strategies for the meeting, and providing intensive support during the meeting. To complicate matters, the seeming competence of such individuals may mask their need for explanation, advice, encouragement, and so forth.

Finally, the provision of inclusion-oriented supports to individuals with mild disabilities may be further complicated by the fact that some individuals may be caught up in other human services systems in which the support instinct is neither strong nor similar in character to that in the mental retardation system. For example, some individuals with mild cognitive limitations may be receiving income supports from the Temporary Assistance for Needy Families (TANF) program, others may be caught up in the child welfare system, some may have dual diagnoses and be served primarily through the mental health system, and still others may be ensnared in the criminal justice system. None of these public programs has the same commitment to inclusion that can be found (albeit nascent in some states) in the mental retardation system.

BASIS FOR A NEW APPROACH

The major structural constraints to people with mild cognitive limitations— even if they were able to gain access to the formal mental retardation system— are the "all-or-nothing" approach to support, the lack of individualization, and the conventional nature of case management. Although people with mild cognitive limitations experience these constraints differently, they are the same constraints that prevent people with more severe mental retardation from being included in their communities. Therefore, any solution that increases the flexibility and participant-driven character of the system will be of benefit to people regardless of the intensity of their disability. The three pillars upon which this new and more malleable approach depends are self-determination, circles of support, and the presence of brokers or facilitators.

Self-Determination

In a number of areas in the country, local and state mental retardation systems are exploring the ways in which people with mental retardation can influence the character and configuration of the supports they receive through increased self-determination. Emphasis on the choices and preferences of individuals, which forms the core or heart of this emerging practice, represents a significant departure from conventional practice.

The dominant approach to the provision of services since the late 1980s has been the implementation of a partnership between the public and private sectors resulting in a system that allocates public funds through contracts to community services providers. Public funds are used to purchase program "slots" that in turn are made available to those individuals that the system's gatekeepers deem as eligible and in need of such services. This partnership, however, does not include the participation of people with mental retardation and their families in the design of services or in the allocation of resources.

The goal of self-determination is to alter significantly these power relationships by placing the choices, preferences, and individual gifts of people with mental retardation at the center of the system and by encouraging a range of traditional and nontraditional providers to compete for the opportunity to supply needed supports.

An emphasis on the preferences of people with disabilities alone, however, is not sufficient to change the direction of a service system; change also requires the power over resources. Therefore, self-determination also includes individually controlled budgets that can be dispersed based on an agreed-on person-driven plan. Finally, to ensure that people receive the information necessary to make decisions in their best interests, some form of service brokerage characteristically is carried out by individuals who do not have a direct interest in the choices made by participants.

Circles of Support

The notion of a circle of support or a circle of friends first gained currency in the United States through the work of two women from Canada—Judith Snow and Marsha Forest (1987). The idea advances the prominence of natural supports, such as family, friends, and neighbors, as a complement to, and at times in lieu of, specialized or paid supports. George Ducharme and his colleagues at Communitas in Connecticut describe circles of support as follows:

> The members of a circle of support are usually friends, family members, coworkers, neighbors, people at a house of worship, and sometimes service providers. The majority of people in a circle of support are not paid to be there. They are involved because they care about the person or family and they have made a commitment to work together on behalf of the

person or family. The circle members come together to pursue the vision by identifying and understanding the challenges and opportunities and working on strategies to overcome certain obstacles and take advantage of opportunities. (Ducharme, Beeman, DeMarasse, & Ludlum, 1994, p. 348)

Circles of support are critical focal points for mobilizing natural supports and frameworks to organize the contributions and participation of individuals who are connected to and who care about the individual with mental retardation. The identified supports can substitute for and/or augment public or specialized services but do require facilitation and commitment on an ongoing basis.

At their best, circles of support can assist individuals to make social connections in their communities, get access to needed services and supports, minimize risks to health and safety, and greatly enrich the everyday lives of people with disabilities as well as the individuals who participate in the circle.

Service/Support Brokers

A third element of this new more flexible vision for people with mental retardation is the service/support broker—an individual who arranges and facilitates self-determination and circles of support. Nerney and Shumway (1996) offered useful guidance on the role of service brokers in a more participant-centered system:

[Service/support brokers] arrange with others to carry out the plans developed by the person with a disability or family and arrange for all necessary supports. They do not provide these supports. They become "personal agents" for the person with a disability and that person's circle or social support network. Of all the roles a broker may assume there are several that seem to fit well with this function:

1. Assisting in defining support needs and life dreams
2. Assisting in providing information and resources
3. Assisting in identifying potential formal and informal service providers and supports
4. Assisting in arranging/contracting for services and supports
5. Assisting in ongoing evaluation and other considerations

One of the primary skills necessary to perform this function is the ability to build on informal supports that may already be present in a person's life or assist the person to help create these informal supports over time, assisting the person to become connected to their community. Skills in bartering or exchange would be helpful. (p. 13)

The service/support broker acts as a knowledgeable guide and advocate, assisting the person with mental retardation to develop a person-centered plan and budget and to secure needed services and supports. Specifically, the broker 1) works closely with the person with cognitive limitations to develop a plan and an appropriate budget, 2) searches for ways through the informal and formal support systems to meet the individual's needs, and 3) represents the person's interests in dealing with providers on an individual basis. In many ways, the broker is the essential pivot point to a more individually tailored, "deconstructed" system.

EXEMPLARY PRACTICE[1]

These types of approaches to managing supports are not new. A number of precedents exist at the state and local level in family support, personal assistance services, and supported employment. More direct examples can be seen in two initiatives launched by the Robert Wood Johnson Foundation, a national philanthropy established in 1972 that is devoted to improving the health and health care of all Americans. These initiatives are the Cash and Counseling projects, aimed at senior citizens and people with disabilities, and the Self-Determination demonstrations, designed to help states create cost-effective participant-centered supports. The United Cerebral Palsy (UCP) Choice demonstration projects in supported employment are another direct example. In addition, several state developmental disability agencies are implementing system reform plans that build explicitly on these individually tailored strategies. These experiences testify to the viability of an individually responsive system and may have direct application to the provision of inclusion-oriented supports for people with mild cognitive limitations.

Personal Assistance Services

Personal assistance is "one person assisting another with tasks individuals would normally do for themselves if they did not have a disability" (Litvak, Zukas, & Heumann, 1987, p. 1). Personal assistance services (PAS) have gone through numerous "incarnations," from a home health/nursing model to a comprehensive array of home- and community-based supports. The major impetus for this shift has been activism by people with disabilities concerned about increasing their control over the delivery of personal assistance services. The broadest definition of PAS includes the conventional assistance with personal care, mobility, and household affairs; however, it also reaches into the arenas of employment, transportation, community participation, communication, and even parenting.

---

[1]The sections, "Exemplary Practice" and "Emerging State Approaches" were adapted from Agosta, J., & Kimmich, M. (1997). *Managing our own supports: A primer on participant-driven managed supports.* Alexandria, VA: Center for Managed Long-Term Supports for People with Disabilities.

Personal assistance is variously provided—sometimes services are purchased directly by the consumer with cash or a voucher; at other times services are provided directly by agencies. In 1987, nearly 150 different state programs provided PAS of some type; less than a quarter could be characterized as consumer directed (Litvak et al., 1987). The latest survey of states (World Institute on Disability, 1996) reveals that there are now approximately 300 PAS programs in the United States, but only about 50 of them, or one sixth, are consumer directed. Hence, while personal assistance needs are gaining more attention in the United States, the movement toward consumer control has not kept pace, largely due to regulatory constraints imposed by funding sources. Nonetheless, advocates of consumer-directed PAS continue to plow ahead, demonstrating in numerous locales that consumer control and choice can be financially viable and politically acceptable (Flanagan, 1996).

The core tenets of consumer-directed PAS are synonymous with the essential elements of the flexible support approaches discussed previously. Vision has always been a strong factor in the development of consumer-directed PAS. The vision of consumer-directed assistance was described aptly by the National Institute on Consumer-Directed Long-Term Services:

> Consumer direction is a philosophy and orientation to the delivery of home and community-based services whereby informed consumers make choices about the services they receive. . . . The unifying force in the range of consumer-directed and consumer choice models is that individuals have the primary authority to make choices that work best for them, regardless of the nature or extent of their disability or the source of payment for services. (1996, p. 2)

Self-determination is also central to PAS. Most often, the funding agency decides on a fixed budget or a maximum number of hours of PAS for each individual. Within that budget, participant choice and control can be exercised in a variety of areas, such as 1) hiring the personal assistant, 2) firing the personal assistant, if necessary, 3) deciding the tasks and the schedule for the personal assistant, 4) training the personal assistant, 5) supervising the personal assistant, and 6) paying the personal assistant. Different PAS programs offer varying opportunities for participants to have such control.

The degree of control exercised by PAS participants depends not only on the opportunities provided but more often on the individual's ability and willingness to take on the responsibilities. Control is not an all-or-nothing experience; for example, a participant may be very active in deciding which tasks are to be performed, may choose to be only somewhat involved in training the personal assistant, and may not want to deal at all with actually paying the assistant. Research has shown that people with all types of disabilities are capable of taking control of their personal assistance services (Kimmich & Godfrey, 1991; Litvak et al., 1987); indeed, people with developmental disabilities have been found to exercise more control over their services than seniors and nearly equal control to that of people with physical disabilities.

Family Support Programs

Contemporary family support programs include support services and/or cash assistance (Agosta & Melda, 1995). Family support programs also offer a large variety of delivery approaches that give families flexibility insofar as where and how they obtain their services and supports. Family support programs are a proven means of providing flexible supports and of increasing the family's participation and presence in their community. The vision is strong—to empower and support families in caring for their children with disabilities. Self-determination and flexible services are at the heart of the family support model, whether through cash or a voucher approach. Having a personal agent is also an important characteristic—family support programs offer various forms of service coordination and individual advocacy. They also explicitly foster the development of community and familial networks and partnerships to better meet the individual needs of families while stretching resources to reach unserved families.

Cash and Counseling Experiments

Cash and counseling programs take consumer choice one step further than personal assistance services in many states. The Robert Wood Johnson Foundation has launched a multi-pronged initiative to explore the use of cash grants to seniors and individuals with disabilities to purchase long-term care. Under the Cash and Counseling option, individuals receive a monthly monetary allowance in addition to information and assistance in choosing and arranging for long-term supports. The Cash and Counseling program can be incorporated into any existing state or federally funded long-term supports program. This allows the individual to choose between a traditional case-managed service benefit or a monthly cash allowance of a lesser monetary value. The individual can use the cash to purchase services from a home care agency or referral service, to pay a friend or relative to provide care or to live with them, or to move to an assisted living facility or other new housing arrangement. The Robert Wood Johnson Foundation has funded the National Council on the Aging to develop and disseminate information on cash and counseling programs to help states design and implement programs (Cameron, 1995; United States Health Cooperative, 1994). The Robert Wood Johnson Foundation also is collaborating with the Office of the Assistant Secretary for Planning and Evaluation (ASPE) in the U.S. Department of Health and Human Services to evaluate two statewide cash and counseling demonstrations.

The range of services for which the cash can be used is extensive, as is the type of provider from whom the individual may purchase the services. However, unlike traditional managed care approaches, financial risk is not passed to the individual in this arrangement. If the individual becomes seriously ill and has to be hospitalized, the cost of the hospitalization is covered by state funds, Medicaid, Medicare, or private insurance, not through the limited cash grants.

The "counseling" portion makes a personal agent or broker available to the individual to use as much or as little as he or she chooses. The counselor assists the individual to draw on existing personal support networks as well as community resources, thus "cultivating the informal care system" (University of Maryland Center on Aging, 1995) and building partnerships. In most cases, the Cash and Counseling programs have some quality assurance mechanisms to ensure positive outcomes—that individuals get what they paid for and that they are safe and healthy. At this point in time, it is not clear what funding streams are being used in the Robert Wood Johnson Foundation's demonstration project states; however, funding does remain categorical, with the demonstrations using various waivers and other approaches to minimize the constraints on how funds can be used.

Supported Employment Demonstrations

Several interesting developments in the area of supported employment similarly provide insight into how to design participant-driven managed support systems. The Arc of Tallahassee, Florida, has a grant from the Florida Developmental Disabilities Council and the Florida Developmental Services State Program Office to demonstrate the effectiveness of vouchers to support employment for people with disabilities (Linton, Persons, & Leatzow, 1996). Unlike the traditional supported employment model in which the individual interacts with a professional job coach, the voucher approach has three key players—the individual, an employment liaison, and a support person. The process encourages the involvement of nontraditional support providers by enabling the individual, with the assistance of the employment liaison, to choose support people from among friends, family, neighbors, co-workers, and others in the community.

Carrying the participant-driven model farther, the UCP Choice demonstration projects in three states put the participant clearly in control of not only who the support person is, but also what specific outcome is desired and what amount should be paid for achieving that outcome. With a federal grant from the Rehabilitation Services Administration, UCPA is testing ways to get people with severe physical disabilities into competitive employment using a consumer-driven approach outside of the traditional rehabilitation system. The Choice demonstration projects are staffed by Choice coordinators, who recruit participants and assist in developing an individual "futures plan for employment." Participants not only can choose the providers who will serve them but also can choose a payment process. Specific payment amounts are set for achieving each of a series of "products," which are expected to lead to the final outcome.

Central to the demonstrations is consumer self-determination and service flexibility, with consumers deciding what they want to purchase, from whom, and at what price. The consumers are encouraged to hire an Employment Advisor (a personal advocate/broker) to help them negotiate with service providers. At this point, the funding is solely federal rehabilitation money, with $10,666 drawn down and put into an individual account for each participant ($8,466 is for specific products, with an additional $2,200 set aside to cover Choice Coordinator and Employment Advisor services).

The projects are actively building community partnerships through a Local Referral Committee in each site, which selects 15 participants per year. The committee includes, at a minimum, a person with a disability, a family member of a person with a disability, an agency representative, a local vocational rehabilitation counselor, and a local school representative. In addition, the Choice Coordinator develops a pool of providers in the community to offer the range of services and supports that the participants want to purchase. The biggest problem that projects have faced is that traditional providers have been reluctant to serve the Choice participants. As a result, individuals and generic agencies have come forward to receive appropriate training to fill the gap and to afford participants real choices among providers.

The Robert Wood Johnson Foundation
Self-Determination Project: The Monadnock Experience

In 1993, the Robert Wood Johnson Foundation agreed to fund an innovative means for financing and delivering supports to a target group of fewer than 50 people in a single service area in New Hampshire.[2] Monadnock Developmental Services (MDS) of Keene, New Hampshire, is the state's contracted regional authority for services for people with developmental disabilities and is the agent for the Robert Wood Johnson Foundation demonstration project. As a regional provider, MDS serves 444 people annually, through both direct services and subcontracts, within a budget of $11.6 million; a growing waiting list contains 122 names. The purpose of the project, which initially served about 30 people with disabilities, was to test whether the proposed method of self-determination would both decrease per capita spending and increase the quality of life for individuals in the project. The project was guided by six principles:

---

[2]This information has been adapted from the following source: An affirmation of community: A revolution of vision and goals—The New Hampshire Self Determination Project. *TASH Newsletter, 21*(7), 21–27 and *TASH Newsletter, 21*(9), 19–23.

1. *Community life:* People with developmental disabilities are vital and integral members of our community and associational life.
2. *Support:* People will be supported to be members of the community rather than clients of programs/services.
3. *Self-determination:* People (with appropriate assistance from family and friends) will determine their own futures and contract for their own supports.
4. *Community capacity:* Communities and ordinary citizens will see themselves as competent and willing to become involved in the lives of people with developmental disabilities.
5. *Contributions:* Through gainful employment, people with disabilities have the opportunity and support to accumulate wealth. People who are accumulating wealth also will be expected to contribute to their own support.
6. *Fiscal conservatism:* Fiscal conservatism and fiscal efficiency are the hallmarks of the new system of supports and services.

The Robert Wood Johnson Foundation Self-Determination project operated under a block grant funding arrangement, with individual capitation rates set initially at 75%–90% of current service costs. However, because MDS received a single large allotment of funds, essentially as a group-capitated rate, individual plans could exceed the ceiling if necessary.

Each individual with developmental disabilities was given the opportunity to control a set sum of Medicaid and state funds to accommodate all of their individual needs. They could secure assistance from any family member or friend they chose, and they had the authority to spend resources on residential, employment, and personal needs as they chose, using discrete contracts with traditional providers or others. In essence, the entire "system" was reorganized to support individual budgets and choice rather than long-term "lump sum" arrangements between payers and providers. Individual budgets may change as individual needs and desires change. Finally, professionally dominated planning teams were replaced by teams that function more as circles of support.

The Robert Wood Johnson Foundation Self-Determination Initiative[3]

Based in great part on the experience of the Monadnock project, the Robert Wood Johnson Foundation gave 19 grants to explore related innovations. The foundation made available up to $5 million over 3 years for grants to states to implement changes in state policy and to enact reforms in at least two localities in each state. The grant program was managed by staff of the Robert Wood Johnson Foundation National Program Office, located at the Institute on Disability at the University of New Hampshire.

---

[3]Much of this section is taken from the Call for Proposals, issued by the Robert Wood Johnson Foundation (1996) concerning its Putting People First initiative.

The major objective of the Robert Wood Johnson Foundation initiative was to help states establish self-determination policies and local options, to improve the quality of life of people with developmental disabilities, and to do so cost effectively. Although states were encouraged to design their reforms based on their own experiences, changes were expected to promote independence with supports, inclusion in the community, and self-determined lifestyles. Some of the features emphasized by the Robert Wood Johnson Foundation staff included the following:

- Implementing individual budgets that were spent based on decisions made by people with disabilities, their family members, and other individuals whom they choose; these individual budgets were based, for example, on a percentage of current per person costs
- Establishing individual planning, operating, and financing structures and corresponding monitoring activities that were consistent with the requirements of individual budgets and decentralized management
- Helping provider agencies retrain their employees to enable self-directed service brokerage
- Introducing people with developmental disabilities and their families to the new opportunities that were available under a reformed system (e.g., how funds could be used more flexibly to enable individuals to arrange the formal and informal supports that they choose)
- Rethinking state quality assurance measures to ensure their consistency with consumer and family values

EMERGING STATE APPROACHES

Facing the competing pressures of declining revenues and increasing needs, numerous states are moving forward with plans to reform existing developmental disabilities systems. Many of these plans embrace, to varying extents, the three major ingredients of a more flexible service system—choice and self-determination, circles of support, and service/support brokers. This section summarizes the plans and activities in three selected states—Rhode Island, Vermont, and Colorado.

Rhode Island's Choices Waiver[4]

Rhode Island officials have submitted a 5-year research and demonstration proposal to the U.S. Health Care Financing Administration to test the applicability of a capitated managed care model for acute and long-term care services for people with developmental disabilities. The proposed "Section 1115" CHOICES

---

[4]This section draws on a description of Rhode Island Choices compiled by Smith & Ashbaugh, 1996. Special thanks to Sue Babin for editorial suggestions.

waiver application combines current Medicaid and other state funding mechanisms into a single coherent system to promote more cost-effective service delivery and to move the system from one that is provider-driven to one that is consumer-driven. The fundamental change that the state is proposing is a shift to an individually tailored system. The CHOICES proposal has six central objectives:

1. Ensure personal voice and control by consumers and their families in decision making.
2. Provide equitable, accessible, and quality health care for people with disabilities.
3. Manage resources more effectively.
4. Build/enhance opportunities for people to have meaningful lives and access to meaningful community participation.
5. Structure the system to be more accessible, responsive, equitable, and understandable to people with disabilities.
6. Make easily available all information about service options and opportunities so that personal voice and participation in decision making and choice are real.

Rhode Island proposes to combine Medicaid funds with state dollars to pay for long-term and acute health care. Present categorical program requirements would be dropped in favor of a unified, cross-cutting set of consumer-centered service and outcome standards. Service categories would be eliminated. In addition to case management, however, four general service areas would exist: 1) residential supports, 2) family supports, 3) day/activity supports, and 4) health care supports. Furthermore, state-operated programs would compete with private agencies to provide the services.

The proposal replaces program-based funding with the allocation of capitated dollar amounts to individuals. An Individualized Funding Authorization (IFA) would be assigned to each person rather than paid directly to a managed-care organization or provider agency. Consumers would have the power to use these dollars flexibly to obtain services and supports identified in a Personal Support Plan. Two percent of available funds would be withheld to cover the cost of emergencies. The individual has the option of either managing the plan him- or herself or electing to have an agency do it. If the individual chooses to manage the plan, then he or she would be required to use an approved fiscal intermediary to handle billings, payments, payroll, and so forth. Direct cash payments would not be made to consumers.

The Rhode Island Choices proposal shares many of the characteristics of a participant-driven supports model. It offers a vision of a reformed system that contains costs while fostering consumer self-determination. It has a unified funding stream, and it offers a wide array of services and providers to allow consumers to flexibly meet their needs as defined in a personal support plan.

Vermont's Systemwide Reform[5]

In the late 1990s, planners in Vermont's Division of Developmental Services (DDS) have explored ways to reform their community-based service system (the only state institution in Vermont closed in 1993). The reforms are based on principles of community integration and self-determination for people with disabilities. The current Vermont plan is to designate a number of private, non-profit agencies in the state as managed service organizations; these will be known as Designated Service Agencies (DSAs). Each DSA will receive an allocation to meet the service needs of all the eligible consumers in its region. Consumers will have limited control over how their individual funds are used through the use of vouchers. Each DSA's aggregate allocation will include individual spending authorizations for each current consumer plus an additional amount to support new users—people who are receiving services for the first time. Many of the details of the plan still have to be worked out, but some specifics can be detailed:

- The DSA will be responsible for identifying the needs of people with mental retardation who meet the state eligibility criteria and who reside in the counties for which they are responsible. The DSA care manager will be responsible for preparing the individual plan and budget for each consumer. In accordance with the plan, the DSA may then provide services directly or through contracts with other service providers certified by the state.
- State payments (allocations) to each DSA will be based on cumulative voucher amounts and actual expenditures, contingent on the achievement of certain system outcome expectations. These outcomes, focused on overall system performance, will be stipulated in the contract, and performance of these outcomes will directly influence contract negotiations. (There also will be system performance measures, targeted to individual performance, which will be assessed annually as a way to fine tune the aggregate system outcome expectations over time). Agencies spending less than the cumulative voucher amounts will receive a portion of the savings to be used to serve new (unserved) or underserved eligibles and for other approved purposes.
- The Vermont Department of Mental Retardation will authorize an individual spending limit for each consumer. This amount will be capped at a level close to what is currently being expended for the person's support. This "individual budget" will be reviewed each year. Consumers/families may be permitted to accrue a portion of their unspent funds each year as an incentive to conserve.

---

[5]This section is drawn from several documents produced by the Division of Developmental Services, including *A Preliminary Plan for Managing Long-Term Services and Supports for Vermont's Citizens with Mental Retardation* and *Vermont Developmental Services: A Preliminary Plan for System Change*. Special thanks to Chas Mosley for editorial suggestions.

- The consumer will be able to direct the use of his or her individual budget, in accordance with an individual plan. Consumers will use vouchers to pay for the services they receive; the vouchers will be issued against their annual spending authorization. The consumer may choose to receive services from the DSA or from a separate certified provider or may organize services for themselves, using a number of individual support people. Although the DSA's care manager will be responsible for preparing each individual plan and budget, the consumer may choose others to counsel and assist him or her, including paid agents or brokers. The consumer may also choose a fiscal intermediary other than the DSA (e.g., a private payroll service).
- An emergency fund will serve as the risk reserve to cover the costs of unplanned but needed supports for individuals using the service and to respond to the critical demands of other individuals who are eligible but unserved. In general, DSAs will be expected to manage the changing needs of people currently in their service areas within their existing allocations.
- The provider may be the DSA, a private certified agency, or an employee of the consumer. As a rule, consumers will not be allowed to switch providers for one year (prior to the annual review). To receive payments from the DSA for services delivered, the provider will cosign the voucher with the consumer or authorized family member/guardian.

Colorado Systems Change Project[6]

In 1995, Colorado Developmental Disabilities participated in a process that yielded a "Blueprint for Change," which outlines significant reforms in state developmental disabilities policy and practice. This initiative and its continuing refinement have three central goals:

1. To promote simplicity, flexibility, and efficiencies while maintaining accountability and commitment to the stated DDS mission: This will be achieved through 1) a reduction in categorical funding, 2) implementation of various cost-containment measures including maximization of federal funds and encouragement of the use of natural supports, 3) limits placed on administrative and overhead expenditures, and 4) improved accountability mechanisms to ensure quality.
2. To increase decision making at the local level to better individualize services and to provide more options and choice for individuals receiving services: This will be achieved by 1) maintaining the important role that Community Centered Boards (CCB) already play in the system; 2) creating options to promote self-determination through intensified person-

---

[6]Information for this section was found through the Internet at the State of Colorado web site (http://www.state.com.us_dir/govmenu.html). The information has been adapted and summarized here. Special thanks to Judy Brown for editorial suggestions.

centered planning, voucher-based options, and pilot of some options outside the CCBs; and 3) promotion of enhanced partnership among all concerned parties.

3. To promote a fairer means of distributing resources to enable more people
    on the waiting list to receive services and supports: This will be achieved
    through 1) crafting more efficient guidelines to promote consistency and
    fairness in how resource levels are assigned to address individual needs,[7]
    2) providing some level of support to all adults on the waiting list over the
    next 2 years, and 3) developing means for reducing the risk to individuals
    and families who participate in the reformed system by establishing state
    and local assessment pools to address emergencies.

Consumers will have considerable control over service delivery. The local
service organizations will work in partnership with the consumer to select providers that are best suited to meeting the needs of the individual with disabilities as identified through the person-centered planning process. Rather than
trying to fit the individual into a predefined program vacancy, a flexible menu
of services and supports will be offered. Options for choice and self-direction
of supports will be explained, including the availability of alternative providers.
In the case of supported living services, consumers also can choose who they
want as a supported living consultant and how much help they want in making
service arrangements. Some individuals may want to exercise a great deal of
control over service arrangements, whereas others may want responsibility for
just some aspects of the supports they receive. Still others may be satisfied with
letting professionals handle the details of implementing their person-centered
plan or just may want to have a choice of providers.

All eligible individuals will be provided with a case manager, who will
work with the consumer to develop the person-centered plan and will be responsible for updating it annually. The consumer will have a choice of case
managers whenever possible and may also choose others to counsel and assist
him or her in developing this plan.

The Colorado Systems Reform plan is still in evolution. It clearly is
designed to tackle the major challenge facing all developmental disabilities
systems—meeting growing demands for services with reduced resources. It
builds on a very strong vision and mission statement; it addresses the issues of
consumer self-determination and flexible services by offering choice among
payment methods, service oganizations, providers, and services; it fosters development of community partnerships through decentralization of authority to the
local level and increased reliance on natural supports; and it promises to lead
to more unified funding through the various service blocks.

---

[7]The Division of Developmental Services (DDS) has commissioned the Human Services
Research Institute to explore means of improved "rate setting" under the new system.

RECOMMENDED ACTIONS

Policy Development

Individual- or participant-driven supports that are self-determined and facilitated by circles of support and service brokers can successfully meet the needs of people with a range of disabilities, including people with mild cognitive limitations. Implementation policies to stimulate the development of such models for the individuals in question, however, are constrained by a variety of factors:

*   In most states, eligibility for publicly funded services and supports is limited to individuals with more severe and profound disabilities. Thus, reforms in these systems may not benefit people with mild cognitive limitations.
*   People with mild disabilities—if they are receiving public services at all—are likely to be participating in a range of generic rather than categorical programs, including Temporary Aid to Needy Families (TANF), child welfare services, juvenile or adult corrections, Social Security Administration services, and so forth.
*   Given the stigma that is still part of the experience of disability, many individuals with mild cognitive limitations may resist identifying themselves as being in need of supports.
*   The definition of developmental disabilities is limited to individuals with severe disabilities, thereby limiting the availability of grant and demonstration funds either at the federal or state developmental disabilities council level.

This suggests that somewhat more indirect methods should be used to ensure that flexible, participant-driven supports are available. Specific policy initiatives might include the following:

*   Expand the services and supports that independent living centers can provide to include service brokerage and broad training programs aimed at self-determination and choice-making for people with mild cognitive limitations.
*   Ensure that state juvenile and adult criminal law includes diversion programs for people with mild cognitive limitations that can be accessed by judges, probation officials, and law enforcement personnel. Such diversion programs could include service brokerage and the use of flexible funds to pay for those supports necessary to keep individuals out of the criminal justice system.
*   Include in family preservation and family support programs funded through federal legislation specific training and supports initiatives aimed at parents with mild cognitive limitations.

- Review vocational rehabilitation legislation to determine the possibility of providing clients with mild cognitive limitations more control over the resources necessary to secure and be supported in a job.
- Explore the expansion of eligibility for public developmental disabilities services to individuals with mild cognitive impairments. Funds could be allocated in a per capita fashion to sub-state organizations (both specialized and generic) to provide limited, periodic supports.
- Create interagency pools of resources drawn from the multiple agencies that provide some services to people with mild cognitive limitations (e.g., social services, mental health, child protection, law enforcement, HMOs) to provide service brokerage as well as limited supports.

Information Development and Access

Another way that these concepts can be adapted to the needs of people with mild cognitive limitations is by providing training and orientation programs through public school programs. The notion of a circle of support is adaptable to any age group and has been used by teachers and families around the country (Jorgensen, 1992; Strully & Strully, 1992). Ensuring that students with cognitive disabilities have such supports will require the following:

- Development of competencies among teachers and interested family members regarding the creation and maintenance of circles of support as well as the facilitation of relationships
- Development and dissemination of materials that can assist circle facilitators and introduce the concepts to students, families, and friends
- Creation of self-advocacy organizations within schools that stress empowerment and choice-making skills
- Interaction with parent-to-parent organizations to introduce the notions of circles and to develop expectations regarding opportunities for flexible adult supports

With respect to adults with mild cognitive limitations, the introduction of more supportive and facilitative models can take place in a variety of settings:

- Introduce the notions of circles of support to spiritual communities around the country. There are many analogues to such an effort, including church networks involved in providing respite services to families with children with disabilities.
- Work with state and local self-advocacy organizations to develop training programs, speakers, bureaus, self-help groups, and other means of disseminating information regarding circles of support.

Demonstration, Evaluation, and Research

There are also several ways in which the expenditure of research and demonstration funds can assist in enriching the provision of supports that will enhance the inclusion and social participation of individuals with mild cognitive limitations:

- Interest foundations in the development of demonstration activities to test the feasibility of interagency collaborative approaches to the provision supports that enhance community inclusion.
- Expand on the experience in the Robert Wood Johnson Foundation Self-Determination projects to set up and expand participant-driven supports.
- Interest individuals with mild cognitive limitations in collaborative, participatory research projects regarding emerging best practices.
- Conduct a survey of people with mild cognitive limitations to determine which types of intervention are most likely to enhance their social participation and community presence.

CONCLUSION

In sum, several criteria should be used to judge the wisdom of policy, informational, and/or research and development initiatives to enhance the social and community participation of children and adults with mild cognitive limitations:

1. *Vision:* Are the values underlying the intervention reflective of participants' beliefs? Will the activity improve the community inclusion, independence, and quality of life of people with mild cognitive limitations?
2. *Participant self-determination:* Do people have a real say in the design of the policy or intervention? At an individual level, do people have real authority over how funds are spent? Can they freely choose among services and among providers?
3. *Flexible array of services:* Are there real choices to be made? Are there different types of services available? Are there different types of providers?
4. *Personal advocates/brokers:* Do brokers work *for* the individual? Can they be replaced? Is the broker knowledgeable about the available services and supports?
5. *Community partnerships:* Does the initiative foster the creation of community and familial networks? Are there incentives for organizations to collaborate?
6. *Outcome focus:* Is the intervention assessed based on how well participants have achieved their desired goals? Does payment hinge on whether the participant is satisfied with the services and supports received?

If these criteria are adhered to, we can be assured that initiatives on behalf of people with mild cognitive limitations will in fact result in increased quality of life and community inclusion.

REFERENCES

Agosta, J., & Kimmich, M. (1997). *Managing our own supports: A primer on participant-driven supports.* Alexandria, VA: Center for Managed Long-Term Supports for People with Disabilities.

Agosta, J., & Melda, K. (1995). *Results of a national survey of family support programs for people with disabilities and their families.* Salem, OR: Human Services Research Institute.

Bradley, V.J., Ashbaugh, J.W., & Blaney, B.C. (Eds.). (1994). *Creating individual supports for people with developmental disabilities: A mandate for change at many levels.* Baltimore: Paul H. Brookes Publishing Co.

Cameron, K. (1995, July–September). Cash and counseling: A model for empowerment and choice for long-term care. *Perspective on Aging, 22–25.*

Ducharme, G., Beeman, P., DeMarasse, R., & Ludlum, C. (1994). Building community one person at a time: One candle power. In V.J. Bradley, J.W. Ashbaugh, & B.C. Blaney (Eds.), *Creating individual supports for people with developmental disabilities: A mandate for change at many levels* (pp. 347–360). Baltimore: Paul H. Brookes Publishing Co.

Flanagan, S. (1996). *Using fiscal and supportive intermediary service models to facilitate the development and implementation of consumer-directed service programs.* Cambridge, MA: The MEDSTAT Group.

Heal, L.W., Haney, J.I., & Novak Amado, A.R. (1988). *Integration of developmentally disabled individuals into the community.* Baltimore: Paul H. Brookes Publishing Co.

Jorgensen, C.M. (1992). Natural supports in inclusive schools: Circular and teaching strategies. In J. Nisbet (Ed.), *Natural supports in school, at work, and in the community for people with severe disabilities* (pp. 179–215). Baltimore: Paul H. Brookes Publishing Co.

Kimmich, M., & Godfrey, T. (1991). *New models for the provision of personal assistance services: Final report.* Cambridge, MA: Human Services Research Institute.

Knoll, J., & Peterson, M. (1992). *Inclusive communities: Better lives for all.* Detroit, MI: Wayne State University, Institute on Developmental Disabilities.

Linton, D., Persons, L., & Leatzow, M. (1996). Vouchers in supported employment. *Supported Employment InfoLines, 7*(1), 1f.

Litvak, S., Zukas, H., & Heumann, J. (1987). *Attending to America: Personal assistance for independent living.* Berkeley, CA: World Institute on Disability.

National Institute on Consumer-Directed Long-Term Services. (1996). *Principles of consumer-directed home and community-based services.* Washington, DC: The National Council on Aging, Inc.

Nerney, T., & Shumway, D. (1996). *Beyond managed care: Self-determination for people with disabilities.* Concord: University of New Hampshire, Institute on Disability, Self Determination Project.

Nisbet, J. (1992). *Natural supports in school, at work, and in the community for people with severe disabilities.* Baltimore. Paul H. Brookes Publishing Co.

Pennhurst State School & Hospital v. Halderman, 451 U.S. 1, 17 (1981).

Robert Wood Johnson Foundation. (1996). *Call for proposals: Self-determination for persons with developmental disabilities.* Concord: University of New Hampshire, Institute on Disability, Self Determination Project.

Smith, G., & Ashbaugh, J. (1996). *Managed care and people with developmental disabilities: A guidebook.* Washington, DC: National Association of State Directors of Developmental Disabilities Services.

Snow, J., & Forest, M. (1987). Circles. In M. Forest (Ed.), *More education integration.* Downsview, Ontario, Canada: G. Allan Roeher Institute.

Strully, J.L., & Strully, C.F. (1992). The struggle toward inclusion and the fulfillment of friendship. In J. Nisbet (Ed.), *Natural supports in school, at work, and in the community for people with severe disabilities* (pp. 165–178). Baltimore: Paul H. Brookes Publishing Co.

Taylor, S., Bogdan, R., & Racino, J.A. (1991). *Life in the community: Case studies of organizations supporting people with disabilities.* Baltimore: Paul H. Brookes Publishing Co.

Towell, D., & Beardshaw, V. (1991). *Enabling community organization: The role of public authorities in promoting an ordinary life for people with learning disabilities in the 1990s.* London: Kings Fund College.

United States Health Cooperative. (1994). *Description of the cash and counseling research project for long-term care funded by the Robert Wood Johnson Foundation.* Washington, DC: Author.

University of Maryland Center on Aging. (1995). *Cash and counseling: A national initiative supported by the Robert Wood Johnson Foundation and the U.S. Department of Health and Human Services.* College Park: Author.

Wolfensberger, W. (1972). *The principle of normalization in human services.* Toronto: National Institute on Mental Retardation.

10

Building Stronger
Communities for All

Thoughts About Community Participation
for Individuals with Developmental Disabilities

Robert Bogdan and Steven J. Taylor

Professionals in the field of developmental disabilities have been trendsetters in talking about *community*, advocating that people with developmental disabilities should not be segregated from society in institutions but instead should be included in the community. The initial conception of *community*, however, was vague—a hazy picture of a place where people lived with one another in harmony, where they had meaningful and satisfying face-to-face relationships, and where they cared about and looked out for each other.

Eventually, other people outside of the developmental disabilities field started to become concerned with community. However, their concerns related to their own lives and their fears that they were losing a sense of community. While we were fighting to get people with developmental disabilities into the community, social critics declared that community was declining in the United States (McKnight, 1980). Rather than people experiencing where they live as a place where people have close face-to-face relationships, know each other, and are neighborly, too much of our society has become a place where people are isolated and estranged from each other. Malls and super stores have replaced more neighborhood-centered institutions, such as the local merchant, the corner store, the butcher, and the baker. Mass media and the Internet have become substitutes for church, civic organizations, community associations, and so forth.

The preparation of this chapter was supported by the Center on Human Policy, School of Education, Syracuse University, through a subcontract with the Research and Training Center on Community Living, University of Minnesota, supported by the U.S. Department of Education, Office of Special Education and Rehabilitative Services (OSERS), National Institute on Disability and Rehabilitation Research (NIDRR), through Contract No. H133B980047. Members of the Center are encouraged to express their opinions; however, these do not necessarily represent the official position of NIDRR and no endorsement should be inferred.

How can we think about including people with disabilities in the community when a sense of community has become so problematic for everyone—when the community itself is under siege? It is important to approach the challenge of helping people with disabilities become part of the community with full appreciation of what is at stake. Thinking about community for people with developmental disabilities might help us think about it for ourselves. What we want for them—a sense of belonging to a community—is what we search for for ourselves. To try to solve their problem is to address our own. It is what we share that ties us together. That is our humanity. This is what makes "them" really part of "us."

This chapter presents some thoughts and observations about what it means for people with developmental disabilities to be part of the community.

BEING PART OF THE COMMUNITY

Being *in* a community is not the same as being *part of* a community. Early formulations of community living for people with developmental disabilities were generated out of concern with deinstitutionalization. We wanted individuals with disabilities to leave institutions, but we were not clear enough in distinguishing that they should be *part of* the community. People can live in the community and experience segregation, isolation, and loneliness. Community placement is merely a first step. Being *in* the community points only to physical presence; being *part of* the community means having the opportunity to interact and form relationships with other community members. Today, this is referred to as inclusion.

What Does It Mean to Be Part of the Community?

Being part of the community means having meaningful relationships with community members. To be part of the community is to be a family member, a neighbor, a schoolmate, a friend, a casual acquaintance, a church member, a shopper, a co-worker, and a significant other. It means belonging to clubs, organizations, and associations and sometimes being a consumer of services as well. Being part of the community means much more than being treated nicely by staff or even having a citizen advocate or volunteer. It means being known as an individual, a unique person—not as a label, a ward of the state, a client of an agency, a consumer of services, or the recipient of another's charity.

Early sociological and anthropological studies concentrated on how people with disabilities were stigmatized and excluded from the community (Bogdan & Taylor, 1976; Edgerton, 1967; Goffman, 1963). We now understand the dynamics of labeling, stereotyping, and the self-fulfilling prophecy. Unfortunately, we know far less about how people make friends and how those who are different come to be accepted. We still need a sociology of acceptance (Bogdan & Taylor, 1987b).

Being part of the community means contributing to the community. It means being a good citizen. Although this usually involves holding a job, it also means contributing in other ways—volunteering, celebrating when the community celebrates, grieving when tragedy strikes, and engaging in neighborly acts. Ties to the community are fragile when they are not based on reciprocity. The inclusion of people with developmental disabilities in a neighborhood should make the community a better place to live.

Being part of the community requires being supported by services and agencies in such a way as to become less dependent on those services and agencies. When individuals with developmental disabilities have to rely exclusively on the services of agencies, they are destined not to become part of the community. The more agencies provide services for these individuals, the less others will be involved in the individuals' lives. Only when support is spread throughout the community can individuals with developmental disabilities be fully included in their communities.

Institutionalization has been defined largely in terms of physical placement in remote facilities, but it can be much more insidious. It also can be described as total consumption of a person's life by an agency or a program. When this happens, the person becomes defined by his or her disability label; the "client" role takes over, and the person becomes lost. When, however, a person has a range of contacts in the community, he or she becomes a "consumer" of services, rather than a client. It is important to define community inclusion not simply in terms of the demise of deinstitutionalization but in terms of breaking down the control that services, programs, and agencies have over the lives of individuals with disabilities. Professionals and staff must view themselves not as people who are all things to their so-called clients, but as community organizers and mobilizers—people who help the people they serve become part of their communities.

Being part of the community should never be confused with neglect, indifference, or denial of support. Although the goal is for people with developmental disabilities to become part of their communities, this cannot be used to excuse the denial of supports and services to these individuals. Being part of a community does not mean that people with developmental disabilities or their families must do without support from publicly funded agencies.

This is a particularly salient issue with individuals with mild cognitive limitations. Because of the current anti-welfare mentality, they are most vulnerable to being abandoned by governmental agencies that search for less inclusive definitions of what constitutes need.

Being part of the community ultimately means doing away with concepts such as normalization, integration, quality of life, and inclusion. These and other concepts are only vehicles for change and not the end result. When a state of full acceptance and inclusion of people with developmental disabilities is reached, these ideas no longer will be necessary. That we have these concepts does not mean that we have arrived; it only means that we recognize that people with developmental disabilities have been denied. In other words, we only examine people's quality of life when we suspect that it is lacking (Taylor, 1994).

Normalization, integration, and inclusion can carry with them a level of self-consciousness that can interfere with people becoming part of the community. Normalization is not normal. Inclusion is not inclusive. When individuals in a community focus on such concepts, they can find it difficult to have spontaneous and natural relationships with people with developmental disabilities. Spontaneity is characteristic of mutual relationships.

We can envision a society that would perplex the most adamant believers in normalization or inclusion. That society would be marked by a natural acceptance of people with disabilities. Members of this society would not have the faintest understanding of normalization principles. If one asked them about inclusion, they would not know how to respond. The society would not operate on normalization; instead, they would operate on spontaneous, natural acceptance. Here the use of concepts such as normalization, quality of life, and inclusion would represent a step backward.

Being part of the community is an end in itself. People with developmental disabilities who are part of their communities act in more typical and socially appropriate ways. They may indeed become more independent and economically productive. However, the strongest argument in favor of enabling people to become part of their communities is that they lead better, more fulfilling lives.

It is important for agencies to operate under the assumption that people can change and learn new skills and that the most difficult behavior problems can be overcome. However, even if people do not change dramatically and become more independent and productive, they still should be able to be part of the community. The right to lead a decent life as part of the community should not be made contingent on becoming "nondisabled" or "normal" (Ferguson & Ferguson, 1986).

Being part of the community cannot be "packaged." Just because an idea, model, or approach seems to work in one place at one time does not mean that it can work anywhere or at any time (Lyle O'Brien, O'Brien, & Mount, 1997). To be sure, we can all learn good ideas from other people, and some models are inherently superior to others. We cannot assume, however, that every good idea can be replicated with equal success. We all know that there is a difference between having a home-cooked meal and eating in a franchise restaurant. What makes the difference is not the recipe but the care, attention, and personal touch that go into the cooking.

Reliance on specific models or approaches can interfere with helping people become part of the community. Just as we have learned not to invest in the bricks and mortar of institutions, we must not bet on one particular approach to inclusion.

Steadfast adherence to a particular approach can prevent new professionals in the field from having the opportunity to contribute to the creativity and insight required to develop better ways of doing things. As more and more community programs develop, recruitment of staff is becoming more routine; it is no longer like joining a spirited movement as it has been in the past. It is necessary to find ways of helping new professionals develop a sense of the history of the struggles that brought us to where we are today, while at the same time being open to fresh ideas. For people with developmental disabilities to become part of the community, a strong commitment, a sense of mission, and clear values will be necessary (Provencal, 1987; Taylor, Bogdan, & Racino, 1991). None of these things can be packaged.

Being part of the community is not an unrealistic goal. Although the history of the treatment of people with disabilities in the United States is rife with instances of discrimination and exclusion, this is not inevitable. To the contrary, an increasing number of examples of full participation of people with developmental disabilities in the community can be found (Andrews, 1995; Bogdan, 1995; Bogdan & Taylor, 1989; Taylor, Bogdan, & Lutfiyya, 1995). Ironically, some of the richest examples of inclusion have resulted not from professional engineering, but as a consequence of ordinary social processes (Andrews, 1995).

Too often we have expected rejection and exclusion of people with developmental disabilities. When such people are not accepted in neighborhoods or included in community groups, it is viewed as a normal and natural outcome of backward attitudes and prejudice. We need to pay more attention to how our own practices, such as grouping people with developmental disabilities, tend to discourage inclusion; we also need to devote greater attention to identifying the kinds of communities or associations in which people with developmental disabilities will be accepted.

Being part of the community will require a return to communal values. As an understandable reaction to the anonymity and block treatment of people with developmental disabilities in institutions and segregated environments, the field has turned to a set of new concepts that endorse individual autonomy: self-advocacy, self-determination, person-centered planning, homeownership, individualized services, and so forth. Although these concepts can help us move toward a service system that is more respectful of the uniqueness of all people with developmental disabilities, an exclusive focus on individualism will prevent people with developmental disabilities from being part of the community. Community has to do with *we,* not *I.* An emphasis on the individual must be balanced with communal values (O'Brien & Lyle O'Brien, 1996).

Being part of the community means recognizing that people with disabilities are more than mere victims. Despite the fact that people with developmental disabilities and their families have been subjected to prejudice, discrimination, and even abuse, they should not be regarded as passive objects that happily conform to what is expected of them. Although the phenomena known as the "self-fulfilling prophecy" (Wolfensberger, 1972) and the "client role" are real and undoubtedly exercise a strong influence on the way in which individuals and families feel and act, to define people solely as victims is just as dehumanizing as defining them solely as clients of human services. Because they are human beings, people with developmental disabilities and their families sometimes conform to the dictates of the human services system and societal expectations and sometimes do not. Families may reject negative stereotypes and construct positive definitions of their children (Bogdan & Taylor, 1989; O'Connor, 1995). People with developmental disabilities do not always view themselves in terms of their impairments, and they are able to take an active role in controlling their lives (Shoultz, 1995; Taylor, 1994, 2000). One of the most striking aspects of deinstitutionalization is that some individuals with disabilities emerged from the experience as survivors with their dignity and self-respect intact.

When people with developmental disabilities have become part of the community, it has often been at their own initiative. Inclusion was not something done for them by others but something that resulted from their own contributions and characteristics.

Being part of the community will take time. Frustrations and setbacks will occur in helping people with mental retardation and developmental disabilities to become part of the community. Communities may not always welcome people with developmental disabilities with open arms. Relationships may not always form spontaneously. Acceptance and inclusion will not be accomplished overnight.

When people with developmental disabilities are visible and involved in their communities—in schools, workplaces, and neighborhoods—good things happen. If community members do not step forward to take over for agency staff, this should not be cause for despair. Progress toward the goal of inclusion should be measured in terms of kind words and subtle gestures, a greeting on the street, an offer of a ride home, or an invitation to dinner or a party.

Being part of the community will require changes in the society. For people with developmental disabilities to become part of the community, society will have to change. Personal relationships are the cornerstone of being part of the community; however, social policies and practices can systematically thwart opportunities for individuals to come together. Until vested interests, funding mechanisms, economic policies, counter-ideologies, agency policies, architectural barriers, and other forces supporting segregation are confronted and changed, large numbers of people with developmental disabilities will not become part of the community.

One of the major barriers to full community participation for people with developmental disabilities is the economic structure in the United States. Most adults with developmental disabilities, even those who work, are poor. Poverty severely limits where and how people can live.

The concept of normalization, which was popularized in the United States by Wolfensberger (1972) in the 1970s, had its origins in the Nordic countries. We also can learn from how the Nordic countries approach equality. A central premise in the Nordic countries is that all people have a right to a decent standard of living. Reforms in developmental disabilities have been tied to this idea. It is not that people with developmental disabilities have a right to a decent life because they have disabilities; they have the right because they are citizens.

The link between normalization and equality is clear in the Nordic countries. In the United States, people with disabilities receive government benefits such as Supplemental Security Income (SSI) or Social Security Disability Insurance (SSDI) not because they are citizens entitled to a decent standard of living but because they have disabilities and presumably are unable to work and contribute to the society. Government support is based on presumed differences from other people. Disability becomes central to a person's status as a citizen. Public policy on welfare and equality runs counter to the ideal of inclusion and of being defined as a human being rather than as someone who is different.

CONCLUSION

For people with developmental disabilities to be part of the community, we must have stronger communities with stronger ties among members. Where do we start? "Before you seek to change the world," wrote the late Burton Blatt, "change yourself" (Taylor & Blatt, 1999, p. 165). Small, modest acts of neighborliness can make a difference, or at least that is the hope. Join neighborhood organizations.[1] Lift your head when you walk. Say "hello" to people. Sit outside. Plant flowers. Buy from your local merchants, even if you have to pay a bit more. Share some of what you have. Take children to the park. Fix it even if you did not break it. Have potlucks. Take an older person grocery shopping. Pick up litter. Talk to the mail carrier. Help someone carry something heavy. Start a tradition. Ask a question. Hire people for odd jobs who do not seem to have anything to do. Organize a block party. Bake extra and share. Ask for help when you need it. Open your shades. Share your skills. Turn up the music. Turn down the music. Listen before you react with anger. Mediate a conflict, rather than take sides. Learn from new and uncomfortable angles. Work at listening.

Building stronger community ties is also something that we can try to do in our professional lives. Avoid gratuitous put-downs of people who are not as sophisticated as you are. Treat ideological opponents with respect, simply be-

---

[1]The following points are inspired by the poster, "How To Build Community," designed by Karen Kerney and published by The Syracuse Cultural Workers.

cause all human beings are valuable. Take the time to answer questions from a student or a colleague. Acknowledge others' contributions to your own accomplishments. Go out of your way to introduce your staff or students to important visitors.

Understand that by making communities stronger for people with developmental disabilities, you just might make life better for yourself. As Blatt concluded, "The individual's life is irrevocably bound to the welfare of the masses, and only good people can save us and, thus, themselves" (Taylor & Blatt, 1999, p. 167).

REFERENCES

Andrews, S.S. (1995). Life in Mendocino: A young man with Down syndrome in a small town in Northern California. In S.J. Taylor, R. Bogdan, & Z.M. Lutfiyya (Eds.), *The variety of community experience: Qualitative studies of family and community life* (pp. 101–116). Baltimore: Paul H. Brookes Publishing Co.

Bogdan, R. (1995). Singing for an inclusive society: The community choir. In S.J. Taylor, R. Bogdan, & Z.M. Lutfiyya (Eds.), *The variety of community experience: Qualitative studies of family and community life* (pp. 141–154). Baltimore: Paul H. Brookes Publishing Co.

Bogdan, R., & Taylor, S.J. (1976). The judged, not the judges: An insider's view of mental retardation. *American Psychologist, 31*(1), 47–52.

Bogdan, R., & Taylor, S.J. (1987a). Conclusion: The next wave. In S.J. Taylor, D. Biklen, & J. Knoll (Eds.), *Community integration for people with severe disabilities* (pp. 209–213). New York: Teachers College Press.

Bogdan, R., & Taylor, S.J. (1987b). Toward a sociology of acceptance: The other side of the study of deviance. *Social Policy, 18*(2), 34–39.

Bogdan, R., & Taylor, S.J. (1989). Relationships with severely disabled people: The social construction of humanness. *Social Problems, 36*(2), 135–148.

Edgerton, R.B. (1967). *The cloak of competence: Stigma in the lives of the mentally retarded.* Berkeley: University of California Press.

Ferguson, D.L., & Ferguson, P.M. (1986). The new victors: A progressive policy analysis of work reform for people with very severe handicaps. *Mental Retardation, 24*(6), 331–338.

Goffman, E. (1963). *Stigma: Notes on the management of spoiled identity.* Englewood Cliffs, NJ: Prentice-Hall.

Lyle O'Brien, C., O'Brien, J., & Mount, B. (1997, December). Person-centered planning has arrived...or has it? [Perspectives]. *Mental Retardation, 35*(6), 480–484.

McKnight, J. (1980, Fall). A nation of clients? *Public Welfare,* 15–19.

O'Brien, J., & Lyle O'Brien, C. (1996). *Members of each other: Building community in company with people with developmental disabilities.* Toronto: Inclusion Press.

O'Connor, S. (1995). "We're all one family": The positive construction of people with disabilities by family members. In S.J. Taylor, R. Bogdan, & Z.M. Lutfiyya (Eds.), *The variety of community experience: Qualitative studies of family and community life* (pp. 67–77). Baltimore: Paul H. Brookes Publishing Co.

Provencal, G. (1987). Culturing commitment. In S.J. Taylor, D. Biklen, & J. Knoll (Eds.), *Community integration for people with severe disabilities* (pp. 67–84). New York: Teachers College Press.

Shoultz, B. (1995). "But they need me!": The story of Anna London. In S.J. Taylor, R. Bogdan, & Z.M. Lutfiyya (Eds.), *The variety of community experience: Qualitative studies of family and community life* (pp. 9–22). Baltimore: Paul H. Brookes Publishing Co.

Taylor, S.J. (1994). In support of research on quality of life, but against QOL. In D. Goode (Ed.), *Quality of life for persons with disabilities: International perspectives and issues* (pp. 260–265). Cambridge, MA: Brookline Books.

Taylor, S.J. (2000). "You're not a retard, you're just wise": Disability, social identity, and family networks. *Journal of Contemporary Ethnography, 29*(1), 58–92.

Taylor, S.J., & Blatt, S. (Eds.). (1999). *In search of the promised land: The collected papers of Burton Blatt.* Washington, DC: American Association on Mental Retardation.

Taylor, S.J., Bogdan, R., & Lutfiyya, Z.M. (Eds.). (1995). *The variety of community experience: Qualitative studies of family and community life.* Baltimore: Paul H. Brookes Publishing Co.

Taylor, S.J., Bogdan, R., & Racino, J.A. (Eds.). (1991). *Life in the community: Case studies of organizations supporting people with disabilities.* Baltimore: Paul H. Brookes Publishing Co.

Wolfensberger, W. (1972). *The principle of normalization in human services.* Toronto: National Institute on Mental Retardation.

IV

Health and Well-Being

Access to Health Services

Improving the Availability and Quality of Health Services for People with Mild Cognitive Limitations

Deborah M. Spitalnik and Sheryl White-Scott

The delivery of health care to individuals with mild cognitive limitations is beset by many of the same barriers to health care experienced by individuals without disabilities. Access to primary health care, the financing of health services, adequate benefit packages, continuity of providers and care, and access to subspecialist and hospital care are barriers to health care experienced by many Americans.

POVERTY STATUS, MEDICAL DISADVANTAGE, AND ACCESS TO HEALTH CARE

As a group, people with cognitive limitations tend to be of low socioeconomic status. They share a common history with other groups of people who are poor and disenfranchised and have difficulty gaining access to health care services. The health care patterns of people with cognitive limitations are a result of their disability status but are also tied to their poverty status. Like other low-income citizens, these individuals are more likely to depend on publicly financed care. They are less likely to have an identified provider or a "medical home," where they are known individually and where their health history and records reside.

Ethnicity and Disability

Disability is strongly associated with race and poverty (Fujiura & Yamaki, 1997). Impoverished minorities have a higher occurrence of disability than the majority population. Individuals with disabilities who are minorities are more likely to be poorer than nonminority individuals with a disability. The association among disability, race, and poverty contributes to difficulties in health care access and increased health risks.

Welfare Reform and Mild Cognitive Limitations

Federal legislation and states' activities in Welfare Reform have begun to focus attention on the nature of the population that has not yet moved off of the Temporary Assistance to Needy Families (TANF; formerly Aid to Families with Dependent Children [AFDC]), rolls. Mothers with disabilities, particularly cognitive limitations, constitute a growing portion of the decreasing TANF caseload (Sweeney, 2000). The available national data group together mothers and children with disabilities (Loprest & Acs, 1996). State data on mothers with disabilities independent of data regarding their children have more utility in projecting the needs of adults with cognitive limitations. A Kansas study (commissioned by the state welfare agency) revealed that 30% of the adults receiving TANF had learning disabilities, and 26% had IQ scores of 80 or below (Gerry & Shively, 1999). Similar findings were found in a state of Washington study, which concluded that 54% of adult TANF recipients had special learning needs, 35% of adult recipients had learning disabilities, 14% of adult recipients were slow learners (IQ scores of 70–80) and 5% of adult TANF recipients had mild mental retardation (IQ scores of less than 70) (State of Washington Department of Social and Health Services, 1998).

CHANGES IN THE HEALTH CARE SYSTEM: MANAGED HEALTH CARE

The health care delivery system in the United States is undergoing major change. The driving force in the system is cost containment, and managed care is the primary vehicle. Managed care is a comprehensive and coordinated system of medical and health care delivery, including preventive, primary, specialty, and ancillary services as well as acute in-patient care. Managed care emphasizes access to primary care to increase the utilization of clinical preventive and primary care services, reducing the unnecessary use of emergency rooms for ambulatory care and attempting to strongly limit hospitalizations.

Managed care continues to grow as the principal method of financing health care as well as the dominant mode of health care delivery in the United States. Increasingly, individuals with mild cognitive limitations gain access to health care through managed care, usually by means of publicly funded health care and, rarely, through commercial insurance provided by employers. Typically, people with mild cognitive limitations are employed in jobs that do not provide health insurance.

Medicaid Managed Care

As a payer for health care, Medicaid is oriented largely toward managed care. Most states have sought and received waivers from the Health Care Financing

Administration to make managed care mandatory for beneficiaries who receive Medicaid coverage through TANF. Many states are in the planning stage, and other states already have moved beneficiaries who receive Medicaid through their Supplemental Security Income (SSI) eligibility into managed care. People with mild cognitive limitations often receive TANF or SSI and now are confronting, or will be confronting, the challenges of a managed care delivery system. People with mild cognitive limitations who receive their access to Medicaid through their TANF status may be more at risk in the movement to managed care as a result of a lack of specific provisions in Medicaid contracts to safeguard the rights of individuals with cognitive limitations and to ensure access to health care.

Individuals who receive Medicaid through their SSI eligibility are identified in Medicaid data collection as SSI recipients and, therefore, as disabled. A serious issue, from both an evaluation and advocacy perspective, is the invisibility of people with mild cognitive limitations who receive Medicaid through their TANF status. In most states, no descriptors that identify these individuals as having cognitive limitations are included within Medicaid data. Although this may be considered less stigmatizing, it makes it very difficult to track the experiences of individuals with mild cognitive limitations in the health care system. Measures of quality cannot be applied to this cohort if they cannot be identified. Similarly, available consumer protections can only be applied to a specific identified individual. This limits the systematic evaluation of the performance of health plans for people with mild cognitive limitations and deprives individuals of performance information, such as "HMO report cards," in choosing a plan. In addition, this lack of information deprives state funding agencies of valuable information regarding the managed care organization's ability to serve particularly vulnerable individuals. This raises a fundamental tension between self-determination and freedom from stigma and access to adequate protections.

Managed care is predicated on a heavily controlled system. The expected efficiencies in a managed care system can only be achieved through strict routines and procedures reinforced by strong behavioral expectations that individuals will conform to these routines. These routines and requirements, such as obtaining appropriate referral authorization and referral forms and seeking assistance through on-call services rather than through the use of emergency rooms, are very difficult for individuals with mild cognitive limitations.

Managed health care makes it more difficult for individuals with mild cognitive limitations to gain access to and utilize health care. Participation in an HMO (health maintenance organization) or other managed care plan is complicated and often requires a level of understanding and activity that is beyond the capabilities of many individuals with mild cognitive limitations.

Exercising choice of health plan and, within that plan, choice of health care provider illustrates the potential pitfalls for individuals with mild cognitive limitations as they move into managed health care. The Medicaid waivers that make it possible for states not to offer fee-for-service as a choice of health coverage still require that beneficiaries have a choice of health plans to join.

Because of the nature of mild cognitive limitations, these elements of choice often are rendered meaningless. For example, individuals with mild cognitive limitations may be automatically assigned to a health care plan because they could not process the instructions they received explaining how to choose a plan and, consequently, did not make a choice. Or an individual may sign papers enrolling in a health plan but may not understand that the act of enrolling restricts them to going to that plan for his or her care.

HEALTH CARE SERVICES FOR PEOPLE WITH COGNITIVE LIMITATIONS

People with cognitive limitations have a history of difficulty in obtaining access to health care services, and often when access is obtained these individuals receive inadequate or inappropriate care. Individuals with mild cognitive limitations as well as people with more severe disabilities are at a medical disadvantage and share similar disincentives to health care. These disincentives include lack of access to care, nonexistent or unavailable medical histories, fragmentation of medical care, lack of trained health professionals in the area of disabilities, lack of transportation, and lack of continuity of care.

People with cognitive limitations whose disabilities originated early in life and have persisted throughout their life span have typically been disenfranchised by the health care system. Traditionally, these individuals receive medical care for their disabilities rather than a holistic approach to their health as individuals themselves who also have disabilities.

Although institutions for people with mental retardation and other developmental disabilities often were organized on the basis of a "medical model," health care in most large congregate settings was notoriously poor. Care often was provided in a "batch" framework. For example, everyone with seizures was prescribed Dilantin (phenytoin), everyone with behavior challenges was prescribed Mellaril (thioridazine), and everyone with bowel problems was prescribed stool softeners. Individuals did not receive care on a personal basis, based on an evaluation of their particular needs. Often congregate facilities such as public institutions were last-resort employers for physicians who were not employable in other settings. Many congregate settings were total institutions, including infirmaries and actual hospitals within their scope and on the grounds of the institution. Institutional segregation also extended to medical care; health care practitioners typically were isolated and often lacked exposure to state-of-the art medical practice and ongoing medical and scientific developments. The standards for practice were variable. As a way of raising standards in institutions, the Intermediate Care Facilities/Mental Retardation (ICF/MR) regulations, introduced in 1977, mandated address of health and safety issues (Boggs, 1979); however, they did little to raise the standards of practice or the qualifications of practitioners.

Class action litigation in the 1970s that focused on improving institutional conditions to secure the rights of individuals with cognitive limitations as well as subsequent cases directed toward deinstutionalization and community placement for individuals with developmental disabilities disclosed the inadequacy of medical care in large, state-operated facilities. Neglect of basic health maintenance, including adequate dental care, provision of appropriate eyeglasses or hearing aids, and basic health screenings for adults, was revealed by the courts and was apparent in the appearance of many of the individuals with mild cognitive limitations who previously were confined to these facilities.

Although deinstitutionalization became a public policy direction as early as 1971, planning for health care services in the community to support and complement deinstitutionalization efforts received little address despite the extent of the need (Garrard, 1982; Minihan, 1986; Yankauer, 1986). Deinstutionalization assumed the availability and, more significantly, the accessibility of generic health services, despite the lack of evidence to support the assumption that services would be delivered to people with cognitive limitations (Gold, 1987; Yankauer, 1986).

Age-Appropriate Health Care

The perception in the 1950s that "mental retardation was a childhood problem" (Boggs, personal communication, 1987) led pediatrics to become the medical area of concentration and expertise within the developmental disabilities field. Through developmental pediatrics or neurodevelopmental pediatrics, the care of and knowledge about children with cognitive limitations and developmental disabilities has become a subspecialty within the pediatric field. Knowledge about disabilities also was infused into general pediatric practice. Although innovations have occurred within particular training programs (Spitalnik, 1996), no comparable systematic development in expertise has been seen within internal medicine or family medicine, those specialties that deal with adult primary health care.

Because people with mild cognitive limitations are living well into middle and old age, age-related conditions complicate their needs for health care services. These conditions include cataracts, hearing loss, hypertension, atherosclerotic heart disease, diabetes, hypercholesterolemia, arthritis, benign prostatic hypertrophy, hemorrhoids, and incontinence.

Unfortunately, individuals with cognitive limitations eventually "age out" of health care. Many pediatricians have struggled to continue to provide care to their patients with developmental disabilities, despite severe limitations. Pediatricians are not trained to recognize adult diseases or provide age-appropriate screening tests, including gynecologic or prostate exams. When the need for hospitalization arises, individuals with developmental disabilities often have difficulty in receiving the appropriate level of nursing and other care. Hospitalization on a pediatric floor is inappropriate, but individuals with cognitive limitations often lack some of the communication skills necessary to maintain themselves in an adult hospital unit. Some hospitals utilize their geriatric beds for people with developmental disabilities, which is also inappropriate for adults with cognitive limitations who have not reached old age.

Training of Practitioners

The lack of awareness and lack of training of health care professionals in treating individuals with disabilities often complicate health care for individuals with mild cognitive limitations. No formal curriculum, analogous to neurodevelopmental pediatrics, exists for training physicians in the care of adults with developmental disabilities. Although the basic medical school science curriculum may include lectures on genetic syndromes, the majority of adult providers trained in internal medicine and subspecialties have no formal exposure to individuals with mild cognitive limitations unless they have a personal interest or connection. Some opportunities for training in family medicine residencies are beginning to arise. Adult practitioners may be uncomfortable with and unwilling to care for adults with developmental disabilities. The need to educate and sensitize adult practitioners in the care of individuals with cognitive limitations is a major challenge.

Limited Knowledge Base

The lack of a practice base in adult medicine for people with disabilities, particularly cognitive disabilities, has contributed to a corresponding lack of a research and knowledge base about the manifestations and consequences of aging for people with developmental disabilities. Although more attention is being focused on secondary conditions (Spitalnik & Cohen, 1995), much of that attention is focused on physical, not cognitive, impairments.

Primary Care Models

Individuals with mild cognitive limitations are less likely than individuals without disabilities to have continuity of health care; in fact, they typically have access only to clinic or emergency room environments. The primary care models in most outpatient environments usually are resident-based clinics that provide primary and subspecialty care through an affiliated hospital to an indigent population. Often, there is a lack of continuity of health care providers, and time available for patients may be limited. During the patient visit, an initial history is obtained, often completed, at least in part, by the patient. The history is followed by a brief dialogue with the physician, a physical exam, laboratory tests, and recommendations. An individual with mild cognitive limitations often may be treated in general medical clinics without his or her disability being specifically identified by practitioners.

Fluctuating Eligibility

Access to care also is affected by individuals' financial situations, which may be marked by a lack of stable income. It is typical for the Medicaid eligibility of people with mild cognitive limitations to fluctuate because of their variable access to employment. Health care coverage is discontinuous, which in turn prevents continuity of care.

Health Risks

People with cognitive limitations are, as a group, less likely to receive comprehensive care. As a result of the kind of care they receive, particularly the lack of continuity in care, they are unlikely to engage in health promotion activities. This is compounded by the dearth of health education targeted to their cognitive level and lifestyle. Individuals with cognitive limitations often are at health risk because of poor nutrition and eating habits and are more vulnerable to other risk behaviors, especially cigarette smoking as in the following case study.

> Mr. Tiles is a 40-year old male with hypertension, hypercholesterolemia, and obesity. He smokes two packs of cigarettes per day, drinks occasional beers, and denies drug use. He plays the organ for a local church weekly. Mr. Tiles has a new girlfriend after recently ending a year-long relationship with a previous girlfriend.
>
> Mr. Tiles has medication for his hypertension and is on a special diet to control his hypercholesterolemia. His diet is complicated by the fact that he lives in a rooming house with limited cooking facilities. He eats out for most of his meals. His money is limited, although he gets paid each week by the church; he spends most of his money on his girlfriend and on take-out meals. He asks for condoms but is also requesting an HIV test because of the change in relationships.
>
> Mr. Tiles presented to an adult primary care clinic for HIV testing. During the pretest counseling session, the physician realized that Mr. Tiles did not fully comprehend the testing issues. He was referred for psychological testing and was found to have mild cognitive limitations. The HIV testing was completed with more information and more time allotted for counseling.

Mr. Tiles has his appropriate medications and is saving money for a bicycle to help with weight loss efforts. His girlfriend, church, and friends provide a rich support network. Because he enjoys smoking, he continues to refuse to try smoking cessation classes.

Mr. Tiles's physical exam identified early stages of end organ damage due to poorly controlled hypertension. Mr. Tiles had been cared for in the medical clinic, with sporadic medical follow-up. The increased awareness of his disability by his network and health providers has helped in setting up appropriate health prevention strategies.

CHALLENGES POSED BY COGNITIVE LIMITATIONS: IMPLICATIONS FOR GAINING ACCESS TO HEALTH CARE

The intellectual and behavioral manifestations of mild cognitive limitations influence and provide many challenges for the interactions among health care providers, the larger health care system, and the affected individuals.

Appearance, Passing, and Compliance with Authority

Health care providers, particularly during a patient's initial visit, may be unaware of the cognitive limitations of the individual they are serving. The individual may have no written or historical information identifying him or her as having cognitive limitations; this is particularly true for individuals who live independently, who may not be connected to specialized services or may not have a "medical home." Initially, the individual may be perceived as being similar to a larger group of individuals with publicly funded health insurance—the "Medicaid population"—and as sharing the stereotypical characteristics of "an impoverished population" rather than the characteristics of a person with a mild disability.

This lack of identification as a person with disabilities is also often reinforced by the individual's own wish to conceal his or her status as a person with a disability and to "pass for normal." The individual's desire to appear normal and capable coupled with his or her tendency to be compliant and to please authority often constrains the interaction between the individual and the health care provider and setting. Individuals with mild cognitive limitations are less likely to admit when they have not understood the physician. Individuals with mild cognitive limitation also are less likely to admit when they have not followed through with a treatment plan; however, it is unclear as to whether this is because they did not understand the instructions or the relationship among their symptoms, concerns, and treatment or because of a desire to please the health care provider.

The individual may report improvement in a condition that has not improved or has even worsened because he or she believes that the physician or nurse expects that response. This pattern of interaction, often coupled with an inadequate or nonexistent health history, makes it difficult for the provider to accurately assess the individual's health problems and to prescribe or conduct the appropriate interventions.

Information and Skills

Individuals with mild cognitive limitations typically have little or poor information regarding their own health. This may be because a provider has not communicated well or in a manner that the individual understands or because the provider did not consider it important to share information with the person directly. The presence of family members beyond the age at which their presence would be a typical developmental expectation often limits the information received directly by the person about his or her own health status. This is compounded by the individual's difficulties in adequately processing information when it is provided in a rushed atmosphere or is highly technical and the individual is in pain or discomfort and is most likely anxious.

Educational disadvantages as well as a lack of exposure to learning independent living skills during childhood and young adulthood may have left the individual unable to care for his or her own health. Understanding how to take his or her own temperature, read the thermometer, and make appropriate health care decisions as a consequence is an example of basic, personal health maintenance that the individual may never have had the opportunity to master.

Abstract Thinking

The limitations in abstract thinking that characterize mild cognitive limitations also may interfere with the individual's participation in health care interactions. Accurate reporting and description of symptoms and illness—including duration, intensity, and sequencing of symptoms as well as antecedents and consequences—rely on concepts that are mathematical in nature. Direct questions such as, "How long have you had this symptom?" or, "Is the symptom different at different times of the day?"—commonplace questions in the health care encounter—all require a fair amount of abstract thinking. "Have you had this before?" and, "What medications helped you?" illustrate the extent of abstract thinking—reporting of time and retention of specific technical knowledge—often involved in the interaction.

Abstract concepts related to time and timing are deeply embedded in the business of health care. "If it's not better in a few days," and "If your fever goes above 101," are implicit or explicit instructions to the patient to utilize mathematical concepts.

Reasoning Skills and Compliance   Compliance with health regimens for people with mild cognitive limitations is complicated by their reasoning skills, their ability to think abstractly, and their living and social situations. The instruction, "Take [the prescription] four times per day" given to a person with cognitive limitations is an abstraction that he or she likely will not be able to comprehend or follow through on. "Four times per day" is a highly abstract concept related to time, mathematics in creating intervals, and scheduling. Instructions need to be given in more concrete language and reinforced by connecting them to other established routines in the person's day. "Take one pill at breakfast, one at lunch, one at dinner, and one at bedtime" is a much more accessible set of instructions. To further ensure compliance, the health care practitioner or health educator may need to know more about the person's specific life situation. Does the person eat lunch at home or at school or elsewhere? Does he or she carry the pills during the day? Does he or she have a pillbox or other container? This attention to detail in utilizing language and creating expectations that are accessible to individuals with mild cognitive limitations enhances compliance. The lack of attention to these considerations mitigates compliance.

The need for precision and appropriateness of language is one of the reasons that providing health care services to individuals with mild cognitive limitations may be so time consuming for providers and, at times, so frustrating. The provider gives what he or she thinks are clear instructions, the individual may not understand them or may be unaware that he or she does not understand them, and the individual expends energy to appear to understand and be a good patient. A cyclic dynamic of miscommunication is launched. The need for health care providers to understand the communication abilities of their patients with cognitive limitations and to develop strategies to communicate directly is essential for meaningful access to all components of care for people with cognitive limitations.

Compliance with regimens for individuals without disabilities is enhanced when the regimen, medication, or treatment diminishes a painful or uncomfortable symptom or condition. Compliance to benefit or remedy an unseen or unfelt symptom, such as high cholesterol, is more difficult to achieve. Achieving and maintaining compliance often is influenced and reinforced by a patient's understanding and the extent to which he or she processes abstract information regarding risks and benefits. For example, a patient without disabilities may generalize from the experience of a family member his or her own health risks: "My father and two of his brothers and my grandfather all died of heart disease. This is something I need to pay attention to."

Compliance with regimens is difficult for the general population, as exemplified by the rate of obesity and sedentary behavior in the adult population or the number of people who do not finish taking a course of antibiotics because their symptoms have disappeared. For individuals with mild cognitive limitations, the task of achieving compliance is all the more onerous because compliance requires a significant amount of abstract reasoning, planning, structure, and organization. Compliance also requires patient education that is targeted to the patient's skills and that makes an affective connection. Individuals with more severe disabilities are more likely to be in supervised settings, and their inability to comply with regimens without assistance is understood. This clarity often does not exist for people with mild cognitive limitations. Even if there is clarity, the social supports and appropriate, targeted health education, which could assist the person, usually are not available.

The Ability to Organize Oneself to Gain Access to and Participate in Health Care

To access, receive, and follow through in one's own health care requires a high degree of personal organization—the ability to plan, sequence events, and process information. Managed care, with the responsibility upon the patient to seek and present referral forms and follow administrative requirements, exaggerates these demands on the individual. Many of the same skills are required in utilizing traditional indemnity fee-for-service care or uncompensated care.

For example, making an appointment is a complex task. The individual needs to have adequate communication skills and information such as telephone numbers and location. Also, he or she must perform a series of processing tasks in which options are weighed against constraints. A time sequence also is employed, and diverse pieces of information are juxtaposed and evaluated. It has been our experience that, upon leaving a medical visit and going to the receptionist's desk to make another appointment, an individual with mild cognitive limitations may make an appointment at a time when he or she is working or has no transportation. Sometimes, individuals agree to appointments without thinking through any logistic considerations, merely because the desk staff suggested a particular day and time. These elements of planning and prioritizing require a high degree of cognitive skill and organization.

Projecting into the Future: Understanding the Consequences of Behavior

People with mild cognitive limitations may have difficulty projecting into the future and imagining the consequences of their own behavior. These difficulties in seeing or recognizing consequences may jeopardize the individual's health. For example, individuals with cognitive disabilities may be unable to foresee the consequences of high-risk sexual behaviors—resulting in sexually transmitted diseases, including HIV infection, or unplanned pregnancies—cigarette smoking, and alcohol and substance abuse. For many people, engaging in these high-risk behaviors arises, in part, out of a desire to be like everyone else.

Problems and Responses to Individuals with
Mild Cognitive Limitations in Health Care Environments

Health care providers and environments may be one of the primary social supports for people with mild cognitive limitations who do not receive specialized services or who have limited social supports and networks. In some instances, the utilization of health care as a substitute for other supports in the individual's life may occur.

Individuals with mild cognitive limitations may call their health care providers frequently; sometimes they will call without a specific reason, or they may create a reason to keep in close contact. This often creates frustration on the part of the provider, who may feel that he or she cannot dedicate so much time to these interactions or that he or she is being put in a difficult position because of the failure of other services. The decreased ability to read social cues or the norms of a social situation, which often affects people with mild cognitive limitations, may lead to burn-out by providers who began the relationship with abundant good will.

The difficulties experienced by many people with mild cognitive limitations in organizing themselves for health care appointments and following the procedures of a health care setting often create tension in the relationship between the individual and the health care environment. Most medical practices and health care settings have rules about canceling and missing appointments with which the person with mild cognitive limitations may have difficulty complying. Practice policies, including the number of noncancelled missed appointments permitted before the person is terminated from the practice, are difficult to reconcile with the person's need for support in gaining access to and receiving health care.

Managed care, with its stringent procedural requirements, including referral forms and prior authorization, may not be compatible with the skills and lifestyle of individuals with mild cognitive limitations. Without extensive patient education and support in gaining access to managed health care, individuals with mild cognitive limitations may be further disadvantaged.

If a person with mild cognitive limitations has children, another pathway to a relationship with the health care environment is created. Often the parent's cognitive limitation is revealed when his or her child presents with a behavior, school, or health problem. Coping with their children's developmental or health needs often focuses adults with mild cognitive limitations on the health care setting as a resource and source of support, as illustrated in the following case study.

> *Ms. Marian James went to the outpatient medical clinic for ongoing health services. Her medical diagnosis prior to evaluation included migraine headaches, asthma, and hypertension. Ms James was seen in the medical clinic for 3 years before she was referred for psychological test-*

ing. Her daughter, CiCi, was 8 years old and was having difficulties in school. The pediatrician referred the daughter for evaluation by a clinical psychologist.

Discussions with the mother revealed difficulties in CiCi's behavior at home as well as in school. During her own evaluation, Ms. James revealed that she spent many years in a special girl's school. Once she aged out of school she returned home. She went to work in a factory and met CiCi's father. They were not married, and Ms. James lost contact with the father when CiCi was born. Ms. James has raised CiCi on her own with a small amount of support from her mother. Recently, CiCi refuses to listen to her mother and has become verbally abusive.

Psychological testing of Ms. James identified mild cognitive limitations. Upon further questioning, it became apparent that Ms. James and CiCi's missed appointments were a result of Ms. James's limited reading skills. The noncompliance with medications noted in Ms. James's chart by adult medical practitioners was a result of her inability to read medication bottles and keep appointments. All of her medications were mixed together in one bottle; Ms. James could not distinguish the individual pills and their uses.

Ms. James refused to identify herself as having cognitive limitations. She received services for her daughter through the school system but not for herself. She did accept a referral to an adult literacy program but left the program within a few weeks.

Ms. James continues to have ongoing issues with her daughter and they both receive limited counseling in the clinic. Ms. James's medical providers are now aware of her mild cognitive limitations and have made adjustments in her medical regimen, which have been successful.

PROBLEMS THAT IMPEDE GOAL ATTAINMENT: CHOICE, CONSENT, AND GUARDIANSHIP

Although most people with mild cognitive limitations are their own guardians and have never been adjudicated "in need of guardianship services" or "incompetent," decision making and consent for health care procedures often is problematic. Many of the health care choices with which adults are confronted require abstract thinking. Benefits and risks must be weighed, and future consequences must be assessed. Individuals with mild cognitive limitations are more capable of giving consent to things with which they have had direct experience. It is easier for a person to consent to a behavior program if he or she has experienced it previously than it is to consent to surgery or chemotherapy for which he or she has no concrete experience.

Many individuals make decisions regarding health care based on concrete and short-range outcomes rather than on larger issues of life trajectory and life quality. For example, a young woman deciding to have an abortion so she can stay in her residential placement may be making the right decision for herself but may not have the cognitive flexibility to explore other alternatives or weigh her own long-term goals and considerations. A challenge of health education is to provide supports in decision making that allow the individual to maximize control over his or her own life.

Even when adults with mild cognitive limitations are their own guardians and have been adjudicated competent to make decisions by the court, many physicians and health care settings will not accept consent for procedures or treatment from a person with cognitive limitations. When a guardian *ad litem,* a temporary guardian for medical decision making, is sought, efforts need to be made to ensure that the preferences and wishes of the individual with mild cognitive limitations are considered and given maximum weight. As the population ages, decision making for the last part of life will become more prevalent as well as difficult. The training of health professionals to explore consent issues is critical to ensuring the rights of people with cognitive limitations.

PROMISING RESPONSES: THE HEALTH STATUS OF ADULTS WITH MILD COGNITIVE LIMITATIONS

The data available on the health status of individuals with developmental disabilities does not demonstrate differences in the rates or causes of death. Until additional data are available, the same medical standards applied to the typical population also are indicated for adults with mild cognitive limitations.

Health Promotion and Disease Prevention

Standards or guidelines for adults with mild cognitive limitations should follow the age-specific suggestions for preventative screenings that apply to individuals without disabilities. The U.S. Preventive Services Task Force Recommendations (1996) would apply the following screenings for adults with mild cognitive limitations as well as for other adults:

- Blood pressure checks every 2 years until age 50, then yearly
- Clinical breast exam
- Mammography
- Pap smear/pelvic exam: Onset of sexual activity or age 18; after 3 consecutive normal Paps, repeat every 1–3 years
- Digital rectal exam
- Fecal occult blood test
- Sigmoidoscopy
- Immunizations: influenza, pneumococcal, tetanus, and hepatitis B

Women's Health Issues

Health issues for women with mild cognitive limitations have historically been unrecognized and ignored. Women with mild cognitive limitations are at increased risk for physical and sexual abuse—and, consequently, at increased risk for sexually transmitted diseases (Pringle, Young, & Aries, 1996).

The lack of access to health care and trained professionals may contribute to the lack of identification and treatment of preventable diseases. The data available on women with physical disabilities demonstrate that reproductive and postmenopausal health problems are not treated adequately within a traditional system designed for women in the general population. Women with learning disabilities also were reported to have a relatively low rate of cervical cancer screenings (24%) compared with an 82% rate for the general population of women. Practitioners' reasons for not screening included "not a requirement," "cognitive limitations," and "not sexually active."

The health care needs of women with mild cognitive limitations are similar to the needs of the general population. They include

- Initial history, including menarche, gynecological surgery, and medications
- Physical exam, including breast and pelvic exams
- Laboratory tests: wet prep, chlamydia, and gonorrhea
- Counseling: contraception, sexuality, sexually transmitted diseases, violence and abuse protection
- Radiology: Mammography, ultrasound and/or CT scan as clinically appropriate

> *Ms. Booth is a 22-year-old woman with a diagnosis of seizure disorder, obesity, and borderline hypertension. She uses oral contraceptives for birth control. Her blood pressure has been elevated since she started the birth control pills. During the last 2 years, she has completed high school and 1 year of college.*
>
> *Ms. Booth is interested in finding a job working with children. She currently works at a local dry cleaners. Her boyfriend is supportive and works evenings. Ms. Booth and her boyfriend plan to get married in 7 months. Both families are in agreement with the wedding.*
>
> *Ms. Booth is interested in getting pregnant and is concerned about the medications that she is taking for her seizure disorder. She was seen by internal medicine, neurology, and gynecology practitioners for follow-up and to review her medications and discuss clinical options.*
>
> *Ms. Evans is a 35-year-old woman with a psychiatric history and recurrent abdominal pain. Gall bladder surgery was recommended by the surgery clinic. Her psychiatric needs require ongoing counseling and daily medications.*

Ms. Evans and her fiancé are getting married this summer. Her mother gave them some assistance in locating a place to live. Her previous residence was shared with another couple who often stole money and food from Ms. Evans. Her hope in the new apartment is to get married and begin a family.

Ms. Evans and her fiancé presented for medical evaluations and infertility workup. Her mother relays information about a hormonal imbalance; previous workups revealed no definitive diagnosis. Present evaluation revealed no physiological reason for Ms. Evans's difficulty conceiving. She continues to come to the doctor despite the fact that her fiancé works in a restaurant without health benefits. He is unable to get the time or the money to see the doctor regularly.

The difficulties they both had with the medical encounters improved once additional information was provided to them. Ms. Evans's fiancé still has limited access to medical care. Ms. Evans continues with ongoing medical care to assess fertility and to evaluate the impact of her psychotropic medications on a potential pregnancy.

Ms. Mayer is a 64-year-old woman with mild cognitive limitations who lives at home. Ms. Mayer cared for her mother until her mother's death 2 months ago. Ms. Mayer's mother had a stroke about 6 months earlier and went to rehab but never fully recovered. Ms. Mayer has two brothers and a sister.

Ms. Mayer was the primary caregiver for her mother. She has a history of congestive heart failure and borderline hypertension and has not been to a doctor regularly since her mother became ill. Her physician noted that her hypertension was poorly controlled. Increasing medication changes were made but with limited effect. A referral was made to the clinic social worker, and additional history was obtained.

Ms. Mayer's mother died at home, and Ms. Mayer was grief-stricken. She would like to continue living in her home with her single brother. A plan was developed to provide grief counseling, a referral to a senior citizen's center, and homemaker assistance as needed. The long-range plan is for Ms. Mayer to move to Texas in 3 years to live with her sister.

Ms. Mayer's blood pressure was brought under control with a medication change to a single, once-a-day agent. Her blood pressure returned to normal limits as soon as she started the new plan.

COMMUNITY ORIENTED PRIMARY CARE: A POTENTIAL MODEL FOR CARE FOR PEOPLE WITH MILD COGNITIVE LIMITATIONS

Individuals with mild cognitive limitations and individuals with other developmental disabilities receiving health care in the generic health care system may benefit from the recent emphasis on primary health care, particularly community oriented primary care (COPC). COPC is a combination of primary health care and community medicine administered in a coordinated practice or health care setting. In a COPC practice, the primary care practitioner accepts a larger than usual share of responsibility for improving the health of a community. The health care practitioner reaches out to offer services that are truly needed and follows through by taking action beyond the traditional method of treating the complaints and problems of patients in the practice. Community members accept responsibility for becoming involved in improving services and individual behavior to maximize the health of the community as a whole.

The COPC model offers a variety of health care services that are accessible and acceptable to the patient. Services are comprehensive in scope, coordinated, and continual over time. The practitioner is accountable for the quality and potential effects of the service.

The COPC basic model involves a primary care program that emphasizes wellness and health promotion, a defined population, and a process by which the major health problems of the community are addressed. This model was the basis for the initial primary care network for the Montefiore Ambulatory Network. The network identified individuals with developmental disabilities as a population that was underserved in 1987 and has since provided services within its health centers for this population.

Evaluation of the COPC model and its services has been limited and would benefit from the analysis of health outcomes to assess the efficacy of the system. It also needs to be tested for replicability.

THE EFFICACY AND IMPORTANCE OF CARE COORDINATION: THE NEED FOR STRUCTURED SUPPORT IN GAINING ACCESS TO CARE

In managed care plans, case management or care coordination typically is condition specific, such as care for asthma, diabetes, or cardiac problems. In the developmental disabilities field, numerous examples of health care demonstration projects point conclusively to the efficacy of care coordination for creating access to and ensuring receipt of care by people with cognitive limitations. As many states move into Medicaid managed care, they conceptualize care coordination as a service or support for individuals with severe disabilities. The difficulties that accrue to people with mild cognitive limitations in accessing and utilizing the health care system would argue for extending care coordination and other forms of structured facilitation to support individuals with mild cognitive limitations.

REFERENCES

Boggs, E.M. (1979). Who is putting whose head in the sand or in the clouds as the case may be? In A.P. Turnbull & H.R. Turnbull, III (Eds.), *Parents speak out: Growing with a handicapped child* (pp. 50–68).Columbus: Charles E. Merrill Publishing Co.

Fujiura, G.T., & Yamaki, K. (1997). Analysis of ethnic variations of developmental disability prevalence and household economic status. *Mental Retardation, 35*(4), 286–294.

Garrard, S.D. (1982). Health services for mentally retarded people in community residences: Problems and questions. *American Journal of Public Health, 72,* 1226–1228.

Gerry, M., & Shively, C. (1999, January). *The Kansas Learning Disabilities Initiative, National Technical Assistance Center for Welfare Reform.* Lawrence: University of Kansas and Kansas Department of Social and Rehabilitative Services.

Gold, H. (1987). *Orchestrating a major policy change in health care services for mentally retarded: Developmentally disabled clients.* Presentation at the annual meeting of the American Association on Mental Retardation, Los Angeles.

Loprest, P., & Acs, G. (1996). *Profile of disability among families on AFDC.* Washington, DC: The Urban Institute.

Minihan, P. (1986). Planning for community physician services prior to deinstitutionalization of mentally retarded persons. *American Journal of Public Health, 76,* 1202–1206.

Pringle, J., Young, D., & Aries, B. (1996, July). *Health matters: Creating health related information for women with disabilities and service providers.* Calgary, Alberta, Canada: The Vocational and Rehabilitation Research Institute.

Spitalnik, D.M. (1996). *Training family physicians in developmental disabilities—A research and training project.* Piscataway, NJ: University Affiliated Program of New Jersey; the Department of Family Medicine, UMDNJ-RWJMS; and the Family Practice Center, Inc., St. Peter's Medical Center.

Spitalnik, D.M., & Cohen, D.E. (1995). *Primary and secondary disabilities: An introduction in health promotion and disability prevention for people with disabilities. A companion to healthy people 2000.* Washington, DC: American Association of University Affiliated Programs for Persons with Developmental Disabilities.

Spitalnik, D.M., & Like, R.C. (1987). *The provision of primary health care to adults with chronic disabilities. Proposal to the Robert Wood Johnson Foundation.* New Brunswick: University Affiliated Program of New Jersey.

State of Washington Department of Social and Health Services. (1998, February). *A baseline analysis of TANF one-parent families: Findings from 1997 client survey.* Author.

Sweeney, E.P. (2000). *Recent studies make clear that many parents who are current or former welfare recipients have disabilities and other medical conditions.* Washington, DC: Center on Budget and Policy Priorities.

U.S. Preventive Services Task Force. (1996). *Guide to clinical preventive services* (2nd ed.). Baltimore: Williams & Wilkins.

Yankauer, A. (1986). Community health services for mentally retarded adults. *American Journal of Public Health, 76,* 1187–1189.

The Healthy People 2010 Process

Difficulties Related to Surveillance and Data Collection

Vincent A. Campbell and Holly J. Fedeyko

This chapter provides an overview of public health activities that relate to people with mild cognitive limitations. The objectives are to 1) review briefly the development of public policy with regard to people with cognitive limitations, particularly those individuals who are mildly affected, 2) describe a national health initiative, Healthy People 2010, and its potential impact on people with mild cognitive limitations, 3) note problems in public health surveillance of mild cognitive limitations, 4) review a selection of health-related studies that suggest increased risk for a variety of health conditions, and 5) make recommendations.

Public health objectives related to mental retardation have changed considerably over the course of U.S. history. Historically, public policy emphasized segregation of people with mental retardation from the rest of the population—first for therapeutic reasons and later for the protection of society (MacMillan, 1982). During the latter part of the 19th century and in the early 20th century, the eugenics movement influenced public health policy related to mental retardation. Authorities such as Goddard (1912) and Pitkin (1928) called for segregation and sterilization of "feebleminded" people; most of these individuals had mild cognitive disabilities.

Beginning in the 1960s and gaining strength in the 1970s, public policy and practice changed with regard to the education and treatment of individuals with cognitive limitations. Clinical and administrative practices began to reflect empirical findings that learning and improvements in adaptive behavior were enhanced by treatment in less restrictive community-based environments, residential training, and work, as opposed to large, overcrowded, and understaffed institutions. A series of court cases (e.g., *Pennsylvania Association for Retarded Children v. Commonwealth of Pennsylvania,* 1971; *Wyatt v. Stickney,* 1972) and legislative actions (e.g., Education for All Handicapped Children Act of 1975 [PL 94-142]) provided people with mental retardation with the opportunity to live more typical lives (Braddock, Hemp, Parish, & Westrich, 1998).

The image of the "six-hour retarded child" was introduced in 1969 (President's Committee on Mental Retardation, 1969) and has been revisited several times since (e.g., Koegel & Edgerton, 1982, 1984; Mercer, 1973). The "six-hour retarded child" was posited to display mental retardation during the period of time he or she spent in school but not to demonstrate disability outside of the academic environment. In effect, the disability was only apparent under the demands of academic performance but not in day-to-day life apart from school. The situation-specific nature of the cognitive limitations in this group of children and their association with academic demands has been supported by epidemiologic investigators who consistently have found that the majority of children with mild cognitive limitations are not readily detectable once they leave school (Gruenberg, 1964; Richardson & Koller, 1996).

This gap between school-age academic impairment and performance of activities in everyday life may be misleading, however. In their 1984 report of a qualitative follow-up study of young African American adults who were formerly enrolled in special education programs for mild mental retardation, Koegel and Edgerton documented initial impressions from their field staff that the research participants had been misplaced in special education. Subsequent reports from these staff, however, indicated that extended contact with these young adults revealed deficiencies in performance of instrumental activities of daily living, such as money management and use of community resources, which supported the earlier diagnoses. As Richardson and Koller stated, it may be that

> During the school years, compulsory education makes age-specific demands on children to meet minimum standards of school performance and behavior. After they leave school, the demands made on young adults are far more flexible, because the tasks and roles expected of them offer a much wider set of options. In school, the demands of literacy, numeracy, and language usage are primary. In some jobs, however, such as unskilled manual labor, these are far less important. Although some young adults classified as mentally retarded during the school years might be able to function in the postschool world without the need for adult MR services, others require these services for some or all of their adult lives. (1996, p. 74)

The focus on academic activities in school brought greater attention to the specific areas of limitation of the "six-hour retarded child" that were not as discernible in environments that were less focused on cognitive performance. Richardson, Katz, and Koller (1993) noted that little is known about cognitive disability persisting into adulthood, despite the passage of 30 years since the issue of school-related mental retardation first was raised. Many adults with mental retardation disappear from the formal mental retardation service system; however, they continue to experience the limitations apparent during their school years.

In the three decades since the "six-hour retarded child" first was conceptualized, profound changes have occurred in the educational rights of people with mental retardation and other cognitive impairments and in the nature of the special education services to which they are entitled. More generally, the rights of people with disabilities have been protected by law in the form of the Americans with Disabilities Act (ADA) of 1990 (PL 101-336). Moreover, since the late 1980s the nation's public health system has formally recognized the health needs of people with disabilities (Institute of Medicine, 1991) and, consequently, has developed programs to address their specific health concerns and set goals to eliminate health disparities relative to people without disabilities. People with mild cognitive impairments, particularly impairments characteristic of the "six-hour retarded child," pose unique problems to public health systems as efforts are made to improve the health and quality of life of people with disabilities in general. The major problem that this chapter addresses is the identification of individuals with mild cognitive limitations for public health surveillance.

In addition to new treatment approaches and increased regard for the civil rights of people with cognitive limitations, a major reconceptualization of disability emerged during the 1990s, which has broadened the perspective of public health to include quality of life and environmental factors that promote or impede social participation (Institute of Medicine, 1991; World Health Organization, 1980, 2000). This change reflects a paradigm shift from diagnosis and impairment to activity limitation and from a medical to an ecological model of disability in which adaptive behavior, or typical functioning, of a person must be examined as an interaction between the person and his or her social and physical environment (Coulter, 1992). The traditional public health approach to disabilities, including mild cognitive impairments, was based on a medical model of disease and directed toward primary prevention (Rioux, 1997). Mental retardation and other developmental disabilities were seen as conditions to be prevented outright, and relatively little attention was given to the health status of the people with disabilities. In keeping with the changing focus, however, efforts have begun to be made in the area of prevention of secondary conditions among people with disabilities. *Secondary conditions* are defined as medical, social, and personal conditions for which the person with a disability is at increased risk because of the primary, preexisting condition (Marge, 1988; Pope, 1992). Although the term *secondary conditions* is relatively new and is rarely used with regard to mild cognitive limitations, numerous studies in the mental retardation literature have described medical, social, and emotional conditions for which people with mental retardation may be at increased risk. Some of these conditions are described briefly in this chapter.

OVERVIEW OF HEALTHY PEOPLE

With the 1979 publication of *Healthy People: The Surgeon General's Report on Health Promotion and Disease Prevention*, the U.S. Public Health Service established a process of setting health promotion goals and objectives to increase the health status and life expectancy of the U.S. population (U.S. Department of Health and Human Services, 1997). As a consequence of this initiative, federal and state health agencies were encouraged to set objectives, develop recommendations for action, and identify data sources to evaluate progress toward meeting the objectives, with a 1990 target date. By 1990, the goals of reducing mortality among infants, children, and adults were achieved; however, the goal of reduction of mortality in adolescents was not. Another goal, to increase independence in older Americans, lacked documenting data and as a result was not considered to have been achieved. For each of these goals, there was a strong emphasis on identifying and using data to document status.

Healthy People 2000

Healthy People 2000 (HP2000) served as a continuation and expansion of the first Surgeon General's report. Representatives of governmental public health organizations, special interest groups, private and professional organizations, businesses, and other interested parties established goals and objectives. HP2000 was an ambitious endeavor resulting in more than 300 objectives in 22 priority areas that addressed three broad goals for all Americans: 1) increasing the healthy period of life, 2) reducing health disparities, and 3) increasing the provision of preventive services (U. S. Department of Health and Human Services, 1997). Basic to all of the objectives was an emphasis on surveillance and data systems necessary to identify baseline and progress. Within the framework of HP2000, objectives were established for mental health, cognitive disorders, and disabilities; however, the focus was on primary prevention of these conditions and did not address the quality of life for people with disabilities or the prevention of secondary conditions within this population.

Healthy People 2010

Healthy People 2010 (HP2010) is the third in this series of prevention initiatives that involves the setting of formal goals and objectives for improving the health of the citizens and residents of the United States (U.S. Department of Health and Human Services, 2000). The public interest that grew throughout the process of developing HP2000 and the alliances and partnerships that were formed served as a basis for the development of the HP2010 goals and objectives. In November 1996, an organizational meeting was held to discuss HP2000, evaluate process and progress, and lay the groundwork for HP2010. Draft goals and objectives were developed during the following 3 years and were presented at a series of public meetings in the latter half of 1999.

The final HP2010 initiative was released in January 2000 (U.S. Department of Health and Human Services, 2000). It has two goals: 1) to increase the quality and years of healthy life and 2) to eliminate health disparities. Ten health indicators are included in HP2010 to track the health of the U.S. population—physical activity, overweight and obesity, tobacco use, substance abuse, responsible sexual behavior, mental health, injury and violence, environmental quality, immunization, and access to health care. These 10 indicators are reflected through 467 objectives in 28 focus areas. It is the first national health strategy to recognize people with disabilities as a select population.

Because of the difficulty identifying people with mild cognitive limitations, it is safe to say that the health status of individuals with mild cognitive limitations will not be affected, except incidentally, by the HP2010 effort. The chapter in HP2010 on disability and secondary conditions contains 13 specific and 111 reference objectives from other focus areas that are designed to improve the health of people with disabilities (refer to the appendix at the end of this chapter for disability-related objectives); however, because of the general nature of the survey questions that will be used to identify people with disabilities, those individuals with mild cognitive limitations will not be distinguishable for most of the health objectives. As a result, HP2010 will be largely irrelevant to the segment of the population with mild cognitive limitations during the first decade of the 21st century. A fundamental problem for population-based surveillance of mild cognitive limitations is the difficulty of developing sensitive and specific questions in framing it operationally for use in surveys, which are the primary vehicles for documenting objectives for HP2010.

IDENTIFICATION AND PREVALENCE OF MILD COGNITIVE LIMITATIONS

Mild cognitive limitations, in the form of mild mental retardation, are hypothesized to represent the low end of the normal distribution of intelligence (e.g., Balla & Zigler, 1979). Generally, the IQ criterion for mental retardation has been recognized to be two or more standard deviations below the mean of 100 (see Figure 2.1 on page 29 for an illustration of the Gaussian distribution of intelligence). Using this criterion, one could expect approximately 2.3% of the general population to have mental retardation. Based on IQ alone, more than 85% of that segment, or roughly 2% of the population, could be expected to have mild mental retardation. Diagnostic criteria, however, require that there be significant limitations in at least two areas of adaptive behavior (Luckasson et al., 1992), which reduces the prevalence considerably, most likely to the range of approximately 1% of the general population (e.g., Baroff, 1982; Heber, 1970).

Various classification schemes have been proposed for intelligence. The two most commonly used are that of the American Association on Mental Retardation (AAMR) and that used in special education. Under its current classification system (Luckasson et al., 1992), AAMR does not classify cognitive impairment on the basis of severity (i.e., mild, moderate, severe, and profound) but, rather, on the basis of the intensity of supports required by the person (i.e., intermittent, limited, extensive, and pervasive). Earlier versions of the AAMR system, in which severity levels were promulgated, indicated mild mental retardation to exist when an adaptive behavior deficiency coincided with an IQ in the range of 55 to 70–75 (Grossman, 1983). The *Diagnostic and Statistical Manual of Mental Disorders, Fourth Edition* (American Psychiatric Association, 1994)—which in earlier editions had paralleled the AAMR classification system—maintained the use of severity levels despite the publication of support levels by AAMR and indicates that mild mental retardation IQ scores range from 50–55 to 70. Looking across these varied classification systems, mild cognitive limitation appears to exist in the IQ range of 50–75, theoretically affecting roughly 4.5% of the general population. Even slight changes in cutoff criteria result in relatively large changes in potential prevalence. As pointed out by MacMillan, Gresham, and Siperstein (1993), the modification of the upper IQ criterion for mental retardation by AAMR in 1992 from 70 to 70–75 increases the proportion of the population falling below the threshold from 2.2% to 5.5%. Certainly, it was not the intent of AAMR to increase the prevalence of mental retardation arbitrarily but, instead, to give the diagnostician flexibility in classifying people in need of supports (Reiss, 1994). The adaptive behavior criterion inhibits the prevalence of mental retardation. The educational system, which has the resources necessary for diagnosis and placement, provides a focus on one aspect of adaptive behavior—academic performance—which highlights limited cognitive ability.

It is possible to distinguish between individuals who have and do not have mental retardation when results of intelligence tests and assessments of adaptive behavior are available; however, it becomes impractical to use evaluation-based diagnosis for population-based surveillance in the absence of preexisting records. Murphy and her colleagues reported a prevalence rate for mild mental retardation of approximately 0.8% among 10-year-old children in the population-based Metropolitan Atlanta Developmental Disabilities Study (MADDS; Murphy, Yeargin-Allsopp, Decouflé, & Drews, 1995); however, it should be noted that even in this rigorously controlled surveillance program, case identification is based on IQ alone.

The term *mild cognitive limitation* is a disability category consistent with the taxonomy currently under revision by the World Health Organization (1980, 2000). In this system, activities are classified in 10 chapters: sensory (seeing and hearing), learning, movement, daily life activities, domestic activities, interpersonal behaviors, responding to particular situations, dealing with particular situations, and using assistive devices. As noted earlier, Koegel and Edgerton (1984) indicated that the cognitive limitations of young adults were most obviously apparent in practical skills that, in the International Classification of Functioning, Disability, and Health (ICIDH-2; World Health Organization, 1997) classification system, are most likely in the chapters about domestic activities and responding to particular situations.

The literature that addresses the prevalence of mental retardation includes a wide range of estimates (e.g., Kiely, 1987). The 19th annual report to Congress on the Individuals with Disabilities Education Act (U.S. Department of Education, 1997) includes percentages of the student population who are classified as having mental retardation for special education services. The percentages for the 1995–1996 school year ranged from 0.3% in New Jersey to 2.4% in Alabama, an eight-fold difference. Similar disparities were reported in a study that used 1993 special education enrollment data for children ages 6–17 and Social Security benefits data for adults ages 18–64 to identify individuals with mental retardation (Centers for Disease Control and Prevention, 1986).

Within individual studies, a wide variation in prevalence is age-related, with a sharp decline in detectable cases occurring in late adolescence. This drop in prevalence is characteristic of these studies and is accounted for mainly by a precipitous drop in cases of mild mental retardation. Many epidemiological studies of mental retardation that have differentiated between severe and less severe forms of mental retardation have found a distinctive variation in prevalence over the life course. Mild cognitive limitation rarely is detected prior to entry into school; prevalence slowly increases throughout childhood, reaches a platcau during early to mid adolescence, and rapidly declines during late adolescence and early adulthood. Kiely (1987) reviewed epidemiological studies of mental retardation from the 20th century, and his research revealed similar age-specific variations in prevalence. Figure 12.1 depicts graphically a summary of prevalence rates reported by Kiely (1987). Dupont (1989), reporting on prevalence studies conducted in Denmark in 1888, 1965, and 1979, included in his study a chart that graphically demonstrated this positively skewed age curve, with a steady decline in prevalence through the oldest age categories. Administratively identified cases of mental retardation from service agencies also have demonstrated this distinctive distribution across the life course (Campbell et al., 1995; Campbell, Hovinga, & Brezausek, 1996). Of course, not all individuals with mild cognitive limitations have been identified by the formal mental retardation service system. An additional problem is that, even when service rosters are accurate, many states do not track clients waiting for services (e.g., Hayden & DePaepe, 1994).

Mild cognitive limitation presents a challenge for instruments designed to gauge the nation's health, such as the National Health Interview Survey (NHIS; Centers for Disease Control and Prevention, 1994), which, with its recurring core set of questions, determines disability on the basis of limitation in age-related major activities—engaging in play (ages younger than 6), attending school (ages 6–17 years), working or keeping house (ages 18–64 years), living independently (ages older than 65) or in other activities, such as recreation (Adams & Marano, 1995). These criteria are unlikely to identify people with mild cognitive limitations. More detailed data was obtained by the NHIS in a special supplemental questionnaire on disability in 1994/1995. Larson, Lakin,

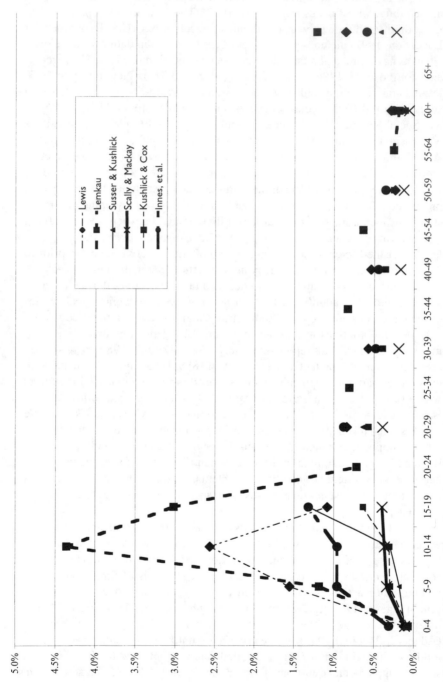

Figure 12.1.   Life course prevalence of mental retardation. (Adapted from Kiely, 1987.)

Anderson, and Kwak (1999) used the 1994 *NHIS Disability Supplement, Phase 1,* to identify people with mental retardation or developmental disabilities. Using a combination of more than 30 variables, these researchers estimated mental retardation prevalences of 3.4%, 2.6%, and 0.5% for age groups of birth to 5 years, 6–18 years and 19 years and older, respectively. Unfortunately, for concerns bearing on mild cognitive limitations, this creative analytic approach does not distinguish between levels of severity. In addition, the *NHIS Disability Supplement* is not ongoing and, as a result, will not provide continuing surveillance data to help inform the HP2010 process.

Additional problems exist with national health surveys with regard to estimating the prevalence of mild cognitive limitation and the health status of the people who are affected. By definition, mild cognitive limitation impairs a person's ability to understand written or spoken language, which may reduce the reliability of responses to survey questions. Proxy respondents may or may not provide reliable answers. In addition, most national surveys exclude people in institutions. The Behavioral Risk Factor Surveillance System (BRFSS; Centers for Disease Control and Prevention, 1998), which is used as the surveillance vehicle for several HP2010 disability objectives, does not sample children—an age group with an especially high prevalence of identified mild cognitive limitation. Using ethnographic research techniques with a sample of 45 African American adults receiving services by virtue of having been identified as having mild cognitive limitations, Koegel and Edgerton (1982) found that only 4% of the adults identified themselves as having a "mild mental handicap," although more than 60% indicated other, more vague types of impairment. The word "slow" was the most commonly used term to describe their condition. Parents or caregivers interviewed during this study were much more likely than the individuals themselves to make direct or indirect reference to the disability. Most of the participants and their caregivers reported that the participants had limitations in basic cognitive activities, such as performing simple arithmetic, reading, handling money, and telling time. Their parents also cited these areas as well as a concern for their children being taken advantage of by others.

The National Health and Nutrition Examination Survey (NHANES) (Centers for Disease Control and Prevention, 1994)— a continuous data collection instrument that gathers information from clinical examinations, interviews, and laboratory tests—potentially could provide valuable information on children with mild cognitive limitations. The survey is designed to make national estimates of health and nutritional status for the noninstitutionalized population of the United States. Among the data gathered on children between the ages of 6 and 16 are block design and digit span raw and scaled scores from the Weschsler Intelligence Scale for Children, Third Edition (Weschler, 1991), and math and reading raw scores from the Wide Range Achievement Test–Revised (Jastak & Wilkinson, 1984). These data, although insufficient to make a definitive diagnosis of mental retardation, provide more objective and reliable information than self- or proxy reports. This survey, however, provides limited insight into social participation and, consequently, may not provide robust indication of the impact of mild cognitive limitations on the lives of the people affected.

Chamie (1994) and Stein, Durkin, and Belmont (1986) reported on the use of a set of 10 questions used to identify children with disabilities in developing countries. The questions, which do not employ medical jargon and, in some instances, may use insensitive language, refer to activities, sensory impairments, and comparisons of the reference child to other children of similar age and are used to gather information on which to base prevention policy and interventions. Although the set of questions is very brief, it emphasizes activities from five of the eight domains used in the revised ICIDH-2 taxonomy (World Health Organization, 2000) that are most pertinent for children: seeing and hearing, learning, moving, moving around, and communication. The development of such questions for adults, and their use in targeted surveys, may increase the ability to detect mild cognitive limitations.

Because of the limits of national surveys for use in surveillance of mental retardation in the general population, and in children specifically, special education enrollment would be valuable for tracking this population. However, many, if not most, state special education departments have moved away from reporting mild mental retardation or EMR as a category. Some, with the admirable objective of reducing stigma, have gone to a completely noncategorical system of special education. Although this decision may diminish the effects of labeling, such a loss of data is unfortunate for public health surveillance.

Unfortunately, there is little population-based data on school-age people with mental retardation or on individuals with mental retardation who have exited school. Richardson and Koller (1996) have reported on a long-term, follow-up, population-based study of adults with mental retardation in Aberdeen, Scotland. Although the information on this group is valuable in a number of areas, the study sheds little light on the health status of these individuals. Beyond the difficulties of establishing a true prevalence rate for mild mental retardation, the problems involved in identifying affected individuals limit the effectiveness of public health efforts such as HP2010 to improve their quality of life and eliminate health disparities relative to people without disabilities.

ASSOCIATED SECONDARY CONDITIONS AND CONCERNS

When compared with people without mental retardation, individuals with mental retardation have been documented to be at increased risk for a number of health conditions and concerns. Study samples for these investigations typically are drawn from people residing in institutions or supervised community residential environments; although, increasingly, people residing alone or with their families are included. Most studies include people with mild mental retardation as well as people with more severe impairments. Because of the difficulty of identifying adults with mental retardation who are not involved in the formal mental retardation services system, very few studies have focused specifically on this population or have included them in population-based research.

The following sections provide a brief overview of some of the health conditions and health concerns reported to be relatively prevalent among people with mild mental retardation and may provide a sense of the scope of the problem of establishing and evaluating public health objectives for this population. These conditions present additional risk for other secondary conditions that have the potential to further reduce quality of life and health status.

Mortality

Naturally, the leading indicator of relative poor health in a subgroup of a population is its mortality rate when compared with the general population and with other subgroups. As documented by Eyman, Grossman, Tarjan, and Miller (1987), numerous studies have demonstrated that people with mental retardation are at higher risk for premature death than their peers without mental retardation. These authors indicate that although relative death rates have decreased for people with mental retardation, people with mild mental retardation had a mortality rate 1.7 times that of the general population as recently as 1970.

Hayden (1998), reporting a 1991 study by Miller, indicated that heart disease was the leading cause of death for people with less severe mental retardation. An October 1998 issue of the journal *Mental Retardation* was devoted to the subject of comparative death rates between individuals residing in institutions and those residing in community residential environments. Much of the material was concerned with the differences between death rates in these different types of environments and the methodologies employed to study the issue. However, the larger issue—that studies of mortality in people with mental retardation are not likely to be definitive because an unknown number of individuals are missing from the numerator in the calculations—was not addressed.

Obesity

Fox and Rotatori (1982) and Kelly, Rimmer, and Ness (1986) have reported that adults with mild to moderate mental retardation are at increased risk for obesity. People with mental retardation have been reported to be at a much higher risk for obesity than their peers without retardation (Rimmer, Braddock, & Fujiura, 1993), with 46% of individuals with mild mental retardation in their study reported to be obese. Type of living arrangement also was strongly linked to obesity; higher percentages of obesity were noted among people in community residential environments. Especially troubling was the finding that 55.3%

of individuals with mild cognitive limitations residing with their natural families were found to be obese. These investigators noted the strong link between obesity and coronary heart disease, cancer, and social discrimination.

Osteoporosis

Center, Beange, and McElduff (1998) reported significantly lower bone mineral density and an increased risk for osteoporosis for a group of people with moderate to mild mental retardation with a mean age of 35 years when compared with age-matched controls.

Lack of Fitness and Exercise

Rimmer (1994) provided a good overview of the research that has been conducted on fitness and exercise in people with mental retardation; however, he makes no distinction for people with mild mental retardation. As he pointed out, not as much research has been focused on individuals with mental retardation as has been focused on other disability groups. Physical education and activity programs for people with mental retardation are provided, for the most part, to school-age children through their special education or other school programs. The extent to which people with mild mental retardation engage in conditioning activities once they exit school is not well documented. Adult programs for individuals with mental retardation that do exist are largely recreational and do not stress the sort of physical activity that is necessary for fitness.

Rimmer reviews a number of studies that demonstrate that adults with mental retardation compare unfavorably with their peers without mental retardation in terms of activity and fitness levels, obesity, resulting in increased risk for disease and poor quality of life (e.g., McConaughy & Salzburg, 1988), cardiovascular fitness and cholesterol levels (e.g., Pitetti, Jackson, Stubbs, Campbell, & Saraswathy, 1989), muscular strength and endurance (e.g., Reid, Montgomery, & Seidl, 1985), and onset of cardiovascular disease (Pitetti & Campbell, 1991). Rimmer's chapter also contains useful material on the benefits and challenges of providing fitness programs to people with mental retardation. Rimmer identifies level of motivation and cognitive limitations as factors that make fitness programming difficult with these adults. The recommendations for the design of a sound program to increase fitness and activity levels in this population include reduction in sedentary activities, the use of behavior modification techniques using individually tailored reinforcers to promote involvement in fitness activities, incremental increases in exertion levels, and knowledge of comorbid conditions.

Unfortunately, little information is available for individuals who do not live in a supervised environment or otherwise participate in habilitation programs. The importance of fitness and healthy lifestyles must be incorporated into special education and rehabilitation programs that serve this population during childhood, adolescence, and young adulthood.

Mental Illness

As reported by Dorn and Prout (1993), people with mental retardation have been reported to be at higher risk for behavior and emotional difficulties than the general population, with prevalence ranging from 20% to 40%. They noted that caution is required in interpreting these findings because of the compounding effects of including people in institutions in the samples of people with mental retardation. In their study of mental health service patterns, these investigators found that adults with mild mental retardation were likely to receive fewer services and a different pattern of care than clients without mental retardation.

Risk Behaviors

In one of the few studies focusing on mild mental retardation, Pack, Wallander, and Browne (1998) reported the results of a comparison of risk behaviors between a sample of adolescent African Americans with mild mental retardation and their peers without mental retardation. They reported increased risk for carrying weapons and reduced likelihood of using alcohol but increased risk for binge drinking among the adolescents with mental retardation. These authors also reported that health education programs rarely took the limited cognitive capacity of adolescents into account.

Christian and Poling (1997) reviewed the literature on drug abuse among people with mental retardation and noted that relatively few studies have been conducted to determine the extent to which drugs and alcohol are used or abused. Most of the studies are small in terms of sample size, focus on a few intoxicants such as alcohol and marijuana, and are not population based. Essentially, the authors cited a limitation in the studies that is characteristic of research with this group of people—difficulty in obtaining accurate information using traditional data collection methods such as written and telephone-based surveys. The studies reviewed suggest that people with mental retardation use drugs and alcohol less frequently than their peers without mental retardation; however, the reviewers expressed concern over the possibility of an increase in substance abuse as individuals with mental retardation are integrated more fully into society. The authors also expressed special concern about the limited substance abuse treatment resources accessible to people with mental retardation.

HEALTH COVERAGE

Most Americans obtain their health care coverage through job-related insurance, either as the primary beneficiary or under dependent coverage. People with mild mental retardation are at a disadvantage under these circumstances because of the high correlation between mental retardation and low socioeconomic status and because of the low level of vocational involvement of many of these people.

Supplemental Security Income (SSI) benefits, which entitle a person to Medicaid coverage, are available to people with mental retardation with an IQ of less than 60 and to individuals whose IQ is in the range of 60–70 who have other physical or mental impairments that result in substantial work-related functional limitation (Social Security Administration, 1994).

SUMMARY AND RECOMMENDATIONS

The surveillance of mild cognitive limitation presents public health programs with a number of serious problems that limit the effectiveness of health promotion efforts and initiatives such as HP2010 with individuals with mild cognitive limitation. The circumstances that most commonly bring attention to mild cognitive limitations are the academic demands of schoolwork, and identification and classification is primarily for the purpose of determining eligibility for special education. Postschool demands appear to be sufficiently diverse and environmental accommodations and supports sufficiently flexible and informal for people who were identified as having mild cognitive limitations during their school years to "disappear" from service rolls and administrative datasets specific to their cognitive limitation after leaving school (Richardson & Koller, 1996). The relatively uniform detection system in place during the school years and the diagnostic resources available to educational systems do not exist during adulthood. This is not to say that adaptive behavior impairments no longer exist. However, performance deficiencies are likely to be outside the scope of the mental retardation service systems. Unless they have severe behavior disorders, people with mild cognitive limitations are likely to go unserved by the formal service system, to work at low skill jobs, and to receive informal supports from family and friends as needs arise. Deficiencies in adaptive behaviors or antisocial activities may be addressed by service programs and systems that are not specifically designed to serve people with mild cognitive limitations. Poor vocational skills, for example, may result in frequent periods of unemployment. Antisocial behavior may come to the attention of the legal system and result in incarceration.

Surveys will provide much of the data that will be used to determine baselines and to evaluate outcomes of HP2010; however, existing survey-based public health surveillance in the United States is inadequate for identifying individuals with mild cognitive limitations. Self-identification by people with mild cognitive limitations is unreliable. Because of increased likelihood of limitation in instrumental activities of daily living such as using a telephone, people with mild cognitive limitations may not be represented adequately in samples used by telephone-based surveys. Face-to-face surveys can provide the detailed data that increase the likelihood of identifying people with developmental disabilities or cognitive impairments; however, their utility for distinguishing people with mild cognitive limitations from people with more severe disibilities has not been demonstrated. Unfortunately, face-to-face surveys such as the NHIS do not routinely include questions that are sensitive to the population with mild cognitive limitations.

Health-related research involving people with mental retardation suggests that people with mild cognitive limitations are at increased risk for a variety of social, emotional, and physical problems. However, most of the studies in this area are based on samples of convenience drawn from mental retardation service programs and do not include comparison groups of individuals without disabilities. For the most part, conclusions cannot be drawn with specific regard to people with mild cognitive limitations because the samples include people with more severe disabilities. Cohort and group effects, such as those related to institutional experience and residential status, are generally poorly controlled.

In large measure, few formal connections exist between public health agencies and educational systems and other agencies that serve people with mild cognitive limitations. As a result, little is done to determine the prevalence of mild cognitive limitations, to identify special health care needs of this population, or to develop mechanisms to provide health promotion programs. The education system is the major identification resource for mild cognitive limitations. Administrative data such as special education enrollment should be evaluated to determine their utility in informing a surveillance program for mild cognitive limitations, even within an age-restricted population such as that between the ages of 10 and 18 years.

The following recommendations are made on the basis of reviewed material and the need for information about the large number of people with mild cognitive limitations who are identified in school but "lost" to the system once they exit school. Solid, population-based data are needed to identify the activity limitations that are experienced by this group, the physical and social barriers to their participation in all aspects of society, and the supports that would enhance their access.

1. Diagnostic and classification systems such as those promulgated by AAMR and the APA are compatible, in terms of emphases on adaptive behavior, with the activity classification in the ICIDH-2 that is being revised by the World Health Organization. Given that the World Health Organization taxonomy attempts to bring together all aspects of the disablement process (i.e., impairment, activities, participation, environmental factors) into a broader picture of the person in society, it is recommended that AAMR and APA become familiar with ICIDH-2 and broaden the conceptualization of the person with mild cognitive limitations in the wider disability community.

2. Parties interested in the welfare and quality of life of people with mild cognitive limitations need to organize and coordinate efforts bearing on the policy issues and research needs related to this population. Beyond the health issues raised by HP2010 and the likelihood that people with mild cognitive limitations will not be included adequately in the data systems used to monitor this process are questions regarding the postschool experiences of these individuals. Although formal services for people with mild cognitive limitations most frequently are provided by educational systems, other governmental sectors are responsible for programs and services that may be used or needed by people with mild cognitive limitations disproportionately more frequently. To what extent are individuals with mild cognitive limitations affected by welfare reform? What proportion of people receiving services under Temporary Assistance to Needy Families (TANF) are former special education students with mild cognitive limitations? What proportion of the incarcerated population has mild cognitive limitations? What vocational supports are effective with people with mild cognitive limitations? The President's Committee on Mental Retardation can provide leadership and coordination of this activity.

   3.   Research is needed to develop questions for use in national telephone-based and face-to-face surveys to reliably identify people with mild cognitive limitations. Telephone-based surveys require short, concise questions that are few in number and that can reliably identify people with disabilities, including cognitive limitations. Follow-up questions need to be developed that identify people with cognitive limitations, distinguish between mild and more severe impairments, and draw distinctions between limitations resulting from developmental processes and those brought on by such conditions as traumatic brain injury and Alzheimer's disease.

   4.   Data sets, including those related to vital statistics, health care, and administrative records such as service enrollment should be evaluated to determine their utility for conducting health-related research on people with mild cognitive limitations. Is it possible or practical to carry out research on mortality of people with mild cognitive limitations by linking special education and National Death Index data sets? What birth record variables are predictive of mild cognitive limitations as reflected in special education enrollment? What are the privacy and confidentiality implications of linking these records? What privacy protections can be developed to permit file and record linkages to conduct such investigations? Can a unique identifier be developed that is useful across vital statistics and health-related and other administrative datasets? It is critical that data-sharing approaches be sensitive to concerns of confidentiality of information and privacy of individuals. Relevant federal legislation should be reviewed and adhered to in the design of such systems. The following is a list, not comprehensive, of federal legislation that is in whole or part relevant to privacy and confidentiality of data and that are potentially useful for health issues with people with mild cognitive limitations: Computer Matching and Privacy Protection Act of 1988 (PL 100-503), Privacy Act of 1974 (PL 93-579), Electronic Freedom of Information Act Amendments of 1996 (PL 104-231), Health Insurance Portability and Accountability Act (HIPPAA) of 1996 (PL

104-191), Family Educational Rights and Privacy Act of 1996, Individuals with Disabilities Education Act Amendments of 1997 (PL 105-17), Medical Information Privacy and Security Act of 1999, and the Medical Information Protection and Research Enhancement Act of 1999.

5. Federal agencies should give priority to funding studies in which data are linked from public health and service agencies (e.g., vital statistics data, special education and vocational rehabilitation enrollment, records from agencies [e.g., public assistance Medicaid, courts, correctional agencies]). Special education serves a unique function as a diagnostic entity for children with mental retardation; however, classification data are often not centralized. Population-based studies of people with mild cognitive limitations could be carried out using linked data sets using special education classification as the touchstone for diagnosis. Among the areas in which research would be welcome are the following:

1. Risk factors present at birth that are predictive of later mild cognitive limitations
2. Use of publicly funded services such as Medicaid and SSI; public assistance; Supplemental Nutrition Program for Women, Infants and Children; and so forth
3. Risk for legal difficulties and involvement in the court and correctional system
4. Evidence of intergenerational special education enrollment and study of ecological data bearing on the family
5. Mortality

   Until specific steps are taken to determine the health status of people with mild cognitive limitations, we will continue to undercount people with mild cognitive limitations, and the public health system will continue to lack meaningful data on which to base sound policy decisions. Questions will remain about the quality of their lives, their health status, and the extent to which secondary conditions diminish their health status and impair participation in society. The consequence, of course, is that many people with mild cognitive limitations will remain overlooked and forgotten by the nation's public health system.

REFERENCES

Adams, P.F., & Marano, M.A. (1995). *Current estimates from the National Health Interview Survey, 1994* (Vital Health Stat 10[193]). Washington DC: National Centers for Health Statistics.

American Psychiatric Association. (1994). *Diagnostic and statistical manual of mental disorders* (4th ed.). Washington, DC: American Psychiatric Association.

Anderson, L., Larson, S., & Lakin, C. (1998, November). *1994 National Health Interview Survey, Disability Supplement: Identifying people with mental retardation or developmental disabilities.* Paper presented at the American Public Health Association conference, Washington, DC.

Balla, D., & Zigler, E. (1979). Personality development in retarded persons. In N.R. Ellis (Ed.), *Handbook of mental deficiency, psychological theory and research*, (2nd ed., pp. 143–168). Mahwah, NJ: Lawrence Erlbaum Associates.

Braddock, D., Hemp, R., Parish, S., & Westrich, J. (1998). *The state of the states in developmental disabilities* (5th ed.). Washington, DC: American Association on Mental Retardation.

Campbell, V.A., Causey, J., Collier, C.B., Ramey, C.T., Shearer, D.S., & Stokes, B.R. (1995, May). *A comprehensive statewide interagency approach to prevention of mental retardation.* Symposium at annual meeting of the American Association on Mental Retardation, San Francisco.

Campbell, V.A., Hovinga, M.E., & Brezausek, C. (1996, December). *Alabama's mental retardation surveillance program: Interagency administrative ascertainment across the lifespan.* Paper presented at the annual Maternal, Infant, and Child Health Epidemiology Workshop, Atlanta.

Center, J., Beange, H., & McElduff, A. (1998). People with mental retardation have an increased prevalence of osteoporosis: A population study. *American Journal of Mental Retardation, 103,* 19–28.

Centers for Disease Control and Prevention. (1994). *National Health and Nutrition Examination Survey.* Hyattsville, MD: U.S. Department of Health and Human Services, National Center for Health Statistics.

Centers for Disease Control and Prevention. (1998). *Behavioral Risk Factor Surveillance System.* Atlanta, GA: U.S. Department of Health and Human Services, Center for Chronic Disease Prevention and Health Promotion.

Chamie, M. (1994). Can childhood disability be ascertained simply in surveys? *Epidemiology, 5,* 273–275.

Christian, L., & Poling, A. (1997). Drug abuse in people with mental retardation: A review. *American Journal on Mental Retardation, 102,* 126–136.

Computer Matching and Privacy Protection Act of 1988, PL 100-503, 5 U.S.C. §§ 552a *et seq.*

Coulter, D.L. (1992). An ecology of prevention for the future. *Mental Retardation, 30,* 363–369.

Dorn, T.A., & Prout, H.T. (1993). Service delivery patterns for adults with mild mental retardation at community mental health centers. *Mental Retardation, 31,* 292–296.

Dupont, A. (1989). 140 years of Danish studies on the prevalence of mental retardation. *Acta Psychiatrica Scandanavica, 79,* 105–112.

Education for All Handicapped Children Act of 1975, PL 94–142, 20 U.S.C. §§ 1400 *et seq.*

Electronic Freedom of Information Act of 1996, PL 104-231, 5 U.S.C. §§ 552 *et seq.*

Eyman, R.K., Grossman, H.J., Tarjan, G., & Miller, C.R. (1987). Life expectancy and mental retardation: A longitudinal study in a state residential facility. *Monographs of the American Association on Mental Deficiency, No. 7.* Washington, DC: American Association on Mental Retardation.

Fox, R. & Rotatori, A.F. (1982). Prevalence of obesity among mentally retarded adults. *American Journal on Mental Retardation, 87,* 228–230.

Goddard, H.H. (1912). *The Kallikak family.* New York: MacMillan.

Grossman, H.J. (Ed.). (1983). *Classification in mental retardation.* Washington, DC: American Association on Mental Retardation.

Gruenberg, E.M. (1964). Epidemiology. In H.A. Stevens & R. Heber (Eds.), *Mental retardation: A review of research* (pp. 259–306). Chicago: University of Chicago Press.

Hayden, M.F. (1998). Mortality among people with mental retardation living in the United States: Research review and policy application. *Mental Retardation, 36,* 345–359.

Hayden, M.F., & DePaepe, P. (1994). Waiting for community services: The impact on persons with mental retardation and other developmental disabilities. In M.F. Hayden & B.H. Abery (Eds.), *Challenges for a service system in transition: Ensuring quality community experiences for persons with developmental disabilities* (pp. 173–206). Baltimore: Paul H. Brookes Publishing Co.

Health Insurance Portability and Accountability Act of 1996, PL 104-191, 42 U.S.C. §§ 201 *et seq.*

Heber, R.F. (1970). *Epidemiology of mental retardation.* Springfield, IL: Charles C. Thomas.

Individuals with Disabilities Education Act (IDEA) of 1990 (PL 101-476), 20 U.S.C. §§ 1400 *et seq.*

Kapell, D., Nightengale, B., Rodrigues, A., Lee, J.H., Zigman, W.B., & Schupf, N. (1998). Prevalence of chronic medical conditions in adults with mental retardation: Comparison with the general population. *Mental Retardation, 36,* 269–279.

Kelly, L.E., Rimmer, J.H., & Ness, R.A. (1986). Obesity levels in institutionalized mentally retarded adults. *Adapted Physical Activity Quarterly, 3,* 167–176.

Kiely, M. (1987). The prevalence of mental retardation. *Epidemiologic Reviews, 9,* 194–218.

Koegel, P., & Edgerton, R.B. (1982). Labeling and the perception of handicap among black mildly mentally retarded adults. *American Journal on Mental Deficiency, 87,* 266–276.

Koegel, P., & Edgerton, R.B. (1984). Black "six-hour retarded children" as young adults. In R.B. Edgerton (Ed.), *Lives in process: Mildly retarded adults in a large city* (Monographs of the American Association on Mental Retardation, No. 6, pp. 145–171). Washington, DC: American Association on Mental Retardation.

Luckasson, R., Coulter, D.L., Polloway, E.A., Reiss, S., Schalock, R.L., Snell, M.E., Spitalnik, D.M., & Stark, J. (1992). *Mental retardation: Definition, classification, and system of supports* (9th ed.). Washington, DC: American Association on Mental Retardation.

MacMillan, D.L. (1982). *Mental retardation in school and society.* Boston: Little, Brown.

MacMillan, D.L., Gresham, F.M., & Siperstein, G.N. (1993). Conceptual and psychometric concerns about the 1992 AAMR definition of mental retardation. *American Journal on Mental Retardation, 98,* 325–335.

Marge, M. (1988). Health promotion for people with disabilities: Moving beyond rehabilitation. *American Journal of Health Promotion, 2,* 29–44.

Massey, P.S., & McDermott, S. (1996). State-specific rates of mental retardation— United States, 1993. *Morbidity and Mortality Weekly Report, 45,* 61–65.

McConaughy, E.K., & Salzburg, C.L. (1988). Physical fitness of mentally retarded individuals. In N.W. Bray (Ed.), *International review of research in mental retardation* (pp. 227–258). New York: Academic Press.

Pack, R.P., Wallander, J.L., & Browne, D. (1998). Health risk behaviors of African American adolescents with mild mental retardation. *American Journal on Mental Retardation, 102,* 409–420.

Pennsylvania Association for Retarded Children v. Commonwealth of Pennsylvania. 334 F. Supp. 1257 (1971).

Pitetti, K.H., & Campbell, K.D. (1991). Mentally retarded individuals: A population at risk? *Medicine and Science in Sports and Exercise, 23,* 586–593.

Pitetti, K.H., Jackson, J.A., Stubbs, N.B., Campbell, K.D., & Saraswathy, S.B. (1989). Fitness levels of adult Special Olympic participants. *Adapted Physical Activity Quarterly, 6,* 354–370.

Pitkin, W.B. (1928). *Twilight of the American mind.* New York: Simon & Schuster.

Pope, A.M. (1992). Preventing secondary conditions. *Mental Retardation, 30,* 347–354.

Privacy Act of 1974, PL 93-579, 5 U.S.C. §§ 552a *et seq.*

Reid, G., Montgomery, D.L., & Seidl, C. (1985). Performance of mentally retarded adults on the Canadian Standardized Test of Fitness. *Canadian Journal of Public Health, 76,* 187–190.

Reiss, S. (1994). Issues in defining mental retardation. *American Journal on Mental Retardation, 99,* 1–7.

Richardson, S.A., & Koller, H. (1996). *Twenty-two years: Causes and consequences of mental retardation.* Cambridge, MA: Harvard University Press.

Richardson, S.A., Katz, M., & Koller, H. (1993). Patterns of leisure activities of young adults with mild mental retardation. *American Journal on Mental Retardation, 97,* 431–442.

Rimmer, J.H. (1994). *Fitness and rehabilitation programs for special populations.* Madison, WI: Brown & Benchmark.

Rimmer, J.H., Braddock, D., & Fujiura, G. (1993). Prevalence of obesity in adults with mental retardation: Implications for health promotion and disease prevention. *Mental Retardation, 31,* 105–110.

Rioux, M.H. (1997). Disability: The place of judgment in a world of fact. *Journal of Intellectual Disability Research, 41,* 102–111.

Social Security Administration. (1994). Disability evaluation under Social Security Publication No. SSA64-039. Washington, DC: U.S. Department of Health and Human Services.

Stein, Z., Durkin, M., & Belmont, L. (1986). "Serious" mental retardation in developing countries: An epidemiologic approach. *Annals of the New York Academy of Sciences, 477,* 8–21. (1986).

Tarlov, A.M., & Pope, A.R. (1991). *Disability in America.* Washington, DC: National Academy Press.

U.S. Department of Education. (1997). *To assure the free appropriate public education of all children with disabilities.* Nineteenth Annual Report to Congress on the Implementation of the Individuals with Disabilities Act. Washington, DC: Author.

U.S. Department of Health and Human Services. (1997). *Developing objectives for Healthy People 2010.* Washington, DC: Office of Disease Prevention and Health Promotion.

U.S. Department of Health and Human Services. (2000a). *Healthy people 2010* (Conference Edition, Vols. 1 & 2). Washington, DC: Author.

U.S. Department of Health and Human Services. (2000b). *Healthy People 2010: Understanding and improving health* (2nd ed.). Washington, DC: U.S. Government Printing Office.

World Health Organization. (1980). *International classification of impairments, disabilities, and handicaps.* Geneva: Author.

World Health Organization. (2000). *ICIDH-2: International classification of functioning, disability, and health: Prefinal draft.* Geneva: Author.

Wyatt v. Stickney, 325 F. Supp. 781 (M.D. Ala. 1971), enforced in 334 F. Supp. 1341 (1971); 344 F. Supp. 387 (1972); Wyatt v. Aderholt, 503 F. 2d. 1305 (5th Cir. 1974).

Appendix
Disability-Specific and Related Objectives of Healthy People 2010

Vincent A. Campbell and Holly J. Fedeyko

Chapter 6 Goal and Objectives for Disability and Secondary Conditions

Goal: Promote the health of people with disabilities, prevent secondary conditions, and eliminate disparities between people with and without disabilities in the U.S. population.

Disability-Specific Objectives and Data Sources:

1   Include in the core of all relevant Healthy People 2010 surveillance instruments a standardized set of questions that identify "people with disabilities."
    Data source: CDC, National Center for Environmental Health will report on this objective.

2   Reduce the proportion of children and adolescents with disabilities who are reported to be sad, unhappy, or depressed.
    Data source: National Health Interview Survey (NHIS)—CDC, National Center for Health Statistics.

3   Reduce the proportion of adults with disabilities who report feelings such as sadness, unhappiness, or depression that prevent then from being active.
    Data source: National Health Interview Survey National Health Interview Survey (NHIS)—CDC, National Center for Health Statistics.

4   Increase the proportion of adults with disabilities who participate in social activities.
    Data source: National Health Interview Survey (NHIS)—CDC, National Center for Health Statistics.

This appendix is reprinted from U.S. Department of Health and Human Services. (2000). *Healthy People 2010: Understanding and improving health* (2nd ed.). Washington, DC: Author.

5   Increase the proportion of adults with disabilities reporting sufficient emotional support.
    Data source: Behavioral Risk Factor Surveillance System (BRFSS)—CDC, National Center for Chronic Disease Prevention and Health Promotion.

6   Increase the proportion of adults with disabilities reporting satisfaction with life.
    Data source: Behavioral Risk Factor Surveillance System (BRFSS)—CDC, National Center for Chronic Disease Prevention and Health Promotion.

7   Reduce the number of people with disabilities in congregate care facilities, consistent with permanency planning principles.
    Data source: Survey of Residential Facilities, University of Minnesota (data for population groups currently are not collected).

8   Eliminate disparities in employment rates between working-aged adults with and without disabilities.
    Data source: Survey of Income and Program Participation (SIPP), U.S. Department of Commerce, Bureau of the Census.

9   Increase the proportion of children and youth with disabilities who spend at least 80% of their time in general education programs.
    Data source: Data Analysis System (DANS), U.S. Department of Education, Office of Special Education (data for population groups currently are not analyzed).

10 Increase the proportion of health and wellness and treatment programs and facilities that provide full access for people with disabilities.
    Potential data source: National Independent Living Centers Network

11 Reduce the proportion of people with disabilities who report not having the assistive devices and technology needed.
    Potential data source: National Health Interview Survey (NHIS)—CDC, National Center for Health Statistics.

12 Reduce the proportion of people with disabilities reporting environmental barriers to participation in home, school, work, or community activities.
    Potential data source: Behavioral Risk Factor Surveillance System (BRFSS)—CDC, National Center for Chronic Disease Prevention and Health Promotion.

13 Increase the number of tribes, states, and the District of Columbia that have public health surveillance and health promotion programs for people with disabilities and caregivers.
    Data sources: Tribal, state, and District of Columbia reports; Office on Disability and Health, CDC.

Related Objectives From Other Focus Areas in HP2010

1[a] Access to Quality Health Services

1[b] People with health insurance
4 Source of ongoing care
5 Usual primary care provider
6 Difficulties or delays in obtaining health care
16 Pressure ulcers among nursing home residents

2 Arthritis, Osteoporosis, and Chronic Back Conditions

3 Personal care limitations
5 Employment rates
8 Arthritis education
11 Activity limitations due to chronic back conditions

3 Cancer

9 Sun exposure
11 Pap tests
12 Colorectal cancer screening
13 Mammograms

4 Chronic Kidney Disease

2 Cardiovascular disease deaths in persons with chronic kidney disease
7 Kidney failure due to diabetes

5 Diabetes

1 Diabetes education
2 Prevent diabetes
3 Reduce diabetes
4 Diagnosis of diabetes
9 Foot ulcers
10 Lower extremity amputations

7 Educational and Community-Based Programs

1 High school completion
3 Health-risk behavior information for college and university students
6 Participation in employer-sponsored health promotion activities
11 Culturally appropriate community health promotion programs
12 Older adult participation in community health promotion activities

9 Family Planning

2 Birth spacing
4 Contraceptive failure
7 Adolescent pregnancy

---

[a]These numbers correspond to chapter numbers in *Healthy People 2010*.
[b]These numbers correspond to objectives within the chapters of *Health People 2010*.

12   Heart Disease and Stroke

   1   Coronary heart disease (CHD) deaths
   7   Stroke deaths
   9   High blood pressure
  10 High blood pressure control
  11 Action to help control blood pressure
  12 Blood pressure monitoring
  13 Mean total cholesterol levels
  14 High blood cholesterol levels
  15 Blood cholesterol screening

14   Immunization and Infectious Diseases

  22 Universally recommended vaccination among children aged 19 to 35 months
  24 Fully immunized children aged 19 to 35 months
  26 State/community population-based immunization registries for children
  29 Flu and pneumococcal vaccination of high-risk adults

16   Maternal, Infant, and Child Health

   1   Fetal and infant deaths
   2   Child deaths
   3   Adolescent and young adult deaths
   4   Maternal deaths
   6   Prenatal care
   9   Cesarean deliveries
  10 Low birth weight and very low birth weight
  11 Preterm birth
  13 Infants put to sleep on their backs
  16 Optimum folic acid
  17 Prenatal substance exposure
  19 Breastfeeding
  21 Sepsis among infants with sickle cell disease
  22 Medical homes for children with special health care needs
  23 Service systems for children with special health care needs

17   Medical Product Safety

   3   Provider review of medications taken by patients

18   Mental Health and Mental Disorders

   4   Employment of persons with serious mental illness
   9   Treatment for adults with mental disorders

19   Nutrition and Overweight

   1   Healthy weight in adults

   2   Obesity in adults
   3   Overweight or obesity in children and adolescents
   4   Growth retardation in children
   5   Fruit intake
   6   Vegetable intake
   7   Grain product intake
   8   Saturated fat intake
   9   Total fat intake
  10   Sodium intake
  11   Calcium intake
  12   Iron deficiency in young children and in females of childbearing age
  13   Anemia in low-income pregnant females
  17   Nutrition counseling for medical conditions
  18   Food security

20 Occupational Safety and Health
   1   Work-related injury deaths

21 Oral Health
   1   Dental caries experience
   2   Untreated dental decay
   3   No permanent tooth loss
   4   Complete tooth loss
   5   Periodontal disease
   6   Early detection of oral and pharyngeal cancer
   8   Dental sealants
  10   Use of the oral health care system
  15   Referral for cleft lip or palate
  16   Oral and craniofacial stats-based surveillance system

22 Physical Activity and Fitness
   1   No leisure-time physical activity
   2   Moderate physical activity
   3   Vigorous physical activity
   4   Muscular strength and endurance
   5   Flexibility

23 Public Health Infrastructure
   4   Data for all population groups
   5   Data for Leading Health Indicators, Health Status Indicators, and Priority Data Needs at Tribal, State, and local levels
   6   National tracking of Healthy People 2010 objectives

24 Respiratory Diseases
   1   Deaths from asthma

2   Hospitalizations for asthma
3   Hospital emergency department visits for asthma
4   Activity limitations
5   School or work days missed
6   Patient education
7   Appropriate asthma care
8   Surveillance systems
9   Activity limitations due to chronic lung and breathing problems
10 Deaths from chronic obstructive pulmonary disease (COPD)

27 Tobacco Use

1   Adult tobacco use
5   Smoking cessation by adults
6   Smoking cessation during pregnancy

28 Vision and Hearing

4   Impairment in children and adolescents
10 Vision rehabilitation services and devices
12 Otitis media
13 Rehabilitation hearing impairment

V

Familial, Psychological,
and Spiritual Well-Being

Family Life

Experiences of People with Mild Cognitive Limitations

Alexander J. Tymchuk

The majority of individuals with mild cognitive limitations live in poverty because they are either unemployed or employed in low-paying jobs. Families living in poverty today are faced with the serious challenge of trying to live satisfactory lives while coping with the consequences of living in a changing society over which they have little control. Families in which one or both parents have mild cognitive limitations[1] are faced with even greater challenges. The challenges for these families have changed significantly since the 1980s—in many respects for the worse. Service providers, researchers, and policy makers also have been faced with significant and changing challenges in their struggle to help ensure an evenness in supports for these families.

This chapter discusses some of the challenges faced by families in which one or both parents have mild cognitive limitations and by service providers, researchers, and policy makers. The ways in which some of these challenges have been addressed and the degree to which they have met with success also are discussed. Recommendations regarding needed research as well as programmatic and policy initiatives are given.

OLD CHALLENGES REMAIN

Some of the old challenges faced by individuals with mild cognitive limitations as they moved from institutions to the community or from school to independence in the mid-1970s remain today (Gan, Tymchuk, & Nishihara, 1977; Lorber, 1974; Tymchuk, 1971)[2]. Although they invariably were ill-prepared for

---

[1]See Chapter 2. The term *mild cognitive limitations* is used to describe individuals who may have fulfilled criteria for a diagnosis of mild mental retardation at some time in their lives, typically during their school years. It also is used for those individuals who no longer fulfill existing criteria as well as those who fell outside the diagnostic criteria but nonetheless displayed virtually the same learning characteristics and living circumstances and for communities of individuals with a diagnosis.

[2]Not so long ago the idea of people diagnosed as having mild mental retardation participating in interpersonal relationships, expressing their sexuality, marrying, bearing children, and parenting

community life, people with mild cognitive limitations had to participate in the community using available resources to be able to care for themselves and for their children. For those individuals who had been institutionalized, this meant learning how to function within a society from which they had been removed or whose members really did not know how to intereact with or help them once they exited schools (Edgerton, 1967, 1984). More specifically, for these individuals, community participation meant finding friends, building relationships, and, most of all, ensuring their own health and livelihoods over all of the stages of their lives. To perform these tasks, these individuals had to communicate with physicians, their children's teachers, support personnel, and, perhaps, child protective agencies, courts, and police officers. They had to read, comprehend, and be able to follow employment, rental, social security, welfare, bank, and other applications and information. They had to do the same with service and contract guidelines and product labels, instructions, and warnings and liabilities; and they had to be able to calculate budgets, making decisions gradually while attempting to build a lifetime of experience. In the absence of knowledge regarding what society expected of them, suitable preparation and practice to meet those expectations, and suitable services and supports, the challenges of maintaining a marital or other relationship, maintaining a household, caring for oneself while caring for a child, working, and all of the other things a family and its members do, while perhaps being the target of increased scrutiny, were overwhelming (Tymchuk & Andron, 1988, 1990, 1992). Some families managed; none flourished (Feldman, 1994; Keltner, 1994).

At any given time across the nation, supports and services for family life have been sparse and uneven, and the legacies of this past still remain (Tymchuk, 1990, 1998a). Questions regarding the competency of parents with mild cognitive limitations continue (Campion, 1995; Hayman, 1990).

NEW CHALLENGES

During the 1990s, substantial shifts within society presented new challenges to low-income families (Miringoff, Miringoff, & Opdycke, 1996). Continuing federal devolution and changes in private enterprise associated with an eco-

---

children to their own independence was anathema to some (e.g., Andron & Sturm, 1973; Brantlinger, 1992). In fact involuntary and forced sterilization of people *who appeared to* fulfill the existing criteria of mental retardation was practiced until recently and even still may be in some jurisdictions *sub rosa* (e.g., Brady & Grover, 1997; Broberg & Roll-Hansen, 1996; The National Film Board of Canada, 1996). Actually being instructed in how to form and maintain rewarding relationships rarely was considered. Women (and men) who were never instructed in relationships including effective decision making, in partner safety, or in self-protection but yet who were in the community may have been the unwitting victims of the absence of such instruction. In fact the current silence on issues of violence against women with mild cognitive limitations probably is related to this earlier silence (e.g., Browne, 1993; Cruz, Price-Williams, & Andron, 1988; Hickson, Golden, Khemka, Urv, & Yamusah, 1998; Stromsness, 1993). Such silence continues to raise serious ethical issues.

nomic downturn and an evolving political landscape have translated directly into disruption, reduction, and significant changes in health care, education, and social and other services for low-income families (Children's Defense Fund, 1997; The California Wellness Foundation, 1996). Federal devolution also has seriously disrupted and reduced opportunities for research in these areas (e.g., Gardner & Wilcox, 1993). Cumulatively, families have been the victims of an intergenerational, downward spiraling of services and opportunities, recent improvements notwithstanding (Children's Defense Fund, 1997).

Within health care, for example, the shift to managed health care and the reduction in public health expenditures have had a dramatic, probably permanent, deleterious impact upon the health status of this generation of low-income families. And while the impact of these changes were at least considered for individuals with a diagnosis of mental retardation or other developmental disability, no considerations were made for families headed by a person with such a diagnosis (Kastner, Walsh, & Criscione, 1997; Pulcini & Howard, 1997). Similarly, no consideration was given to the potential impact of these changes on parents who once fulfilled the criteria for a diagnosis but no longer do or on parents who fell just outside the criteria for a diagnosis and, consequently, were not considered for categorical services but had needs similar to families who met the criteria. In public health, a system in which many people in poverty, including recent immigrants, turned for basic health care, not only was the amount of care significantly reduced, but also the type of care was severely limited (e.g., Breslow, 1997; Jorgensen, 1994).

In response to economic and political shifts, the resultant realignments, and subsequent increases in staff demoralization and turnover, even disability-specific services ceased or became more limited and then were provided only to individuals fulfilling categorical definitions. Already limited crossover services, such as mental health for children or for adults with a history of mental retardation, became even more restrictive. The extent and consequences of untreated depression, stress, and hopelessness can only be assumed. Most significantly, because governmental devolution was accompanied by reduced funding levels and a major time lag between termination of previous services and full establishment of new replacement services, the amount and quality of service was diminished (DiSimone, 1996). The health status of families deteriorated as a result of a lack of knowledge of these new initiatives (e.g., welfare reform) or services and their usage rules (Zambrana & Dorrington, 1998). While the process of familiarizing families and advocates with the new rules continues, services and rules continue to change, thereby adding to the already significant stresses experienced by these families (Geen, Zimmerman, Douglas, Zedlewski, & Waters, 1997).

The service gaps created by governmental devolution directly resulted in significant increases in the numbers of children living in poverty (Children's Defense Fund, 1997), in reported cases of child maltreatment (National Research Council, 1993; Sedlak & Broadhurst, 1996), in reports of domestic violence, in the numbers of families who were unserved or underserved by health and other social services, and in lowered health status of people living in poverty (Miringoff et al., 1996). These service gaps also are related to other events adversely affecting families living in poverty, some of which we believe have had an even greater adverse effect on parents with mild cognitive limitations. Adverse effects include continuing increases in homelessness, residential mobility, and deteriorating living circumstances (e.g., living in motel rooms, residential or group homes sometimes separating families); increased substance abuse; continuing high rates of adolescent and out-of-marriage pregnancy (Kirby, 1997); increased dropout rates from school (U.S. Department of Education, 1997); lowered overall educational attainment; and increased victimization. Despite these adverse effects, service fragmentation continues.

In the absence of accurate epidemiological data, it is estimated that parents with mild cognitive limitations, invariably women, and their families have suffered disproportionately (Edgerton, 1999). Both parents and their children have continued to be at heightened risk for impaired health status and health outcomes due to preventable diseases and disorders, unintentional home or community injuries, and injuries from violence (Tymchuk, 1999). Heightened risk status places these families increasingly under the scrutiny of child protective services and other agencies (Glaun & Brown, 1999; Taylor et al., 1991; Tymchuk, 1996). As a result, families not only are faced with the demands of life and their child's development but also are faced with coping with the intensity of outside scrutiny. This multiple risk status continues lifelong and places the family at substantial risk for partial or complete disintegration. Services are ill-prepared to address family needs, often providing brief, stop-gap, unvalidated measures (Carter, 1996). All of these factors have placed serious strains on families and their supports who continue to struggle to work within the evolving systems (Kagan & Pritchard, 1996).

At the same time, these families are less likely to be aware of, participate in, and enjoy activities that enhance their well-being and satisfaction with life and that might help to mitigate difficulties to inoculate them against further poor health. Unlike the members of many other groups who have been affected similarly, families in which one or both parents have mild cognitive limitations also seldom participate in political self-advocacy or have someone lobby on their behalf. These families are in fact "hidden."

SOCIAL CONTEXTUAL DEVELOPMENTS FACILITATING SERVICE DEVELOPMENT

There have been several social contextual developments that could be seen as potentially helpful to parents with mild cognitive limitations and their families. However, in order for families to benefit, they must be included and their needs must be addressed within each of these developments. In addition, they must be aware of and be able to utilize the available services. Social contextual developments have included the continuing implementation of the Americans with Disabilities Act (ADA) of 1990 (PL 101-336); the establishment of private foundations or other organizations developed especially to address the issues of people in poverty[3]; the re-direction of existing foundations or private organizations to target the service gaps caused by federal devolution[4]; and increased cooperation between federal agencies to move more quickly in addressing societal needs in order to avoid duplication of effort and to increase "institutional" memory, thus allowing for progressive and cumulative developments. In addition, the private and public sectors have begun to attempt to coordinate efforts. However, it does not appear that the needs of parents with mild cognitive limitations and their families have been addressed in any of these potentially facilitating developments.

Although other developments, such as welfare reform, continue, it is unclear to what extent, if any, the needs of parents with mild cognitive limitations and their families have been addressed within these developments (DiSimone, 1996; Geen et al., 1997). In the absence of attention to these needs, families continue to be in jeopardy (e.g., what happens when the Temporary Aid to Needy Families [TANF] benefits cease?).

Within the larger context of health care, a factor that has significant potential in the development of an effective system of health care delivery for all people has been the belated move from a system that has been solely ameliorative or palliative in nature to one that has included a focus upon increased self-health care responsibility and an emphasis on prevention and well-being (U.S. Department of Health and Human Services, 1990). However, Healthy People 2000, and now 2010, as these initiatives are termed, does not provide for ways in which parents, or, for that matter, individuals who are not parents who have limited education; limited reading, conceptual, or numeracy abilities; or individualized learning needs can achieve self-health care responsibility or practice prevention and wellness strategies (U.S. Department of Health and Human Services, 1995; 2000; Weissbourd, Gullota, Hampton, Ryan, & Adams, 1997). It also is unclear to what extent managed health care has adopted and implemented a similar philosophy (McManus & Fox, 1995). Further, because it is unlikely that parents with mild cognitive limitations have health insurance or belong to a managed care plan and because they appear to rely upon limited public health, emergency rooms, and publicly funded shelters or clinics for basic health care, it is unlikely that they will be provided with self-health care, prevention, and well-being education. Although Healthy Families, a division of

---

[3]In health care a number of foundations have been formed as a result of managed health care plans being allowed to move from their original nonprofit status to a for-profit company.

[4]There has been increasing cooperation of all foundations to pool resources in order to thoughtfully mitigate the adverse consequences of the changing role of governments upon families in poverty. However, despite these intentions, the total funds available amount only to a fraction of what had been available previously. Also, there has been a significant time lag between governmental devolution and new foundation support.

Healthy People, may be one vehicle through which prevention can occur, it has just begun to provide primary care for low-income families. As recent as 1998, the threat of not providing health care or other services for immigrants (documented or undocumented) has introduced a continuing cloud of fear for these families, thereby reducing the potential impacts of such initiatives. Such fears of government among people of low socioeconomic and minority status have appeared in part to have contributed to their unwillingness to participate in other public health initiatives (e.g., HIV/AIDS education).

Healthy People 2010 also does not consider preparing people to assume the more common aspects of self-health care. These aspects include taking a temperature and understanding the relationship of temperature to normal or abnormal health; recognizing symptoms of illness in oneself or in one's children early enough in the disease process to prevent exacerbation of symptoms, which has been shown to reduce the higher costs associated with treatment of more serious illnesses; learning how to use everyday products such as prescription or over-the-counter medications, the misuse of which can seriously injure an individual; or using and maintaining home precautionary measures such as electrical outlet covers, fire extinguishers, or smoke detectors. The absence of such preparatory normative self-health care education presumes that parents will obtain the requisite knowledge and skills and will adapt to the changing circumstances over the child's development on their own and/or with available resources. In this situation only parents with higher formal education attainment and with adequate finances, supports, and other resources are likely to be able to obtain such self-health care knowledge or to be able to make changes as they change residences and as their children develop. However, the absence of self-health care education places parents with lowered educational attainment or supports, such as those with mild cognitive limitations, and their families at a significant disadvantage and risk. Empirical studies of parents with or without mild cognitive limitations living in poverty have demonstrated that parents have limited self- and child-preparatory health care or injury and disease prevention knowledge and few if any supports and opportunities to obtain assistance (e.g., Tymchuk, 1992a, 1994c).

Clearly, an anticipatory step to ensuring adequate health of all families must begin with a determination of their knowledge and skills and be followed by the provision of preparatory normative self-health care education if needed. Much, if not all of this, can be successfully achieved during the school years.

WHAT WE KNOW

Although literature exists regarding parents with a history of mental retardation[5], it has only been since the 1980s that a growing research base has been

---

[5]These parents include those who have a current diagnosis of mental retardation; those who no longer fulfill the criteria but who once did (usually during their school years); and those who

developed (e.g., Feldman, 1994; Tymchuk, 1990; Tymchuk, Andron, & Unger, 1987; Tymchuk & Feldman, 1991). Thus, care must be taken in examining reported findings. Because of the absence of theoretical and practical infrastructures suitable for use in clinical applications or in empirical studies involving parents with a history of mental retardation, part of this empirical work has involved the establishment of theoretical perspectives within which empirical development of suitable assessment instruments, curricula, and instructional and parent-use materials has occurred (e.g., American Red Cross, 1989; Feldman, 1998; Tymchuk, 1990, 1992b, 1998b; Tymchuk, Andron, Bavolek, Quattrociocchi, & Henderson, 1990; Tymchuk, Hamada, Andron, & Anderson, 1990a; Tymchuk, Lang, Dolyniuk, Berney-Ficklin, & Spitz, 1999). These instruments, curricula, and materials then were used within clinical support programs. Some development of effective delivery procedures and processes across service sectors also has occurred (Feldman, 1998; Keltner & Tymchuk, 1992; Tymchuk, 1998a, 1998b; Tymchuk, 1999). As examples of this development, Figures 13.1 and 13.2 display in black and white two of the six empirically developed color illustrations used to assist young parents in the identification of dangers in the home associated with family injury and in the development of suitable precautions (Tymchuk, Lang, Lieberman, & Koo, in press).

Other research has demonstrated that when services take into account the living circumstances of the parents and the parental learning needs, health and safety risk status can be reduced and well-being can be promoted for both parents and children (Feldman, 1994; Llewellyn, 1996; Tymchuk, 1990, 1992a; Tymchuk & Feldman, 1991). Mother–child interaction can be facilitated with resultant positive child outcomes (Feldman, Case, Rincover, Towns, & Betel, 1989; Keltner, Wise, & Taylor, 1999; Tymchuk & Andron, 1992). Parents, too, may feel more comfortable in their parenting roles. Such efforts can be preparatory, preventive, and responsive.[6] Predictors of positive and negative family

---

never fulfilled criteria for a diagnosis of mental retardation but who demonstrated lowered cognitive abilities accompanied by lowered functional abilities. Some may have fulfilled criteria for other diagnoses such as learning disabilities or behavioral disorders. They also may have had comorbid conditions.

[6]*Preparatory* refers to the development of knowledge and skills in order to prepare for parenting. An example of preparation is the development of knowledge and skills related to the area of self-health care that a student receives during school years which then can be applied to child-health care upon becoming a parent. Such knowledge and skills can include the identification and usage of suitable supports in order to achieve competence in any functional area. *Preventive* refers to the development of knowledge and skills related to an area of life in which there often are difficulties in order to decrease the probability of their occurrence. Examples include the prevention of injuries within the home, victimization, substance abuse, child abuse, unwanted pregnancy, dropping out of school, stress, depression, suicide, community violence, etc. *Responsive* refers to the provision of a service in response to a specific need. It often refers to health care provision in response to an identified health need (perhaps within emergent care), but also can refer to the provision of education that is adapted to the individual's learning preferences in area. *Health promotion* refers to activities that seek to foster both healthy living as well as a healthy life in progressive and cumulative fashion. *Health* usually refers both to psychological as well as physical health and can include such concepts as promotion of attributes related to decision making, planning, re-

Figure 13.1.   Empirically developed home illustration for the kitchen.

outcomes also have been identified (Tymchuk, 1992a; Tymchuk & Keltner, 1991). This work has demonstrated that in the absence of suitable supports, positive outcomes may be limited.

However, because difficulties continue regarding the adequacy of information concerning parents with mental retardation, addressing the needs of this population during this "new federalism" is problematic (Geen et al., 1997; Tymchuk, 1990, 1999). The lack of attention to individuals with mild cognitive limitations, including the continued unavailability of funding, has left a serious and widening knowledge gap. Difficulties include a lack of continuous longitudinal epidemiological data regarding this population as they move from high school through adult life[7] within key service sectors (e.g., in public or private health care; within social services, including child protection; within the courts; within ancillary services, including child care or housing). Another major difficulty has been the need to conceptualize family life and parenting as they relate to

---

siliency, hardiness, and coping. Well-being refers to the general satisfaction an individual has with life or in this case, parenting. It can be related to all aspects of life including vocation and careers, relationships, spirituality, health status, citizenship, and so forth.

[7]While the National Longitudinal Study of Youth (*youth* is defined as those between the ages of 15 and 20 between 1979 and 1983 who were in secondary school) did not examine family life (or crimes, victimization, health care, or violence) (Wagner & Blackorby, 1996), Gene Edgar (Levine & Edgar, 1994) inserted a parenting variable in a second study of postschool outcomes of students in special education.

Figure 13.2.   Empirically developed home illustration for the living room.

the circumstances of parents with mild cognitive limitations who live in poverty, have limited supports, and have limited educational or other experiences.

Families Are Involved with Many Service Sectors

Evidence shows that families are involved with many service sectors. This involvement can either be voluntary or involuntary (e.g., being required to attend an infant class in order to obtain another service or to maintain involvement with a child). Although specific agencies within service sectors may change as a child develops or as the family moves through life, the sectors remain the same. These sectors include disabilities; public and perhaps private health care; education (including early intervention when the child is young); housing; welfare; vocational, mental health, and other social services, as well as child and adult protective services; and the juvenile and adult court systems. Because each of these service sectors focuses on different aspects of family life, with disparate requirements perhaps involving different terminology and processes, they seldom work together in an integrated and cohesive manner for the benefit of a family or its members (England & Cole, 1995). Despite involvement with the same family, ample evidence suggests that agencies in these sectors work at cross-purposes. Sometimes, agencies have an adversarial relationship with families. Outside of the disability sector, few services are prepared to meet the needs of these families; in fact, personnel employed by these services seldom understand the families' needs (Blanch, Nicholson, & Purcell, 1994; Tymchuk, 1999). Even within disability services, parents who exhibit emotional or other conditions that require attention may be excluded from receiving services. Further, parents who no longer fulfill criteria for categorical services are left to their own devices. Both groups of families simply "fall through the cracks" of the various service systems. Both the absence of a single broker or service coordinator and the absence of support collaboration and coordination place severe strain on these families (Tymchuk, 1992b). Faced with these demands, they are also unlikely to advocate for themselves (Tymchuk, Llewellyn, & Feldman, 1999).

CHARACTERISTICS, CIRCUMSTANCES, AND ENVIRONMENTS OF PARENTS AND FAMILIES

Despite the variability in descriptions of parents with mild cognitive limitations and their family circumstances, the environments in which they live noticeably have changed for the worse as a result of the past economic downturn. However, there is a clear need for accurate epidemiological data. Families now often are comprised of a woman and her child or children. Although there may be male partners, the woman often bears primary responsibility for the family as well as the sole brunt of questions regarding her competence. As a result, she feels the impact on her identity and confidence as a person, a woman, and a mother (Glaun & Brown, 1999; Pixa-Kettner, 1999; Tymchuk, 1991).

Although examples of assisted housing, alternative residential options, and supported living arrangements exist, these vary across region and often face immutable housing or welfare codes (Wark, Andron, & Tymchuk, 1989). Because experiences from varying sites seldom are shared and built upon, each new court case or new program invariably requires starting from scratch. Whereas referred families once lived a relatively stable life, residing one family to an apartment or home, several families may now live together and may change residences frequently. Women and their children may live in a motel room or reside in a shelter during a transition from one housing situation to another. Many women, especially those who are younger, perhaps minors, live with the families of a male partner. Women with mild cognitive limitations experience more symptoms of depression (Tymchuk, 1994a), stress (Feldman, 1998), and anxiety (Tymchuk, 1991) than do women without mild cognitive limitations. They also have a significantly lowered self-concept (Tymchuk, 1991). A substantial number of women with cognitive limitations also indicate that they have been physically or sexually abused as children and continue to be abused as adults by a partner. These women are often unaware of opportunities to safely report the offender (who may be a relative) or of how to safely extricate themselves from the abusive situation (Cruz et al., 1988). Unfortunately, they also may believe that abuse is typical in many relationships and that they will not be able to change their circumstances so they must put up with the abuse. Unlike the

women in Edgerton's classic study (Edgerton, 1967) who had benefactors looking out for them, during this era of reduced societal supports, women with mild
cognitive limitations may be preyed upon. Mothers with mild cognitive limitations also are at heightened risk for being reported to child protection, in part
based on an *a priori* view of incompetency (Hayman, 1990; Miller, 1994).
Although parental substance use and abuse is prevalent in reports of maltreatment within the United States, it is unclear what the prevalence rate is among
parents with mild cognitive limitations. Furthermore, due to an absence of needed
supports, adequacy of child care may be seen as neglectful, and instances of
abuse are mostly perpetrated by the male partner of the mother—not by the
mother herself (Tymchuk & Andron, 1990). This is a significantly unstudied
area.

Educational Characteristics

The educational histories of parents with mild cognitive limitations were not reported in earlier studies; similarly, the actual maternal performances in academic
subjects that have been shown to be related to intervention efficacy, such as reading or other communication skills, were never assessed, even though recent
reports state that most parents with mild cognitive limitations participated in
special education. This is a salient factor to emphasize as level of education can
directly impinge upon the success or failure of direct-service interventions.

   Students with disabilities are more likely to drop out of school early (U.S.
Department of Education, 1997), and once they have exited school, females are
five times more likely to become a parent within 5 years than are their peers
without disabilities (Levine & Edgar, 1994). Students with disabilities also exit
school performing at several grade levels below expectations; students with
mild cognitive limitations typically are four to six grades behind their peers
without mental retardation. Recent data show that young or expectant referred
parents are four to eight grades below age expectations in reading recognition
and comprehension (Tymchuk, Groen, & Dolyniuk, 2000). Functionally, they
also are unable to read and/or comprehend words that are commonly used by
parents to ensure the health and safety of their children. For example, more than
50% of these individuals are unable to read words such as *corrosive* or to know
what *corrosive* means.

   Although these data demonstrate the importance of ensuring that all parents can read and comprehend words associated with prescription and over-the-
counter medications or with other high-risk household products, these findings
have even greater significance when mothers with mild cognitive limitations
are older than age 25. In comparison to mothers who were minors (younger
than age 18) and to mothers who were young adults (18–25), mothers older
than age 25 demonstrated significantly lower scores on both academic tests and
on functional reading recognition and comprehension tests. These data are dis-

played in Figure 13.3. Whereas the average reading recognition and comprehension performance for the two younger groups was four grade levels below
age expectations, mothers older than age 25 read and comprehended information at around a fourth-grade average.

Most of the mothers in the study displayed better reading comprehension
than recognition. However, comprehension was improved over recognition due
to information being read to the mother rather than the mother having to read
it herself. Nonetheless, mothers often were unable to read or to comprehend
more complex words or symbols such as *Celsius* and *Fahrenheit* even when
these words were read to them. These parents also had difficulty conceptualizing relationships between external symptoms and internal physiological processes. Effective communication between parents and supports may be limited,
and maternal and child health may suffer (Baker et al., 1997; Koegel & Edgerton, 1984) unless these needs are recognized and adaptations are made (Davis
et al., 1994).

Psychological and Functional Characteristics

Psychologically, mothers with mild cognitive limitations follow limited patterns of decision making (Tymchuk, Yokota, & Rahbar, 1990); however, with
specific interventions, they can learn to be deliberate and effective decision

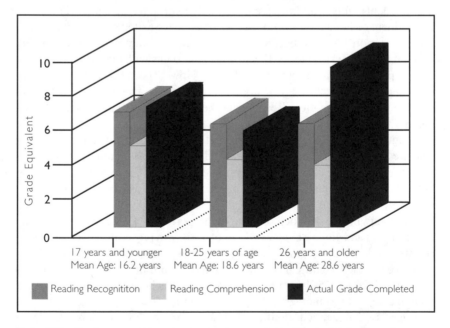

Figure 13.3. Reading recognition and comparison compared with actual grade achieved.

makers (Tymchuk, Andron, & Rahbar, 1988). Other studies have demonstrated that mothers with mild cognitive limitations may not perform well on psychometrically standardized instruments designed to assess functional aspects of child care. These instruments are observational, illustrated, or performance-based (Tymchuk, Lang, et al., 1999; Tymchuk, Lang, et al., in press). However, with adaptation of interventions, performance can be significantly improved and maintained (Tymchuk, Lang, et al., 1999). Improved maternal performance not only translates into improved quality of communication with support personnel but also into increased satisfaction with such tailored services. Clinically, many of these parents show remarkable endurance and resiliency.

Social Supports

Although parents with mild cognitive limitations have been portrayed in the past as having limited supports, supports have become even more limited during the 1990s as all low-income families have struggled (Ford, Tio, & Tymchuk, 1990). Some variability exists among families, however. Llewellyn, McConnell, Cant, and Westbrook (1999) developed a typology of social supports describing mothers who live with their own parents, mothers who live alone with their children, and mothers living with a partner. Although Llewellyn and her colleagues did not examine type of support and parental or family outcomes, other data show a positive relationship between the extent of suitable support and elements of child care adequacy (Feldman, Case, & Sparks, 1992; Tymchuk, 1992b).

Effects of Tailored Educational Interventions

It is now known that educational approaches that are tailored to the educational and learning characteristics of the parents, the living circumstances of the families, the community environments and supports, and the families' culture facilitate family success (Feldman, 1994; Tymchuk & Feldman, 1991; Tymchuk, 1998b). Areas of family life that have been addressed include general infant care (Feldman, 1998); injury prevention through the recognition and remediation of home dangers and the implementation of home precautions (Tymchuk, Hamada, et al., 1990a); preparation for responding to common home emergencies (Tymchuk, Hamada, Andron, & Anderson, 1990b); illness symptom recognition and response; comprehension of child development; promotion of positive child interactions (Feldman et al., 1989; Tymchuk & Andron, 1992; Tymchuk, Andron, & Tymchuk, 1990); and effective decision making (Tymchuk, Andron, & Rahbar, 1988). However, gains may be lost without continued support.

As an example of such tailoring, Figure 13.4 displays several of the 60 empirically developed illustrations portraying critical elements of child care; in these instances, the elements are ear discharge and symptoms of choking (Tymchuk, 1994c, 1998a).

Another example of tailoring is the use of simplified text in large print with illustrations accompanying instructions for the correct use of home safety and health care devices. The association of symbols with words they portray facilitates learning even with mothers who have limited reading recognition skills. Such an approach is encouraging given the primacy of the printed word in health care communication. This work has demonstrated that it is implausible to expect parents with mild cognitive limitations to identify and remediate all home dangers, to purchase and implement home precautions, and then to maintain such diligence in each new residence as they move on their own. However, when actual safety devices are provided and implemented with assistance, parental maintenance with continuing assistance becomes achievable and feasible.

SUPPORT SERVICES FOR FAMILIES

Since the mid-1970s, a number of support services have existed for families in which the parents have mild cognitive limitations. In a report for the President's Committee on Mental Retardation, Tymchuk (1990) traced the history and evolution of those services, outlined the substantial issues faced by those services,

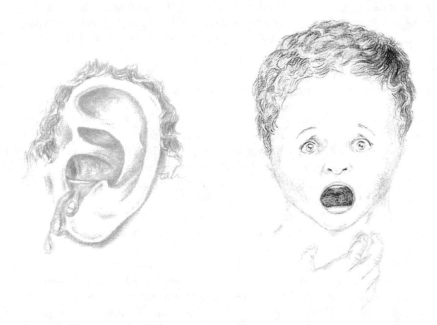

Figure 13.4.   Empirically developed health illustrations.

and presented a number of recommendations. Most often, delimited programs had been established in response to a need within a local community serving a few families. Sometimes, they were established in response to court orders. Many of these services have been short-lived, often because of the demands placed upon service providers who had to work within multiple sectors in order to achieve some success. Several programs have longevity. However, interest in parents with mild cognitive limitations continues to be sporadic.

Although there has been some movement toward addressing the needs of these families in some locales since 1990, all of the issues outlined in this chapter remain. Unfortunately, many of the issues were exacerbated during the economic downturn of the 1990s and continue despite general economic improvements. Regardless, last-resort safety nets have not and do not exist for these families, making them vulnerable to the consequences of new shifts in social policy.

The most significant challenge that service providers face continues to be ensuring stability for families that is relatively immune to economic or political events. Clearly, in order to achieve such stability, a successful integration of services is needed so that families in which the parents have mild cognitive limitations can receive services that are matched to their needs. Integration must be accompanied by increased opportunities for self-reliance and maintenance of family integrity.

Such integration, however, must recognize the changing social systems and the impact these changes have had on families. Specifically, processes must be developed to facilitate services to families in each of the sectors with which they are involved. In order to achieve these goals, however, there must be a dedicated, collaborative, and longitudinal effort. Such efforts have been unsuccessful with other types of families (Kagan & Pritchard, 1996).

MOVING TOWARD SUCCESSFUL INTEGRATION

Based on experience and in response to wider community interests regarding parents with mild cognitive limitations, a planning process was undertaken between 1990 and 1992 in Sacramento and Los Angeles, California. Health care, education, social services, and child protective and legal agencies involved with families in these regions participated in identifying the disparate ways in which parents with mild cognitive limitations were identified, described, and served (Tymchuk, 1999). This process also identified reasons for cooperation or lack of cooperation across sectors and identified agencies and ways to plan for the seamless delivery of a collaborative integration of services that focused upon the strengths and abilities of these families. Family focus groups also were conducted. From this process, The UCLA Parent/Child Health & Wellness Project was begun in 1995 as a random clinical trial of two approaches to self- and child health care, injury and illness prevention, and wellness home education for young parents with individual learning needs. The first year allowed for the revisiting and testing of materials, curricula, and delivery processes across all sectors. All materials were translated into Spanish. Table 13.1 contains the components considered to form the basis of successful family life that were incorporated into the Wellness Project.

The intervention phase, which involved several hundred young families over a 3-year period, has been completed. Overall results showed that families that received home instruction showed significant improvement over those who received materials only. Other results showed improvement on the dependent variables in some families that were receiving materials only. Outcome was influenced in part by maternal communication abilities, educational history, health and disability status, and injury prevention and health care knowledge and skills at entry. Outcome also was influenced by the type and quality of the families' residence and the frequency with which the family moved. Further, outcome was influenced by infant health and disability status. In addition to the empirical results, however, the results of all phases (preparatory, development and piloting, intervention, follow-up, and policy) have direct applicability to other locales. Careful preparation, for example, allowed for the identification of barriers and potential facilitators to service integration. Memoranda of understanding between agencies in which responsibilities were specified as well as procedures for successive feedback were adopted. Parents provided poignant examples of service breakdown. The Wellness Project has been replicated at the University of Sydney (Llewellyn, 1996) and is being pilot-tested in 10 Colorado counties as a service model involving child welfare, developmental disabilities, and health care.

Recommendations and Strategies to Address Needs of Families

Parents with mild cognitive limitations and their families clearly have been and will continue to be a vulnerable group. These families also have been significantly underserved and understudied. To address this group within our evolving society, a focused approach is required. However, it is unclear how initiatives that cut across sectors through different levels of government can be funded. One strategy may be to bring together a foundation and governmental task force.

A Compelling Need: Recognition of
Parent and Family Needs for Ongoing Services

There is an immediate and compelling need to provide information about parents with mild cognitive limitations and their families to the private and public health care sectors; to child protection services and the courts; and to the educational, welfare, housing, and other service sectors. When parents appear not to be succeeding, specific recognition must be made of their family circum-

Table 13.1.   Component areas considered to be critical for family life

Fundamental Knowledge and Skills for Parents	Safety

Fundamental Knowledge and Skills for Parents

Support relationships
  • Social supports
  • Service supports
Effective short and long-term planning
Effective decision making
Effective coping
Effective observation skills
Finances and budget
Meal planning
House cleanliness
Hygiene

Health

Body works
  • Understanding health comprehension
  • Parts of the body
  • Common problems associated with body parts
  • Understanding of sickness and health
  • Knowing when you are sick
  • Knowing when your child is sick
Diagnostics
  • Body temperature
  • Pulse
  • Breathing
  • Common health problems
  • Diagnosing common health problems
Life-threatening emergencies
  • Knowledge of life-threatening emergencies
  • Causes of life-threatening emergencies
  • Prevention of life-threatening emergencies
  • Emergency planning
  • When a life-threatening emergency occurs
Calling the doctor: knowing when to call and what to do
  • Symptoms to call the doctor about
  • Calling the doctor
  • Understanding the doctor's directions
Medicines
  • Asking questions about prescription medicine
  • Getting a prescription filled
  • Getting over-the-counter medicine
  • Using prescription medicine
  • Using over-the-counter medicine

Safety

Partner safety
Safety in the home or the apartment
  • Phone safety
  • Door safety
  • On vacation
Community safety
  • Going out
    – Before going out
    – While out in the community
    – Returning home
  • Reporting a crime
Home safety: home dangers and precautions inventory
  • Fire
  • Electrical
  • Danger of choking from small objects
  • Suffocation
  • Firearm and other projectile weapons
  • Poisons
  • Falling heavy objects
  • Sharp/pointed objects
  • Clutter
  • Inappropriate edibles
  • Dangerous toys or animals
  • Cooking
  • General dangers
  • Yard/outdoors
  • Danger & safety maps

Parent and Child Enjoying Each Other

Child safe
Parent and child playing
Parent reading and singing to child

Source: The UCLA Parent/Child Health & Wellness Project.

stances and of their practical reading, comprehension, and other communication skills, and specific adaptations must be made to accommodate for those circumstances and skills. Further, collaborative strategies must be adopted to ensure that these families do not fall between the cracks of the social systems with which they are involved during their lives.

HOLISTIC APPROACH TO FAMILY LIFE FOR PEOPLE WITH MILD COGNITIVE LIMITATIONS

Although studies of the family life of adults with mild cognitive limitations have been limited, what is known emphasizes the importance of a holistic approach spanning the longevity of the family. Such an approach would enhance family integrity. Instead of a coordinated longitudinal and more comprehensive approach to the facilitation and study of family life, what we now know has been skewed by a piecemeal approach. Often, service providers have responded to the needs of families when a child is young, often adapting existing materials and procedures. Some of these adaptations are suitable. Whether they can be replicated is unsure. Less is known about services to families caring for adolescents (Booth & Booth, 1997). Individual researchers who also are clinicians have been faced with a dearth of empirical information and have had to design and implement clinical studies in order to build an empirical database. Simultaneously, these clinical researchers have had to ensure the care of the family while handling issues of child protection and domestic violence.

Conceptualizations of Family Life with Mild Cognitive Limitations

In addition to the need for a holistic approach, there is a need to examine conceptualizations of family life within an evolving society. Such conceptualizations must take into consideration the many challenges faced by families in which one or both parents have mild cognitive limitations. And while complex, such conceptualizations must allow the public and the private sectors to become familiar with the needs of these families. Figure 13.5 portrays one conceptualization that takes into consideration historical and current factors that might influence current parental child care as well as parental ability to learn and maintain what they have learned.

The Need for New Evaluation and Research Models

To undertake studies of families that address the complexities of life within an evolving new society, new research models, which may not follow a randomized design, are needed. These models, too, must be tested. One example of this is based on the results within The Wellness Project. Currently, relationships among maternal disability status, infant/child disability/health status, and effectiveness of injury prevention education are being examined (see Figure 13.6).

Economic Studies

Further, economic comparisons between the provision of preparatory education for young families and the provision of later services are needed (Bryant & Daro, 1994; Caldwell, 1992; Carter, 1996). All available evidence supports the contention that provision of prevention education is significantly more cost-effective.

Development of Suitable Processes to Address Ethical Issues in Research

Development and dissemination of processes that address the ethical dilemmas that researchers, clinicians, and other providers face in the conduct of their work with this population also are needed (Tymchuk, 1998a).

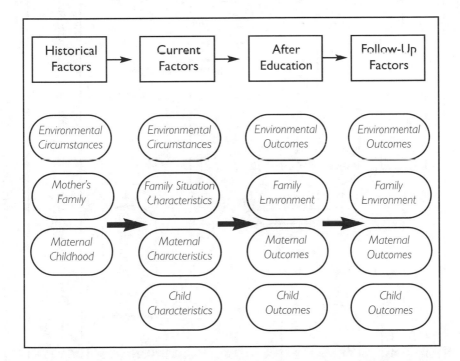

Figure 13.5. Temporal working model to examine injury prevention with mothers with cognitive limitations.

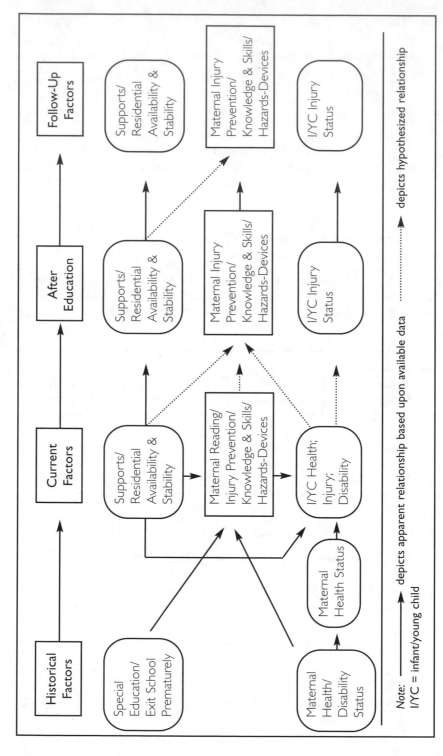

Figure 13.6. Sample hypothetical relationships among mother's early life, preintervention performance on selected measures, and selected outcomes at posttest and follow-up.

Coordination of Public and Private Efforts

In addition to the cross-sector task force, there is a need for coordination of public and private efforts related to these families. A number of recent efforts within the federal government have emphasized the coordination of federal efforts across agencies in addressing significant needs. For example, there is a federal coordinating council on child maltreatment (National Research Council, 1993; U.S. Department of Health and Human Services, 1993). Similarly, the National Institutes of Health (NIH) requires applicants submitting grant proposals to relate their projects to Healthy People 2000 objectives. In the private sector, the focus of The Annie E. Casey Foundation's Family to Family (1992) initiative is to improve foster care. Efforts must be made regarding the inclusion of families with mild cognitive limitations into these initiatives in order to ensure their inclusion in last-resort safety net programs (Geen et al., 1997).

Technical Assistance and Sharing of Information

Funding is required to establish a program that can develop a database regarding families from which technical assistance can be provided. Further, this program can serve as a facilitator of information sharing regarding this population.

CONCLUSION

Social planners recognize the concept of "critical mass," in which a critical number of people are needed before a group and its needs become noticeable. Before this critical mass status is attained, supports and services are uneven across localities, are easily disrupted, and are seldom suitably matched to familial needs. Families then continue to be adversely affected. Because parents with mild cognitive limitations are an emerging population, it does not appear that critical mass status has been attained. However, sufficient and cumulating interest has been shown regarding this population; therefore, perhaps this population will soon get the attention and resources it so desperately needs.

REFERENCES

American Red Cross. (1989). *Parenting for parents with special learning needs*. Los Angeles: Author.

Americans with Disabilities Act (ADA) of 1990, PL 101–336, 42 U.S.C. §§ 12101 *et seq.*

Andron, L., & Sturm, M. (1973). Is "I do" in the repertoire of the retarded? A study of the functioning of married retarded couples. *Mental Retardation, 11*(1), 31–34.

The Annie E. Casey Foundation. (1992). *Family to family: Reconstructing foster care*. Baltimore: Author.

Baker, D., Parker, R., Williams, M., Scott Clark, W., & Nurss, J. (1997). The relationship of patient reading ability to self-reported health and use of health services. *American Journal of Public Health, 87,* 1027–1030.

Blanch, A., Nicholson, J., & Purcell, J. (1994). Parents with severe mental illness and their children: The need for human services integration. *The Journal of Mental Health Administration, 21,* 388–396.

Booth, T., & Booth, W. (1997). *Exceptional childhoods, unexceptional children: Growing up with parents who have learning difficulties.* London: Family Policy Studies Centre.

Brady, S., & Grover, S. (1997). *The sterilisation of girls and young women in Australia.* Canberra, Australia: Human Rights and Equal Opportunity Commission.

Brantlinger, E. (1992). Professionals' attitudes toward the sterilization of people with disabilities. *Journal of The Association for Persons with Severe Handicaps, 17,* 4–18.

Breslow, L. (1997). *Report of review of public health programs and services in Los Angeles County, Department of Health Services.* Los Angeles: University of California, Los Angeles, School of Public Health.

Broberg, G., & Roll-Hansen, N. (Eds.). (1996). *Eugenics and the welfare state. Sterilization policy in Denmark, Sweden, Norway, and Finland.* East Lansing: Michigan State University Press.

Browne, A. (1993). Violence against women by male partners. Prevalence, outcomes, and policy implications. *American Psychologist, 48,* 1077–1087.

Bryant, P., & Daro, D. (1994). *A comparison of the cost of child maltreatment to the cost of providing ALL new parents parent education and support.* Chicago: The National Committee to Prevent Child Abuse.

Caldwell, R. (1992). *The costs of child abuse vs. child abuse prevention: Michigan's experience.* East Lansing: Michigan State University Press.

The California Wellness Foundation. (1996). *Devolution: How will California respond? Annual report.* Woodland Hills: Author.

Campion, M. (1995). *Who's fit to be a parent?* London: Routledge.

Carter, N. (1996). *See how we grow: A report on the status of parenting education in the U.S.* Philadelphia: The Pew Charitable Trusts.

Children's Defense Fund. (1997). *The state of America's children yearbook 1997.* Washington, DC: Author.

Cruz, V.K., Price-Williams, D., & Andron, L. (1998). Developmentally disabled women who were molested as children. *Social Casework,* 69(7), 411–419.

Davis, T., Mayeaux, E., Fredrickson, D., Bocchini, J., Jackson, R., & Murphy, P. (1994). Reading ability of parents compared with reading level of pediatric patient education materials. *Pediatrics, 93,* 460–468.

DiSimone, R. (1996). Major welfare reforms enacted in 1996. *Social Security Bulletin, 59,* 56–63.

Edgerton, R. (1967). *The cloak of competence: Stigma in the lives of the mentally retarded.* Berkeley: University of California Press.

Edgerton, R. (Ed.). (1984). *Lives in process: Mildly retarded adults in a large city.* Washington, DC: American Association on Mental Retardation.

England, M., & Cole, R. (1995). Children and mental health: How can the system be improved? *Health Affairs, 14,* 131–138.

Feldman, M. (1994). Parenting education for parents with intellectual disabilities: A review of outcome studies. *Research in Developmental Disabilities, 15,* 299–332.

Feldman, M. (1998). Parents with intellectual disabilities. In J. Lutzker (Ed.), *Handbook of child abuse research and treatment* (pp. 401–420). New York: Plenum.

Feldman, M., Case, L., Rincover, A., Towns, F., & Betel, J. (1989). Parent education project, III. Increasing affection and responsivity in developmentally handicapped mothers: Component analysis, generalization, and effects on child language. *Journal of Applied Behavior Analysis, 22,* 211–222.

Feldman, M., Case, L., & Sparks, B. (1992). Effectiveness of a child-care training program for parents at-risk for child neglect. *Canadian Journal of Behavioral Science, 24,* 14–28.

Ford, K., Tio, I., & Tymchuk, A. (1990). An analysis of supports of mothers who are labeled and non-labeled as mentally retarded. *Pacific State Archives, 15,* 105–111.

Gan, J., Tymchuk, A., & Nishihara, A. (1977). Mildly retarded adults: Their attitudes toward retardation. *Mental Retardation, 15,* 5–9.

Gardner, W., & Wilcox, B. (1993). Political intervention in scientific peer review. *American Psychologist, 48,* 972–983.

Geen, R., Zimmerman, W., Douglas, T., Zedlewski, S., & Waters, S. (1997). *Income support and social services for low-income people in California.* Washington, DC: Urban Institute.

Glaun, D., & Brown, P. (1999). Motherhood, intellectual disability, and child protection: Characteristics of a court sample. *Journal of Intellectual and Developmental Disabilities, 24,* 95–105.

Hayman, R. (1990). Presumptions of justice: Law, politics, and the mentally retarded parent. *Harvard Law Review, 103,* 1202–1271.

Hickson, L., Golden, H., Khemka, I., Urv, T., & Yamusah, S. (1998). A closer look at interpersonal decision-making in adults with and without mental retardation. *American Journal on Mental Retardation, 103,* 209–224.

Jorgensen, C. (1994). Health education: What can it look like after health care reform? *Health Education Quarterly, 21,* 11–26.

Kagan, S., & Pritchard, E. (1996). Linking services for children and families: Past legacy, future possibilities. In E. Zigler, S. Kagan, & N. Hall (Eds.), *Children, families, and government* (pp. 378–393). New York: Cambridge University Press.

Kastner, T., Walsh, K., & Criscione, T. (1997). Overview and implications of Medicaid managed care for people with developmental disabilities. *Mental Retardation, 35,* 257–269.

Keltner, B. (1994). Home environments of mothers with mental retardation. *Mental Retardation, 32,* 123–127.

Keltner, B., & Tymchuk, A. (1992). Parents with mental retardation: A challenge to nurses. *MCN the American Journal of Maternal/Child Nursing, 17,* 136–140.

Keltner, B., Wise, L., & Taylor, G. (1999). Mothers with intellectual limitations and their 2-year-old children's developmental outcomes. *Journal of Intellectual and Developmental Disability, 24,* 27–44.

Kirby, D. (1997). *No easy answers. Research findings on programs to reduce teen pregnancy.* Washington, DC: The National Campaign to Prevent Teen Pregnancy.

Koegel, P., & Edgerton, R. (1984). Black "six-hour retarded children" as young adults. In R. Edgerton (Ed.), *Lives in process: mildly retarded adults in a large city* (pp. 145–171). Washington, DC: American Association on Mental Retardation.

Levine, P., & Edgar, E. (1994). An analysis by gender of long-term postschool outcomes for youth with and without disabilities. *Exceptional Children, 61,* 282–300.

Llewellyn, G. (1996). *The NSW Parent-Child Health and Wellbeing Project.* Sydney, Australia: University of Sydney Faculty of Health Sciences.

Llewellyn, G., McConnell, D., Cant, R., & Westbrook, M. (1999). Support networks of mothers with intellectual disability: An exploratory study. *Journal of Intellectual and Developmental Disabilities, 24,* 7–26.

Lorber, S. (1974). *Consulting the mentally retarded: An approach to the definition of mental retardation by experts.* Unpublished doctoral dissertation, Department of Psychology, University of California, Los Angeles.

McManus, M., & Fox, H. (1995). *Strategies to enhance preventive and primary care services for high-risk children in health maintenance organizations.* Washington, DC: Fox Health Policy Consultants.

Miller, W. (1994, April 10–12). State of neglect. Judged unfit before they try. Mentally retarded rarely allowed to raise their babies. *The Spokesman Review,* Spokane, WA, pp. H1, H4.

Miringoff, M., Miringoff, M-L., & Opdycke, S. (1996). Monitoring the nation's social performance: The Index of Social Health. In E. Zigler, S. Kagan, & N. Hall. (Eds.). *Children, families, and government* (pp. 10–20). New York: Cambridge University Press.

The National Film Board of Canada. (1996). *The sterilization of Leilani Muir.* Montreal, Quebec, Canada: Author.

National Research Council. (1993). *Understanding child abuse and neglect.* Washington, DC: National Academy Press.

Pixa-Kettner, U. (1999). Follow-up study on parenting with intellectual disability in Germany. *Journal of Intellectual and Developmental Disabilities, 24,* 75–93.

Pulcini, J., & Howard, A. (1997). Framework for analyzing health care models serving adults with mental retardation and other developmental disabilities. *Mental Retardation, 35,* 209–217.

Sedlak, A., & Broadhurst, D. (1996). *Third national incidence study of child abuse and neglect. Final Report.* Washington, DC: U.S. Department of Health and Human Services.

Stromsness, M. (1993). Sexually abused women and mental retardation: Hidden victims with mental retardation, absent resources. In M. Willmuth & L. Holcomb (Eds.), *Women with disabilities* (pp. 139–152). New York: Harrington Park Press.

Taylor, C., Norma, D., Murphy, J., Jellinek, M., Quinn, D.., Poitrast, F., & Goshko, M. (1991). Diagnosed intellectual and emotional impairment among parents who seriously mistreat their children: Prevalence, type, and outcome in a court sample. *Child Abuse and Neglect, 15,* 389–401.

Tymchuk, A. (1971). Token economy and motivating environment for mildly retarded adolescent boys. *Mental Retardation, 9,* 8.

Tymchuk, A. (1990). Parents with mental retardation: A national strategy. A white paper prepared for the President's Committee on Mental Retardation. *Journal of Disability Policy Studies, 1,* 43–55.

Tymchuk, A. (1991). Self-concepts of mothers with mental retardation. *Psychological Reports, 68,* 503–510.

Tymchuk, A. (1992a). Do mothers with or without mental retardation know what to report when they think their child is ill? *Childrens' Health Care, 21,* 53–57.

Tymchuk, A. (1992b). Predicting adequacy and inadequacy of parenting by persons with mental retardation. *Child Abuse and Neglect, 16,* 165–178.

Tymchuk, A. (1994a). Depression symptomatology in mothers with mental retardation: An exploratory study. *Australia and New Zealand Journal of Developmental Disabilities, 19,* 111–119.

Tymchuk, A. (1994b, April 24–26). *Recommendations for assessing and enhancing self-healthcare competence of persons with mental retardation.* Presented as part of the President's Committee on Mental Retardation's "A Presidential Forum: The President's Reforms Agenda and People with Mental Retardation: 21st Century Realities," Washington, DC.

Tymchuk, A. (1994c). *The UCLA Parent-Child Health & Wellness Project.* Los Angeles: University of California, Los Angeles, School of Medicine.

Tymchuk, A. (1996). *Parents with 'functional or categorical' disabilities: Risk assess-ment, case management, and techniques for improving parenting skills. A training manual for caseworkers.* Los Angeles: University of Southern California, Center on Child Welfare.

Tymchuk, A. (1998a). Addressing current and planning for future ethical issues in child maltreatment research. In J. Lutzker (Ed.), *Handbook of child abuse research and treatment* (pp. 543–560). New York: Plenum.

Tymchuk, A. (1998b). The importance of matching educational interventions to parent needs in child maltreatment: Issues, methods, and recommendations. In J. Lutzker, (Ed.), *Handbook of child abuse research and treatment* (pp. 421–448). New York: Plenum.

Tymchuk, A. (1999). Moving towards integration of services for parents with intellec-tual disabilities. *Journal of Intellectual and Developmental Disabilities, 24,* 59–74.

Tymchuk, A., & Andron, L. (1988). Clinic and home parent training of a mother with mental handicap caring for three children with developmental delay. *Mental Handi-cap Research, 1,* 24–38.

Tymchuk, A., & Andron, L. (1990). Mothers with mental retardation who do or do not abuse or neglect their children. *Child Abuse and Neglect, 14,* 313–323.

Tymchuk, A., & Andron, L. (1992). Project Parenting: Child interactional training with mothers who are mentally handicapped. *Mental Handicap Research, 5,* 4–32.

Tymchuk, A., Andron, L., Bavolek, S., Quattrociocchi, A., & Henderson, H. (1990). *Nurturing program for parents with special learning needs and their children.* Park City, UT: Family Development Resources.

Tymchuk, A., Andron, L., & Rahbar, B. (1988). Effective decision-making/problem-solving training with mothers who have mental retardation. *American Journal on Mental Retardation, 92,* 510–516.

Tymchuk, A., Andron, L., & Tymchuk, M. (1990). Training mothers with mental hand-icaps to understand behavioural and developmental principles. *Mental Handicap Re-search, 3,* 51–59.

Tymchuk, A., Andron, L., & Unger, O. (1987). Parents with mental handicaps and ade-quate childcare: A review. *Mental Handicap, 15,* 49–54.

Tymchuk, A., & Feldman, M. (1991). Parents with mental retardation and their children: Review of research relevant to professional practice. *Canadian Psychology, 32*(3) 486–496.

Tymchuk, A., Groen, A., & Dolyniuk, C. (2000). Health, safety, and well-being: Read-ing recognition abilities of young parents with functional disabilities. Construction and preliminary validation of a prescriptive instrument. *Journal of Developmental and Physical Disabilities, 12*(4), 349–366.

Tymchuk, A., Hamada, D., Andron, L., & Anderson, S. (1990a). Emergency training with mothers who are mentally retarded. *Education and Training in Mental Retarda-tion, 25*(2), 142–149.

Tymchuk, A., Hamada, D., Andron, L. & Anderson, S. (1990b). Emergency training with mothers with mental retardation. *Child and Family Behavior Therapy, 12,* 31–47.

Tymchuk, A., & Keltner, B. (1991). Advantage profiles: A tool for health care profes-sionals working with parents with mental retardation. *Issues in Comprehensive Pedi-atric Nursing, 14*(3), 155–161.

Tymchuk, A., Lang, C., Dolyniuk, C., Berney-Ficklin, K., & Spitz, R. (1999). The home inventory of dangers and safety precautions–2: Addressing critical needs for pre-scriptive assessment devices in child maltreatment and in healthcare. *Child Abuse & Neglect, 23*(1), 1–14.

Tymchuk, A., Lang, C., Lieberman, S., & Koo, S. (in press). *Development and validation of the illustrated version of the Home Inventory for dangers and safety precautions: Continuing to address learning needs of parents*. Submitted manuscript.

Tymchuk, A., Llewellyn, G., & Feldman, M. (1999). Parents with intellectual disabilities: A timely international perspective. *Journal of Intellectual and Developmental Disabilities, 24*, 3–6.

Tymchuk, A., Yokota, A., & Rahbar, B. (1990). Decision making abilities of mothers with mental retardation. *Research in Developmental Disabilities, 11*, 97–109.

U.S. Department of Education. National Center for Education Statistics. (1997). *Dropout rates in the United States: 1995*. Washington, DC: Author.

U.S. Department of Health and Human Services. (1990). *Healthy People 2000: National health promotion and disease prevention objectives*. Washington, DC: Author.

U.S. Department of Health and Human Services. (1993). *Neighbors helping neighbors: A new national strategy for the protection of children*. Washington, DC: Author

U.S. Department of Health and Human Services. (1995). *Healthy People 2000: An update*. Washington, DC: Author.

U.S. Department of Health and Human Services. (2000). *Healthy People 2010*. Washington, DC: Author.

Wagner, M., & Blackorby, J. (1996). Transition from high school to work or college: How special education students fare. *The Future of Children, 6*, 103–120.

Wark, R., Andron, L., & Tymchuk, A. (1989). *A continuum of services for parents who are developmentally disabled*. Los Angeles: University of California, Los Angeles, Department of Psychiatry.

Weissbourd, R., Gullota, T., Hampton, R., Ryan, B., & Adams, G. (Eds.). (1997). *Healthy Children 2010: Establishing preventive services*. Thousand Oaks, CA: Sage Publications.

Zambrana, R., & Dorrington, C. (1998). Economic and social vulnerability of Latino children and families by subgroup: Implications for child welfare. *Child Welfare, LXXVII*, 5–27.

14

People with a Dual Diagnosis

America's Powerless Population

Steven Reiss

> For 87 days, Mark Wheatley has been locked in a psychiatric ward at Johns
> Hopkins Hospital. The Baltimore man was ready to leave two months ago,
> but no person, no agency would take him: In addition to having a psychi-
> atric problem he is also mentally retarded.
>
> While waiting for a home, Wheatley, 29, endured the taunts of other
> patients, who were troubled mentally but of normal intelligence. He was
> restrained and shut in seclusion. He had to watch everyone else go home.
> (Sugg, 1999, 1A)

This chapter addresses people who have a "dual diagnosis," that is, a mental
health disorder as well as mental retardation. As illustrated in the story of Mark
Wheatley, people with a dual diagnosis truly are forgotten and powerless. Because of the nature of their disabilities, these individuals have difficulty finding
people to help them.

For the purposes of the chapter, the following terminology is used: *Maladaptive behavior* refers to the symptoms of mental health disorders. *Mental
health disorders* consist of three main subtypes: mental illnesses, personality
disorders, and severe behavioral disorders. *Mental illnesses* have onsets and
are associated with significant deteriorations in functioning called *regressions*.
Examples include anxiety disorder, somatoform disorder, mood disorder, and
schizophrenia. *Personality disorders* are deeply ingrained, chronic patterns of
maladaptive behavior with no definite period of onset. They are seen in people
with and without mental retardation. Examples include conduct disorder,
avoidant personality disorder, borderline personality disorder, and paranoid
personality disorder. *Severe behavior disorders* are significant conduct problems, including self-injurious behavior, severe destructive behavior, and stereotypic behavior. Depending on the individual case, the occurrence of a severe
behavior disorder may or may not be associated with a mental illness or a personality disorder.

Many people confuse mental health disorders and mental retardation, but
they are distinct categories of disabilities. Mental health disorders are psycho-

logical disabilities associated with emotional, social, and personality dysfunctioning. Mental retardation is a cognitive disability that affects a person's interaction with his or her living environments (Luckasson et al., 1992). Most people who have a mental health disorder do not have mental retardation, and most people who have mental retardation do not have a mental health disorder. However, it is possible for people with mental retardation to experience any of the mental health disorders that people with average intelligence experience. Personality disorders and severe behavior disorders are much more common in people with mental retardation than in the general population. Mental illnesses are about equally common in both populations. As psychologists George Tarjan and Herbert Grossman are fond of saying, "Mental retardation is not an antidote for mental illness." People with mental retardation can develop a psychosis, such as schizophrenia, or an anxiety disorder, such as obsessive-compulsive disorder. They can become depressed and develop mood disorders. They also are vulnerable to maladaptive personality traits such as excessive dependency, suspiciousness, or impulsivity.

People with a dual diagnosis constitute one of the most underserved populations in the United States (Reiss, Levitan, & McNally, 1982). For a number of reasons, these individuals often do not receive the mental health supports they need. They have difficulty obtaining adequate residential, mental health, and educational services. This population has few advocates. Although many more services are available today than were available in 1980, the vast majority of people with a dual diagnosis still do not receive minimally adequate services.

Individuals with a dual diagnosis are among the most powerless groups in our society. The vast majority are unable to advocate for themselves, and few advocates or organizations represent their interests. In medical schools, dual diagnosis falls through a crack between pediatrics and psychiatry; therefore, few physicians are trained to provide appropriate medical supports to this population. In the community, individuals with a dual diagnosis may be referred back and forth between mental health and developmental disabilities programs. Generally speaking, people with a dual diagnosis are nobody's priority.

CONSEQUENCES AND PERSISTENCE OF DUAL DIAGNOSIS

Mental health disorders have a number of unfortunate consequences for people with mental retardation. They impair the individual's quality of life by delaying personal growth and creating barriers to community living (Larson & Lakin, 1992; Schalock & Keith, 1993), and they often cause a deterioration in overall adaptive functioning, called *regression*. In some cases, intellectual functioning also is impaired by mental health disorders (Russell & Tanguay, 1981).

Some mental health disorders are associated with emotional suffering. For example, anxiety disorders may lead to experiences of intense fear, repeated panic attacks, and chronic anxiety states. Mood disorders may lead to experiences of despair, hopelessness, and self-hatred. Schizophrenia may lead to withdrawal from the interpersonal environment and overwhelming feelings of resentment. Personality disorders may lead to suicide attempts, alcoholism, prostitution, and crime. Severe behavior disorders may lead to self-injury, self-mutilation, chronic pain, irritability, and overactivity.

Mental health disorders create barriers toward inclusion in educational, social, employment, and community settings. Maladaptive behavior is a major factor in limiting community access of individuals with mental retardation (e.g., Beier, 1964; Eyman & Borthwick, 1980). Scheerenberger (1980) found that behavior problems were the primary obstacle to deinstitutionalization. Maladaptive behavior is a major cause of failure in community placements (Bruininks, Hill, & Morreau, 1988). Poor social skills and maladaptive behavior also lead to failure in employment settings (Greenspan & Shoultz, 1981; Schalock & Harper, 1978).

Mental health disorders in individuals with mental retardation can persist for years with little change. Reid, Ballinger, Heather, and Melvin (1984) found considerable persistence of behavior problems among people with severe mental retardation over a 6-year period. James (1986) reported a number of older adults with an IQ of less than 50 who had behavior or affective problems for decades. Linden and Forness (1986) found poor adjustments in about 70% of a sample of 40 people with mild mental retardation 10 years after they had received treatment for various psychiatric disorders.

Laman (1989) found evidence of stability of depressed mood in 36 adults with mental retardation over a time period of 14–30 months. The participants had been administered the informant-rated version of the depression scale from the Psychopathology Inventory for Mentally Retarded Adults (Matson, 1988) and the Illinois-Chicago Informant Rating Scale for Depression (Reiss & Benson, 1985). There was a significant correlation over time of .40, *probability* < .01.

Matson, Coe, Gardner, and Sovner (1991) evaluated 506 residents of four institutions in two states for frequency, severity, and duration of behavior problems. They found that 91.6% of maladaptive behaviors had been evident for at least 12 months. The findings that behavioral disorders persist through time provide additional evidence for the need for services. Researchers have found that challenging behavior has the potential for creating devastating effects on both the individual and his or her family over periods of years. Without services, these problems rarely are resolved.

PREVALENCE

Researchers have found that between 30% and 40% of all individuals with mental retardation who have been identified by the government and services system require mental health services (Nezu, Nezu, & Gill-Weiss, 1992). Prevalence is probably much lower among the 80% of people with mental retardation who live at home and receive no publicly funded services other than public education. Given a prevalence rate of mental retardation of about 1% of the total population—or about 3 million people in the United States—it can be estimated that 300,000–600,000 Americans have a dual diagnosis. This estimate, moreover, reflects only the 1-day prevalence rate—that is, the rate of mental health disorders on any given day. Because some people who are healthy today may develop a mental health disorder in the future, the percentage of people with mental retardation who will require mental health services at some point in their life is likely to be much higher than the estimated 1-day prevalence rates. Unfortunately, there is no research on lifetime or even 1-year prevalence rates for mental health disorders in individuals with mental retardation.

Studies Comparing People with and without Mental Retardation

Maladaptive behavior is much more common in people with mental retardation than in the general population. For example, Hollingworth, as quoted in Eysenck (1943), administered hundreds of IQ tests to soldiers with neurosis and found that, in general, they had below average IQ scores. However, Eysenck (1943) examined data on 3,000 people and questioned the validity of Hollingworth's conclusion, suggesting instead that people with neurosis had either above- or below-average IQ scores. Both Hollingworth and Eysenck agreed that an unusual number of people with low IQ test scores were highly anxious (neurotic), but they disagreed regarding the numbers of people with high IQ scores who were highly anxious.

A number of studies have directly compared the rates of mental health disorders for individuals with and without mental retardation. The best known of these studies is the research conducted on the Isle of Wight in the United Kingdom (Rutter, Tizard, & Whitmore, 1970). This research was based on a survey of the entire population of children ages 9, 10, and 11 on the Isle of Wight. The rate of mental health disorders in these children with mental retardation was estimated at 30% based on parent interviews and at 42% based on teacher ratings. These numbers compared with an overall rate of only 7% for the general population. Thus, the Isle of Wight studies found that prevalence rates of mental health disorders were five to seven times higher for children with mental retardation than for children without mental retardation.

In 1995, McNally and Shin studied the relationship between intelligence and recovery from posttraumatic stress disorder (PTSD). They administered a battery of psychological measures to 105 Vietnam combat veterans and found that low IQ scores were associated with severe PTSD symptoms. They concluded that intelligence may affect one's ability to cope with trauma, affecting whether a person develops chronic PTSD.

Cullinan, Epstein, and Olinger (1983) compared ratings on the Revised Behavior Problem Checklist (RBPC; Quay & Peterson, 1987) for 146 females with mild mental retardation and 228 females without mental retardation. All of the girls were between the ages of 7 and 18.9 years. The group with mild mental retardation scored higher for occurrence of conduct problems, personality disorders, social inadequacy, and social delinquency. In a follow-up study, Epstein, Cullinan, and Polloway (1986) compared ratings for 360 students with educable mental retardation (EMR) and 360 students with no mental retardation. The students with educable mental retardation had significantly higher scores for aggression, attention-deficit disorder (ADD), anxiety-inferiority, and social incompetence. Koller, Richardson, Katz, and McLaren (1983) evaluated 221 22-year-olds with mental retardation for emotional disturbance, hyperactive behavior, aggressive behavior, and antisocial behavior. Compared with matched peer controls, people with mental retardation were found to be two and one half times more likely to have a mental health disorder and seven times more likely to have a severe behavior disorder.

Dewan (1948), surveying the records of the Canadian army, studied 2,055 men with mental retardation and 28,192 without mental retardation. The men varied in age from 18 to 40 (average 25). An IQ score was estimated from the M test (IQ test administered by the army); psychiatrists who had access to the men's historical data, including previous medical and psychiatric records, interviewed the recruits and rated their emotional stability. They found that 47.7% of the men with mental retardation were rated as emotionally unstable by psychiatrists, versus 19.7% of men without mental retardation. Thus, the prevalence of emotional instability was twice as great in men with mental retardation compared with their control peers.

RESIDENTIAL SETTINGS

A large body of data indicates that challenging behavior increases referral to institutions and creates barriers to community and social integration (Bruininks et al., 1988; Eyman & Borthwick, 1980). For these reasons, the rate of severe behavior disorder is very high in state-operated, institutional environments.

Lakin, Hill, Hauber, Bruininks, and Heal (1983) have conducted a series of comprehensive studies on the prevalence of severe behavior disorders in individuals living in various residential settings. This research, which was national in scope, analyzed behavior disorders in terms of frequency, severity, and consequences. The data were summarized in terms of the categories of *injures self,* *injures other people,* and *destructive to property* (Bruininks, Hill, Weatherman, & Woodcock, 1986). The research found very high rates of severe behavior disorders in large state-operated facilities. Only three states had rates of less than 30%, whereas 20 states had rates of 50% or more.

Although most studies have found that rates for challenging behavior in noninstitutional settings are much lower than those in large state institutions, the rates are still significant. Bruininks and his colleagues found that rates for behavior that is hurtful to self varied from 10% for semi-independent living environments to 31.0% for group homes. Similarly, rates for behavior that is hurtful to others varied from 14.1% in semi-independent living to 35.6% in group homes. In this study, the rates for family and foster care living arrangements were in between those for semi-independent living and institutions.

TYPES OF PSYCHIATRIC DISORDERS

Philips (1967), summarizing the results of his work with 227 children with mental retardation, described a number of children who showed symptoms of sadness, withdrawal, and phobic fears. He concluded that mental health disorders appeared to result from an interaction of delayed development and negative social conditions.

Corbett (1979) surveyed all individuals with mental retardation listed in the Camberwell (United Kingdom) register on December 31, 1971. Corbett had nurses, supervisors, teachers, or relatives rate each survey participant on the Social and Physical Incapacity Scale (Kushlick, Blunden, & Cox, 1973). A mental health disorder was found in 186 of the 402 participants, a rate of 46%.

Eaton and Menolascino (1982) summarized the results of psychiatric work with 798 individuals with mental retardation who were seen at the Nebraska Psychiatric Institute. The participants ranged in age from 6 to 76. Using the psychiatric categories defined in the *Diagnostic and Statistical Manual of Mental Disorders, Second Edition,* the researchers found high rates of personality disorder (27.2%) and psychotic reactions (29.8%).

Reiss (1990) surveyed a random sample of 205 adolescents and adults who were recipients of community-based mental retardation services in the greater Chicago area. In this study, the Reiss Screen for Maladaptive Behavior (Reiss, 1988) was completed by caregivers who were familiar with the study participants. According to the results, the single most prevalent mental health problem was social inadequacy, which was rated as a "problem" in the lives of 36.5% of the sample and as a "major problem" in the lives of an additional 8.9%. Thus, nearly 46% of the individuals were rated as socially inadequate to the extent that it caused a problem or a major problem in their lives. Further, personality disorders were especially common in the Chicago sample. Approximately 30% of the participants were found to show personality problems that negatively affected their lives, sometimes to a significant extent.

Similarly, other studies have shown very high rates of personality disorder among individuals with IQ scores between 35 and 70. Craft (1959) diagnosed personality disorder in 39 of 104 people (37.5%) with both mental retardation and challenging behavior. Reid and Ballinger (1987) found evidence of mild personality disorder in 56% of a sample of 100 individuals with IQs between 35 and 70; the rate for severe personality disorder was 22%. Goldberg, Gitta, and Puddephatt (1992) reported rates of personality disorder in 80% of a community sample of individuals with mental retardation seeking psychiatric treatment in Canada.

EFFECTS OF AGE

Although additional research is needed before any firm conclusions can be drawn, mental health disorders appear to be much less prevalent among young children compared with other age groups. In a study of 583 children and adolescents, for example, Reiss and Valenti-Hein (1994) found that mean symptom scores were significantly lower for children younger than age 11 versus children and adolescents between 11 and 21.

Researchers have reported inconsistent results regarding the prevalence rate of mental health disorders in older adults with mental retardation. Some researchers have reported high rates for older adults (Coyle, 1988; Davidson et al., 1992; Harper & Wadsworth, 1990; Jacobson & Harper, 1989). Day (1985) found that, except for dementia, overall rates are lower for elderly adults than for other age groups. Jacobson and Harper (1989) found no differences in rates for elderly adults versus young and middle-age adults.

In the Jacobson and Harper (1989) study, questionnaires were sent to 1,000 randomly selected facilities serving elderly adults. A total of 597 questionnaires were returned. A psychiatric diagnosis was reported for 21.6% of the 379 people in the sample age 55 or older. The researchers did not report a breakdown of specific psychiatric diagnoses. The presence of at least one maladaptive behavior was reported for 77.0% of the sample. There were a number of inconsistencies in the data, such as much higher rates of mental health disorders for individuals between the ages of 60 and 74 than for individuals between the ages of 50 and 55 or those 75 or older. Nevertheless, the study provided some support for a significant rate of mental health disorders among older adults with mental retardation.

James (1986) studied a sample of 50 people, age 60 or older, with IQ scores of 50 or lower. The participants were ambulatory and had had a continuous period of admission to an English hospital for developmental disabilities for at least 20 years. Significant rates of behavior disorder and affective disorder were found. In some cases, the disorders had persisted for years and even decades. In other cases, affective disorders developed following a recent loss, such as the death of a family member or a friend. James suggested that older adults with mental retardation may be especially vulnerable to loss because of low self-esteem.

Dementia is among the disorders commonly seen in older adults. Dementia is indicated by personality change and impairments in memory, abstract thinking, judgment, and other brain functions. In studies reviewed by Jacobson and Harper (1989), dementia added between 2% and 22.2% to the reported prevalence rates for mental health disorders in older adults. Abnormalities of the brain, similar to those seen in individuals with Alzheimer's disease, are virtually universally present in adults with Down syndrome older than age 40. However, only 15%–25% ever actually display the clinical symptoms of Alzheimer's disease (Pueschel, 2001).

CAUSES OF DUAL DIAGNOSIS

Reiss and Havercamp's (1997) sensitivity theory divides the causes of dual diagnosis into three categories: 1) *negative contingencies*, which refer to the direct reinforcement of maladaptive behavior (discussed extensively in the literature on applied behavior analysis), 2) *negative environments*, such as large institutions, that do not satisfy ordinary desires and psychological needs (the psychological effects of negative environments have been evaluated by many researchers, including Zigler (1971) who put forth the idea of outerdirectedness), and 3) *unusual motivation*, which refers mostly to the desire for excessive amounts of some reward or to hypersensitivity to aversive stimuli. Examples of unusual motivation include children who are "addicted" to attention, adults who are "addicted" to sex, and adolescents who are hypersensitive to frustration or anxiety.

According to sensitivity theory, the amount of reinforcement that is being given may be the simplest way to estimate whether a mental health disorder is caused by contingencies, environment, or motivation. For example, when a person with a conduct problem is receiving about the same amount of total attention (positive and negative forms) compared with his or her well-behaved peers, odds are that his or her behavior is caused by negative contingencies. When a person is receiving noticeably less total attention compared with his or her well-behaved peers, odds are that the behavior is caused by negative environments. When a person is receiving noticeably more total attention compared with his or her peers, the odds favor unusual motivation as the cause of the maladaptive behavior.

Negative Reinforcement Contingencies

People with mental retardation need positive reinforcement contingencies to support the development of interpersonal and other skills important for positive mental health. They need educational programs that are tailored to their rate of learning. One of the most beneficial applications of applied behavior analysis, for example, has been to teach skills in a systematic fashion that can be grasped by slow learners. Two skills that are especially relevant for positive mental health are communication skills and social skills.

A number of investigators have cited a lack of communication skills as a possible developmental risk factor for mental health disorders. As Mundy, Seibert, and Hogan stated, "Level of communication skill is directly related to children's ability to interact effectively with others. Thus, it is reasonable to expect that individual differences in communication skills are related to emotional problems in mentally retarded children" (1985, p. 65).

Furthermore, Carr and Durand (1985a, 1985b) proposed that some people with mental retardation and poor communication skills develop severe behavioral disorders as an alternative means of communication. The behavior problem may communicate a need for sustained adult attention.

A number of limitations in social skills are associated with challenging behavior (Kopp, Baker, & Brown, 1992). Difficulty solving everyday social problems has been related to maladjustment in children with mental retardation (Healey & Masterpasqua, 1992); inappropriate assertiveness has been related to problems in anger management (Benson, 1986; Wolpe, 1958); and inadequate leisure skills increase vulnerability to stress and irritability.

Generalization can be a major problem when teaching social problem-solving skills to people with mental retardation. For these individuals, the skills that are learned in an educational or experimental situation rarely transfer to natural environments. Foxx and his colleagues have been at the forefront of addressing this issue (Foxx, Bittle, & Faw, 1989; Foxx & Faw, 1992). Foxx trains people with developmental disabilities to ask themselves a set of simple questions such as, "Who should I talk to?" "Where should I look for help?" and "What should I say?" It is hoped that these self-directing questions will help mediate the transfer of learning from educational to natural environments.

Negative Environments

Some people with mental retardation experience environments that expose them to conditions that lead to or worsen mental health disorders. The following is a list of seven negative social conditions (Reiss & Benson, 1984) that may increase the risk of mental health disorders among individuals with mental retardation:

1. Few labels are more devastating psychologically than "mental retardation." Childish taunts of "retard" create perceptions of inferiority, difference, and exclusion. As noted by Edgerton (1967), many people view mental retardation as forever dooming the individual to incompetence in managing his or her own affairs. People with mental retardation may become defensive about their competencies and try to mask their disabilities. They try to "pass" as typical.

2. Many children perceive placement in a residential program as a rejection; they may think that they were "sent away" because they were unworthy of parental love. Children blame themselves for the loss of parents and family, and this can be psychologically damaging for many years. After an initial placement in a residential facility, children with mental retardation can experience a high degree of social disruption and loss when they are moved from one residential program to another (Sarason & Gladwin, 1958). With each residential relocation, the individual experiences an abrupt loss of parental figures, peers, and familiar surroundings. At the moment of abrupt loss, moreover, the individual is surrounded by strangers and is living in an unfamiliar setting. Berkson and colleagues were among the first researchers to document the negative impact of residential relocations on an individual's friendships (Berkson & Romer, 1980).

A number of studies have documented that children with mental retardation often are socially rejected or neglected and that feelings of loneliness are common (e.g., Luftig, 1988). For example, Baker, Blacher, and Pfeiffer (1993) found that about one third of children with mental retardation in residential treatment settings had no family contact. The level of family involvement with children with maladaptive behavior was found to be significantly less than for children with mental retardation and no mental health disorders or for children with a psychiatric disorder and no mental retardation.

3.   People with mental retardation experience varying degrees of segregation from society. This includes placement in state institutions and in other large congregate residential facilities. In these facilities, individuals live apart from society and may receive segregated services for education, health, and recreation. Although the population of individuals living in state institutions in the United States has declined from 1.9 million in 1967 to approximately 50,000 in 1999, large numbers of individuals with mental retardation still are served in large congregate residential facilities (Cunningham & Mueller, 1991).

Even people who live at home with their families may experience a significant degree of segregation. Access to many community or social situations may be limited; for example, a child may not participate in Little League softball or go to summer camp with classmates. In addition, families sometimes control the individual's access to public events in order to protect him or her or to avoid inconvenience or embarrassment.

Many researchers have documented the negative effects of segregation associated with institutionalization. For example, institutionalization impairs performance on language tasks, tasks of emotional understanding, and learning tasks (Lustman & Zigler, 1982; Zigler, 1971).

4.   Individuals with mental retardation do not have the usual opportunities for a rewarding life. For example, the vast majority of people with mental retardation will not marry or have a romantic relationship for any length of time. The overwhelming majority will not experience parenthood. Although some individuals with mental retardation may obtain jobs, their opportunities are restricted. The majority of people with mental retardation will not find competitive employment or satisfying work. Unemployment is very high among people with mental retardation.

The transition from high school to adult life is particularly difficult for individuals with mental retardation (Rusch, DeStefano, Chadsey-Rusch, Phelps, & Szymanski, 1992). When peers obtain a driver's license, start dating, and go to work or college, the person with mental retardation may be left behind—no driver's license, no girlfriend or boyfriend, no college, and no job.

5. Mental retardation is associated with an increased risk of victimization (Edgerton, 1967), including physical abuse, robbery, or being taken advantage of by an employer. Individuals with mental retardation are more vulnerable to sexual exploitation than people without mental retardation (Valenti-Hein & Mueser, 1990). One survey found that as many as one fourth to one third of women with mental retardation were abused. In some cases, women with mental retardation have been found to have PTSD as a result of sexual abuse (Ryan, 1993).

6. People with mental retardation often are referred to as "children" even when they are adults (Philips, 1967). They are often treated inconsistently with regard to the issue of independence. Encouraged to be dependent when they were younger, today the current generation of people with mental retardation are encouraged to become independent, advocating for their own rights, holding jobs in the community, and living apart from their parents as adults.

7. People with mental retardation receive less positive social support from significant others. Krauss, Seltzer, and Goodman (1992) evaluated the social support networks of 418 adults who lived at home. Although the study found wide individual variations in social support, 42.3% of the sample had no friends. Instead, their social support networks comprised mostly family members. The study provided support for the hypothesis that people with mental retardation who live at home have difficulty finding age-appropriate friends.

Many people with mental retardation who are relocated from an institution to a community residence may have difficulty finding friends (Smith, Valenti-Hein, & Heller, 1985). Schalock, Harper, and Genung (1981) found that one third of 27 former residents of an institution had no friends after having been placed in the community. The remainder of the individuals in the sample had only one or two friends.

Williams and Asher (1992) evaluated the loneliness of 62 students with mild mental retardation and 62 typically developing students. The study found that boys with mental retardation were significantly more lonely than their peers who were typical. However, this correlation did not hold true for the girls in the study.

Social support not only affects the stress level of children but also affects the stress level of parents. McKinney and Peterson (1987) found that spouse support and the parent's perceived locus of control were two important factors in the stress level of parents with children with developmental disabilities. The participants in this study were 67 mothers of children between the ages of 7 and 41 months. All children had a developmental disability such as Down syndrome or cerebral palsy. Ninety-seven percent of the mothers were living with their spouses. The level of parental stress to which the children were exposed was modulated to a considerable degree by support from the spouse. In families in which spouses helped out and provided support, the mother's stress was much lower and the mood was much better than in families in which spouses provided little support.

Lunsky and Havercamp (1999) made the important point that all forms of social support are not positive. They reported a study in which stressful social interaction, called *social strain*, positive social support, and maladaptive behavior were rated for 104 adults with mental retardation. The results showed that social strain is more strongly associated with maladaptive behavior than are overall low levels of social support.

Unusual Goals and Desires

Unusual or extreme behavior is often a consequence of unusual or extreme goals and desires. When people do not care about the same goals or reinforcers as everybody else, they behave differently. Why would a person be very slow to learn grooming behavior? Perhaps because the individual does not care much about what other people think of his or her appearance. Why would a person cling to a particular object and become upset when it is lost or taken away? Perhaps because the individual cares enormously about maintaining a sense of security that comes from order.

Reiss and Havercamp (1998) empirically derived a list of 15 basic desires based on a survey of 2,548 people with and without mental retardation. The 15 basic desires are shown in Table 14.1. Overall, the research results showed that people with mental retardation, as well as individuals without mental retardation, want the same things from life. In terms of happiness, individuals with mental retardation have the same needs as all people. For example, they need acceptance, attention, order, independence, and exercise, and they need to minimize anxiety, frustration, and pain.

Reiss (2000) has argued that the 15 basic desires make us individuals. When a person experiences a particular motive intensely or frequently, that individual is said to be "high" for that motive. For example, people with high attention needs are comfortable in situations in which they are the center of attention. In contrast, people with low attention needs feel uncomfortable when they are the center of attention. Whereas the former individual seeks to maximize attention, the latter individual seeks to minimize it.

When unusual motives become functionally related to maladaptive behavior, sensitivity theory provides a goal-oriented analysis as to how this may have occurred. Because maladaptive behavior usually leads to a great deal of attention, individuals with a high need for attention are predicted to be more likely to engage in maladaptive behavior. The attention that is experienced when a person misbehaves is reinforcing for a person with a high need for attention but punishing for a person with a low need for attention.

Table 14.1.   The 15 basic desires

Acceptance	The desire to be included and approved of; associated with general feelings of self-worth
Attention	The desire for attention from adults; associated with a desire for status and a sense of importance
Anxiety sensitivity	The desire for tranquility; associated with fear
Curiosity	The desire to explore novel stimuli; associated with a desire to learn
Eating	The desire for food; associated with feelings of appetite
Frustration sensitivity	The desire for immediate gratification; associated with impatience
Helping others	Concern for the welfare of others; associated with feelings of compassion and parenting
Independence	The desire for self-reliance; associated with feelings of personal freedom
Morality	The desire for loyalty; associated with feelings of honor
Order	The desire for stability and predictability; associated with feelings of security
Pain sensitivity	The desire for tranquility; associated with feeling hurt
Physical activity	The desire for muscle exercise; associated with feelings of energy
Sex	The desire for sensual pleasures; associated with feelings of lust
Social contact	The desire to socialize; associated with optimism
Vengeance	The desire for revenge; associated with feelings of anger and hatred

Some evidence has been obtained supporting the hypothesis that mental health disorders are associated with maladaptive behavior. Table 14.2 shows means differences in standard scores on the Reiss Profile of Fundamental Goals and Motivational Sensitivities (mental retardation/developmental disabilities version). For the samples studied, a high sensitivity for frustration was the most common motivational difference associated with dual diagnosis. The desires for independence and physical activity were unrelated to dual diagnosis.

In addition, there is evidence that specific developmental disorders are associated with specific Reiss profiles. Dykens and Rosner (1999) published Reiss motivational profiles for various genetically determined, developmental syndromes. They found that diagnostic group membership could be predicted with up to 94% accuracy by motivational items on the Reiss Profile of Fundamental Goals and Motivational Sensitivities (mental retardation/developmental disabilities version). People with Prader-Willi syndrome (a genetic syndrome caused by a disorder of chromosome 15, marked by decreased muscle tone and failure to thrive during infancy and obesity and developmental delays as time passes) were more likely to enjoy puzzles or mysteries and order and showed relatively strong maternal/paternal instincts.

Table 14.2. Differences between mean standardized scores on the Reiss Profile of Fundamental Goals and Motivational Sensitivities (Reiss, 1988)

Scale	Mean difference	$F(1,939)$	$p <$
Frustration sensitivity	0.8	99.9+	.001
Anxiety sensitivity	0.7	74.7	.001
Vengeance	0.6	80.5	.001
Morality	−0.5	52.1	.001
Helping others	−0.4	30.6	.001
Attention	0.4	26.4	.001
Social contact	−0.3	25.5	.001
Order	0.3	24.5	.001
Pain Sensitivity	0.2	8.3	.03
Eating	0.4	18.9	.001
Acceptance	0.3	18.9	.001
Curiosity	−0.3	17.1	.001
Independence	0.0	0.4	ns
Physical activity	0.0	0.2	ns

Scores from people with a dual diagnosis ($n = 596$) minus scores from people with mental retardation only ($n = 395$); ns, not significant.

Under the system of 15 basic desires, the need for a positive self-concept falls under the need for acceptance. Many people with mental retardation need a more positive view of themselves (Zetlin & Turner, 1984). Their desire for acceptance can sometimes motivate defensiveness. For example, people with mental retardation hide their disabilities from others and pretend to understand more than they do. Edgerton (1967) called this behavior the "cloak of competence." Stephens (1953) suggested that the self-concept of people with mental retardation is influenced by how others view their disabilities. Strong feelings of inadequacy can frustrate the desire for acceptance. When this happens, individuals may be motivated to turn to unusual behavior to gain the acceptance they need.

Under sensitivity theory, the desire to minimize anxiety falls under anxiety sensitivity. Although it is widely presumed that people with mental retardation have special difficulties handling stress, the available research does not consistently support this hypothesis. Researchers have found few differences in how people with and without mental retardation respond to frustration (Angelino & Shedd, 1965; Libb, 1972; Portnoy & Stacey, 1954; Talkington & Hall, 1968; Tebeest & Dickie, 1976; Thorne, 1947; Viney, Clark, & Lord, 1973). For example, people with mental retardation react to frustrative nonreinforcement by increasing the rate of responses, which is similar to how most people react.

Nucci and Reiss (1988) directly tested the hypothesis that people with mental retardation handle stress poorly. In a 2 x 3 (groups x conditions) factorial experiment, people with and without mental retardation waited to perform a counting task under conditions designed to induce stress, no particular emotional state, or relaxation. Physiological, behavior, and self-report measures confirmed that the *stress condition* actually induced stress. Contrary to prediction, the study found that stress led to similar improvements in task performance for both groups of participants—those with mental retardation and those without mental retardation. The authors concluded the following:

> The idea that mentally retarded people readily fall apart when frustrated or stressed might be an invalid, stereotypic conception. Although some mentally retarded people might have great difficulty handling stress, others might be able to cope very well, so that overall there is little or no association between intelligence and the capacity of handling stress. In this regard, the first author observed an incident in which a mentally retarded woman fell down while leaving the experiment. The woman bruised herself and was in obvious pain. Nevertheless, she kept her wits about her, remained calm during the ride to the university hospital, and was able to respond effectively to the physicians' questions about the incident. . . . The woman handled the stress of the accident quite well, contradicting stereotypic notions that mentally retarded people readily fall apart under conditions of stress. (p. 166)

FORGOTTEN POPULATION

People with mental retardation are underserved with regard to their mental health needs (Reiss, Levitan, & McNally, 1982). Paradoxically, mental retardation has been found to both increase the risk of mental health disorders and to decrease the opportunity for mental health services. As Fletcher put it, "The mentally retarded have been characterized as worry-free and thus mentally healthy. The severely retarded have been considered to express no feelings and therefore do not experience emotional stress" (1988, p. 255). In 1980, Szymanski and Tanguay published an influential book titled *Emotional Disorders of Mentally Retarded Persons,* which noted "Many mental health clinics still categorically exclude retarded people from their services" (p. 4).

Diagnostic Overshadowing

Part of the problem in establishing a priority for dual diagnosis has to do with how society thinks about mental retardation. When a child with mental retardation misbehaves, we assume that the inappropriate behavior may be related to mental retardation rather than to a mental health disorder. For this reason, the need for services to treat mental health disorders in this population has been inadequately recognized.

The experimental phenomenon of diagnostic overshadowing lends support to the hypothesis of a general tendency to attribute maladaptive behavior to mental retardation (Reiss, Levitan, & Szyszko, 1982). The term *diagnostic overshadowing* refers to instances in which the presence of mental retardation decreases the diagnostic significance of accompanying emotional and behavioral disorders. Just as a 6-inch line appears smaller than it really is when viewed next to a 10-inch line, the debilitating effects of mental health disorders appear less significant than they really are when viewed in the context of the debilitating effects of mental retardation.

In the first experimental study on diagnostic overshadowing, a case description of a debilitating fear was presented to three groups of psychologists. The case described a young man who had commuted to and from work at a fast-food restaurant for more than a year. One day the man took the wrong bus home, was robbed, and subsequently stopped riding the bus and lost his job. The psychologists were asked to rate the suggested fear on a number of psychological scales and to provide diagnostic impressions and recommendations for interventions.

The three groups differed only in terms of the information that was added to the basic case description. One group rated the fear for an individual who was suggested to have mental retardation; a second group rated the fear for an individual who was suggested to have alcoholism; and a third group rated the fear for an individual who was suggested to have average intelligence.

The results indicated that the same debilitating fear was less likely to be considered an example of a mental health disorder when the subject was suggested to have mental retardation as compared to when the subject was suggested to have average intelligence. In other words, the presence of mental retardation overshadowed the diagnostic significance of an accompanying maladaptive behavior (avoidance of commuting resulting in loss of job) that is usually considered indicative of phobia. In addition, the psychologists were significantly less likely to recommend the appropriate therapy (desensitization) for people with mental retardation. Diagnostic overshadowing also occurred for the person with alcoholism.

The results of subsequent experiments extended the diagnostic overshadowing phenomenon to cases involving schizophrenia and personality disorder (Reiss, Levitan, & Szyszko, 1982). The amount of previous clinical experience with people with mental retardation was found to be unrelated to overshadowing (Reiss & Szyszko, 1983). The phenomenon was demonstrated with both social workers and psychologists (Levitan & Reiss, 1983).

Goldsmith and Schloss (1984) replicated and extended the diagnostic overshadowing findings to case descriptions in which the primary diagnoses were learning disabilities and hearing impairment. They used a hypothetical case of a 17-year-old female who accidentally rode the wrong bus and ended up in an alley where she was accosted by a man. Subsequently, the woman refused to take public transportation and lost her job. The researchers found that school psychologists' ratings of this case differed when the case included a primary diagnosis of hearing impairment or learning disability versus no primary diagnosis. The school psychologists were less likely to apply the diagnosis of mental health disorder to and recommend appropriate services for a student previously diagnosed as having a learning disability or hearing impairment.

Sprengler, Strohmer, and Prout (1990) reported evidence of a diagnostic overshadowing phenomenon at an IQ of 58 but not at an IQ of 70 or 80. Inspection of their data, however, actually shows a virtual straight line relationship in which diagnoses of schizophrenia are increasingly less likely as IQ decreases. These researchers also replicated the earlier Reiss and Szyszko finding that diagnostic overshadowing is unrelated to professional experience (as measured by the number of individuals treated); however, they found that professional experience as measured by longevity in the field diminished the tendency for diagnostic overshadowing.

The potential impact of diagnostic overshadowing on mental health services was summarized by Reiss and Szyszko as follows:

> Service delivery typically requires interdisciplinary staffing leading to a diagnosis of an emotional problem and a recommendation for treatment, a case manager who acts on the recommendation, state administrators who recognize the emotional aspects of mental retardation to be sufficiently important to fund appropriate services, and community clinics capable of providing the relevant services. If overshadowing is interpreted as a tendency to view emotional problems in mentally retarded people as less important than they really are, the phenomenon can influence the delivery of services at any of a variety of points in the case management process. For example, even in instances in which a diagnosis and treatment recommendation are made, the service might not be delivered if the case manager assumes that the recommendation for psychotherapy is less important than the recommendation for other services. (1983, p. 401)

AGENDA FOR PROGRESS

The most important goal for individuals with mental retardation is community-based care. All too often, people with a dual diagnosis live in institutions or special residential facilities that preclude or significantly limit their access to the community. In fact, it has become clear that the United States will not be able to close a significant number of existing institutions until community care options are created for individuals with mental retardation.

Unfortunately, there are obstacles to community care for individuals with mental retardation; perhaps the most detrimental obstacle is the absence of trained professional personnel to provide necessary supports or dispense appropriate medications. Because of a lack of trained physicians and child or adult psychiatrists, medical care often is dispensed by physicians who have limited understanding of developmental disorders and mental health disorders. This results in common problems such as polypharmacy, poor follow-up, and ineffective care. For example, when an individual with a dual diagnosis becomes very upset emotionally, case managers or community personnel usually refer the individual to a physician. If the physician has no specific training in dual diagnosis, odds are high that a sedating or inappropriate neuroleptic medication will be prescribed, too. If the person does not calm down in a day or so, the physician may prescribe a higher dosage or additional medications. Either way, the potential exists for inappropriate use of medications.

The National Institutes of Health (NIH) should fund fellowships to train psychiatrists in developmental disabilities. The fellowships should pay for residents or fellows in child psychiatry, adult psychiatry, or behavioral pediatrics. If physicians were better trained, there would be far fewer concerns about inappropriate uses of medications. The various university affiliated programs located across the country are well suited to providing the needed training.

Furthermore, few clinical psychologists work in the field of mental retardation, creating shortages of people who have been trained in programs approved by the American Psychological Association. In addition, there is a growing shortage of doctorate-level applied behavior analysts. The NIH should fund fellowships to train clinical psychologists or applied behavior analysts.

In addition to training, we need to support research on dual diagnosis. The National Institute of Child Health and Human Development needs to increase significantly its annual mental retardation research budget for issues directly relevant to finding cures or to developing supports for dual diagnosis or related issues. At the local level, communities need to develop crisis intervention programs to maintain people in the community. Rapid response is sometimes the key to preventing hospital or institutional care.

Finally, training and coordination are needed among service systems. In addition to greater cooperation among developmental disabilities and mental health agencies, we need better responses from HMOs. A high priority in many localities should be to train staff physicians and psychologists at HMOs that provide crisis intervention services.

Although much remains to be done, much also has been accomplished. Only 20 years ago, the existence of dual diagnosis was not even recognized. Thousands of people with a dual diagnosis now enjoy community life. We have developed objective and valid instruments to screen and assess various types of dual diagnosis. Many new medications are available that offer partial but significant benefits in some cases. A consensus handbook on best practices was developed with the participation of the field's leading medical and scientific authorities (Reiss & Aman, 1998). The use of aversive methods has been greatly reduced and, in some places, eliminated entirely. We have made significant progress in developing a needed base of scientific knowledge. If we can now move forward with an agenda based on national training, we should see additional progress.

REFERENCES

American Psychiatric Association. (1968). *Diagnostic and statistical manual of mental disorders* (2nd ed.). Washington, DC: Author.

Angelino, R., & Shedd, C.L. (1965). A study of the reactions to "frustration" of a group of mentally retarded children as measured by the Rosenzweig Picture-Frustration Study. *Psychological Newsletter, 8,* 49–54.

Baker, B.L., Blacher, J., & Pfeiffer, S. (1993). Family involvement in residential treatment of children with psychiatric disorder and mental retardation. *Hospital and Community Psychiatry, 44,* 561–566.

Beier, D.C. (1964). Behavioral disturbances in the mentally retarded. In H. Stevens & R. Huber (Eds.), *Mental retardation.* Chicago: University of Chicago Press.

Benson, B.A. (1986). Anger management training. *Psychiatric Aspects of Mental Retardation Reviews, 5,* 51–55.

Berkson, G., & Romer, D. (1980). Social ecology of supervised communal facilities for mentally disabled adults: I. Introduction. *American Journal of Mental Deficiency, 85,* 219–228.

Bruininks, R.H., Hill, B.K., & Morreau, L.E. (1988). Prevalence and implications of maladaptive behaviors and dual diagnosis in residential and other service programs. In J.A. Stark, F.J. Menolascino, M.H. Albarelli, & V.C. Gray (Eds.), *Mental retardation and mental health. Classification, diagnosis, treatment, services* (pp. 3–29). New York: Springer-Verlag.

Bruininks, R.H., Hill, B.K., Weatherman, R.F., & Woodcock, R.W. (1986). *Technical summary for the Inventory for Client and Agency Planning.* Allen, TX: DLM Teaching Resources.

Carr, E.G., & Durand, V.M. (1985a). Reducing behavior problems through functional communication training. *Journal of Applied Behavior Analysis, 18,* 111–126.

Carr, E.G., & Durand, V.M. (1985b). The social-communicative basis of severe behavior problems in children. In S. Reiss & R.R. Bootzin (Eds.), *Theoretical issues in behavior therapy.* New York: Academic Press.

Corbett, J.A. (1979). Psychiatric morbidity and mental retardation. In F.E. James & R.P. Snaith (Eds.), *Psychiatric illness and mental handicap* (pp. 11–25). London: Gaskell Press.

Coyle, J.T. (1988). Psychiatry, neuroscience, and the double disabilities. In J.A. Stark, F.J. Menolascino, M.H. Albarelli, & V.C. Gray (Eds.), *Mental retardation and mental health. Classification, diagnosis, treatment, services.* New York: Springer-Verlag.

Craft, M. (1959). Mental disorder in the defective: A psychiatric survey of in-patients. *American Journal of Mental Deficiency, 63,* 329–834.

Cullinan, D., Epstein, M., & Olinger, E. (1983). School behavior problems of mentally retarded and normal females. *The Mental Retardation and Learning Disability Bulletin, 11,* 104–109.

Cunningham, P.J., & Mueller, C.D. (1991). Individuals with mental retardation in residential facilities: Findings from the 1987 national medical expenditure survey. *American Journal on Mental Retardation, 96,* 109–117.

Dalton, A.J., & Wisniewski, H.M. (1990). Down's syndrome and the dementia of Alzheimer's disease. *International Reviews of Psychiatry, 2,* 43–52.

Davidson, P.W., Cain, N.N., Sloane-Reeves, J.E., Kramer, B., Quijano, L.E., Van Heyningen, J., & Giesow, V.E. (1992). *Aging effects on severe behavior disorders in community-based clients with mental retardation.* Paper presented at the annual meeting of the Gerontological Society of America, Washington, DC.

Day, K. (1985). Psychiatric disorders in the middle-aged and elderly mentally handicapped. *British Journal of Psychiatry, 147,* 660–667.

Dewan, J.G. (1948). Intelligence and emotional stability. *American Journal of Psychiatry, 104,* 548–554.

Dykens, E.M., & Rosner, B.A. (1999). Refining behavioral phenotypes: Personality-motivation in Williams and Prader-Willi syndromes. *American Journal on Mental Retardation, 104,* 158–169.

Eaton, L.F., & Menolascino, F.J. (1982). Psychiatric disorders in the mentally retarded: Types, problems, and challenges. *American Journal of Psychiatry, 139,* 1297–1303.

Edgerton, R.B. (1967). *The cloak of competence: Stigma in the lives of the mentally retarded.* Berkeley: University of California Press.

Epstein, M.H., Cullinan, D., & Polloway, E.A. (1986). Patterns of maladjustment among mentally retarded children and youth. *American Journal of Mental Deficiency, 91,* 127–134.

Eyman, R.K., & Borthwick, S.A. (1980). Patterns of care for mentally retarded persons. *Mental Retardation, 18,* 63–66.

Eysenck, H.J. (1943). Neurosis and intelligence. *The Lancet,* 362–363.

Fletcher, R. (1988). A county systems model: Comprehensive services for the dually diagnosed. In J.A. Stark, F.J. Menolascino, M.H. Albarelli, & V.C. Gray (Eds.), *Mental retardation and mental health: Classification, diagnosis, treatment, services* (pp. 254–264). New York: Springer-Verlag.

Foxx, R.M., Bittle, R.G., & Faw, G.D. (1989). A long-term maintenance strategy for discontinuing aversive procedures: A 52-month follow-up of the treatment of aggression. *American Journal on Mental Retardation, 94,* 27–36.

Foxx, R.M., & Faw, G.D. (1992). An eight-year follow-up of three social skills training studies. *Mental Retardation, 30,* 63–66.

Gillberg, C., & Steffenburg, S. (1987). Outcome and prognostic factors in infantile autism and similar conditions: A population-based study of 46 cases followed through puberty. *Journal of Autism and Developmental Disorders, 17,* 273–287.

Goldberg, B., Gitta, M.Z., & Puddephatt, A. (1992). *Personality and trait disturbances in an adult mental retardation population: Significance for psychiatric management.* Presented at the International Association for the Scientific Study of Mental Deficiency, Gold Coast, Australia.

Goldsmith, L., & Schloss, P.J. (1984). Diagnostic overshadowing among learning-disabled and hearing-impaired learners with an apparent secondary diagnosis of behavior disorders. *International Journal of Partial Hospitalization, 2,* 209–217.

Greenspan, S., & Shoultz, B. (1981). Why mentally retarded adults lose their jobs: Social competence as a factor in work adjustment. *Applied Research in Mental Retardation, 2,* 23–38.

Harper, D.C., & Wadsworth, J.S. (1990). Dementia and depression in elders with mental retardation: A pilot study. *Research in Developmental Disabilities, 11,* 177–191.

Healey, K.N., & Masterpasqua, F. (1992). Interpersonal cognitive problem-solving among children with mental retardation. *American Journal on Mental Retardation, 96,* 367–372.

Jacobson, J.W., & Harper, M.S. (1989). Mental health status of older persons with mental retardation in residential care settings. *Australia and New Zealand Journal of Developmental Disabilities, 15,* 301–309.

James, D.H. (1986). Psychiatric and behavioral disorders amongst older severely mentally handicapped inpatients. *Journal on Mental Retardation Research, 30,* 341–345.

Koller, H., Richardson, S., Katz, M., & McLaren, J. (1983). Behavior disturbance since childhood among a 5-year birth cohort of all mentally retarded young adults in a city. *American Journal on Mental Deficiency, 87,* 386–395.

Kopp, C.B., Baker, B.L., & Brown, K.W. (1992). Social skills and their correlates: Preschoolers with developmental delays. *American Journal on Mental Retardation, 96,* 357–366.

Krauss, M.W., Seltzer, M.M., & Goodman, S.J. (1992). Social support networks of adults with mental retardation who live at home. *American Journal on Mental Retardation, 96,* 432–441.

Kushlick, A., Blunden, R., & Cox, G. (1973). A method of rating behavior characteristics for use in large scale surveys of mental handicap. *Psychological Medicine, 3,* 466–478.

Lakin, K.C., Hill, B.K, Hauber, F.A., Bruininks, R.H., & Heal, L.W. (1983). New admissions and readmissions to a national sample of public residential facilities. *American Journal of Mental Deficiency, 88,* 13–20.

Laman, D.S. (1989). *A longitudinal investigation of the relationship among depressed mood, social support, and social skills in mentally retarded adults.* Unpublished doctoral dissertation, Department of Psychology, University of Illinois at Chicago.

Larson, S.A., & Lakin, K.C. (1992). *Quality of life for people with challenging behavior living in community settings.* Presented at the 1992 annual American Association on Mental Retardation National Convention in New Orleans.

Levitan, G.W., & Reiss, S. (1983). Generality of diagnostic overshadowing across disciplines. *Applied Research in Mental Retardation, 4,* 59–64.

Libb, W.J. (1972). Stimuli previously associated with reinforcement: Reinforcing or frustrating to the mentally retarded. *Journal of Experimental Child Psychology, 14,* 1–10.

Linden, B.E., & Forness, S.R. (1986). Post-school adjustment of mentally retarded persons with psychiatric disorders: A ten-year follow-up. *Education and Training of the Mentally Retarded, 21,* 157–164.

Luckasson, R., Coulter, D., Polloway, E., Reiss, S., Schalock, R.L., Snell, M., Spitalnik, D., & Stark, J.A. (1992). *Mental retardation: Definition, classification, and systems of supports* (9th ed.). Washington, DC: American Association on Mental Retardation.

Luftig, R.L. (1988). Assessment of the perceived school loneliness and isolation of mentally retarded and nonretarded students. *American Journal on Mental Retardation, 92,* 472–475.

Lunsky, Y., & Havercamp, S.H. (1999). Distinguishing low levels of social support and social strain: Implications for dual diagnosis. *American Journal on Mental Retardation, 104,* 158–169.

Lustman, N., & Zigler, E. (1982). Imitation by institutionalized and noninstitutionalized mentally retarded and nonretarded children. *American Journal of Mental Deficiency, 87,* 252–258.

Marsh, H.W., & Barnes, J. (1982). *Self-description questionnaire: II.* Unpublished manuscript. University of Sydney, Australia.

Matson, J.L. (1988). *The PIMRA manual.* Worthington, OH: IDS Publishing Corporation.

Matson, J.L., Coe, D.A., Gardner, W.I., & Sovner, R. (1991). A factor analytic study of the diagnostic assessment for the severely handicapped scale. *The Journal of Nervous and Mental Disease, 179,* 553–557.

McKinney, B., & Peterson, R.A. (1987). Predictors of stress in parents of developmentally disabled children. *Journal of Pediatric Psychology, 12,* 133–150.

McNally, R.J., & Shin, L.M. (1995). Association of intelligence with severity of posttraumatic stress disorder symptoms in Vietnam combat veterans. *American Journal of Psychiatry, 152,* 936–937.

Mundy, P.C., Seibert, J.M., & Hogan, A.E. (1985). Communication skills in the mentally retarded. In M. Sigman (Ed.), *Children with emotional disorders and developmental disabilities.* Orlando, FL: Grune & Stratton.

Nezu, C.M., Nezu, A.M., & Gill-Weiss, M.J. (1992). *Psychopathology in persons with mental retardation: Clinical guidelines for assessment and treatment.* Champaign, IL: Research Press.

Nucci, M., & Reiss, S. (1988). Mental retardation and emotional disorders: A test for increased vulnerability to stress. *Australia and New Zealand Journal of Developmental Disabilities, 13,* 161–166.

Philips, I. (1967). Psychopathology and mental retardation. *American Journal of Psychiatry, 124,* 67–73.

Portnoy, B., & Stacey, C.L. (1954). A comparative study of Negro and white subnormals on the children's form of the Rosensweig Picture-Frustration Test. *American Journal of Mental Deficiency, 59,* 272–278.

Pueschel, S.M. (2001). *A parent's guide to Down syndrome: Toward a brighter future* (Rev. ed.). Baltimore: Paul H. Brookes Publishing Co.

Quay, H.C., & Peterson, D.R. (1987). *Revised behavior problem checklist—PAR edition (RBPC).* Lutz, FL: Psychological Assessment Resources.

Reid, A.H., & Ballinger, B.R. (1987). Personality disorder in mental handicap. *Psychological Medicine, 17,* 983–987.

Reid, A.H., Ballinger, B.R., Heather, B.B., & Melvin, S.J. (1984). The natural history of behavioral symptoms among severely and profoundly retarded mentally retarded patients. *British Journal of Psychiatry, 145,* 289–293.

Reiss, S. (1988). The development of a screening measure for psychopathology in people with mental retardation. In E. Dibble & D.B. Gray (Eds.), *Assessment of behavior problems in persons with mental retardation living in the community.* Rockville, MD: National Institute of Mental Health.

Reiss, S. (1990). Prevalence of dual diagnosis in community-based day programs in the Chicago metropolitan area. *American Journal on Mental Retardation, 94,* 578–585.

Reiss, S. (2000). *Who am I?: The 16 basic desires that motivate our actions and define our personalities.* New York: Jeremy P. Tarcher.

Reiss, S., & Aman, M.G. (1998). *Psychotropic medications and developmental disabilities: The international consensus handbook.* Columbus: The Ohio State University (Distributed by the American Association on Mental Retardation).

Reiss, S., & Benson, B.A. (1984). Awareness of negative social conditions among mentally retarded, emotionally disturbed outpatients. *American Journal of Psychiatry, 141,* 88–90.

Reiss, S., & Benson, B.A. (1985). Psychosocial correlates of depression in mentally retarded adults: I. Minimal social support and stigmatization. *American Journal of Mental Retardation, 89,* 331–337.

Reiss, S., & Havercamp, S.H. (1997). The sensitivity theory of motivation: Why functional analysis is not enough. *American Journal on Mental Retardation, 101,* 553–566.

Reiss, S., & Havercamp, S.H. (1998). Toward a comprehensive assessment of functional motivation: Factor structure of the Reiss Profiles. *Psychological Assessment, 10,* 97–106.

Reiss, S., Levitan, G.W., & McNally, R.J. (1982). Emotional disturbed mentally retarded people: An underserved population. *American Psychologist, 37,* 361–367.

Reiss, S., Levitan, G.W., & Szyszko, J. (1982). Emotional disturbance and mental retardation: Diagnostic overshadowing. *American Journal on Mental Deficiency, 86,* 567–574.

Reiss, S., & Szyszko, J. (1983). Diagnostic overshadowing and professional experience with retarded persons. *American Journal of Mental Deficiency, 87,* 396–402.

Reiss, S., & Valenti-Hein, D. (1994). Development of psychopathology rating scale for children with mental retardation. *Journal of Consulting and Clinical Psychology, 62,* 28–33.

Rusch, F.R., DeStefano, L., Chadsey-Rusch, J., Phelps, L.A., & Szymanski, E.M. (1992). *Transition from school to adult life: Models, linkages and policy.* Sycamore, IL: Sycamore Publishing.

Russell, A.T., & Tanguay, P.E. (1981). Mental illness and mental retardation: Cause or coincidence? *American Journal on Mental Deficiency, 85,* 570–574.

Rutter, M., Tizard, J., & Whitmore, K. (1970). *Education, health and behavior.* New York: John Wiley & Sons.

Ryan, R. (1993). *Posttraumatic stress disorder in persons with developmental disabilities.* Unpublished manuscript. Boulder: Department of Psychiatry, University of Colorado Health Sciences Center.

Sarason, S.B., & Gladwin, T. (1958). Psychological and cultural problems in mental subnormality. In R. Masland, S. Sarason, & T. Gladwin (Eds.), *Mental subnormality.* New York: Basic Books.

Schalock, R.L., & Harper, R. (1978). Placement from community-based mental retardation programs: How well do clients do? *American Journal of Mental Deficiency, 83,* 240–247.

Schalock, R.L., Harper, R.S., & Genung, T. (1981). Community integration of mentally retarded adults: Community placement and program success. *American Journal of Mental Deficiency, 85,* 478–488.

Schalock, R.L., & Keith, K.D. (1993). *Quality of Life Questionnaire Manual.* Worthington, OH: IDS Publishing Corporation.

Scheerenberger, R.C. (1980). *Public residential services for the mentally retarded, 1979.* Madison, WI: National Association of Superintendents of Public Residential Facilities for the Mentally Retarded.

Smith, D.C., Valenti-Hein, D., & Heller, T. (1985). Interpersonal competence and community adjustment of retarded adults. In M. Sigman (Ed.), *Children with emotional disorders and developmental disabilities: Assessment and treatment* (pp. 71–94). Orlando, FL: Grune & Stratton, Inc.

Sprengler, P.M., Strohmer, D.C., & Prout, H.T. (1990). Testing the robustness of diagnostic overshadowing bias. *American Journal on Mental Retardation, 95,* 204–273.

Stephens, E. (1953). Defensive reactions of mentally retarded adults. *Social Casework, 34,* 119–124.

Sugg, D.K. (1999, December 3). When am I going to go home? *The Baltimore Sun,* pp. A1, A8.

Szymanski, L.S., & Tanguay, P.E. (1980). *Emotional disorders of mentally retarded persons.* Baltimore: University Park Press.

Talkington, L.W., & Hall, S.M. (1968). Use of a frustration technique to reinstate speech in non-verbal retarded. *American Journal of Mental Deficiency, 73,* 496–499.

Tebeest, D.L., & Dickie, J.R. (1976). Responses to frustration: Comparison of institutionalized and noninstitutionalized retarded adolescents and nonretarded children and adolescents. *American Journal of Mental Deficiency, 80,* 407–413.

Thorne, F.C. (1947). The problem of institutional elopements. *American Journal of Mental Deficiency, 51,* 637–643.

Valenti-Hein, D.C., & Mueser, K.T. (1990). *The dating skills program: Teaching social-skills to adults with mental retardation.* Worthington, OH: IDS Publishing Co.

Viney, L., Clark, A., & Lord, J. (1973). Resistance to extinction and frustration in retarded and non-retarded children. *American Journal of Mental Deficiency, 78,* 308–315.

Widaman, F.J., MacMillan, K.F., Hemsley, D.L., Little, R.E., & Balow, I.H. (1992). Differences in adolescents' self-concept as a function of academic level, ethnicity, and gender. *American Journal on Mental Retardation, 96,* 387–403.

Williams, G.A., & Asher, S.R. (1992). Assessment of loneliness at school among children with mild mental retardation. *American Journal on Mental Retardation, 96,* 357–366.

Wolpe, J. (1958). *Psychotherapy by reciprocal inhibition.* Palo Alto, CA: Stanford University Press.

Zetlin, A.G., & Turner, J.L. (1984). Self-perspectives on being handicapped: Stigma and adjustment. In R. Edgerton (Ed.), *Lives in progress: Mentally retarded adults in a large city. AAMD Monographs, 6,* 93–120.

Zigler, E. (1971). The retarded child as a whole person. In H.E. Adams & W.K. Boardman (Eds.), *Advances in experimental clinical psychology* (pp. 47–121). New York: Pergamon Press.

15

Spirituality and Self-Actualization

Recognizing Spiritual Needs and Strengths of Individuals with Cognitive Limitations

William Gaventa and Roger K. Peters

David

David's frame was large and well-developed from disciplined work at his Mennonite father's sawmill. He had a mild cognitive disability and experienced tonic-clonic seizures. However, from his perspective, his biggest challenge was fitting in—he felt as if he did not really belong. One day he was in a house full of Mennonite men. A word was said that he understood as a "put down." David started to swing his mighty fists. The reclusive traditional Mennonites, believing they had no choice, called the state police.

David was committed to a large state-operated center for individuals with mental retardation. This was a new and strange world for David. He retained his Mennonite clothes but found no Mennonite community at the center. David soon developed a reputation as a violent person.

At the center, David sought out a man who dressed more like the Mennonite than the "English." That man was a priest, the Catholic chaplain. One day, in a prayer with David, the priest asked that God would take the fire of hate out of David and put the fire of love into his heart.

After the session, David started back down the hall toward his living area. When someone would pass him in the hall, he would swagger his large body toward them announcing, "The fire of hate is out of my heart. The fire of love is in my heart." Because David's words frightened the professional staff as much as his fists, the psychologist at the center sent David to the psychiatrist. However, David stopped hitting people. Also, he seemed happier than ever—almost euphoric.

The chaplain intervened and explained to the psychiatrist the reason for David's words. Eventually, David was able to return to his community.

He did need spiritual supports to stay in the Mennonite community. David found strength to cope through prayer with the chaplain, who would visit every few weeks. Eventually, through an interested staff person, the chaplain, and David's family, the Mennonite pastor was briefed about David's need for spiritual supports. Once a week, David would walk to his Mennonite pastor's home for his prayer. After the connection was made with the Mennonite pastor, David never returned to the center.

Spirituality may be discovered in the strangest ways and in the strangest places. It may or may not be discovered in and through organized religion (Fowler, 1981). David's spiritual encounter took place through a traditional and sensitive intervention of a priest. Since the 1980s, spirituality has been seen as an important component of self-actualization, relationships, and well-being (Culligan, 1996; Sims, 1998; Wallis, 1996). In spiritual connection and practice, David found both personal affirmation and new meaning that renewed his connection with his own Amish community.

SPIRITUALITY

Defining Spirituality

Words and phrases such as *core* and *depth of the self* are used in the attempt to describe spirituality. Other descriptions include having a sense of ultimate meaning and a connection with the unknown mysteries of living (Anderson & Morgan, 1994). Spirituality often is pictured in terms of values, relatedness, and heart (Moore, 1994). It is a term usually connected with people who are religious. Studies, however, suggest that faith or spirituality is a universal phenomenon for the religious and the nonreligious (Carder, 1984; Fitchett, 1993; Fowler, 1981; Larson & Larson, 1994). The spiritual dimension of people's lives is revealed through the ways people express personal meaning and values and through the ways they express their experience of the ultimate or the sacred (Anderson & Morgan, 1994; Fitchett, 1993).

Spirituality often is expressed in and through the traditions and practice of a religion. These religions include the major faith traditions of Islam, Judaism, and Christianity; they also include other religious traditions such as the eastern religions (e.g., Hinduism, Buddhism), Native American religions, and new age religious expressions. However, religious practice may or may not be an expression of spirituality. In contrast to purely extrinsic religion, intrinsic religion is an integrated and vital part of the adherent's personal life. Spirituality corresponds to intrinsic religion (Culligan, 1996). It is that aspect of religion or personal philosophy of life that transforms living with "the perception of transcendent meaning" (Stevens, 1986, p. 15).

Spiritual Development

Mary

Mary is a beautiful 40-year-old woman. As a result of cerebral palsy, Mary has both cognitive and physical limitations. She uses a power wheelchair for mobility. She is able to communicate her needs, wants, and opinions; however, her speech is sometimes difficult to understand. Currently, Mary lives in a fully accessible home with two other individuals.

Recently, Mary had dinner with several members of the clergy in her community. She was there to advocate for herself and others. When it was her turn to talk about her involvement at the local Catholic church, Mary's speech was articulate and clear. She told the ministers and priests that she really felt like a part of her church, that she loved going to mass, and that she particularly appreciated her friends at the church.

Mary's personality is effervescent. Her smile is pleasing, and her laughter is delightful. She has faced her limitations with a spiritual courage and strength that is remarkable. One day, she talked about her personal experience of faith. She mentioned more than the external observances of her faith. She spoke of the sense of belonging that she feels as part of her religious community, and she spoke of the personal meaning of prayer for her: "I pray for my mom and dad up in heaven. They're looking down on me every day. I believe in heaven."

When asked what problems she has encountered in her faith involvement, Mary did not speak of the usual difficulties with logistics in assuring her inclusion. Instead, she simply said, "My mom died, and my dad died." For Mary, the period of grieving for her parents had been a time of spiritual struggle: "I didn't want to go to mass that first day after my mom died. Later I went back to church. I did a lot of praying in my room." When asked the nature of her prayer, she replied, "Please, God, help me get over this—every day to get over it." Mary speaks with seriousness but also with acceptance about still missing her parents—especially during the holiday season. Then, she relates the comfort and affirmation she experiences through her faith: "God," she says, "is 'friend.'"

The seeds of spiritual expression are sown in human beings during infancy (Fowler, 1981). Erikson pointed "to the first year of life as an extremely crucial period for the development of a basic sense of trust" (as cited in Peters, 1986, p. 11). Erikson saw that "trust born of care" (Erikson, 1963, p. 250) is crucial for later faith expression (Westerhoff, 1976). Although Mary clearly had experienced deprivations due to her disabilities during her development, she also clearly experienced emotional/spiritual reassurance through the consistent caring of her parents. Her faith, while expressed through her religious participation, was rooted in early parental nurture.

Theorists have applied Erikson's and Fowler's research on the development of faith to the expression of faith in people with cognitive limitations.
Schurter, for example, has utilized Fowler's model to describe the spiritual
needs and expressions of individuals with cognitive limitations. The dominant
issues of faith for people with mild cognitive limitations are "affiliation, belonging, being cherished; differentiation of self and one's group from others; learning the lore, legends and language of the religious group; sorting out fact and
fantasy, the real and the 'made up'" (Schurter, 1987, p. 238). When Mary was
asked about her personal faith, she focused her appreciation on friends and
friendship with God. Although she knew and spoke some of the language of her
religion, the focus of her experience of faith was her relationship and affiliation
with others.

Developing an Awareness of Spirituality

The beginning of this chapter described David's remarkable spiritual conversion. The story also described the fearful attitude of professional staff toward
David's religious experience. The professional staff were focusing exclusively
on a socioscientific approach to human services. Perspective can be lost when
exclusive focus is given to the socioscientific model (Berger & Luckmann, 1995;
Danforth, 1997; Jencks, 1995).

The socioscientific world view has influenced the arts and religion. In
fact, Steiner (1989) asserted that in the modern world human beings have
become so adept at analysis, definition, and criticism that the wonder of the arts
can no longer be fully experienced. Religion in the 20th century "has largely
tried to interpret itself as compatible with and supporting . . . science and ra-
tionalism" (Holmes, 1978; Otto, 1926; Peters, 1994; Turner, 1972).

However, in the present day, neither science nor religion should accept
knowledge as static and monolithic. In his famous book, *The Structure of Scientific Revolutions,* Thomas Kuhn (1962) demonstrated the subjectivity of modern scientific thinking. Theologians admit that a doctrine is an attempt to explain
the unexplainable (Marty, 1980), and synergistic thinking is needed (Schaef,
1988).

Synergistic thinking encourages an appreciation for human beings from
many perspectives. It does not diminish scientific methods and inquiry regarding issues related to individuals with cognitive limitations. However, it values
as much or more their experiences and their perspectives and insights (Danforth, 1997; Kvale, 1995). The spiritual awareness and desires of individuals
with cognitive limitations are accepted not because they represent objective
facts but because they are the expressions of real people.

Professionals are now willing to highlight the need for "spiritual supports"
for people with cognitive limitations (Coulter, 1994; Luckasson et al., 1992). A
necessary next step is the recognition of individuals with cognitive limitations

as important facilitators of spiritual awareness. The literature abounds with stories of the spiritual perception and awareness of people with all degrees of cognitive limitation (Hoogewind, 1998; Peters, 1987; Shisler, 1998; Webb-Mitchell, 1993; Wolfensberger, 1976).

The hope for the future is an intentional appreciation for the multidimensional aspects of life. For people like David, supported by agencies in which the expression of spirituality may be misunderstood, the hope is not only for a future of listening ears but also one of open hearts.

Spirituality and Well-Being

Openness to the spiritual dimensions of life can lead to improved quality of life and health for people with cognitive limitations. When Mary was asked about her involvement with a community congregation, she said, "I like it. It makes me feel good." The surprise to modern scientists has been that Mary's feeling of wellness in connection with her faith experience is more than just an emotion. Since the 1980s, a plethora of research has been conducted regarding the effects of spirituality on health. The research overwhelmingly indicates that spirituality is positively correlated with the prevention of disease, with wellness, and with recovery from injury, disease, or surgery (Culligan, 1996; Matthews, Larson, & Barry, 1993; Wallis, 1996).

Research on the healthy connection between spirituality and wellness is not restricted to physical health. Researchers also have noted positive correlations of spirituality with mental health. For example, suicide rates and drug use are significantly lower among people who express their spirituality in religious practice (Comstock & Partridge, 1972; Gorsuch & Butler, 1976; Loch & Hughes, 1985).

Many spiritual assessment instruments and research models have been developed (Farrar, 1995; Larson & Larson, 1994; Matthews et al., 1993; Prins, 1994). Practitioners and researchers have emphasized the importance of community inclusion for people with cognitive limitations. Congregations and spiritual communities are important resources for community life and for building supportive relationships (Amado, 1993). Participation in spiritual communities and activities also has been highlighted in the self-determination movement. Participation gives individuals with cognitive limitations opportunities for self-affirmation and for responsibility through "truly contributing to the associational life of their communities, the spiritual life of our churches and synagogues, and the cultural and artistic life of our cities and towns" (Nerney & Shumway, 1996, p. 6).

Research has highlighted the responsibility of service providers to support the spirituality of people with cognitive limitations (Dudley & Helfgott, 1990; Heifitz, 1987). Research also has focused on the role of spirituality and religion for the families of people with cognitive limitations (e.g., Haworth, Hill, &

Glidden, 1996; Rogers-Dulan & Blacher, 1995). However, little specific research on the effects of spiritual and religious practice on the well-being of people with mild cognitive limitations has been conducted.

Anecdotal evidence, however, is overwhelming. People with cognitive limitations find in their religious experiences a source of emotional/spiritual support for healthy living (Hoogewind, 1998; Hornstein, 1997; Shisler; 1998, Webb-Mitchell, 1993). Practitioners and writers have observed and described in many ways a transparent spirituality in the lives of people with cognitive limitations that not only is a source of personal well-being for the individuals themselves but is also a source of inspiration for other people (Hoogewind, 1998; Hornstein, 1997; Peters, 1987; Shisler, 1998; Webb-Mitchell, 1993).

SPIRITUAL JOURNEYS

Mark, Barbara, and Sandy

On Monday morning, Bill stopped at one of the group homes to talk with the home's supervisor. He asked whether there was any evidence of interest on the part of the people who lived at the home in participating in a religion of their choice. The supervisor assured Bill that the issue of religious interest had been reviewed for each person, and none of the individuals had any interest in religion. Bill then asked another question: "Do any of the people have religious pictures, books, or objects?"

The supervisor immediately began to describe religious behavior observed in Mark, Barbara, and Sandy. The supervisor reported that Mark has a yarmulke that he regularly wears on Saturdays. He also becomes very animated and hyperactive around Passover and other Jewish holy days. Barbara cherishes her rosary and is seen fingering it regularly. Sandy has pictures of Jesus on the walls of her room and has a big Bible beside her bed. When one of the staff members at the home was going to have surgery, Sandy told him that she would be praying for him.

After his interview with the home's supervisor, Bill knew that the problem of the lack of community religious participation was not a lack of interest but, rather, a lack of staff awareness and action. The supervisor and other staff members were not antireligious. They simply did not think about the possibility of community religious inclusion for Mark, Barbara, and Sandy. Staff were conditioned to evaluate maladaptive behaviors, medical needs, and training and educational needs. However, they were not aware of the need for spiritual assessment for the individuals who lived in the home. (Gleason, 1998)

This story is unusual not because of the spiritual needs of these individuals but, rather, because the agency that served them realized that it was ignoring the spiritual needs and gifts of its consumers and the ways that the quality of life of its consumers could be enhanced by more sensitive, proactive supports. The initiative of the agency is what is unusual. By virtue of the congregate setting, the issues were relatively easy to address once the awareness had been raised.

That is not and would not be the case for the vast majority of people with mild cognitive limitations. These people, many of whom have never been in an institution or group home, often fall through the cracks between the intentional initiatives in both "secular" and "spiritual" support systems. The following vignettes tell the stories of some of these individuals.

Robert

Robert, a young man in is twenties, was one of the first people to move out of a state institution in the late 1970s. One of Robert's valued roles at the institution was assisting the chaplain. Once Robert left the institution, he lived first in a group home, then in a supported living arrangement, and finally in his own apartment. Robert's employment life has been characterized by a number of attempts to move beyond the sheltered workshop. All efforts toward independent employment have been impeded by either his physical needs or a lack of effective supports. In his personal life, Robert fulfilled a dream by marrying; however, not long after the marriage, he experienced the trauma of seeing his wife have a stroke and experience other medical conditions. Robert's identity and purpose have been forged since his move from the institution around 1980. He demonstrates support as a spouse by regularly visiting his wife in a nursing home. Robert continues to serve as an usher and be an active member in the nearby congregation where his wedding ceremony took place. He also keeps in touch with the chaplain he assisted at the institution. Robert often comments, "Life in the community is not easy."

When the Supports Are Not Intentional

John

John served as a chaplain's assistant each Sunday when he lived in his state's institution. Then he moved to a group home in a nearby city, then to supported living, and finally to his own apartment. John became a full-time employee on the janitorial staff at another state facility, where he worked successfully for years. Unfortunately, John was forced to take early disability retirement because of failing eyesight and other medical issues. Because he lived in a downtown urban neighborhood, John's social support system became bus drivers, policemen, tavern owners, and professionals from former placements. However, John's street savvy did not extend into confidence about participating in a congregation. Without an active welcome or friendship, his social shyness turned him away from churches. He was reluctant to be part of intentional "special ministries programs" offered at nearby congregations.

Ready to Give But Not Received

Ann

Ann, a young woman of prominence in a self-advocacy organization, grew up in a church-going family. When she moved to another city, she began attending services with a different denomination and participating in their youth group. However, Ann began to get very frustrated by the group's unwillingness to validate her desire to express herself. She wanted to share her own faith journey and story in the ways that were expected of others.

In another example from New Jersey, a self-advocacy group coordinator requested resources and suggestions on ways to assist two self-advocacy groups who wanted the opportunity to talk about the Bible and to do Bible study. Many of the individuals participate in congregations, but they wanted the chance to talk about their spirituality, faith journeys, and the Bible in a setting in which they feel comfortable and the discussion of the Bible was shaped by their questions and concerns.

Transitions to Full Membership

Ray

Ray, a young man who has been educated in an inclusive environment, wanted to be baptized in his church as other teenagers and church members are. The initial pastoral response was that Ray did not need to be baptized because his special needs made him already one of "God's elect." It took both individual and family persistence, in addition to some outside consulting and encouragement, to help the clergy move beyond a cognitive interpretation of a sacrament to recognition of its importance as a coming-of-age ritual and transition.

Jim

Jim wanted to keep attending his church's senior high youth group even though all of his peers had graduated and moved on to college and beyond. His parents saw the group as a major social outlet for Jim. However, new members of the youth group did not see Jim as a peer and struggled with Jim's attempts to date girls in the group. Attempts to deal with the issues felt, to Jim and his family, like congregational rejection.

MILESTONES AND CHALLENGES

In the previous vignettes, one can discern a number of significant achievements for and by individuals with mild cognitive limitations during the past several decades. These achievements include the opportunity to participate in religious education programs in either congregate or inclusive settings and the inclusion of young adults in religious rituals and rites of passage such as baptism, confirmation, bar and bat mitzvahs, and other ceremonies that once would have been closed to them (Hornstein, 1997). The stories also demonstrate personal commitment by individuals, families, and friends that has enabled individuals with cognitive limitations to move beyond participation to contribution in spiritual communities. However, challenges and issues also are evident. Those struggles include the following:

- *The paradox of status gained and status lost in inclusive community settings:* In more restrictive, congregated settings, people with mild cognitive limitations often were the stars, the ones who could and did have positions of responsibility and leadership. But in the community, they often moved from being the stars to being on the fringe in terms of cognitive and social skills and to being on the bottom or certainly on the outside in terms of participation in spiritual communities.
- *The equation of faith and spirituality with reason and cognitive ability:* Although many changes have occurred, remnants of the attitudes that equate faith with cognitive ability still exist. Participation in rites of passage and belonging, such as first communion and bar or bat mitzvahs, often have been restricted by questions about the capacity of an individual with cognitive limitations to understand meaning and significance or to meet other standards. Or sometimes, as was the case with Ray, the assumption is made that the accepted standards do not apply to individuals with cognitive limitations and thus they are not challenged to learn and/or demonstrate their beliefs. Although these attitudes have changed radically in many traditions, it is still difficult for people with mild cognitive limitations to find a place in congregations in which their spiritual questions and journeys are taken seriously. As adults, they do not fit in with religious education programs for children and young people. Most adult religious education programs, such as Bible study courses, rely on more advanced cognitive skills for their participants and/or lack creative teachers or facilitators who could involve people with mild cognitive limitations. Some faith communities may have special religious education programs for adults with cognitive limitations, but what happens with individuals who are sensitive to stigma and labels

and want no part of a "labeled" program but want to participate in more typical ways in congregational life?

- *The equation of disability with the lack of social-cultural-religious skills:* One of the challenges faced by people with mild cognitive limitations in spiritual participation is the assumption that their lack of understanding of social skills or membership skills in a particular faith tradition is diagnosed as a product of their cognitive limitation (Gaventa, 1986). The lack of effective skills in practicing a particular religious faith or tradition is more likely to be the result of a lack of opportunity and practice. Most people who are members of a particular spiritual tradition grew up in that community and had many opportunities to learn and practice how one worships in a particular faith, how you behave at coffee hours and other social functions, and how to be an effective member or contributor. Those particular spiritual traditions are also integral parts of many cultural communities. Thus, "spiritual" and "religious education" happens in the home, in cultural activities and during holidays, in communal practices of celebration and grief, and in so many other parts of life. People with mild cognitive limitations face a challenge because this form of education is more implicit than explicit. They may need the help of teachers or mentors who are sensitive to issues of stigma and lack of self-confidence and self-esteem—issues that many individuals with mild cognitive limitations face in any spiritual community.

- *Poverty:* Although people with mild cognitive limitations may be gainfully employed and may be doing much better than they were as consumers in a sheltered workshop, most are still poor and may lack some of the economic means to practice their own spirituality or religious faith. Poverty makes it difficult for these individuals to buy clothing, find transportation, and participate in congregational activities; often, it also puts people with mild cognitive limitations in the position of being receivers rather than givers.

- *Lack of spiritual guides:* The final challenge faced by many individuals with mild cognitive limitations is the question of who serves as their guides into spiritual communities and in community settings. If individuals with cognitive limitations are living independently, with minimal public supports, those supports rarely have the sophistication or means to honor, respect, and facilitate spiritual development and participation. Put simply, who asks the "forgotten generation" about their spiritual questions, journeys, or preferences? Who takes responsibility for finding ways to meet their needs and to discover their gifts? Who makes the invitations and helps make the introductions? Who, on the side of faith communities, takes responsibility for seeking out and inviting to services individuals with cognitive limitations who may live in their community but who, for whatever reason, are not part of faith communities (Gaventa, 1989, 1993)? It is important to note that these challenges reflect issues that are not solely the result of mild cognitive limitations, but that are issues in spiritual life and participation for many people with varying levels of abilities. Strangers, newcomers, or individuals on the fringe of a spiritual or secular community also face these issues.

BUILDING OPPORTUNITIES FOR SPIRITUAL GROWTH

Cornerstones

As a foundation for more effective responses to the spiritual needs and gifts of individuals with mild cognitive limitations, there are at least three cornerstones that need to be laid in theory and practice in both the spiritual and secular support systems.

First, as has been addressed in other parts of this chapter, both spiritual and secular support systems need to recognize and affirm the integrity and importance of the spiritual journey and spiritual dimensions of the lives of individuals with mild cognitive limitations. Lack of intellectual skills does not equate with a lack of spiritual understanding, needs, and strengths (Luckasson et al., 1992). The basis for affirming the spiritual capacity of individuals with mild cognitive limitations can come from any of the following (Gaventa, 1999):

- Recognition of the spiritual and sacred dimension of life
- Recognition of the multitude of ways that people shape and derive meaning
- Sensitivity to the importance of spiritual traditions in understanding and development of cultural competency
- Honoring and encouraging of the rights of individuals to choose and practice spiritual and religious freedom

Affirmation of the spiritual needs of individuals with mild cognitive limitations also involves recognition of the capacity of congregations to address a variety of needs. In addition to meeting basic spiritual needs for belonging and affirmation, spiritual communities represent opportunities for socialization, recreation, education, service, connection to potential employers, and more (Gaventa, 1986, 1993b). Congregations or other forms of spiritual communities and associations are doorways into wider community life. For example, thousands of congregations in this country have provided multiple levels of support to sponsor the resettlement of refugee families within communities. There is little difference between those supports and the ones needed by people with mild cognitive limitations.

Second, providers need to approach the spiritual lives of individuals with mild cognitive limitations from a gifts perspective rather than from a deficit orientation (Kretzmann & Mcknight, 1993). Stated another way, the question is not just how do spiritual and religious communities serve people with mild cognitive limitations; the question is how do people have the opportunity to explore and develop their own response to the call to service and faithful practice, however it is defined? Nerney and Shumway (1996) cited the spiritual community as a primary path for "responsible contribution" of all individuals using self-determined supports. In more practical terms, this may mean that professionals and supporters should focus on finding ways for individuals to use their gifts and strengths in the context of their own spiritual community. A narrow focus on inclusion in worship and religious education may unintentionally put all of the emphasis on overcoming impairments in understanding or education rather than on finding ways for people to give as well as to receive.

Third, opportunities and programs for spiritual and religious education should focus at least as much on assisting individuals to understand what it means to be part of a particular religious tradition and community as they do on helping these individuals understand basic tenets of faith and scriptural traditions. What if religious education was envisioned as developing "membership skills" as opposed to intellectual understanding? That focus may mean opportunities for both inclusive and segregated spiritual expression. The crucial question is not an ideological battle over either/or but an approach that may offer both options and provide real and meaningful opportunities for choice, contribution, responsibility, and leadership.

Problems in Laying the Cornerstones

So, what gets in the way of these theoretical goals and the practices based on them? Perhaps the problems that impede more effective practice are evident in the story of the agency and in the individual community vignettes presented previously. However, to begin to ensure that the problems are not only noted but addressed, the following questions should be asked:

1. Have support professionals and/or agencies asked individuals about their preferences and traditions (i.e., have they done some form of basic spiritual assessment)? Have professionals and/or agencies been willing to invite or include friends or allies from a person's faith community in interdisciplinary assessment and planning processes?
2. Who is responsible for taking the lead in spiritual development and participation? The individual? The direct support staff? The case managers or agencies? The individual's family? The members of the congregation? Policies, theories, and hospitable theologies may make doors easier to open, but it is real people who help others through them. Whatever their background, the crucial issue is, who will step forward to be the coach (i.e., help make introductions; interpret strengths as well as needs; guide responses to behavior that congregations may misinterpret; or, stated more positively, help people learn membership skills in a given community, association, culture, or tradition)?
3. Although an agency's policy may say religious freedom is respected, are there really opportunities to practice one's faith, to try different traditions,

to go by oneself or with one individual rather than as a group to religious activities, and to participate in congregational activities other than weekly worship and weeknight religious education? Is there sensitivity within congregations and agencies to the importance of religious rituals of transition and belonging (Hornstein, 1997)? Has the agency explored policies to enhance spiritual practice in ways that move beyond perceived barriers of church/state separation? Careful policy, combined with effective staff and congregational education, can make a huge difference (Hoeksema, 1995).

PROMISING RESPONSES

Many of the individual stories and scenarios used in this chapter illustrate some of the promising responses that are taking place in the United States and elsewhere in recognizing the spiritual needs and gifts of individuals with mild cognitive limitations. Creative initiatives include the following:

- Congregations that are working with individuals, agencies, and families in the use of person-centered planning strategies and circles of support to assist individual belonging and growth (Preheim-Bartel & Neufeld, 1986)
- Growing numbers of religious agencies involved in the development of community living arrangements, with intentional connections between the individuals being supported and members of the host congregation; this is happening in Catholic, Jewish, and Protestant circles
- The real and symbolic importance of the L'Arche communities,[1] founded by Jean Vanier, in affirming and recognizing the spiritual dimensions of supports in these intentional residential and support communities in addition to the writings of other L'Arche leaders such as Henri Nouwen and Sue Mostellar, who have helped to interpret the integrity and depth of the spiritual journeys of people with cognitive limitations
- Numerous examples of congregational leadership by people with mild cognitive limitations, including service as Eucharistic ministers within Roman Catholic congregations; service as ushers, deacons, or teacher aides; and participation in faith-based service associations, such as Knights of Columbus, Hadassah, men's and women's clubs, and others
- Religious/spiritual education programs that provide opportunities for the development of friendships, connections, and leadership skills and that provide both skills and motivation to participate in inclusive congregational settings; some national programs include the Friendship Ministries in Protestant congregations, Faith and Light Communities (primarily Catholic, founded as an adjunct to the L'Arche network), YACHAD and other Jewish

---

[1]In L'Arche communities, people with cognitive disabilities live together with supporters in intentional residential settings with a strong focus on spiritual dimensions that create a community of acceptance and celebration for each person.

programs (e.g., Chaverim in Los Angeles) that provide opportunities for socialization, education, and self-advocacy

- Spiritual ministries and services founded in both public and private networks that envision their role explicitly as bridge builders and connectors to help individuals with cognitive limitations to participate in faith traditions of their own choice and tradition. Some Catholic dioceses, Jewish federations, large faith-based service providers, and former institutional chaplaincies have developed these roles. Massachusetts has several creative projects that represent collaborations between state agencies, providers, and interfaith councils. These projects recruit volunteers from area congregations to serve as "faith companions" to assist individuals with cognitive limitations to participate in spiritual activities and communities of their choice (Perkins, 1997).

- The growth in the quantity and quality of resource materials, advocacy initiatives, and networking organizations within denominations, faith communities, and secular associations with the common focus on building effective spiritual supports (Gaventa, 2000). A growing awareness of both opportunity and responsibility within clergy, laity, and congregations has been fostered by national initiatives including the Religion and Spirituality Division of the American Association on Mental Retardation (AAMR), the National Apostolate for Inclusion Ministries (formerly the National Apostolate for Mentally Retarded Persons), the Christian Council for Persons with Disabilities, the Consortium of Jewish Special Educators and programs in many Jewish federations and agencies of education, the National Council of Churches Committee on Disability, and the Religion and Disability Program of the National Organization on Disability.

TOMORROW'S JOURNEY

Policy and Spirituality

Policy development in both public and religious (spiritual) networks can address spiritual development and inclusion not only from the point of view of legal obligation but also from the point of view of natural community supports. A number of positive steps can be taken in the development of policy to help tap the potential of spiritual supports for people with mild cognitive limitations:

   1. Policy development must be informed by self-advocates. In the process of formulating policy, policy makers in both secular and spiritual systems should make deliberate efforts to listen to the aspirations, ideas, and concerns of self-advocates with regard to spirituality and to honor their history, traditions, and current preferences or choices. This process can be performed for individuals with cognitive limitations through assessments and planning processes, but people with mild cognitive limitations can and should have a place at

the table in policy development and the planning of systemic initiatives and supports. As the self-advocacy slogan states, "Nothing about me without me."

2.   Policy development must be clear on the obligation of service providers to support the religious involvement of each person's choice. Confusion has existed regarding church/state separation issues. Those issues must be resolved in favor of religious liberty and opportunity without coercion or proselytizing (Hoeksema, 1995). Policy development must assure the provision of adequate resources to guarantee religious freedom and spiritual supports and welcome partnerships with faith communities to develop those supports. Stated more starkly, freedom of choice without supports may be meaningless.

3.   Religious organizations and community service providers often need assistance in determining how to collaborate in ways that maximize community inclusion (Gaventa, 1993a, 1993b; Thornburgh, 1997). Too often, marginalized people are seen as the responsibility of either a public agency or the religious community. Policy development in the United States is increasingly allowing the exploration of public–private partnerships in faith-based initiatives that combine public resources with volunteer action and commitment. The question of responsibility is "both/and," not "either/or."

4.   Policy development should support the importance of training and education within public agencies *and* within the spiritual community. Policy development in "both directions" may support the role of "bridge-builders"— people who can facilitate connections and collaboration between public agencies and spiritual communities for the sake of more holistic supports to people with mild cognitive limitations.

5.   In both the public and religious/spiritual communities, policy initiatives need to link services and supports to people with disabilities with other services and/or initiatives for people who are marginalized for other reasons. This needs to happen in the religious community and in voluntary associations as well. For example, how might literacy, housing, or parenting programs in faith communities be more fully inclusive of people with disabilities? Or, as already mentioned, how might the model of "wrap-around" supports for refugees by congregations be tapped to assist people with mild cognitive limitations in ways that do not presume life-long dependency but, instead, presume the provision of whatever supports are necessary to help people become contributing members of the community?

Implementing and Demonstrating Spiritually Liberating Policy

The information and resources necessary for enabling the secular and spiritual communities to develop effective training and educational programs and for helping policies become practice (i.e., to practice what is preached) already exist. The question is, who will exercise the will and the motivation to utilize them? In a number of ways, public and private systems and networks are beginning to develop demonstration programs that build on successful experiences and initiatives and that point to possible directions for future practice. These directions include the following:

Statewide Collaborations   A need exists for the development of public–private, religious–secular collaborations at statewide levels, perhaps with the assistance of developmental disabilities councils. Examples include a project in New Jersey to support a survey of congregational supports and development of an interfaith coalition for inclusive ministries, an initiative in Pennsylvania sponsored by the Developmental Disabilities Council to bring together secular and religious communities to develop collaborative projects around their common mission of inclusion, and a Request for Proposals for small grants by the North Carolina Developmental Disabilities Council to support creative local initiatives by congregations and agencies. Although some of these initiatives perhaps raise questions of church and state separation for some, they are evidence of a growing number of ways that public agencies in many areas of human services are attempting to build appropriate collaborations with faith-based communities because of demonstrated outcomes (e.g., the Faith in Action Initiatives of the Robert Wood Johnson Foundation supported by the Interfaith Caregivers Alliance, formerly the National Federation of Interfaith Volunteer Caregivers). The importance of involvement by developmental disabilities councils or other public or secular arenas for building interfaith collaboration is the role they play as a neutral arena in which varying religious and spiritual traditions can come together in places where there may not be strong interfaith organizations. This kind of statewide initiative could also facilitate the creation of relationships between self-advocacy organizations and religious organizations.

Enhancing Bridge Builders and Spiritual Supports Coordinators   By whatever title one calls a role or program, many more intentional efforts need to be made to create roles that facilitate connections between people with mild cognitive limitations and the spiritual communities and associations of their choice and preference. In an era of deinstitutionalization, chaplaincy roles often have disappeared because of the system's belief that "congregations would do it" or would "take over." In some cases, this has been true. However, supports can greatly facilitate the process of involving individuals with mild cognitive limitations in the religious community. For example, supports have been necessary in the area of employment; connections that are effective and inclusive do not happen by waiting for a business to make the first move or by dropping off consumers on the front steps or at the human resources department. What is needed in the area of spirituality is the equivalent of the supported employment coach, or a support broker—a "church coach," that is, an individual who can assist others in negotiating and tapping supports and making contributions. As demonstrated by the Bridges to Faith projects in Massachusetts (Perkins, 1997), community-based chaplaincies in other states, and bridge-building roles developed by religious organizations and some agencies, a variety of people could serve the needed role of building bridges between public and private (or formal and natural) supports.

Including Spirituality in Quality of Life and Consumer Outcomes Initiatives Whether through spiritual assessments, person-centered planning, service evaluation, or quality-of-life/outcomes initiatives, people with mild cognitive limitations need to be asked about, and supported in, their spiritual preferences. Support agencies need to develop and demonstrate appropriate and real ways to assist consumers to exercise choice and preferences in their spiritual lives. Support agencies also need to develop effective means of including spiritual supports and supporters in ongoing life planning, evaluation, and consumer satisfaction instruments. This is happening in isolated locations but, again, needs much wider demonstration.

Training   A basic way to address the need for spirituality supports for individuals with mild cognitive limitations is to include an area of study and opportunities for practice in professional training programs such as graduate schools and seminaries. A wide variety of professional disciplines are developing theory and practice in ways to address spiritual needs in professional practice. A few seminaries have courses, or parts of courses, related to spiritual care for people with disabilities. But very few training programs, with recognized forms of credit, focus on the spiritual needs of persons with disabilities and/or effective support-building strategies. On a national level, this calls for some more creative collaborations between secular and religious training programs, or, for example, between university-affiliated programs and seminaries or pastoral care training programs. The Elizabeth M. Boggs Center on Developmental Disabilities in New Jersey has initiatives in this area, but there are many more possible collaborations. Community-based, accredited clinical-pastoral education programs in systems supporting individuals with disabilities would provide a means for training clergy, laity, and related professionals in the spiritual care of individuals with cognitive limitations and for developing "congregational coaching" models and strategies.

Collaborative Supports without New Walls: Spirituality and Self-Determination   When spiritual communities begin to get involved in supports and services for people with cognitive limitations, they often do so because individuals, families, or advocates have expressed a desire for faith-based supports that demonstrate sensitivity and commitment. The temptation for religious networks is to create their own agencies, supported living arrangements, group homes, and so forth that mirror the kinds of supports and services already provided by public or other private agencies.

In some areas of the country, new collaborations are attempting to provide supports that do not copy other nonspiritual agencies but that represent community-based collaborations between faith communities and public agencies. It can take the form of congregation-based circles of support (Mennonites) or the support of brokering services for families and individuals to do futures planning and support coordination. Brokering and planning can then combine public supports with strategies for maintaining friendships and relationships with community and congregation connections.

Stated another way, as the national self-determination movement and model grows, how might the "support brokering" model be one that truly links and facilitates formal and informal supports in ways that build on and enhance community connection and contribution rather than impede more natural supports? How might self-determination initiatives across the country demonstrate ways of organizing and brokering supports that integrate spiritual supports with other systems of support?

Evaluation and Research   All of the cutting edges in policy, practice, and demonstration call for evaluation and further research. The following three areas call for particular attention:

1. "Supported writing" that assists people with mild cognitive limitations to describe and share their own spiritual journeys and stories in written form or through another way of communicating spiritual issues, such as music, art, prayer, or meditation (Josephson, 1997; Shisler, 1998)
2. Participatory research models that explore the meanings of spirituality from the perspectives of people with mild cognitive limitations, with the goal of learning how to support their needs and gifts more effectively but also of learning from their own unique perspective as people who have been caught "in between" or "on the outside of" the boundaries of systems and theories too often
3. Research that explores the linkages between spiritual supports and quality-of-life outcomes, including health, consumer satisfaction, and community inclusion. Research exploring linkages among spirituality, religious involvement, and health has received increasing national attention in scientific and religious circles as well as in the press (Gaventa, 1999; Larson & Larson, 1994). Many people believe that supports and services that intentionally focus on the spiritual needs and gifts of people with cognitive disabilities will have quality-of-life outcomes. This belief needs to be tested and researched. For example, do spiritual supports make a difference in consumer satisfaction? Does an agency with a commitment to spiritual supports demonstrate quality-of-life outcomes? These questions are simply some of the obvious starting places for research that needs to be published in both secular and religious circles.

CONCLUSION

This book, and the conference that spawned it, provides some of the very opportunities for collaboration that have been described in this chapter. Cruz, a researcher who is doing participatory research with adults with mild cognitive limitations who are also parents with multiple children, some of whom also have been diagnosed with mental retardation, included some questions related to spirituality and congregations in her research. Here are some of the quotes she collected:

"Recently, I found out that I needed to sort through some things in this household to get rid of. To do it by yourself . . . to do organization of his household . . . has been an ongoing battle. When the church offered to come over, to help me sort through things . . . first thing that came into my mind is that I have some pride. My second thought was, forget the pride, you need some help to sort through what the kids no longer need . . . give it to somebody who needs it but at the same time learn to organize visually. . . . So, they've been helping out in regards to cleaning house, helping to sort through things, and to be emotionally there as well."

"In the past year, (my husband) was pulled out of the home and isn't currently in the house. So ongoing with the kids, I've been supporting being a parent to the kids with limited contact with their father. . . . Recently, with me in the past year, I've had to learn how to be both parent in the morning, parent in the afternoon, and parent at night. By nighttime, I'm looking at myself . . . and this is why I went to the church to get some ideas . . . is how to keep my energy level enough there so I can do four kinds when there is chaos going on in the house. The impact is that if the church had not come back into help, I'm sensing this family would be in a whole lot more trouble of having to maintain a household, to put it mildly."

"[My daughter] has a hard time understanding when a person means no, they mean no. With the church, is that they guide them without being judgmental of how to quiet down, to be polite, to sit properly. Manners, in my mind. Most needful, because as they get older . . . [they will need them]."

"You know what keeps me going is the man that's upstairs. At one time, everyone was like, 'Come on [name], let's go to church.' Now I'm going when I get ready. I didn't want to go. I didn't have the time. I was on that alcohol. I was too busy trying to find that next drink. But after I got off the alcohol, K. was off of drugs and she started going to church and then I kinda went with her a couple of times. And I was like, oh, wait a minute, this is it. I like this. And that's how I got into God. And He's there. And I've learned so much how He's been carrying me and my family on His shoulders cause if it wasn't for God, I don't think I'd be here now. He's the one that's got me here. He's the one that said, "Okay, it's going to be [your] job to take care of this family." Without God, there would be no family. I understand the fact that there's agencies that's helping us and some of the family members, but the man upstairs is the one that's doing everything. You know when I get down on my knees at night, I thank Him for everything we have, everything. Because without God, I wouldn't have nothing." (Quotes used with permission from Virginia Cruz)

Spiritual resources are an underutilized treasure in supporting individuals with mild cognitive limitations. Religious and spiritual practice is partly a rights issue, but it is much more. Spirituality is an innate quality of all people. Supporting spiritual aspirations is another way to focus on people as people rather than focusing on their disabilities. For human services systems, spiritual resources offer primary opportunities for real community inclusion and the development of natural supports. For religious organizations, intentional steps toward inclusion are more than charitable acts. Those steps are steps closer to the precepts of religious traditions and steps toward the religious vision of supportive, interdependent communities of faith for all people where all have needs and gifts. For people with cognitive limitations, the opportunity for spiritual practice can be a foundation for a more holistic and inclusive life in the community.

REFERENCES

Amado, A. (Ed.). (1993). *Friendships and community connections between people with and without developmental disabilities.* Baltimore: Paul H. Brookes Publishing Co.

Anderson, P., & Morgan, M. (1994, Summer). Spirituality and sexuality: The healthy connection. *Journal of Religion and Health, 33,* 115–121.

Berger, P.L., & Luckmann, T. (1995). The dehumanized world. In W.T. Anderson (Ed.), *The truth about the truth: Deconfusing and re-constructing the postmodern world.* New York: G.P. Putnam and Sons.

Carder, M. (1984). Spiritual and religious needs of mentally retarded persons. *The Journal of Pastoral Care, 38*(2), 143–154.

Comstock, G.W., & Partridge, K.B. (1972). Church attendance and health. *Journal of Chronic Disease, 25,* 665–672.

Coulter, D. (1994, Fall/Winter). Spiritual supports in the 1992 AAMR system. *National Apostolate for Persons with Mental Retardation (NAPMR) Quarterly, 25*(2), 10–12.

Culligan, K. (1996, August 31). Spirituality and healing in medicine. *America,* 17–21.

Danforth, S. (1997). On what basis hope? Modern progress and postmodern possibilities. *Mental Retardation, 35*(2), 93–106.

Dudley, J., & Helfgott, C. (1990). Exploring a place for spirituality in the social work curriculum. *Journal of Social Work Education, 26,* 287–294.

Erikson, E.H. (1963). *Childhood and society.* Philadelphia: Harper and Row.

Farrar, J. (1995). *Client's spirituality and religious life: Challenging the scope of occupational therapy practice.* Unpublished master's thesis, Tufts University.

Fitchett, G. (1993). *Assessing spiritual needs: A guide for caregivers.* Minneapolis, MN: Augsburg/Fortress Press.

Fowler, J. (1981). *Stages of faith: The psychology of human development and the quest for meaning.* New York: Harper and Row.

Gaventa, W. (1986). Religious ministries and services with adults with developmental disabilities. In J.A. Summers (Ed.), *The right to grow up: An introduction to adults with developmental disabilities* (pp. 191–226). Baltimore: Paul H. Brookes Publishing Co.

Gaventa, W. (1989, Summer). Bring on the church coach. *AAMR News and Notes.*

Gaventa, W. (1993a, September/October). From belief to belonging to belief: Trends in religious ministries and services with people with mental retardation. *The Disability Rag ReSource,* 27–29.

Gaventa, W. (1993b). Gift and call: Recovering the spiritual foundations of friendships. In A. Amado (Ed.), *Friendships and community connections between people with and without developmental disabilities* (pp. 41–66). Baltimore: Paul H. Brookes Publishing Co.

Gaventa, W. (in press). Defining and assessing spirituality and spiritual supports: Moving from benediction to invocation. In S. Greenspan & H. Switzky (Eds.), *What is mental retardation? Ideas for the new century.* Washington, DC: American Association on Mental Retardation.

Gleeson, T. (1998). *Social act, community responsibility.* Presentation at the AAMR national conference, San Diego.

Gorsuch, R.L., & Butler, M.C. (1976). Initial drug abuse: A view of predisposing social factors. *Psychological Bulletin, 3,* 120–137.

Haworth, A., Hill, A., & Glidden, L. (1996). Measuring the religiousness of parents of children with developmental disabilities. *Mental Retardation 34*(5), 271–279

Heifitz, L. (1987). Integrating religious and secular perspectives in the design and delivery of disability services. *American Journal on Mental Retardation, 25,* 127–131.

Hoeksema, T. (1995). Supporting the free exercise of religion in the group home context. *Mental Retardation, 33*(5) 289–294.

Holmes, U.T., III (1978). *The priest in community.* New York: Seabury Press.

Hoogewind, A. (1998). *Parables of hope, inspiring truths from people with disabilities.* Grand Rapids, MI: Zondervan Publishing House.

Hornstein, B. (1997). How the religious community can support the transition to adulthood: A parent's perspective. *Mental Retardation, 35*(6), 485–487.

Jencks, C. (1995). What is post-modernism? In W.T. Anderson (Ed.), *The truth about the truth: Deconfusing and re-constructing the postmodern world.* New York: G.P. Putnam and Sons.

Josephson, G. (1997). *Bus girl.* Boston: Brookline Publishers, Inc.

Kretzmann, J., & Mcknight, J. (1993). *Building communities from the inside out: A path toward finding and mobilizing a community's assets.* Evanston, Illinois: Northwestern University.

Kuhn, T.S. (1962). *The structure of scientific revolutions.* Chicago: University of Chicago Press.

Kvale, S. (1995). Themes of postmodernity. In W.T. Anderson (Ed.), *The truth about the truth: Deconfusing and re-constructing the postmodern world.* New York: G.P. Putnam and Sons.

Larson, D., & Larson, S. (1994). *The forgotten factor in physical and mental health: What does the research show?* Rockville, MD: National Institute of Healthcare Research.

Luckasson, R., Coulter, D., Polloway, E., Reiss, S., Schalock, R., Snell, M., Spitalnik, D., & Stark, J. (1992). *Mental retardation: Definition, classification, and systems of supports.* Washington, DC: American Association on Mental Retardation.

Marty, M.E. (1980). *The Lord's supper.* Philadelphia: Fortress Press.

Matthews, D., Larson, D., & Barry, C. (1993). *The faith factor: An annotated bibliography of clinical research on spiritual subjects.* Rockville, MD: National Institute of Healthcare Research.

Moore, T. (1994). *Soulmates.* New York: HarperCollins.

Nerney, T., & Shumway, D. (1996). *Beyond managed care: Self-determination for people with disabilities.* Concord: University of New Hampshire.

Otto, R. (1926). *The idea of the holy.* [Translated by J.W. Harvey.] New York: Oxford University Press.

Perkins, C. (1997). *Bridges to faith* [Videotape]. (Available from Department of Mental Retardation, 908 Purchase Street, New Bedford, MA 02740)

Peters, R. (1986). *A theological rationale for the administration of communion to persons who are profoundly mentally retarded.* Unpublished doctoral dissertation, University Microfilms International, Ann Arbor.

Peters, R. (1987). Self-advocacy through participation in the Lord's Supper for persons who are conceptually non-expressive. *The Journal of Pastoral Care, 41*(3), 221–233.

Peters, R. (1994). Between the wall and the fall: Ministering to Humpty Dumpty. *Journal of Religion In Disability & Rehabilitation, 1,* 27–38.

Preheim-Bartel, D., & Neufeld, A. (1986). *Supportive care in the congregation.* Goshen, IN: Mennonite Mutual Aid.

Prins, G. (1994). *Spiritual life plan.* Paper presented at the American Association on Mental Retardation national conference, Boston.

Rogers-Dulan, J., & Blacher, J. (1995). African American families, religion, and disability: A conceptual framework. *Mental Retardation, 33*(4), 226–238.

Schaef, A.W. (1988). *When society becomes an addict.* New York: Harper and Row.

Schurter, D.D. (1987). Fowler's faith stages as a guide for ministry to the mentally retarded. *The Journal of Pastoral Care, 41,* 234–240.

Shisler, B. (1998). *Blessed is the meadow.* Harleysville, PA: Indian Creek Foundation.

Sims, C.L. (1998). Toward a postmodern chaplaincy. *The Journal of Pastoral Care, 52,* 249–259.

Steiner, G. (1989). *Real presences.* Chicago: The University of Chicago Press.

Stevens, A. (1986). Thoughts on the psychobiology of religion and the neurobiology of archetypal experience. *Zygon: The Journal of Religion and Science, 21,* 9–29.

Thornburgh, G. (1997). *That all may worship: An interfaith welcome to people with disabilities.* Washington, DC: National Organization on Disability.

Turner, V.W. (1972). Passages, margins, and poverty: Religious symbols of communities. *Worship, 46,* 390–494.

Wallis, C. (1996, June 24). Faith and healing. *Time,* 59–62.

Webb-Mitchell, B. (1993). *God plays the piano too: The spiritual lives of disabled children.* New York: Crossroad.

Westerhoff, J.H., III. (1976). *Will our children have faith?* New York: The Seabury Press.

Wolfensberger, W. (1976). *The moral challenge of mentally retarded persons to human services.* Paper presented at the American Association on Mental Retardation national conference.

VI

Citizenship and Civil Rights

An Overview of the Emerging Disability Policy Framework

A Guidepost for Analyzing Public Policy

Robert Silverstein

INTRODUCTION

Society has historically imposed attitudinal and institutional barriers that subject persons with disabilities to lives of unjust dependency, segregation, isolation, and exclusion. Attitudinal barriers are characterized by beliefs and sentiments held by nondisabled persons about persons with disabilities. Institutional barriers include policies, practices, and procedures adopted by entities such as employers, businesses, and public agencies.[1]

Sometimes, these attitudinal and institutional barriers are the result of deep-seated prejudice.[2] At times, these barriers result from decisions to follow the "old paradigm" of considering people with disabilities as "defective" and in need of "fixing."[3] At other times, these barriers are the result of thoughtlessness, indifference, or lack of understanding.[4] It is often difficult, if not impossible, to ascertain precisely why the barriers exist.

In response to challenges by persons with disabilities, their families, and other advocates, our nation's policymakers have slowly begun to react over the past quarter of a century. They have begun to recognize the debilitating effects of these barriers on persons with disabilities and have rejected the "old paradigm."

---

[1] See Americans with Disabilities Act of 1990 § 2(a), 42 U.S.C. § 12101(a) (1994) (listing congressional findings regarding Americans with disabilities); see also S. REP. NO. 101-116, at 5-20 (1989). Former Senator Lowell Weicker testified before Congress "that people with disabilities spend a lifetime 'overcoming not what God wrought but what man imposed by custom and law.'" Id. at 11.

[2] S. REP. NO. 101-116, at 5-7.

[3] See National Institute on Disability and Rehabilitation Research, 64 Fed. Reg. 68,576 (1999) (providing notice for the final long-range plan for fiscal years 1999–2003 and explaining that the new paradigm of disability is an expectation for the future).

[4] S. REP. NO. 101-116, at 5-7.

A "new paradigm" of disability has emerged that considers disability as a natural and normal part of the human experience. Rather than focusing on "fixing" the individual, the "new paradigm" focuses on taking effective and meaningful actions to "fix" or modify the natural, constructed, cultural, and social environment. In other words, the focus of the "new paradigm" is on eliminating the attitudinal and institutional barriers that preclude persons with disabilities from fully participating in society's mainstream.

Aspects of the "new paradigm" were included in public policies enacted in the early 1970s.[5] Between the 1970s and 1990, lawmakers further defined and society further accepted the "new paradigm."[6] In 1990, the "new paradigm" was explicitly articulated in the landmark Americans with Disabilities Act (ADA)[7] and further refined in subsequent legislation.[8]

Many people have documented the historical mistreatment of persons with disabilities. Others have described and analyzed the ADA as a civil rights statute that prohibits discrimination in the areas of employment, public services, public accommodations, and telecommunications. Few people have stepped back to consider the fundamental beliefs and core policies that were reflected in the 1970s legislation, explicitly articulated in the ADA, and further refined in subsequent legislation. Taken as a whole, these efforts have critical implications regarding the design, implementation and evaluation of programs and policies that affect citizens with disabilities.

The purpose of this overview is to provide a Disability Policy Framework consistent with the "new paradigm" that can be used as a lens or guidepost[9] to design, implement, and evaluate generic,[10] as well as disability-specific, public

---

[5]Rehabilitation Act of 1973, 29 U.S.C. ch. 16 (1994); *See* Education for All Handicapped Children Act of 1975, Pub. L. No. 94-142, 89 Stat. 773 (adding Part B to the Individuals with Disabilities Education Act, 20 U.S.C. ch. 33 [1994]).

[6]Fair Housing Amendments Act of 1988, Pub. L. No. 100-430, 102 Stat. 1619; Developmental Disabilities Assistance and Bill of Rights Act Amendments of 1987, Pub. L. No. 100-146, 101 Stat. 840; Rehabilitation Act Amendments of 1986, Pub. L. No. 99-506, 100 Stat. 1807; Education of the Handicapped Act Amendments of 1986, Pub. L. No. 99-457, 100 Stat. 1145; Air Carrier Access Act of 1986, Pub. L. No. 99-435, 100 Stat. 1080.

[7]42 U.S.C. ch. 126 (1994). President Bush signed the ADA into law on July 26, 1990. *Id.* Senator Tom Harkin (D. Iowa), the chief sponsor of the ADA, often refers to the legislation as the "20th century Emancipation Proclamation for persons with disabilities." 136 CONG. REC. S9689 (daily ed. July 13, 1990).

[8]Ticket to Work and Work Incentives Improvement Act of 1999, Pub. L. No. 106-170, 113 Stat. 1860; Individuals with Disabilities Education Act Amendments of 1997, Pub. L. No. 105-17, 111 Stat. 37; Developmental Disabilities Assistance and Bill of Rights Act Amendments of 1994, Pub. L. No. 103-230, 108 Stat. 284; Rehabilitation Act Amendments of 1992, Pub. L. No. 102-569, 106 Stat. 4344.

[9]*See Re-Charting the Course—First Report of the Presidential Task Force on Employment of Adults with Disabilities* (Nov. 15, 1998).

[10]Generic programs include persons with and without disabilities among the beneficiaries of assistance. An example of a generic program is the recently enacted Workforce Investment Systems Act, 29 U.S.C. ch. 30 (Supp. IV 1998), that establishes an integrated workforce investment preparation and employment system for all job seekers, including individuals with disabilities.

policies and programs to ensure meaningful inclusion of people with disabilities in mainstream society.

To this end, this overview is targeted to the needs of several audiences. For federal, state, and local policymakers as well as persons with disabilities, their families and advocates, this overview offers a guidepost for designing, implementing, and assessing generic, as well as disability-related, programs and policies. For researchers, this overview provides a benchmark for studying the extent to which generic and disability-specific policies and programs reflect the "new paradigm" and achieve its goals. For service providers, this chapter provides a lens for designing, implementing and evaluating the delivery of services to persons with disabilities. Finally, for college and university professors teaching courses that include disability policy, this overview provides a framework for policy analysis.

This overview is divided into two parts. Part I describes the various components of the Emerging Disability Policy Framework. Using the Emerging Disability Policy Framework described in Part I, Part II of the overview includes an audit—a checklist of questions that stakeholders can use to assess the extent to which generic and disability-specific programs or policies reflect the components of the Emerging Disability Policy Framework.

PART I: AN OVERVIEW OF THE
EMERGING DISABILITY POLICY FRAMEWORK

INTRODUCTION

Part I provides an overview of the major components of the Emerging Disability Policy Framework, including:

- Statement of findings and rationale
- Precept and overarching goals
- Definitions of disability
- Core policies
- Methods of administration
- Program support

STATEMENT OF FINDINGS AND RATIONALE

Every piece of disability-specific legislation promulgated since 1973 includes a carefully constructed rationale known as a "Statement of Findings." A well-constructed Statement of Findings includes the following four major items:

1. A description of the historical treatment of persons with disabilities
2. A summary of the nature of the problem addressed by the proposed legislation
3. An explanation of why the issue is important and why change is needed

4. A description of the role of various entities in designing, implementing, and evaluating the legislation

A Statement of Findings facilitates enactment of the legislation by convincing policymakers of its merits. Once the legislation is enacted, the rationale provides a clear statement to guide implementation and enforcement of the law.[11]

PRECEPT AND OVERARCHING GOALS

In addition to the inclusion of a Statement of Findings, most major disability-specific legislation includes a statement of precept and goals. As with the Statement of Findings, a well-constructed precept and statement of goals further facilitates enactment of the legislation by convincing policymakers of the merits of the legislation. Once the legislation is enacted, the precept and goals provide clear statements to guide implementation of the law. In addition, the precepts and goals provide an explanation when there is uncertainty regarding legislative intent.

The statements of precept and goals are either included within the Statement of Findings or within a separate section. They are sometimes referred to as a "Purpose" section or a "Statement of Policy."

The precept of Disability Policy Framework is that disability is a natural and normal part of the human experience that in no way diminishes a person's right to participate fully in all aspects of life, consistent with the unique strengths, resources, priorities, concerns, abilities, and capabilities of the individual.[12]

According to the Americans with Disabilities Act, "the Nation's proper goals regarding individuals with disabilities are to ensure

1. Equality of opportunity
2. Full participation [empowerment]
3. Independent living
4. Economic self-sufficiency . . . ."[13]

DEFINITIONS OF DISABILITY

In addition to constructing a Statement of Finding and the precept and overarching goals of the legislation, stakeholders must define who will be protected

---

[11]*See* Individuals with Disabilities Education Act § 601, 20 U.S.C. § 1400(c) (1994 & Supp. IV 1998) (listing the congressional purpose as "assur[ing] that all children with disabilities" have access to appropriate legislation); Rehabilitation Act of 1973 § 100(a), 29 U.S.C. § 720(a) (1994 & Supp. IV 1998) (listing congressional findings, purpose, and policy behind the Act); ADA § 2(a), 42 U.S.C. § 12101(a) (1994) (listing congressional findings regarding disabled Americans).

[12]*See* IDEA § 601(c)(1), 20 U.S.C. § 1400(c)(1) (1994) (explaining how disability is a "natural part of the human experience"); Rehabilitation Act of 1973 § 2(a)(3), 29 U.S.C. § 701(a)(3) (1994) (same); Developmental Disabilities Assistance and Bill of Rights Act § 101(a)(2), 42 U.S.C. § 6000(a)(2) (1994) (same).

[13]ADA § 2(a)(8), 42 U.S.C. § 12101(a)(8) (1994).

or benefited from the proposed legislation. All laws include definitions of key terms. The definition of the term *disability* within the specific legislation is drafted to accomplish its specific purposes. For example, civil rights statutes contain a definition of disability that enables the reader to determine which individuals will be protected by the legislation.[14] The definition of *person with a disability* is also included in formula grants and entitlement programs to determine which individuals are eligible for benefits or services.[15]

CORE POLICIES

Once the rationale and goals for the proposed legislation are specified and definitions of disability are established, it is critical for stakeholders to specify the core policies. These statements describe the scope and limitations of the protections, the nature and type of benefits and services, and the circumstances under which benefits and services will be provided.

The numerous core policies can best be understood when they are organized under the four goals of disability policy articulated in the ADA—equality of opportunity, full participation (empowerment), independent living, and economic self-sufficiency. Core policies from various categories of legislation affecting people with disabilities are provided below.

Equality of Opportunity

The goal of equality of opportunity (nondiscrimination) articulated in the ADA includes three core components: 1) individualization, 2) genuine, effective, and meaningful opportunity, and 3) inclusion and integration.

Individualization   This is accomplished through the following actions:

---

[14]Two civil rights statutes pertaining to persons with disabilities are of particular relevance. The first is the Americans with Disabilities Act, 42 U.S.C. ch. 126 (1994), and implementing regulations, 28 C.F.R. pt. 35 (1999), which prohibits discrimination by employers, state and local agencies, public accommodations, and telecommunications. The second law is section 504 of the Rehabilitation Act of 1973, 29 U.S.C. § 794 (1994), which prohibits discrimination by recipients of federal financial assistance. Pursuant to Executive Order 12250, the Department of Justice is responsible for coordinating the implementation of section 504 by various federal agencies, each of which is responsible for issuing its own section 504 regulation. The section 504 coordination regulations issued by the Department of Justice are set out in 28 C.F.R. pt. 41 (1999). The ADA definition of "disability" is set out in section 3(2) of the ADA, 42 U.S.C. § 12102(2) (1994). The section 504 definition of "individual with a disability" is set out in section 6(20) of the Rehabilitation Act of 1973, 29 U.S.C. § 705(20) (1994).

[15]*See,* for example, the definition of "disability" for an adult in the Supplemental Security Income program, Social Security Act § 1614(a)(3)(A), 42 U.S.C. § 1382c(a)(3)(A) (1994) ("An individual shall be considered disabled . . . if he is unable to engage in any substantially gainful activity by reason of any medically determinable . . . impairment [lasting—or expected to last—no less than twelve months] . . ."). *See also* the definition included under Part B of the Individuals with Disabilities Education Act under which a child is entitled to special education and related services, IDEA § 602(3), 20 U.S.C. § 1401(3) (Supp. IV 1998) (defining children's disabilities as those encompassing mental retardation and learning disabilities, as well as health impairments and emotional disturbance).

- Making decisions on the basis of the unique strengths, resources, priorities, concerns, abilities, and capabilities of each person with a disability, including individuals with significant disabilities.[16]
- Treating a person with a disability as an individual based on facts and objective evidence, and not based upon generalizations, stereotypes, fear, ignorance, prejudice, or pernicious mythologies.[17]
- Using definitions and eligibility criteria that result in even-handed treatment of a person with a particular disability and other similarly situated individuals, including nondisabled persons and persons with other disabilities[18]
- Satisfying the broad, nondiscriminatory eligibility criteria by ensuring universal access to generic programs for persons with disabilities.[19]
- Using interdisciplinary assessments performed on a timely basis by qualified personnel conducted across multiple environments in making fact-specific decisions. Using information provided by the individual with a disability, the person's family, or the representative.[20]
- Developing individualized plans that identify and describe needs, goals, objectives, services, and accountability measures.[21]

Genuine, Effective, and Meaningful Opportunity   Ensure that the opportunities that are made available to persons with disabilities are genuine, effective, and meaningful.[22] This includes the following actions:

- Providing "appropriate" services and supports that address the unique needs of the individual, not the needs of the "average" person.[23]
- Making reasonable modifications to policies, practices, and procedures, unless it would fundamentally alter the nature of the program.[24]
- Providing auxiliary aids and services, unless it would result in an undue hardship to the covered entity.[25]

---

[16]*See* Developmental Disabilities Assistance and Bill of Rights Act § 101(c)(3), 42 U.S.C. § 6000(c)(3) (1994) (providing that disabled people and their families should be the "primary decisionmakers" about what services they need).

[17]S. REP. NO. 101-116, at 7 (1989).

[18]*See* 28 C.F.R. § 35.130 (1999) (prohibiting a public entity from treating a disabled person unequally or providing substandard services); 28 C.F.R. § 41.51(b)(1) (1999) (prohibiting the same conduct as the previous regulation).

[19]28 C.F.R. § 35.130 (1999); 28 C.F.R. § 41.51(b)(1) (1999).

[20]*See* IDEA § 614(a), 20 U.S.C. § 614(a), (*repealed by* Pub. L. No. 91-230, 84 Stat. 188 (1970); Rehabilitation Act of 1973 § 102, 29 U.S.C. § 722 (1994 & Supp. IV 1998) (stating that decisions will be made by agency officials within a reasonable period of time).

[21]*See* Rehabilitation Act of 1973 § 102, 29 U.S.C. § 722 (1994 & Supp. IV 1998) (listing options for developing individualized plans for employment); IDEA § 614(c), 20 U.S.C. § 1414(c) (Supp. IV 1998), *repealed by* Pub. L. No. 91-230, 84 Stat. 188 (1970).

[22]*See generally* Nondiscrimination on the Basis of Disability, 28 C.F.R. § 35.130 (2000) (stating that no qualified individual shall be subject to discrimination by a public entity); Nondiscrimination on the Basis of Handicap, 28 C.F.R. § 41.51(b) (2000) (stating that handicapped individuals may not be denied opportunities by federally assisted programs on the basis of the handicap).

[23]IDEA § 612(a)(1), 20 U.S.C. § 1412(a)(1) (1994 & Supp. IV 1998).

[24]28 C.F.R. § 35.130(b)(7) (1999); 28 C.F.R. § 41.51(b) (1999).

[25]28 C.F.R. § 35.160(b) (1999); 28 C.F.R. § 41.51(b), (e) (1999).

- Providing reasonable accommodations to employees, unless it would result in an undue hardship to the covered entity.[26]
- Making programs physically accessible.[27]
- Providing accessible communications.[28]

Inclusion and Integration   Foster the inclusion and integration of persons with disabilities in programs, projects, and activities provided by covered entities. Persons with disabilities should not unnecessarily or unjustifiably be isolated, segregated, or denied effective opportunities to interact with nondisabled persons and to participate in mainstream activities. This can be accompanied by the following:

- Administering programs, projects, and activities in the most integrated setting appropriate to the needs of the individual.[29]
- Providing services in the least restrictive environment (continuum of program options).[30]

Full Participation

The second goal of disability policy articulated in the ADA is full participation. This means empowering persons with disabilities, fostering self-determination, allowing real and informed choice, and participating actively in decision-making processes at the individual and system level (including self-advocacy).[31]

Involvement and Choice by the Individual in Decisions Affecting the Individual   Foster the active involvement and real and informed choice of the individual with a disability in decisions directly affecting the individual by encouraging the following:

- Opportunities to receive information about policies that affect the individual
- Assessments of the individual's progress
- Planning
- Services and supports for the individual (including the right to refuse or terminate services)
- Selection of service providers[32]

---

[26]29 C.F.R. § 1630.9 (1999); 28 C.F.R. § 41.53 (1999).

[27]*See* 28 C.F.R. § 35.149-51 (1999) (addressing program accessibility in the ADA); 28 C.F.R. § 41.53 (1999) (containing the section 504 coordination regulations).

[28]*See* 28 C.F.R. § 35.160(b) (1999) (discussing accessible communications in the ADA); 28 C.F.R. § 41.51(b), (e) (1999) (providing the section 504 coordination regulations).

[29]*See* 28 C.F.R. § 35.130(d) (1999) (discussing integration); 28 C.F.R. § 41.51(d) (1999) (providing the section 504 coordination regulations).

[30]*See* 34 C.F.R. §§ 300.550-.551 (1999) (addressing least restrictive environments within the implementation of IDEA).

[31]*See* Rehabilitation Act of 1973 § 2(c)(1), 29 U.S.C. § 701(c)(1) (Supp. IV 1998) (requiring that all programs receiving assistance be carried out in a manner consistent with "respect for individual dignity, personal responsibility, self-determination, and pursuit of meaningful careers, based on informed choice, of individuals with disabilities"); Developmentally Disabled Assistance and Bill of Rights Act § 101, 42 U.S.C. § 6000 (1994) (same).

[32]*See, e.g.,* IDEA § 614(d)-(f), 20 U.S.C. § 1414(d)-(f) (Supp. IV 1998); Rehabilitation Act of

Involvement and Choice by the Individual's Family in Decisions Affecting the Individual   Facilitate active involvement and real and informed choice of family members (under appropriate circumstances) in decisions affecting the individual with a disability and the family, including the following:

• Opportunities to receive information about policies that affect the individual
• Assessments of the individual's progress
• Planning
• Services and supports for the individual (including the right to refuse or terminate services)
• Selection of service providers[33]

Involvement by Individuals and Families at the System Level   Encourage active involvement in policy decisions at the system level, including the following:

• Opportunities to comment on agency proposals and agency responses
• Participation in governing boards or councils that make or recommend policies relating to the program
• Joint sign-off between the public agency and the governing board or council[34]

Independent Living

The third goal of disability policy articulated in the ADA is to foster the ability and capabilities of individuals with disabilities to live independently.

Independent Living Skills Development and Specialized Planning   Support independent living skill development and specialized planning, by the following:

• Training in individual and systems advocacy
• Services related to securing food, clothing, and shelter
• Management of personal assistants and other support personnel
• Use of assistive technology devices[35]

Long-Term Services and Supports, Including Personal Assistance   Support for long-term services and supports, including personal assistance services and supports necessary to enable an individual to live independently in the com-

---

1973 § 102(b), 29 U.S.C. § 722(b) (Supp. IV 1998) (requiring that the eligible individual participate in developing and agreeing to the rehabilitation program); Ticket to Work and Self-Sufficiency Program, Social Security Act as added by Pub. L. No. 106-170, 113 Stat. 1860 (same).

[33]Ticket to Work and Self-Sufficiency Program, Social Security Act as added by Pub. L. No. 106-170, 113 Stat. 1860.

[34]See provisions in the Rehabilitation Act of 1973 pertaining to the State Rehabilitation Advisory Council, 29 U.S.C. § 725 (1994); Statewide Independent Living Council, 29 U.S.C. § 795(d) (1994); Ticket to Work and Work Incentives Advisory Panel, Pub. L. No. 106-170, 113 Stat. 1860.

[35]29 U.S.C. §§ 796, 796f (1994 & Supp. IV 1998).

munity, including consumer-directed and agency-directed personal assistance services and supports.[36]

Cash Assistance and Other Forms of Support   Support for cash assistance and other programs of assistance that enable the individual to live independently in the community include, for example,

- Cash assistance[37]
- Health care[38]
- Transportation
- Housing[39]
- Food[40]

Economic Self-Sufficiency

The fourth goal of disability policy articulated in the ADA is to foster the economic security, stability, and productivity of persons with disabilities consistent with their actual (not perceived) capabilities, strengths, needs, interests, and priorities.

Systems Providing Employment-Related Services and Supports   Systems providing employment-related skills and supports include, for example:

- Education[41]
- Training[42]
- Self-employment (entrepreneurship)[43]
- Ongoing on-the-job assistance[44]

Cash Assistance and Other Assistance Programs   Support for cash assistance and other programs, such as the following:

---

[36]*See, e.g.,* 29 U.S.C. § 723 (1994 & Supp. IV 1998) (offering personal assistance services to those individuals receiving vocational rehabilitation services under the Rehabilitation Act of 1973 § 103); 42 U.S.C. § 1396d (1994) (amended 1999) (explaining that personal assistance services are an optional benefit under the Medicaid program); 42 U.S.C. § 1396n (1994) (amended 1999) (stating that assistance services are also an authorized benefit under the Medicaid home- and community-based services waiver).

[37]*See* 42 U.S.C. § 1381 (1994) (authorizing the Supplemental Social Security Income program, a federally administered cash assistance program designed to provide minimum income for, among others, persons who are blind and disabled); 42 U.S.C. § 401(b) (1994) (initiating a program of federal disability insurance benefits for, among others, workers who have contributed to the Social Security trust fund and become disabled or blind before retirement age).

[38]*See generally* 42 U.S.C. § 1396 (1994) (authorizing the Medicaid program).

[39]*See* Housing Act of 1937 § 8, 42 U.S.C. § 1437f(o) (1999).

[40]Food Stamp Act of 1977, 7 U.S.C. § 2011) (1994).

[41]*See* Rehabilitation Act of 1973 § 103, 29 U.S.C. § 722 (1994 & Supp. IV 1998); IDEA, 20 U.S.C. § 1400 (1994 & Supp. IV 1998).

[42]*See* Rehabilitation Act of 1973, 29 U.S.C. § 720 (1994).

[43]*Id.*

[44]*See* Social Security Act § 1915(c), 42 U.S.C. § 1396n(c) (1994) (amended 1999) (authorizing expenditures under the home-and community-based services waiver program).

- Cash assistance, including worker incentive provisions[45]
- Health care[46]
- Housing[47]
- Food[48]

Tax Policy Providing Incentives   Tax policy that provides incentives to employers, consistent with business objectives, to hire people with disabilities and that provides deductions and credits for employment-related expenditures enabling an individual with a disability to work include incentives for employers[49] and individuals with disabilities.

METHODS OF ADMINISTRATION

After providing the rationale and goals for the proposed legislation, establishing definitions for disability, and specifying the core policies, stakeholders must then consider the inclusion of administrative or accountability provisions. These provisions, which are referred to as "methods of administration," include such provisions as monitoring and enforcement to ensure implementation, procedural safeguards to ensure individuals are afforded due process of law, outcome measures to determine the impact of the legislation, and methods for financing programs.

These methods of administration are designed to maximize the likelihood that the protections afforded by the civil rights statutes are realized and that the services and benefits made available under entitlement and grant-in-aid programs are provided and implemented in accordance with best practices. Examples of methods of administration from various categories of legislation affecting people with disabilities are provided below.

---

[45]Title XVI of the Social Security Act authorizes the Supplemental Security Income program, a federally administered cash assistance program designed to provide a minimum income for, among others, persons who are blind and disabled. 42 U.S.C. § 1381 (1994). Section 1619 of the Social Security Act creates incentives for SSI beneficiaries with disabilities to work, including permitting these individuals to retain eligibility for Medicaid. *See* 42 U.S.C. § 1382h (1994) (enabling these individuals to continue to receive personal assistance services). *See also* Social Security Act § 1905(q), 42 U.S.C. § 1396d(q) (1994); Social Security Act, U.S.C. § 401 (1994) (authorizing a program of federal disability insurance benefits for, among others, workers who have contributed to the Social Security trust fund and become disabled or blind before retirement age); Ticket to Work and Work Incentives Improvement Act of 1999, Pub. L. No. 106-170, 113 Stat. 1860 (amending the Social Security Act and Medicaid to create new work incentives and expand health care for workers with disabilities).

[46]*See generally* 42 U.S.C. § 1396 (1994) (authorizing the Medicaid program).

[47]*See* U.S. Housing Act of 1937 ch. 8, 42 U.S.C. § 1437f(o) (1994) (providing rental vouchers for low income families).

[48]Food Stamp Act of 1977, 7 U.S.C. §§ 2011-2036 (1994 & Supp. IV 1998).

[49]*See* 26 U.S.C. § 44 (1994) (providing a disabled access tax credit for small business); 26 U.S.C. § 51 (1994) (amended 1999) (providing a targeted jobs tax credit).

State Plans, Applications, and Waivers

State plans and applications describe how the public agency plans to satisfy the applicable requirements, including core policies and methods of administration. Waivers provide exemptions or alternative methods of implementation, including testing the provision of new services.[50]

Monitoring and Enforcement by Government Agencies

Monitoring and enforcement maximize the likelihood that recipients and contractors will comply with applicable requirements and implement the program to ensure results for persons with disabilities. This includes preparing monitoring instruments, conducting monitoring reviews, issuing reports, requiring corrective action, imposing sanctions, and securing remedies for individuals.[51]

Procedural Safeguards

Procedural safeguards for individuals include the following:

- The right to notice of rights[52]
- The right to examine records[53]
- The right to file a complaint[54]
- The right to use of mediation and other forms of alternative dispute resolution[55]
- The right to an administrative due process hearing and administrative review[56]
- The right to seek redress through private right of action in court, including remedies and the awarding of attorneys fees to prevailing parties.[57]

---

[50]*See generally* the state plan requirements under the Rehabilitation Act of 1973, 29 U.S.C. § 721 (1994 & Supp. IV 1998); and the state (§ 612) and local (§ 613) eligibility provisions set out in IDEA, 20 U.S.C. §§ 1412-1413 (1994 & Supp. IV 1998). See also waiver provisions in section 1115 of the Social Security Act, 42 U.S.C. §§ 1215, 1396n(c), 1915(c) (1994 & Supp. IV 1998).

[51]*See, e.g.,* IDEA § 616, 20 U.S.C. § 1416 (1994 & Supp. IV 1998) (explaining withholding of payments and judicial review of educational discrimination against children with disabilities); 45 C.F.R. § 84.6 (1999); 28 C.F.R. §§ 35.170-190 (1999) (covering the filing of complaints for disability discrimination); 42 Fed. Reg. 22687 (May 4, 1997).

[52]IDEA § 615(b)(3), 20 U.S.C. § 1415(b)(3) (1994 & Supp. III 1997) (giving a disabled person the opportunity to present complaints); 28 C.F.R. § 35.105 (1999).

[53]IDEA § 615(b)(1), 20 U.S.C. § 1415(b)(1) (1994 & Supp. III 1997).

[54]28 C.F.R. §§ 35.170-.190 (1999); *see* IDEA § 615(b)(6), 20 U.S.C. § 1415(b)(6) (1994 & Supp. III 1997); Rehabilitation Act of 1973 § 102(d), 29 U.S.C. § 722(d) (1994 & Supp. IV 1998) (requiring state agencies to provide written policies and procedures).

[55]IDEA § 615(e), 20 U.S.C. § 1415(e) (1997); ADA § 513, 42 U.S.C. § 12212 (1994 & Supp. IV 1998).

[56]IDEA § 615(f), 20 U.S.C. § 1415(f) (1994 & Supp. III 1997).

[57]IDEA § 615(i), 20 U.S.C. § 1415(i) (1994 & Supp. III 1997); Rehabilitation Act of 1973 § 505, 29 U.S.C. § 795 (1994) (amended 1998); ADA § 203, 42 U.S.C. § 12133 (1994 & Supp. III 1997).

Accountability for Results (Outcome Measures)

This area facilitates accountability for results using standards and performance indicators that reflect the expected outcomes for recipients with disabilities, the use of sanctions for failure to meet expected outcomes,[58] and rewards for exceeding expectations.[59]

Representation at the Individual and Systems Levels

This area facilitates public support for representation and advocacy at the individual and systems level to ensure meaningful involvement and choice. This includes the following:

- Systems providing protection and advocacy at the individual and systems level[60]
- Self-advocacy training[61]

Single Line of Responsibility, Coordination, and Linkages Among Agencies

It is beneficial to place accountability for the administration of a program in a single agency to avoid "buck-passing."[62] At the same time, it is necessary to provide mechanisms for interagency coordination and collaboration to ensure that no one "falls between the cracks" and that agencies provide for the effective delivery of services.[63]

---

[58]IDEA § 614 (d), 20 U.S.C. § 1414(d) (1994 & Supp. III 1997); Rehabilitation Act of 1973 § 106(c), 29 U.S.C. § 726(c) (1994 & Supp. IV 1998).

[59]*See* 20 C.F.R. § 666.20(a) (1999) (expounding the regulations for implementing the Workforce Investment Act).

[60]For example, protection and advocacy systems are funded under the Developmental Disabilities Assistance and Bill of Rights Act, 42 U.S.C. §§ 6041-6043 (1994 & Supp. IV 1998), the Rehabilitation Act of 1973, 29 U.S.C. § 794e (1994) (amended 1998), and the Protection and Advocacy for Mentally Ill Individuals Act, 42 U.S.C. §§ 10801-10851 (1994 & Supp. IV 1998). In addition, advocacy and individual representation is authorized under Title VII of the Rehabilitation Act of 1973, 29 U.S.C. § 796f-4 (1994) (amended 1998); parent training and information centers are authorized under IDEA, 20 U.S.C. § 1482 (Supp. III 1997). *See* Ticket to Work Incentives Improvement Act of 1999, Pub. L. No. 106-170, 113 Stat. 1860 (setting out state grants to protection advocacy systems for work incentives assistance to disabled beneficiaries).

[61]For example, self-advocacy training is authorized under Title VII of the Rehabilitation Act of 1973, 29 U.S.C. § 796f-4 (1994) (amended 1998). In addition, parent training is authorized under the IDEA, 20 U.S.C. § 1482 (Supp. III 1997). It also is an authorized use under the Developmental Disabilities Assistance and Bill of Rights Act, 42 U.S.C. §§ 6000-6083 (1994 & Supp. IV 1998).

[62]IDEA § 612(a)(11), 20 U.S.C. § 1412(a)(11) (1994) (amended 1997); Rehabilitation Act of 1973, § 101 (a)(2), 29 U.S.C. § 721(a)(2) (1994).

[63]*See* Rehabilitation Act of 1973 § 101(a)(11), 29 U.S.C. § 721(a)(11) (1994) (providing for interagency cooperation); IDEA § 612(a)(12), 20 U.S.C. § 1412(a)(12) (1994 & Supp. IV 1998) (charging the Chief Executive Officer with ensuring interagency cooperation).

Service Coordination (Case Management)

It is essential to provide service coordination to assist individuals in receiving necessary services when a comprehensive array of services is required and such services are provided or paid for by multiple agencies.[64]

Financing Service Delivery

This area includes proscribing methods for financing services through the allocation of funds or the establishment of cost reimbursement schemes (including outcome-based reimbursement schemes) that have the effect of denying effective opportunities for persons with the most significant needs[65]

Privacy, Confidentiality, Access to Records, and Informed Consent

Protecting privacy and confidentiality and requiring informed consent minimizes the extent of government intrusion.[66] Access to records ensures that individuals have the necessary information to make informed choices.[67]

Comprehensive System of Personnel Development

Personnel who provide services to beneficiaries must satisfy qualification standards to perform assigned tasks in an effective and efficient manner. Personnel knowledgeable about civil rights statutes and promising practices are preferred because they are able to provide state-of-the-art services to persons with disabilities.[68]

Responsiveness to Cultural Diversity

Services must be provided in a culturally competent manner and be responsive to the beliefs, interpersonal styles, attitudes, language, and behaviors of individuals receiving services to ensure maximum participation in the program.[69]

---

[64]See the early intervention program in Part C of IDEA, 20 U.S.C. § 1435(a) (Supp. IV 1998).

[65]See IDEA § 612(a)(5), 20 U.S.C. § 1412(a)(5) (1994 & Supp. IV 1998) (specifying that state funding schemes may not result in placing a child outside the least restrictive environment).

[66]See, e.g., IDEA § 614(a)(1)(c), 20 U.S.C. § 1414(a)(1)(c) (Supp. IV 1998) (requiring parental consent for a qualification evaluation of a child); IDEA § 617(c), 20 U.S.C. § 1417(c) (1994 & Supp. IV 1998) (assuring confidentiality of personal information); ADA § 102(c)(3)(B), 42 U.S.C. § 12112(c)(3)(B) (1994 & Supp. IV 1998) (requiring that employers keep disability-related medical records confidential).

[67]See 42 U.S.C. § 6042(g) (1994 & Supp. IV 1998) (authorizing a state's system to have access to individual records to address the needs of disabled individuals).

[68]See IDEA § 612(a)(14)-(15), 20 U.S.C. § 1412(a)(14)-(15) (1994 & Supp. IV 1998) (mandating that states put into effect personnel standards and a system of personnel development); Rehabilitation Act of 1973 § 101(a)(7)(A), 29 U.S.C. § 721(a)(7)(A) (1994) (requiring that the state's plan establish standards of care for people with disabilities).

[69]See Rehabilitation Act of 1973 § 101, 29 U.S.C. § 721 (1994 & Supp. IV 1998) (describing outreach procedures to identify and serve individuals with disabilities who are minorities).

Fiscal Provisions

Public agencies must use program funds to supplement—and not supplant—other sources of funding and must maintain their own fiscal effort.[70]

Financial Management and Reporting

Grant funds should be managed in such a way to ensure fiscal control and fund accounting.[71]

PROGRAM SUPPORT

Stakeholders provide the rationale and goals for the proposed legislation, establish definitions for disability, specify the core policies, and develop methods of administration provisions. In addition, stakeholders must ensure that initiatives conform to best practices and are state-of-the-art by adopting program supports, such as grants, to support systemic change, research, training, and technical assistance. Examples of program supports from various categories of legislation affecting people with disabilities are provided below.

Systems Change Initiatives

This includes funding designed to assist public agencies in developing and implementing comprehensive reforms at the system or institutional level (policies, practices, and procedures).[72]

Training of Individuals with Disabilities and Their Families

This area requires supporting model approaches for training individuals with disabilities and their families.[73]

---

[70]*See* IDEA § 612(a)(18)-(19), 20 U.S.C. § 1412(a)(18)-(19) (1994 & Supp. IV 1998) (outlining the rules for public agencies regarding allocation of funding).

[71]*See* 20 U.S.C. § 1232(f) (1994) (defining how records are to be kept).

[72]*See* 20 U.S.C. §§ 1451-1456 (1994 & Supp. IV 1998) (providing assistance in the area of media); 29 U.S.C. § 3001 (1994) (encompassing technological assistance); 42 U.S.C. ch. 75 (1994) (codifying developmental assistance); Ticket to Work and Work Incentives Improvement Act of 1999, Pub. L. No. 106-170, 113 Stat. 1862 (developing grants to establish state infrastructure that will support working individuals with disabilities).

[73]*See, e.g.* 20 U.S.C. §§ 1461, 1462, 1471-1474 (1994), *amended by* 1461, 1471-1474 (Supp. IV 1998) (explaining parent information and training centers); 29 U.S.C. § 796f (1994 & Supp. IV 1998) (explaining centers for independent living under Title VII of the Rehabilitation Act of 1973); 42 U.S.C. ch. 75 (1994) (explaining protection and advocacy systems and university affiliated programs under the Developmental Disabilities Assistance and Bill of Rights Act); *see also* Ticket to Work and Work Incentives Improvement Act of 1999, Pub. L. No. 106-170, 113 Stat. 1860 (detailing Work Incentives Outreach programs under the Social Security Act).

Training of Personnel Regarding Promising Practices

This legislation provides support for personnel preparation and training, including training of specialists, generalists, and leaders.[74]

Research, Technical Assistance, and Information Dissemination

This area includes support research, technical assistance, and information dissemination which all ensure that the programs are effective, state-of-the-art, and efficient.[75]

PART II: GENERAL QUESTIONS FOR ANALYZING THE EXTENT TO WHICH DISABILITY-SPECIFIC OR GENERIC PROGRAMS OR POLICIES REFLECT THE DISABILITY POLICY FRAMEWORK

INTRODUCTION

Using the Disability Policy Framework described in Part I, this part includes general questions for analyzing the extent to which disability-specific and generic programs or policies reflect the precept, goals, definitions, core policies, methods of administration, and program supports set out in the Disability Policy Framework. In other words, this part serves as a guidepost for evaluating, expanding, and improving the design and implementation of public policies affecting persons with disabilities.

Answering these questions may entail, among other things, reviewing previous studies and reports, reviewing data, conducting analyses of proposed and final policy pronouncements, and conducting surveys of stakeholders. Not all questions articulated in this part are applicable to all programs and policies; for example, some questions may only be applicable to generic programs serving nondisabled persons, as well as persons with disabilities.

QUESTIONS RELATING TO STATEMENT OF FINDINGS AND RATIONALE

- Is the program longstanding, undergoing major reform, or new? If new, does it replace an existing program?

---

[74]*See* 20 U.S.C. §§ 1461, 1462, 1471-1474 (1994), *amended by* 20 U.S.C. §§ 1461, 1471-1474 (Supp. IV 1998) (covering training in education); 29 U.S.C. §§ 770-776 (1994 & Supp. IV 1998) (providing general training programs); 42 U.S.C. §§ 6061-6066 (1994 & Supp. IV 1998) (addressing interdisciplinary training by university affiliated programs under the Developmental Disabilities Assistance and Bill of Rights Act).

[75]*See* 20 U.S.C. §§ 1451-1456, 1461, 1471-1474 (1994 & Supp. IV 1998) (regarding assistance in the field of media); 29 U.S.C. §§ 760-765 (1994 & Supp. IV 1998) (funding research by the National Institute on Disability and Rehabilitation Research under Title II of the Rehabilitation Act of 1973).

- Was the program established on a sound premise?
- Has the program historically excluded persons with disabilities or specific categories of persons with disabilities? For example, has a policy, procedure, or accepted practice historically disqualified persons with significant disabilities from receiving services, or has a policy, procedure or accepted practice by a generic program automatically referred all persons with disabilities to disability-specific programs?
- Is there a history of segregation of persons with disabilities into specific slots or components of the program?
- Is there a history of denial of genuine, effective, and meaningful services in the program?
- Is there a history of ensuring that people with disabilities enjoy choice in assessments, planning, services provided, selection of service providers, and measures of progress?
- Is there a history of fostering independent living and ensuring self-sufficiency?
- What efforts have been made to ascertain the prevalence of persons with disabilities among the prospective pool of eligible recipients of a generic program?
- What efforts have been made to ascertain the scope of unmet need?
- Is the public agency considering the historical treatment of persons with disabilities in the development of new policies and procedures and in the methods of administration it uses?

QUESTIONS RELATING TO PRECEPT

Does the program include a statement articulating the core precept on which it is based? Is the core precept of the program consistent with the precept of disability policy that disability is a natural and normal part of the human experience that in no way diminishes a person's right to fully participate in the program, consistent with the unique strengths, resources, priorities, concerns, abilities, and capabilities of the individual?

A QUESTION RELATING TO OVERARCHING GOALS

Do the goals of the program reflect the goals of federal disability policy articulated in the ADA—equality of opportunity, full participation (empowerment), independent living and economic self-sufficiency for persons with disabilities?

QUESTIONS RELATING TO DEFINITION OF DISABILITY

- Does the definition of disability reflect the purposes of the particular legislation?

- How does the definition of disability relate to definitions used in other programs?
- Does it relate to the definition used in Section 504 and the ADA?

QUESTIONS RELATING TO CORE POLICIES

Questions Relating to Equality of Opportunity

Individualization   Do the policies and procedures governing eligibility and application for and delivery of services under the program

- Account for the unique strengths, resources, priorities, concerns, abilities, and capabilities of each person with a disability, including individuals with significant disabilities?
- Account for the added dimension of poverty?
- Use definitions and eligibility criteria that result in even-handed treatment between a person with a particular disability and other similarly situated individuals, including nondisabled persons and persons with other disabilities?
- Satisfy the broad, nondiscriminatory eligibility criteria by ensuring universal access to generic programs for persons with disabilities?
- Support and promote the treatment of persons with a disabilities as individuals based on facts and objective evidence, not based on generalizations, stereotypes, fear, ignorance, or prejudice?
- Use interdisciplinary assessments performed by qualified personnel, conduct timely assessments across multiple environments, and use information provided by the individual with a disability and the person's family or representative in making fact-specific decisions?
- Use individualized plans to identify and describe needs, goals, objectives, services, and accountability measures?

Genuine, Effective, and Meaningful Opportunity   Do the policies and procedures governing eligibility and application for and delivery of services under the program offer opportunities that are genuine, effective, and meaningful? Do the policies and procedures

- Provide "appropriate" services and supports designed to meet the unique needs of the individual, not the needs of the "average" person?
- Make reasonable modifications to policies, practices, and procedures, unless it would fundamentally alter the nature of the program?
- Provide auxiliary aids and services, unless it would result in an undue hardship to the covered entity?
- Provide reasonable accommodations to employees, unless it would result in an undue hardship to the covered entity?

- Make a program physically accessible?
- Provide for communication accessibility?

Inclusion and Integration   Do the policies and procedures governing eligibility and application for and delivery of services under the program foster the inclusion and integration of persons with disabilities, or do the policies and procedures unnecessarily or unjustifiably isolate or segregate persons with disabilities?

Questions Relating to Full Participation

Do the policies and procedures governing the program foster the empowerment of persons with disabilities, real and informed choice, and active participation in decision-making processes at the individual and system level (including self-advocacy)?

More specifically, do the policies and procedures governing the program foster

- Active involvement and real and informed choice of the individual with a disability in areas including
  - Opportunity to receive information about policies that affect the individual?
  - Assessments?
  - Planning?
  - Services?
  - Selection of service providers?
  - Measures of progress?
- Active involvement and real and informed choice of family members and other representatives (under appropriate circumstances) in decisions affecting the individual with a disability and the family, including
  - Opportunity to receive information about policies that affect the individual?
  - Assessments?
  - Planning?
  - Services?
  - Selection of service providers?
  - Measures of progress?
- Active involvement in policy decisions at the system level (respecting the design, implementation and evaluation of a program), including
  - Consideration of input from consumers?
  - Participation on governing boards and councils?
  - Joint sign-off on policies by the governing board/council?

Questions Relating to Independent Living

Do the policies and procedures governing the program foster the ability and capabilities of individuals with disabilities to live independently through support for independent living skill development, including

- Training in individual and systems advocacy?
- Service related to securing food, clothing, and shelter?
- Training the management of personal assistants and the use of assistive technology?
- Specialized planning for transitioning to independent living?
- Do the policies and procedures governing the program enable the person with a disability to live independently through the provision of long-term services and supports, for example, consumer-directed personal assistance services and supports and assistive technology devices and services?
- Do the policies governing the program enable the person with a disability to live independently in the community through cash assistance or other forms of assistance?

Questions Relating to Economic Self-Sufficiency

Do the policies and procedures governing the program foster the economic security, stability, and productivity of persons with disabilities consistent with their actual (not perceived) capabilities, strengths, needs, interests, and priorities through support for

- Systems that include universal access to generic services as well as access to specialized services and supports as an integral component of the system?
- Training, education, and employment of choice (including self-employment)?
- Ongoing on-the-job support?
- Specialized planning (e.g., transition planning for children in high school)?
- Cash assistance programs that reflect the goal of maximizing economic self-sufficiency, including policies that provide incentives to work (e.g., waive or modify income and resource limits, retain eligibility for acute and long-term services and supports)?

QUESTIONS RELATING TO METHODS OF ADMINISTRATION

Questions Relating to State and Local Plans, Applications, and Waivers

- Does the plan/application include specific policies and procedures governing implementation for persons with disabilities?
- Do waiver requests have the effect of enhancing or diminishing opportunities for persons with disabilities? For example, is a waiver request designed to test new strategies for delivering services that reflect the goals of disability

policy articulated in the ADA? Or is the waiver request based on "perceptions" that individuals with disabilities cannot succeed or participate in the program or assessment generally applicable to nondisabled persons?
- Does the plan/application explain how people with disabilities and their representatives were involved in the process of completing the plan/application?
- In addition to the inclusion of an assurance of nondiscrimination, does the plan/application include specific policies and procedures relating to implementation of the program consistent with section 504 of the Rehabilitation Act of 1973 and the ADA?

Questions Relating to Monitoring and Enforcement by Government Agencies

- What are the respective roles and responsibilities of federal, state, and local agencies for monitoring and enforcement?
- Does the monitoring instrument developed by the government agency include specific inquiries related to persons with disabilities? If so, what are they?
- Does the government agency use a monitoring instrument for ascertaining compliance with section 504 of the Rehabilitation Act of 1973 and the ADA? If so, what is included?
- Do on-site monitoring reviews include assessments relating to meeting the needs of persons with disabilities and ensuring nondiscrimination?
- What sanctions are available and used? Under what circumstances?
- What incentives are available and used?
- How are findings of noncompliance used by the agency? Are findings of noncompliance used for purposes of ongoing continuous quality improvement reviews?
- What remedies are available?
- Is there a complaint resolution procedure that includes complaints involving discrimination on the basis of disability?

Questions Relating to Procedural Safeguards for Individuals, Their Families, and Representatives

Do the policies and procedures governing the program provide for

- Notice of rights?
- Examination of records?
- The right to file a complaint?
- The use of mediation and other forms of alternative dispute resolution?
- Administrative due process hearings and administrative review?

- Redress through private right of action in court, including remedies and the awarding of attorneys' fees to prevailing parties?

Questions Relating to
Accountability for Results (Outcome Measures)

- Does the agency include outcome measures that address issues of specific relevance to persons with disabilities?
- Does the agency disaggregate data so the agency can determine whether its program is meeting the needs of persons with disabilities or persons with specific categories of disabilities as part of a process of continuous improvement?

Questions Relating to
Representation at the Individual and Systems Level

Does the public agency provide support for representation and advocacy at the individual and systems level, including support for systems providing protection and advocacy, and self-advocacy training?

Questions Relating to Single Line of
Responsibility/Coordination and Linkages Among Agencies

- Is there a single agency (state or local) responsible for implementation of the program for all beneficiaries, including persons with disabilities? If not, how does the agency ensure compliance for persons with disabilities?
- Does the agency require the assignment of an individual who will be responsible for ensuring implementation of the program for persons with disabilities, particularly with respect to implementation of the program consistent with Section 504 of the Rehabilitation Act of 1973 and the ADA?
- Has the agency developed policies and procedures for collaboration among agencies to ensure meaningful and effective delivery of necessary services to persons with disabilities, including cost sharing arrangements?

A Question Relating to Service Coordination (Case Management)

Has the agency developed policies and procedures for service coordination to ensure that individuals with disabilities, particularly those with the most significant disabilities, receive the services they need, particularly where services are provided by multiple agencies?

Questions Relating to Financing Service Delivery

- Does the system for allocating funds among agencies and service providers facilitate or thwart accomplishment of the goals articulated in the ADA and the policies that effectuate the goals? For example, does the outcome-based reimbursement scheme used to pay service providers recognize and reward those who serve persons with the most significant disabilities and who cost more than the average recipient of services (risk adjustment)?
- Is the network of service providers adequate to address the needs of persons with disabilities eligible for assistance under the program?
- Is the financing system for services (for example, personal assistance services, assistive technology) consumer-directed?

Questions Relating to Privacy, Confidentiality, Access to Records, and Informed Consent

- Does the agency include specific policies and procedures protecting the rights of persons with disabilities to privacy? Confidentiality? Access to records?
- Does the agency include specific policies and procedures requiring informed consent?

Questions Relating to Comprehensive System of Personnel Development

- Does the agency include specific training components regarding the implementation of its program (e.g., policy, "promising practices," and resource allocation) for persons with disabilities?
- Does the agency include specific training for its personnel regarding implementation of its program consistent with Section 504 of the Rehabilitation Act of 1973 and the ADA?

A Question Relating to Responsiveness to Cultural Diversity

Does the agency include policies and procedures that address the special needs of persons with disabilities from diverse cultural backgrounds?

A Question Relating to Fiscal Provisions

Do the "supplement, not supplant" and "maintenance of effort" provisions ensure continuation of funding from state and local sources for services provided to persons with disabilities?

Questions Relating to Financial Management and Reporting

Do the fiscal control and fund accounting procedures enable oversight with respect to the provision of funding for persons with disabilities consistent with legislative intent?

QUESTIONS RELATING TO PROGRAM SUPPORT

To the extent an agency supports efforts to improve the quality of services provided through initiatives (such as systems change grants, training, research, technical assistance, demonstrations, and information dissemination), do these initiatives include specific components or specific initiatives that address the unique needs of persons with disabilities?

This chapter was funded by a grant from The Joseph P. Kennedy, Jr. Foundation, grants from the National Institute on Disability and Rehabilitation Research of the U.S. Department of Education supporting the Rehabilitation Research and Training Center on Workforce Investment and Employment Policy for Persons with Disabilities (No. H133B980042) and the Rehabilitation Research and Training Center on State Systems and Employment (No. H133B30067), and a grant from the Robert Wood Johnson Foundation. Additional support for this chapter was provided by The Public Welfare Foundation, The Peter L. Buttenwieser Fund of the Tides Foundation, Mr. and Mrs. Justin Dart, Fenmore R. Seton, The American Occupational Therapy Association, Inc., The Bernard L. Schwartz Foundation, Inc., Glaxo Wellcome, Inc., Josiah Macy, Jr. Foundation, Kaleidoscope, American Speech-Language-Hearing Association, The Nancy Lurie Marks Family Foundation, The Philanthropic Collaborative, Inc., and The Ada G. Halbreich Revocable Trust. The opinions contained in this chapter are those of the author and do not necessarily reflect those of the U.S. Department of Education or the other grantors.

17

The Criminal Justice System and People with Mild Cognitive Limitations

Ruth Luckasson

If democratic citizenship has genuine meaning, it must include an expectation that all people receive just and fair treatment from all societal institutions, including the criminal justice system. This chapter discusses what has happened, in terms of justice, to the adults who were termed "six-hour retarded children" (President's Committee on Mental Retardation [PCMR], 1969) during their school years. How has this segment of society—people with mild cognitive limitations—fared? The short answer to this question is that they routinely are denied fair treatment in the criminal justice system. This chapter addresses how the principles of justice, fairness, and safety are often distorted in the presence of mild cognitive limitations, how defendants with cognitive limitations are treated, and how crime victims with cognitive limitations are often disregarded in the present criminal justice system. This chapter also explores promising practices and needed program and policy reforms to improve the likelihood that people with cognitive limitations—as either victims of crimes or the accused—can achieve justice.

EXPECTATIONS IN A FAIR SOCIETY

A desire for justice is deeply rooted in American society. In 1620, when the Pilgrim forebears signed the Mayflower Compact before they even landed at Plymouth Rock, they agreed among themselves to pursue a just society. They pledged "solemnly and mutually" to create a civil body politic and just and equal laws. The strands of mutual agreement continued through the creation of the Declaration of Independence and the Constitution. Each American generation was bound by powerful themes of life, liberty, happiness, and property. After the Civil War, constitutional amendments guaranteeing the principles of equal protection and due process were passed and ratified, reinforcing the expectation of justice.

Analyzing these deep roots, John Rawls (1971), the prominent American legal philosopher, developed the idea of justice as fairness, based on a social contract. He rejected the utilitarian explanation for the drive to justice and emphasized that a just society must respect justice for each individual. Rawls explained that the loss of freedom for some cannot be rationalized by gain for others; advantages for the many cannot outweigh sacrifices made by the few. "Each person possesses an inviolability founded on justice that even the welfare of society as a whole cannot override" (Rawls, 1971, p. 3). A public sense of justice is a necessity for a well-ordered society. Americans may disagree over whether certain actions are just, but all agree that justice must be the foundation of our society. This robust ideal so powerfully permeates our society that we take it for granted like the air we breathe. But the everyday reality demands our attention and action. Justice eludes many individuals with mild cognitive limitations when they come into contact with the criminal justice system, and this failure of universal justice undermines trust in the society.

CIRCUMSTANCES OF INDIVIDUALS WITH MILD COGNITIVE LIMITATIONS

Today's converging societal circumstances of economic downturns, everyday technological demands, increased family mobility and separation, recent human services reductions, increased resistance to the stigma of the label of mental retardation, and increased incarceration rates have brought into stark relief the plight of many people with mild cognitive limitations. This plight is dramatically revealed in the criminal justice system, whether the person becomes a defendant accused of committing a crime or a victim upon whom a crime is committed. Daily, the intellectual limitations of individuals with mild cognitive limitations go unrecognized, their rights are denied, their human worth is devalued, and their interactions with the criminal justice system are met with widespread injustices.

The United States imprisons more of its citizens than any other Western country. According to Wilson and Herrnstein (1985), the average IQ score of offenders is approximately 92, slightly below the societywide average of 100. Noble and Conley (1992) reviewed the incidence and prevalence rates of mental retardation in corrections facilities and concluded that approximately 2%–10% of people in the criminal justice system have mental retardation.

However, individuals with mild cognitive limitations comprise a broader segment of the population than that which Noble and Conley investigated, and no reliable research exists on the number of these individuals in the criminal justice system. It is a group larger than that usually included in typical calculations of disability or impairment. The group includes individuals currently identified as having mental retardation with IQ scores at the upper end approaching the ceiling of approximately 70–75, individuals who may qualify technically as having mental retardation but who have avoided using the label, and individuals who may not currently be able to obtain an official diagnosis of mental retardation either because of mistakes in evaluation or because their limitations do not precisely fit current categorical disability definitions. The limitations of most individuals with mild cognitive limitations probably are not physically apparent and, for some, may only be temporary. However, each individual has overall intellectual functioning below what is required to adequately function independently in American society, has reduced ability to intellectually handle interactions in society, needs societal assistance, and is forgotten by both the disability community and society.

The group is both highly invisible, because there are generally no physical markers for mild cognitive limitations, and highly visible, because without supports they are at high risk for many situations that draw negative attention. Unless supports—services, programs, or policy changes—are brought to bear, many of the following circumstances for individuals with mild cognitive limitations are likely: victimization and exploitation, maltreatment, acts of violence against them, incarceration, lowered life satisfaction, lowered living standards, limited competence in parenting skills, child removal, family disintegration, placement of children in out-of-home care, decreased likelihood of justice in the criminal justice system, inadequate physical and mental well-being, school failure, illiteracy, dropping out or being pushed out of school, homelessness, and joblessness.

Let us look more closely at the points at which cognitive limitation decrease the likelihood of justice, first for defendants, then for victims. A cursory review of the sequence of steps of an incident leading to arrest and prosecution or an incident of victimization leading to a complaint reveals the complex, highly verbal, extremely stressful nature of the interaction between citizens with mild cognitive limitations and the criminal justice system. The same confusing aspects pertain to the situation regardless of whether the individual is accused of a crime or is the victim of a crime. For example, most individuals without disabilities experience a considerable amount of stress when stopped by law enforcement personnel for minor traffic violations. Consider the amplified stress of an actual arrest. Then, think about the number of resources a person without disabilities can bring to bear to the situation: verbal ability, negotiating skills, access to people who can help, money for a lawyer and expert witnesses, and so forth. Now, superimpose the situation of most people with cognitive limitations: limited verbal ability, reduced personal skills, few social connections, no money for a lawyer, reduced ability to deal with stress, and so forth. The contrast is striking, and the imbalance sets the stage for injustice.

Logical questions might be, doesn't the criminal justice system contain protections against injustice? Shouldn't the legal system itself ensure justice? It should, of course, and many doctrines, such as the right to a lawyer, protections in search and seizure, and rules concerning trial fairness, contain the seeds of justice for people with mild cognitive limitations. However, these doctrines have been insufficient, and many aspects of the system actually interfere with justice for people with cognitive limitations. Neither the legal doctrines, nor the administrative processing, nor the day-to-day operations ensure justice.

Over the years, certain doctrines have emerged in the criminal law to address differences or disadvantages, including mental disability, among defendants (for a general review, see Ellis & Luckasson, 1984). For example, many competence doctrines exist: competence to stand trial, competence to plead guilty, competence to confess, competence to waive rights, and so forth. Why are these doctrines insufficient for ensuring justice for people with cognitive limitations who are accused of committing crimes? First, all of the aforementioned doctrines evolved in response to the condition of mental illness, which affects more people than cognitive limitations. Therefore, these doctrines arose from concerns about the ways in which schizophrenia and disordered thinking might interfere with justice. Second, in order for these doctrines to be brought to bear during a case, someone in authority—the defense lawyer, prosecutor, or judge—must recognize and successfully raise the issue of the cognitive limitations of the individual. Third, beyond merely recognizing the limitation, a forensic evaluator must take it seriously, measure the nature and extent of the disability, and genuinely explore its legal import. Fourth, the presence of cognitive limitation must be used as a lens for increased understanding of the person and his or her blameworthiness rather than as a vehicle for prejudice or a shorthand means for devaluation and demonization (Conley, Luckasson, & Bouthilet, 1992). The stakes are high: liberty, safety, autonomy, and, in the case of the death penalty, even life itself. (See, for example, the case of Earl Washington, a Virginia man with an IQ of 69 who was incarcerated on death row for 17 years and who came within days of execution based on a "confession." DNA tests finally led to exoneration and pardon [Rimer, 2000].)

For victims of crime, parallel issues arise (Luckasson, 1992; Petersilia, 2000; Sobsey, 1994). Victims with mild cognitive limitations are routinely unrecognized, their complaints go uninvestigated, and they are devalued and dehumanized in analyses of the occurrences against them (National Research Council, 2000).

FOUNDATIONS FOR SOCIAL RESPONSE

The social response should retain at its core the historical societal commitment to justice as fairness for all citizens, including those with mild cognitive limitations. Fairness is only possible if we truly acknowledge individuals with mild cognitive limitations and genuinely implement systemic accommodations for supporting the participation of people with mild cognitive limitations. As Rawls stated in support of a social contract,

> Each member of society is thought to have an inviolability founded on jus-
> tice . . . which even the welfare of every one else cannot override. . . .
> Therefore in a just society the basic liberties are taken for granted and the
> rights secured by justice are not subject to political bargaining or to the
> calculus of social interests. (1971, p. 28)

Historical injustices against individuals with mild cognitive limitations contaminate present social responses to these individuals. At the end of the 19th century, the American ideal of the self-made man linked together intelligence, morality, and success (Trent, 1994). In stories such as those written by Horatio Alger, smart individuals achieved financial success through moral strength. Conversely, failure to achieve material success was believed to be caused by a lack of intelligence and immorality. Therefore, from early in our history, people who did not succeed were thought to be individually at fault for their lack of success. A 19th-century understanding of biological heredity and its pseudoscientific translation into social Darwinism and eugenics seems to have supported these supposed connections. Herbert Spencer's phrase, "survival of the fittest," supposed this part of the natural order of society and the resulting economic and social marginality as fate. Barr referred to individuals with feeble minds as "not conducive to the national prosperity" (as cited in Trent, 1994, p. 143). In addition, individuals with cognitive limitations were regarded as causing vice and crime. These supposed links have subtly persisted.

Supposed connections between "feeblemindedness" and criminality were described in the late 1800s and early 1900s. Early professionals even referred to a group of people they called "moral imbeciles" (Kerlin as cited in Sloan & Stevens, 1976, pp. 14–15). Traditional responses to these individuals included segregation in isolated mental institutions, forced surgical sterilization, statutory marriage restrictions, and denial of necessary lifesaving medical care. Although many of these specific actions largely have been abandoned in their pure forms, remnants of the attitudes persist in the treatment of people with mild cognitive limitations, and variations of the actions remain today, including isolation in certain areas of a city, limits on assistance with childrearing and loss of custody, lack of basic support for families, financial disincentives to marriage, and restricted health care.

The 19th century search for criminal "types" who could then be eugenically rooted out of society implicated people from certain racial and ethnic groups, with certain body types (e.g., long fingers supposedly indicated a thief), and with cranial bumps as well as immigrants and people with cognitive limitations. People with cognitive limitations increasingly came to be seen as the cause of social ills, "the menace of the feebleminded" (Trent, 1994, p. 141) or, in Kerlin's phrase, "moral imbeciles."

In the late 1950s and the 1960s an attempt was again made to formally classify the group of individuals with IQs between 70–75 and 85 as having "borderline mental retardation" (Heber, 1959). This attempt was severely criticized by professionals who feared the stigmatizing effects of the label "mental retardation" and was soon abandoned by the American Association on Mental Retardation in its definition manual of 1973 (Grossman, 1983). When the category of "borderline mental retardation" was eliminated, the prevalence rate for mental retardation decreased from 16% to 3%; however, disability-based eligibility for services also was reduced (Perske, 1991). People with mild cognitive limitations did not disappear—only the label of "borderline mental retardation" that had opened the doors to some services.

Restating versions of historical rationales in contemporary language, many commentators urge quick and punitive fixes—usually involving segregation, such as building more prison beds and exacting longer sentences—to the social problems that arise when citizens whose overall intellectual functioning is below that which is required to adequately function independently in American society get in trouble. Maxine Green (2000), writing about the ambiguities of freedom, criticized the narrowing of options that occurs when people are denied the support systems they need. When individuals without needed supports, who thus must operate within an extremely limited range of options, "choose" certain actions, they often are stigmatized and even criminalized. This injustice was dramatically portrayed in *Les Misérables* (Hugo, 1862).

How should individuals with mild cognitive limitations be acknowledged in the search for justice? Should they be treated as if they have no learning problems because many do not have any type of label? Should they be regarded as ordinary citizens who happen to need extra help? Or, should they be given a special label and designated as atypical?

Promising Responses

To plan for improved responses to the needs of people with mild cognitive limitations in the criminal justice system, it is necessary to ensure certain basics such as education for all children, income support, job training, family assistance, and training in citizenship. In addition, it may be necessary to create some specialized services. In designing the specialized services, it may be helpful to look at successful programs that have addressed the needs of people with mental retardation in the criminal justice system. These specialized services have developed ways to address the needs of people whose cognitive limitations are even more severe than those of the individuals addressed in this book and thus can offer techniques and strategies adaptable to people with mild cognitive limitations. It is essential also to engage the assistance of people who themselves have cognitive limitations, especially those who have direct experience as self-advocates. Their development, as a community, of political skills and their rich history of fighting for recognition of their needs for supports are important resources.

Vulnerable individuals must have advocates, especially when their cognitive limitations interfere with their ability to deal with the system and when the system is complex and the stakes are high. The criminal justice system is complex and the stakes—freedom and sometimes life itself—are extremely high. Specialized advocacy services are essential. For example, the advocacy project of The Arc of Colorado Springs is an excellent model. Employing a multidisciplinary team approach, members of the advocacy project respond quickly when personnel such as police officers, lawyers, or judges identify a person with a disability. The lawyers, judges, and law enforcement personnel know that the project will respond. The Arc of New Mexico created a similar program that provides individual advocacy and technical assistance and promotes system change. The Arc of New Jersey has another excellent program, which has been in place for many years. It conducts training, provides advocacy, and acts as a clearinghouse. At the national level, The Arc of the United States has created important training materials for people with disabilities and for law enforcement officers and other personnel to address the issues. Temple University also has created important training materials and has facilitated the participation of self-advocates in the development and dissemination of resources.

RECOMMENDED SOCIAL RESPONSES

The pursuit of increased fairness for people with mild cognitive limitations in the criminal justice system should include the development of policies that address the needs of this population, the development of improved information, and the creation of demonstration, evaluation, and research models.

Policy Development

Excellent work already has been accomplished in the area of policy development. For example, in 1984 the American Bar Association Delegate Assembly passed model statutes for doctrinally addressing mental disabilities in the criminal justice system (American Bar Association, 1989). Future work needs to be done with regard to adopting the models in the state and federal systems. In addition, the needs of individuals with mild cognitive limitations should be included in the doctrinal work.

The major professional organizations also have established policy statements and legislative goals addressing justice for people with mental retardation (see, e.g., American Association on Mental Retardation, 2000; The Arc of the United States, 1998). However, additional policy work is required, both in the legal area and in general societal supports area. Two immediate needs are 1) a plan for developing appropriate disposition, diversion, and sentencing alternatives and 2) a plan for providing job training, education, therapeutic services, and other necessary supports that reflect best special education practices for individuals with mild cognitive limitations.

Information Development and Access

The limited information and data on the justice issues that affect people with mild cognitive limitations hamper analysis and problem solving. The following recommendations would address some of the immediate information and data needs:

- Establish a transdisciplinary, national, legislatively mandated center for technical assistance, research, and information dissemination regarding individuals with mild cognitive limitations and fair access to justice and equal treatment under the law.
- Require continuing education for lawyers, judges, and law enforcement personnel (Luckasson & Vance, 1995).
- Support increased focus by law schools and state bar associations on the legal needs of individuals with mild cognitive limitations.
- Use technology such as listservs to connect people around the country who are working on these issues.

Demonstration, Evaluation, and Research

Transdisciplinary demonstration, evaluation, and research projects should be initiated to meet the following needs:

- Create techniques, instruments, and standards to be used in the forensic evaluation of juvenile and adult defendants with mild cognitive limitations in the areas of competence to stand trial, competence to confess, competence to waive, and, for victims, competence to testify as a witness.
- Collect data on victimization of individuals with mild cognitive limitations.
- Collect data on defendants with mild cognitive limitations.
- Ensure opportunities and supports for full and genuine citizenship for all.
- Acknowledge and prepare people for the legal status of adulthood.
- Support and prepare people to be sensitive to environmental and personal risks and to learn the skills to manage risks.
- Seek appropriate legal balance between protection and autonomy.
- Ensure that the criminal justice system recognizes and accommodates disability in defendants and victims.
- Enhance and continue to implement civil rights, entitlement, and community supports legislation.
- Ensure justice and fairness in society.

CONCLUSION

The goal of a justice system must be to ensure justice for all. As long as any individuals or groups are excluded from the expectation of justice, the system loses the trust of citizens and does not fulfill the social contract. We have an opportunity to reexamine the lives of "six-hour retarded children" now that they are adults. Does their experience in the justice system satisfy the requirement of justice for all? The answer is no. But to ask the question of an attentive citizenry and government, using words that authentically capture the experiences of individuals with mild cognitive limitations, and to engage in a discussion reflecting the high stakes of the outcome gives hope for the future.

REFERENCES

American Association on Mental Retardation. (2000). *2000 legislative goals*. Washington, DC: Author.

American Bar Association. (1989). *ABA criminal justice mental health standards*. Chicago: Author.

The Arc of the United States. (1998). *Policy statement on criminal justice*. Silver Spring, MD: Author.

Conley, R.W., Luckasson, R., & Bouthilet, G.N. (Eds.). (1992). *The criminal justice system and mental retardation: Defendants and victims*. Baltimore: Paul H. Brookes Publishing Co.

Ellis, J.W., & Luckasson, R.A. (1984). Mentally retarded criminal defendants. *The George Washington Law Review, 53*, 414–493.

Green, M. (2000). The ambiguities of freedom. *English Education, 33*, 8–14.

Grossman, H. (Ed.) (1983). *Classification in mental retardation*. Washington, DC: American Association on Mental Deficiency.

Heber, R. (1959). A manual on terminology and classification in mental retardation. *American Journal on Mental Deficiency, 64*(Monograph Supplement).

Hugo, V. (1862). *Les misérables*. New York: Dodd, Mead.

Luckasson, R. (1992). People with mental retardation as victims of crime. In R.W. Conley, R. Luckasson, & G.N. Bouthilet (Eds.), *The criminal justice system and mental retardation: Defendants and victims* (pp. 209–220). Baltimore: Paul H. Brookes Publishing Co.

Luckasson, R., & Vance, E.E. (Eds.). (1995). *Defendants, victims, and witnesses with mental retardation: An instructional guide for judges and judicial educators*. Reno, NV: The National Judicial College.

National Research Council. (2000). *Crime victims with developmental disabilities: Report of a workshop*. Washington, DC: National Academy.

Noble, J.H, Jr., & Conley, R.W. (1992). Toward an epidemiology of relevant attributes. In R.W. Conley, R. Luckasson, & G.N. Bouthilet (Eds.), *The criminal justice system and mental retardation: Defendants and victims* (pp. 17–53). Baltimore: Paul H. Brookes Publishing Co.

Perske, R. (1991). *Unequal justice: What can happen when persons with mental retardation or other developmental disabilities encounter the criminal justice system*. Nashville, TN: Abingdon Press.

Petersilia, J. (2000). Invisible victims: Violence against persons with developmental disabilities. *Human Rights, 27*, 9–13.

Rawls, J. (1971). *A theory of justice.* Cambridge, MA: Harvard.

Rimer, S. (2000, Dec. 10). Life after death row. *The New York Times Magazine.*

Sloan, W., & Stevens, H.A. (1976). *A century of concern: A history of the American Association on Mental Deficiency 1876-1976.* Washington, DC: American Association on Mental Deficiency.

Sobsey, D. (1994). *Violence and abuse in the lives of people with disabilities: The end of silent acceptance?* Baltimore: Paul H. Brookes Publishing Co.

Trent, J.W., Jr. (1994). *Inventing the feeble mind: A history of mental retardation in the United States.* Berkeley: University of California.

Wilson, J., & Herrnstein, R. (1985). *Crime and human nature.* New York: Simon and Schuster.

18

Enhancing Understanding, Opportunity, and Social Support through Community Programs and Social Policy

Alexander J. Tymchuk, Ruth Luckasson, and K. Charlie Lakin

Individuals with mild cognitive limitations face an uncertain future because of the general lack of attention to their needs and the consequent absence of a coherent policy to address those needs. Although this inattention is a result of a number of factors, a major factor may be the relative "invisibility" of this population; simply put, because people desire to be as self-sufficient as possible and do not want to be seen as different, they do not seek out services. However, this inattention is also in part a result of the continued use of categorically driven service- and age-specific funding on the part of service providers; individuals with cognitive limitations are often told, "You are too young," or "You are too old." "That is the school's responsibility, not ours." "Try disability services." "Why aren't you working?" "You shouldn't have had any children if you knew that you couldn't care for them!" "Sorry, your son can be seen here, but you will have to go to adult services." "I don't understand why you can't read this—my 6-year-old son can read it!"

To obtain categorical funding, an individual must fit established categorical criteria. Although some individuals demonstrate needs that are similar to those demonstrated by people who fit into certain categories (e.g., mental retardation), these individuals may not meet the criteria required to obtain services or they may no longer fit the criteria as they exit school. In effect, these individuals become hidden from the social services system. Although some agencies accept moral responsibility, few can accept the financial responsibility of addressing the needs of people who do not fit criteria for which funding is received. In fact, as a result of the societal changes accompanying federal devolution, service sectors themselves struggle to serve individuals who do fit existing service criteria. Generic services also have been and remain largely unfamiliar with the needs of individuals with mild cognitive limitations.

This lack of attention to the needs of individuals with mild cognitive limitations occurs for other reasons as well. Invariably, as a group, people with mild cognitive limitations are poor, struggling to do the best that they can. However, as a result of the time required to do day-to-day tasks in order to get by, individuals with mild cognitive limitations have neither lobbied for themselves nor have had others do so on their behalf. This lack of activism or advocacy coupled with a society that increasingly demands of its citizens escalating levels of self-sufficiency in all areas of life forces those who do not have adequate knowledge, skills, or supports to remain on the margins of society. For example, individuals with mild cognitive limitations receive little or no routine health care and must rely on emergency rooms or store-front clinics. Often these individuals are uninsured, unemployed or employed periodically in poorly paying jobs, and living in inadequate housing with little residential stability or perhaps in temporary shelters because they have no home of their own. They also are at heightened risk for being reported for suspected child maltreatment, tend to be victims of abuse and domestic violence, and often are recipients of welfare. Individuals with mild cognitive limitations also appear to be at heightened risk for substance use and abuse, depression, stress, social isolation, and loneliness. They also demonstrate significantly lower life satisfaction and well-being. Cumulatively, this confluence of factors has meant a continuing downward intergenerational spiral.

Clearly, because of the complexity of the topic and the cumulative consequences of inattention to this population, a concerted sustained effort is required to address the problems of the forgotten generation. The efforts represented in this book and in the President's Committee on Mental Retardation (PCMR) Report to the President (1969) are initial steps in trying to elucidate the issues that confront adults with mild cognitive limitations. With implementation of the recommendations, perhaps the futures of subsequent generations of individuals with mild cognitive limitations can be more certain and satisfactory.

RESPONDING TO THE CHALLENGES

A number of challenges for individuals with mild cognitive limitations have been identified in this book: community living; income security, employment, and career development; housing; health and physical well-being; family, psychological, and spiritual well-being; and citizenship and civil rights. Although these topics are seemingly disparate and distinct, in reality all of the areas are intertwined and vary slightly over the life span of individuals with mild cognitive limitations. Although researchers, funding agencies, and, most of all, politicians enjoy single issues addressed single-mindedly with a short-term horizon, issues facing individuals with mild cognitive limitations, similar to those facing everyone in poverty, are complex. However, *all of the issues* are addressable. These issues beg for strategies that address the realities faced by individuals with mild cognitive limitations at different periods in their lives. Thus, coordinated, multi-pronged, and sustained research; professional training; service; and self-advocacy efforts are required while individuals with mild cognitive limitations are in school, during their transition from school, during their work lives, while they are caring for their families, and as they get older.

GUIDING PRINCIPLES

The mental retardation/developmental disabilities field has been known for its development of principles to guide the efforts involving individuals with mental retardation or other developmental disabilities. This field also is known for the application of these principles to a large extent. Similar principles, including cultivating respect for the individuals and their cultures; emphasizing individual autonomy, choice, and self-determination; providing nonvaluative individually determined needs-based supports; increasing accessibility to activities that all people enjoy; and advocating for fairness in civil and criminal law have guided the current effort.

HOW CAN THE COMMUNITY LIVES OF INDIVIDUALS WITH MILD COGNITIVE LIMITATIONS BE ENHANCED?

Independence, individual choice, needs-based supports, and self-actualization, among other things, are critical concepts for individuals with mild cognitive limitations. However, as skills increase, as labels or criteria change, or as certain supports become less necessary, one of the chief dilemmas faced by individuals with mild cognitive limitations is whether to identify oneself as having a disability. Disability service providers face a similar problem: Should they encourage the diagnosis of a disability for an individual as a means of obtaining financial or other disability-related supports? Because generic community service systems are largely unfamiliar with the needs of individuals with mild cognitive limitations, little opportunity exists for continuity between systems. However, continuity can be established in a number of ways to enhance the community lives of people with mild cognitive limitations. Although research is needed in all areas of living for individuals with mild cognitive limitations, an overriding need exists for the identification of the things they need at certain times of their lives, the identification of services with which they come in contact during those times, and a judgment regarding how useful those services were to the individual and his or her family. A determination of which methods were used in seeking and obtaining services by individuals also should be made. Once gathered, this information could provide the basis for the development of continuity of services in all sectors that are needs-based and not strictly related to categorical criteria. Consequently, individuals would not fall through a variety of service sector cracks.

Based on information that is currently available, a number of recommendations can be made to enhance the community lives of individuals with mild cognitive limitations. First, information about this population must be effectively disseminated to specific agencies within the federal, state, and local governments, to private foundations, to disability groups, and to organizational groups representing private service sectors including managed care. Professional organizations such as the American Psychological Association and the American Association on Mental Retardation also should be integrally involved. Accrediting groups such as the Joint Council on Accreditation of Healthcare Organizations also must incorporate criteria related to this population.

Second, by working with schools, long-term care organizations, families, and health services, linkages between service sectors must be established whereby integration of services can occur for all people. Technical assistance should be provided to these coalitions or linkages in order to collect data on an ongoing basis regarding who is or is not served. Foundations can play a significant catalytic role. As part of this effort, service brokers can be organized to assist individuals with mild cognitive limitations in obtaining services.

Third, both the information that is available for self-use in all community sectors and the manner in which the information is presented must become more user-friendly. Most often, materials available in the community are written at an advanced level of writing that is only understood by individuals who *do not* have disabilities. This oversight of the needs of individuals with disabilities occludes them from receiving much needed and highly important information.

Fourth, and probably most important, individuals with mild cognitive limitations must learn how to identify their own learning needs, including the types of adaptations that seem to work best for them. With that information, individuals can provide service providers with direction regarding how to best meet the individuals' needs.

HOW CAN EMPLOYMENT AND ECONOMIC SECURITY OF INDIVIDUALS WITH MILD COGNITIVE LIMITATIONS BE ACHIEVED?

Evidence suggests that the needs of students with mild cognitive limitations who do not qualify for special education are largely not addressed while the students are in school. This lack of attention causes significant impediments for the students as they leave school, particularly if they exit school before graduating. The development of models of school-to-work transition programs for students with mild cognitive limitations that consider the continuities of learning abilities are clearly needed. These programs should be developed in partnership with businesses and industries while including students with mild cognitive limitations in the existing School-to-Work Opportunities Act of 1994 (PL 103-239), the Department of Labor's Employment and Training Administration Programs, and the Department of Education's Office of Vocational Education. Generic and specialized services also should participate to help ensure lifelong access to needed community supports. A system of supports for employers, including training regarding employment adaptation methods that maximize accessibility including informational and technological accessibility, also should be developed. An ongoing effort for continuous feedback between school and work and between work and school must be established. To facilitate employment opportunities, the current Work Opportunities Tax Credit should be expanded so that economic incentives to employers are equivalent to those provided by the Welfare-to-Work Tax Credit. To ensure continuity, programs should be established so that individuals can remain eligible for health care and related benefits should they lose their jobs.

HOW CAN INDIVIDUALS WITH MILD COGNITIVE LIMITATIONS BE ASSURED OF ADEQUATE AND STABLE HOUSING?

Quality and stability of housing for all people who live in poverty continue to be major concerns in the United States. Individuals with mild cognitive limitations, particularly those who have families, are especially vulnerable to the lack of suitable housing, not only because of housing unavailability but also because of the lack of suitable employment opportunities. Inadequate educational preparation also limits the abilities of these individuals to utilize existing supports to obtain housing and to sustain their lives. For families, the absence of housing alternatives tied to parenting support availability coupled with restrictive residency codes increases the probability of family disintegration. A number of strategies are recommended. First, as in all avenues of life, the individual often is his or her own best and most effective lifelong advocate. Therefore, he or she must be made aware of housing issues as part of his or her transition from school. School, too, can be seen as a resource for students who exited early. To achieve this, however, the role of the school must expand in such a way as to operate as a resource center for previous and current students. Second, existing and planned housing initiatives should be informed regarding the needs of individuals with mild cognitive limitations, especially those individuals with families. Housing advocate groups should be apprised of ways in which they can assist these individuals. As part of this effort, advocacy groups as well as the individuals themselves should influence how housing funds are spent. One way in which this can be accomplished is through participation in the development of the 5-year consolidated plans that cities and counties receiving federal housing assistance must develop and update annually. Families who no longer qualify for disability services also must be assisted in making their needs known to agencies that receive federal housing assistance. Further, if they come into contact with child protective services, these families must reiterate their housing needs and seek assistance from child protective service contract agencies.

CITIZENSHIP AND CIVIL RIGHTS

In the absence of effective education and supports enabling them to live relatively balanced lives, it is apparent that individuals with mild cognitive limitations have little opportunity to fully participate as citizens and, in effect, have
been disenfranchised. In addition, individuals with mild cognitive limitations
are at high risk for coming into contact with legal or other authorities. Unfortunately, once they are involved with the authorities, it appears that individuals
with mild cognitive limitations have few of the skills necessary to defend or
to extricate themselves from this involvement; therefore, difficulties with authorities may continue throughout their lives. Parents who have mild cognitive
limitations are especially at increased risk for being involved with the legal authorities due to the stigma held by society that they are innately incapable of
being good parents.

A number of steps can be taken to assist individuals with mild cognitive
limitations. First, individuals must be educated regarding what it means to be
involved with legal and other authorities and regarding what strategies they can
use if they do become involved. This education must be part of citizenship education while in school. Legal aid groups must be part of this effort. Second,
information regarding the needs of individuals with mild cognitive limitations
must be disseminated, and judges, attorneys, and civil rights advocates must be
provided with training. Third, a special effort must be made to address the civil
rights of parents with mild cognitive limitations. The Department of Justice
should aggressively examine cases on parental rights under Title II of the Americans with Disabilities Act of 1990 (PL 101-336). Further, established models
of parenting education and support provision should be disseminated and evaluated in a systematic manner. Potentially, web-based instruction and dissemination may be used. It has been demonstrated that lowered educational and
communication skills and inexperience with medical, legal, contractual, and
other complicated terminology coupled with the exigencies of poor living circumstances place individuals with mild cognitive limitations at risk for not
understanding what they consent to. Unfortunately, these individuals may be
unable to refuse, dissent, or withdraw their consent once it has been given. Conversely, sufficient empirical evidence exists to show that presentation of information in easier to understand, larger, and uncluttered print with sufficient time
and supports for processing and assimilation significantly increases understanding as well as the effectiveness of decision making. In addition, the use of
clear uncluttered illustrations adds to the improvement of understanding. Further, this understanding and decision making can be maintained over time.
Based on this evidence, a fourth recommendation is the development of a concerted effort to ensure that various documents and the processes by which they
are presented should follow the proven strategies. This effort could be headed
by the National Institute on Disability and Rehabilitation Research.

FAMILY LIFE

Individuals with mild cognitive limitations who have their own families continue to be given short shrift. Although several researchers as well as a number of service providers struggle to increase our research knowledge base and to develop models of and actually provide family assistance, passive resistance to any systematic approach to addressing needs of families with cognitive limitations continues. Anecdotal evidence illustrates, for example, that among parents who are first reported for suspected child maltreatment, between 30% and 70% display learning difficulties associated with mental retardation or learning disabilities. Usually, these learning difficulties had been identified while the parent was in school. Invariably, reported parents display limited communication skills, including low reading abilities, and limited self-health care knowledge and skills and are involved in complicated and sometimes threatening relationships. They also may have co-morbid psychological disorders. It is unknown what portion of those individuals who are reported lose their children either temporarily or permanently; what is known, however, is that the parenting education to which all families are referred upon being accused of child maltreatment invariably follows the typical "cookie cutter" approach in which one type of service is meant to fit all. Invariably, families with mild cognitive limitations fail. Despite the need, initiatives related to the prevention of child maltreatment have not included parents with mild cognitive limitations.

There are obvious needs for a systematic approach to family life when a parent has functional needs associated with mild cognitive limitations. First, dissemination of information to federal, state, and local government as well as other agencies and organizations about the needs of parents with mild cognitive limitations and their families is needed. This information must address issues of housing, health care, and child protection. Second, self-health care, injury prevention, and well-being education should be provided to all students while they are in school. These efforts should focus particularly on children who are living in poverty who may not have access to other avenues by which they might obtain such information. Preparatory education for self-health care will at least provide youngsters who become parents with a foundation upon which to build child care skills. Third, specially constituted task forces of private and public groups need to be assembled to address the needs of individuals with mild cognitive limitations and their children. Further, we need to know what happens to children with mild cognitive limitations as they get older. And later, what happens to families as parents age?

PSYCHOLOGICAL HEALTH AND WELL-BEING

Individuals with mild cognitive limitations are affected by the same psychological difficulties that affect individuals without cognitive disabilities. However, in their attempt to foster their own psychological health and well-being, those with cognitive disabilities experience similar, yet greater, difficulties than individuals without disabilities. Individuals with mild cognitive limitations are faced with time constraints and are forced to decipher complex, often contradictory, media or other messages. This daily compounding of difficulties faced by individuals with mild cognitive limitations leads to frustrations that build and lead to more serious internal anxiety and psychological complications. Some individuals with cognitive limitations seek assistance. Invariably, however, when a person with mild cognitive limitations demonstrates symptoms that are associated with a psychological disorder, these symptoms go unrecognized or are recognized only when they become severe. Often, these psychological impairments are untreated or undertreated. Further, because of the unavailability of assistance to foster enjoyment of life, satisfaction with attainments, and psychological wellness and because of limited educational backgrounds, which severely limit the self-development and fostering of positive mental health, individuals with mild cognitive limitations may suffer from lifelong and, sadly, often preventable mental disorders.

This problem continues despite clear needs. Specifically, organizations involved in the provision of mental health services must be informed of the mental health needs of individuals with mild cognitive limitations during different age periods. In particular, private mental health maintenance organizations must share in assuming responsibility in the development of continuity of care models for this population. Culturally relevant faith-based organizations also should participate. Research also is required to identify which mental health and well-being needs exist and which treatments appear to be the most beneficial. Based upon the results of this effort, successful preventive and palliative models can be developed across the life span.

HEALTH AND PHYSICAL WELL-BEING

As health care systems continue to evolve, the health and physical well-being of all people in poverty continues to be fragmented and minimal in nature. Individuals who have any type of impairment, including mild cognitive limitations, and their families have been, and continue to be, disproportionately adversely affected during this evolution. Although the precise extent of the adverse health consequences are unknown, they appear to be substantial and intergenerational. It appears that instead of usual care, individuals with mild cognitive limitations are more likely to utilize emergent or public health or to go untreated. Although Healthy People 2010 and its predecessor, Healthy People 2000, have emphasized increased self-health care responsibilities, no recommended strategies are provided by which individuals who are unable to utilize available resources can develop these skills. Therefore, in the absence of effective and basic self-health care preparatory knowledge while in school, in a workplace, or in a health care system, individuals with mild cognitive limitations have difficulty conceptualizing the relationship between external symptomatology and internal physiological disease processes. They also lack access to preventive health services. Also, as a result of lowered reading and other communication skills, individuals with cognitive limitations are unable to use available self-care resources. However, it is known that matching disease and medical treatment regimen information to the learning needs of individuals, perhaps coupled with suitable supports, dramatically improves their understanding, compliance, and health outcomes. Logically, health care costs would be significantly lowered as well. Additional strategies such as probing, questioning, and role playing add to these improvements. In injury prevention, for example, the use of illustrations and the actual provision of home safety devices are inexpensive but effective ways to prevent infant and child injury—the number one killer of children. In addition, nonfatal injuries are the primary cause of hospitalization and medical treatment of infants younger than the age of 1 year. The consequences of single injuries can be long-lasting. Effective strategies should be disseminated to training programs, health care delivery systems, and "on-the-ground" direct health care providers. Further, there are obvious research needs to identify the actual health and economic consequences of the absence of a usual care system to individuals with mild cognitive limitations.

OTHER NEEDS: ISSUES RELATED TO DEFINING THE POPULATION

A method of describing a particular population must be found for ease of communication. Terms such as *hidden majority* or *invisible disability* have been used to describe individuals with mild cognitive limitations who do not appear to have a disability. In part, this lack of visibility of a disability (or perhaps lack of seeing or knowing or recognizing on the part of society) has contributed to the difficulties that adults with mild cognitive limitations now face. For the current effort and for the time being, the term *mild cognitive limitation* was chosen to describe a substantial number of people whose learning, information processing, and other cognitive processes are such that some adaptations of mainstream practices may be required to help them succeed. These adaptations may be needed in some areas of living but not in all, and the need for such adaptations may vary over a life span. Therefore, *mild cognitive limitations* is a term used to describe functional learning needs. Other terms also could be used, such as *parenting learning needs, financial learning needs, vocational learning needs, health care learning needs, housing learning needs, legal learning needs,* and so on. The important factor, however, is to recognize that learning is multi-faceted and takes place on a continuum. We also struggled with the use of the term *mild* because the comparison is only to people with more severe disabilities, and *mild* does not accurately capture the serious learning and functioning disadvantages these individuals face.

Although it is tempting to return to the use of terms such as *mild mental retardation* or even *borderline mental retardation,* these terms appear to have lost their usefulness because individuals to whom they have been applied reject them. In addition, because of their categorical, either/or, all-or-none nature, the use of these categories does not mirror the complexities of life. People can fall outside of any criterion but still have similar needs for service and have those services denied. Therefore, although there is a need to examine nomenclature, this examination must not divert attention from the people involved.

CONCLUSION

Despite the increased recognition that adults with mild cognitive limitations are at heightened risk of failure within the general society, only small measures of progress have been achieved. Only by elucidating and accommodating the strengths and weaknesses of these individuals; providing a continuation to fill the gaps of support and service provision; and, overall, respecting the rights and needs of all citizens can the quality of lives of adults with mild cognitive limitations be improved.

REFERENCES

Americans with Disabilities Act (ADA) of 1990, PL 101-336, 42 U.S.C. §§ 201 *et seq.*
School-to-Work Opportunities Act of 1994, PL 103-239, 20 U.S.C. §§ 6101 *et seq.*

Index

Page numbers followed by f indicate figures; those followed by t indicate tables; and those followed by n indicate notes.

AAMR, *see* American Association on Mental Retardation
Accessibility
  Air Carrier Access Act of 1986 (PL 99-345), 324n6
  Rehabilitation Act of 1973 (PL 93-112), 155, 329nn27, 28
  wheelchair, 156
Accommodations
  Code of Federal Regulations (C.F.R.), 328–329, 328nn24, 25, 329n26, 339nn27, 28
  student achievement tests, 122, 130
  workplace, 101–102, 113–114, 114t
ADA, *see* Americans with Disabilities Act of 1990 (PL 101-336)
Adaptive behavior
  cultural differences in, 60, 75–76
  improvements with time, 12, 57
  link with IQ score, 50–51, 57–58, 225, 226
  regression of due to mental health disorders, 276
  success rates of, 5
Adolescents
  African American, 233
  lack of information about, 266
  and pregnancy, unplanned, 213, 243, 252
Adult activity centers, 91
Advocacy
  employers as advocates, 76
  housing assistance, 148–149, 153–154, 165, 361
  importance of to quality of life, 74
  need for, 16, 353, 358
  public policy and, 334, 334n60, 343
  in schools, 186
  self-advocacy training, 334n61
  service/support brokers, 173–174
  spirituality advocates, 312–313

AFDC, *see* Aid to Families with Dependent Children
AFIA, *see* Assets for Independence Act
African Americans
  demographic data, 61
  dropout rates of, 29
  informal care of individuals with disabilities, 76
  prevalence of developmental disabilities among, 62
  risk behaviors in, 233
  school-to-work transitions for, 6–8, 12
  self-identification of mild cognitive limitations among, 229
  special education programs for, 222
Aggression, mental retardation and, 279
Aging
  demographics, 46, 281–282
  dual diagnosis in older adults, 281–282
  effects on social competence, 12–13
  health care issues for, 13–16
  impact on special services, 49
  individuals with developmental disabilities, 208
  long-term care, 15, 176–177
  mental health disorders, 281–282
  National Council on Aging, 176
  role of senior citizens in shaping public policy, 46–48
  senior citizens as primary caregivers, 49
Aid to Families with Dependent Children (AFDC), replaced by Temporary Assistance to Needy Families (TANF), 44, 143
Air Carrier Access Act of 1986 (PL 99-435), 324n6
Alcohol abuse, 213, 233, 277
Alternative employment, *see* Employment; Supported employment

Alzheimer's disease, 281–282
American Association on Mental Retar-
    dation (AAMR)
  classification system, 225–226, 235,
    352
  definition of mental retardation, 57
  legislative and policy goals, 353
  need for dissemination of information,
    360
American Bar Association Delegate
    Assembly, model statutes for mental
    disabilities, 353
American Housing Survey, 146
American Indians and Alaskan Natives
  cultural values of, 75
  decision-making rights of, 77
  demographic data on, 61
  prevalence of developmental disabili-
    ties, 62
American Psychiatric Association (APA)
  classification of mental retardation,
    226, 235
  need for dissemination of information,
    360
Americans with Disabilities Act (ADA)
    of 1990 (PL 101-336)
  accessibility, 329nn27, 28
  confidentiality, 335n66
  congressional findings, 323n1
  description of protected individuals,
    327n14
  focus on elimination of barriers, 324,
    324n7
  goals and core policies, 326, 326n13,
    327–332
  influence on employment of individu-
    als with disabilities, 89, 119
  parental rights, 362
  passage and implementation, 21,
    87–88, 253
  rationale, 326n11
  shortcomings, 89, 97
  workplace supports, 102t
Annie E. Casey Foundation, Family to
    Family initiative, 269
Anthropology
  definition of culture, 64–65
  health care issues, 66
Antisocial behaviors, 51, 279
Anxiety disorders, 275, 276, 279
APA, see American Psychiatric Association

Apprenticeship programs, see Tech-prep
    programs
The Arc of the United States, 353
Asian Americans and Pacific Islanders
  cultural values of Fijians, 75, 78
  demographic data on, 61
  prevalence of developmental disabili-
    ties among, 62
ASPE, see Office of the Assistant Secre-
    tary for Planning and Evaluation
Assessment
  accommodations, 122, 130
  alternative, 122, 130
  clinical judgment in IQ testing, 58
  cultural differences, 57–58, 75–76
  interdisciplinary, 328, 328n20
  lack of valid instruments, 60
  quality of life, 8–11
  student achievement tests, 122, 130
Assets for Independence Act (AFIA; PL
    105-285), 162
Assistive technology
  Healthy People (HP) 2010 goals, 242
  for independent living, 330, 330n35
Asthma, Healthy People 2010 goals on,
    245–246
Attention-deficit disorders, mental retar-
    dation and, 279

Barriers
  to affordable housing, 148–149
  Americans with Disabilities Act
    (ADA) of 1990 (PL 101-336), 324,
    324n7
  attitudinal, 323, 323n1
  to community-based care, 276–277,
    279, 291–292
  to cross-system cooperation, 53
  elimination of, 324, 324n7
  ethnocentrism, 67
  to health care, 203, 210–216
  to homeownership, 159t
  to inclusion, 191–192, 196–197, 277
  institutional, 323
  mental health disorders as, 276, 279
  student achievement tests, 122
Behavior disorders, severe
  defined, 275, 277
  persistence of, 277
  in residential institutions, 279

Behavioral Risk Factor Surveillance System (BRFSS), 229
Benign prostatic hypertrophy, 207
Bias, cultural, *see* Cultural differences; Ethnocentrism; Minority groups
Blatt, Burton, 97, 197, 198
Block grant programs
  allocated through HUD, 149–150
  federal government shift to, 44, 129
  Robert Wood Johnson Foundation Self-Determination project, 178–179
  Temporary Assistance to Needy Families (TANF), 143
  Workforce Investment Act of 1998, 129
Bond, Kit, section 8 vouchers, 152
BRFSS, *see* Behavioral Risk Factor Surveillance System
Bush, George Herbert Walker, and Americans with Disabilities Act (ADA) of 1990 (PL 101-336), 324n7

Cancer
  Healthy People 2010 goals, 243
  link to obesity, 232
Cardiovascular disease
  adults with cognitive limitations, 207, 231, 232
  Healthy People 2010 goals, 244
Career development
  after exit from school, 128–129
  agencies, recommendations to, 132–133
  career academies, 127–128
  characteristics of successful approaches, 122–124
  educators, recommendations to, 131–132
  employers, recommendations to, 133–134
  National Occupational Information Coordinating Committee (NOICC) guidelines, 121
  school-to-work transitions, 6–8, 9–10, 88, 119, 121, 125–126
  students and families, recommendations to, 129–130
  tech-prep programs, 127
  trends, 124–129

  see also Vocational education
Carl D. Perkins Vocational and Applied Technology Education Act Amendments of 1990 (PL 101-392), 119, 120–121, 124, 127
Cash assistance, 176–177, 331–332, 331n37, 332n45
  see also Supplemental Security Income (SSI)
CCD, *see* Consortium for Citizens with Disabilities Housing Task Force
Cerebral palsy
  case study about, 301
  stress levels among mothers of children with, 285–286
C.F.R., *see* Code of Federal Regulations
Child abuse, 251, 269
  individuals with mild cognitive limitations, 259
  need for prevention measures, 363
  risk factors for, 358, 363
Child care, UCLA Parent/Child Health & Wellness Project, 263–264
Child protection system
  failure to address needs of parents, 34
  mothers with mild cognitive limitations, 259
Chronic disabilities, prevention of, 15–16
Civil Rights Act of 1964 (PL 88-352), 40
Classification, individuals with disabilities
  American Association on Mental Retardation (AAMR), 225–226, 235
  American Psychiatric Association (APA), 226, 235
  borderline mental retardation, 351–352
  categorical versus functional approach, 23–24, 23n2–24n2, 57–60, 223
  diagnostic categories, 30f
  mild cognitive limitations, 23, 23n1, 57, 225–227, 229–230, 235
  World Health Organization (WHO), International Classification of Functioning, Disability, and Health (ICIDH-2), 226, 230, 235
Clinton, Bill, and use of budget surplus for Social Security and Medicare Trust Fund, 46
Code of Federal Regulations (C.F.R.)
  discrimination against people with disabilities, 328nn18, 19, 22
  integration (inclusion), 329nn29, 30

Code of Federal Regulations (C.F.R.)—
    continued
  modifications and auxiliary aids,
    328nn24, 25 329nn26, 27, 28
Communication
  accessibility requirement, 329, 329n28
  importance of for adequate health care,
    212–213
  poor skills linked to dual diagnosis,
    282–283
  requirements under Section 504 of the
    Rehabilitation Act of 1973 (PL 93-
    112), 155
Community, concept of
  circles of support, 172–173, 186
  decision-making rights, 77
  defined, 63, 191
  empowerment, 70–72
  mental health disorders as barrier,
    276–277, 279
  role in career development, 123
  social supports, enhancing, 123,
    185–187, 192–198, 359–360
  spiritual communities, circles of sup-
    port, 186
  strategies for community organization,
    69–74
Community oriented primary care
    (COPC), 218–219
Community-based services
  barriers to, 276–277, 279, 291–292
  importance of, 63–64, 68
  inclusion, 141, 169–174, 191–198
  involvement of religious agencies, 311
  L'Arche communities, 311, 311n1
  living arrangements, 48, 276–277, 279
  paternalistic model of services, 69–70
  recommendations for enhancing, 123,
    185–187, 192–198, 359–360
  state programs of support, 177–184
  strategies for community organization,
    69–74
  sustainability of programs, 72–73
  transitions to, 4–6, 170, 192, 193
  workplace supports, 114t, 115, 123
Competence, see Adaptive behavior
Computer Matching and Privacy Protec-
    tion Act of 1988 (PL 100-503), 236
Conduct disorders, 275, 279
Confidentiality issues, 236–237, 335,
    335n66, 344

Consent
  civil and legal rights, 335, 344, 362
  for health care, 215–216
  parental, 335n66
Consortium for Citizens with Disabilities
    (CCD) Housing Task Force, housing
    affordability problem, 146–147
Consumer direction, social support ser-
    vices, 175
COPC, see Community oriented primary
    care
Corporate liaisons, supported employment
  guidelines for, 106–111, 109t
  role of, 102, 104
Corporate-initiated workplace supports
  proactive corporate culture, 90–91,
    101, 134
  supported employment programs,
    90–91, 101–116, 109t, 114t
Correctional facilities, see Prisons
Crime, among individuals with mild cog-
    nitive limitations
  increased risk of, 6, 7, 26, 349, 350
  prediction regarding imprisonment,
    4–5
Criminal justice system
  competence doctrines, 350
  failure of, 26, 34
  historical perspective on, 350–352
  justice, concept of, 347–348
  legal protections among, 349–350
  limitations of, 348–350
  recommendations for, 185, 353–354,
    362
  successful programs, 352–353
  see also Prisons
Cultural differences
  as assessment consideration, 57–58
  competition versus cooperation, 77–78
  environmental risk factors, 68–69
  family support, 76
  health care issues, 61, 65–66
  perception of disability, 55–56
  professional ethnocentrism, 66–67
  public policy, 335, 335n69, 344
  role in school-to-work transitions, 6–8
  views of important adaptive skills, 60,
    75–76
  see also Minority groups
Culture, concept of
  anthropological view of, 64–65, 66

defined, 62, 64–65
multiculturalism and pluralism, 78
proactive corporate culture, 90–91,
    101, 134
as subordinator, 66

Databases
    list of, 27
    need for cross-system data manage-
        ment, 51–53, 235–236, 237, 269
Day service programs, 91
Dementia, 281–282
Demographic data
    aging, 46, 281–282
    databases, 27, 236–237
    dementia, 281–282
    disabilities, 144–145, 203–204
    dropout rates, 29, 121–122, 252
    dual diagnosis, individuals with,
        277–282
    estimates based on educational place-
        ment, 28–29, 30f, 31
    federal benefits recipients, 47n4, 204
    homeownership, 156
    housing, 42–43, 48–49
    hypothetical accomplishment curve,
        33f
    IQ scores, normal distribution of, 28,
        29f, 225–226
    IQ scores in prisons and corrections
        facilities, 348
    life span, 32, 33f, 49
    low-income households, 41–42,
        44–45, 61–62, 203–204
    mental health disorders, 277–282
    mental retardation, 41, 52, 61–62, 204,
        225–227, 228f, 229–230, 277–282
    mild cognitive limitations, 27–29,
        60–63, 91, 204, 226
    minority groups, 61, 62, 78, 203
    Social Security, 47n4
    specific learning disabilities, 28
    Supplemental Security Income (SSI),
        47n4, 143, 147–148
    Survey of Income and Program Partic-
        ipation (SIPP), 42–43
    Temporary Assistance to Needy Fami-
        lies (TANF), 204
    unemployment rates, 87, 99, 119–120,
        144

Dental care
    Denti-Cal program, 13–14
    Healthy People 2010 goals, 245
Depression
    Healthy People 2010 goals, 241
    increased risk, 358
    persistence of, 277
Designated Service Agencies (DSAs),
    182–183
Developmental disabilities, see Disabili-
    ties; Mental retardation; Mild cogni-
    tive limitations
Developmental Disabilities Assistance
        and Bill of Rights Act
    advocacy, 334n60, 336n73
    focus on "new paradigm," 324nn6, 8
    full participation, 329n31
    funding needs, 16
    parent training, 334n61
    personnel training, 337n74
    precept, 326n12
    university affiliated programs, 336n73,
        337n74
Devolution of services, 25–26, 44–45,
    251
Diabetes
    Healthy People 2010 goals for, 243
    And individuals with cognitive limita-
        tions, 207
Diagnostic and Statistical Manual of
        Mental Disorders, Fourth Edition,
        classification of mental retardation,
        226
Diagnostic overshadowing, dual diagno-
    sis, 289–291
Disabilities, individuals with
    attitudes about, 323–324, 323n1, 351
    cultural differences in perception,
        55–56
    health care issues among, 203–210
    homeownership, 156–165, 159t, 164t
    mothers of, 204
    public policy framework, 325–337
    relationship to race and poverty,
        203–204
    stigmatization of, 56, 58–60, 192–193
    see also Mental retardation; Mild cog-
        nitive limitations
Discrimination
    avoidance of in core public policies,
        328, 328nn18, 19, 22, 333n51

Discrimination—*continued*
   housing, 142, 148, 155–156
   link to obesity, 232
   toward individuals with disabilities,
      323, 323n1, 351
   see also Minority groups; Stigmatization
Disease model for describing disabilities,
   67–68
Diversity, *see* Cultural differences;
   Ethnocentrism; Minority groups
DNA testing, 350
Down syndrome
   and Alzheimer's disease, 282
   increase in life span, 49
   stress levels of mothers who have chil-
      dren with, 285–286
Dropout rates, 29, 121–122, 252, 259, 349
Drug abuse, *see* Substance abuse
DSAs, *see* Designated Service Agencies
Dual diagnosis, individuals with
   barriers to community-based care,
      291–292
   basic desires of, 286–287, 287t, 288t
   case study about, 275
   causes of mental health disorders,
      282–289
   diagnostic overshadowing, 289–291
   lack of physician training, 276,
      291–292
   mental health disorders, 275–282
   negative environments, 283–286
   negative reinforcement contingencies,
      282–283
   and older adults, 281–282
   prevalence, 277–282
   sensitivity theory, 282–289
   terminology, 275–276
   unusual motivation, 286–289

Early intervention
   effects of, 67
   need for, 52–53
Economy
   overview, 99–100
   public policy, effect on, 24–25
   school-to-work transitions, effect on, 6
   welfare reform, effect, 44
Education
   cost-effectiveness of prevention educa-
      tion, 267

   of individuals with disabilities, 144
   of individuals with mild cognitive lim-
      itations, 222–223
   educational placement, 28–29, 30f, 31
   grants-in-aid, 40
   parents with mild cognitive limita-
      tions, 259–260
   reform initiatives in career develop-
      ment, 124–128
   role in development of successful
      adaptation skills, 6–8
   social support options, training in,
      186
   spiritual, 308, 310, 311–312
   spiritual support training, 315
   tailored educational interventions for
      families, 261–262, 262f
Education for All Handicapped Children
   Act of 1975 (PL 94-142)
   focus on "new paradigm," 324n5
   lack of attention to vocational skills,
      120
Education of the Handicapped Act
   Amendments of 1986 (PL 99-457),
      324n6
Educators
   circles of support, competence in cre-
      ating and maintaining, 186
   professional development, 132
   recommendations to enhance career
      development, 131–132
Elderly population, *see* Aging
Elizabeth M. Boggs Center on Develop-
   mental Disabilities, 315
Emotional disorders, mental retardation
   and, 279
*Emotional Disorders of Mentally
   Retarded Persons,* 289
Employment
   accommodations, 101–102, 113–114,
      114t
   advantages of business partnerships,
      101, 103t
   Americans with Disabilities Act
      (ADA) of 1990 (PL 101-336), 89,
      119
   corporate-initiated workplace support
      model, 101–116, 109t, 114t
   employer education topics, 109t
   federal programs, 95–96, 129
   Healthy People 2010 goals, 242

Individuals with Disabilities Education
Act (IDEA), 92
loss of health insurance as disincentive, 94–95
mentoring programs, 102t, 111–113
predictors of success, 8
preemployment support, 102–103
President's Committee on Mental
Retardation, employment summit,
92–95
recommendations for improvement,
360–361
Rehabilitation Act of 1973 (PL 93-
112), 328n21, 331nn41, 42, 43
school-to-work transitions, 6–8, 9–10
segregated systems, 91–92
Social Security Act of 1935 (PL 74-
271), 331n44
state programs, 92–93, 177
supported employment programs,
90–91, 113–116, 114t, 177–178
unemployment of individuals with
mild cognitive limitations, 87, 284,
349, 358
unemployment statistics, 87, 99,
119–120, 144
Workforce Investment Systems Act,
324n10
workplace supports, 100–104, 101–104,
102t, 103t, 113–116, 114t
see also Career development; Vocational education
Employment and Training Administration Programs, 360–361
Epidemiological data
lack of for individuals with mild cognitive limitations, 252, 256
need for, 14–15, 16, 60–63, 258
prevalence of mental retardation, 227,
228f
Ethnic minorities, see Minority groups
Ethnicity, defined, 62
Ethnocentrism, 66–67, 75–76
Exemplary practice approaches to social
supports
cash and counseling experiments,
176–177
family support programs, 176
personal assistance services (PAS),
174–176
self-determination projects, 178–180

supported employment demonstrations, 177–178

Fair Housing Amendments Act of 1988
(PL 100-403), 154, 324n6
Faith, see Spirituality
Family Educational Rights and Privacy
Act of 1996, 237
Family planning, Healthy People 2010
goals, 243
Family support
career development, 122–123
components of successful family life,
265t
cultural differences, 76
effects of social support on adequacy
of child care, 261
effects on school-to-work transitions, 6
empowerment, 70–72, 176
holistic approach, 266–267, 267f, 268f
home instruction, 264
housing, 43
inadequacies of services, 249–252
instability of, 262–263
integration of services, 263–264, 269
need for information about families to
service providers, 264–266
obesity associated with, 231–232
parents with mental retardation,
254–257, 254n5
parent-use materials, 255, 256f, 257f,
265, 265t
programs, 176
recommendations for improvement,
363
reliance on means-tested benefits,
43–44
service sectors, 257–258
tailored educational interventions,
261–262, 262f
Federal expenditures
Medicaid, 46–47
Medicare, 46–47
Social Security Disability Insurance
(SSDI), 93
Supplemental Security Income (SSI),
93
Fitness and exercise
Healthy People 2010 goals, 245
lack of, 232–233

Food stamps
  family reliance on, 44
  Food Stamp Act of 1964, 40
  Food Stamp Act of 1977 (PL 88-525),
    331n40, 332n48
Foster care, 50, 269, 280
Functional approach for describing indi-
    viduals with disabilities, 23–24,
    23n2–24n2, 57–60, 223
Funding
  cash and counseling experiments, 174,
    176–177
  categorical funding of individuals, 357
  dual diagnosis research, 292
  effects of reduction in government
    funding, 24–25
  for housing, 149–153
  individual development accounts
    (IDAs), 161–162
  integrated employment alternatives, 92
  private foundations, 25, 150, 253,
    253nn3, 4, 269
  Robert Wood Johnson Foundation,
    174, 176–177, 314
  special services, 48

Gender issues
  child abuse, 259
  depression, 258
  employment, 8
  individuals with mild cognitive limita-
    tions, 26
  likelihood of becoming a parent, 259
  loneliness, 285
  school-to-work transitions, 8
  self-concept, 258
  single-parent households, 258
  violence against women, 250n, 258,
    285
  women's health care, 41, 217–218
Grade level expectations, 29, 31, 31f, 41,
    259
Grants-in-aid, establishment of, 40
Great Society programs, 40–43
Guardianship, for medical decision-
    making, 216

*Halderman, Pennhurst State School &
    Hospital v.,* 170

Happiness, *see* Quality of life
Health care
  age-appropriate, 207–208
  aging and, 13–16
  authorization of Medicaid program,
    331n38, 332n46
  barriers to, 203, 210–216
  behavioral model, 69
  community oriented primary care
    (COPC), 218–219
  consent, 215–216
  costs for seniors, 46
  cultural differences, 61, 65–66
  diagnostic overshadowing, 289–291
  disease model, 67–68
  disincentives to, 206, 253–254
  effects of spirituality, 303
  empowerment, 70–72
  funding, 16
  health promotion concept, 71, 255n6
  inadequacy of, 26, 145, 206–210, 223,
    253–254
  insurance coverage, 45, 94–95,
    233–234, 236–237, 253, 358
  lack of compliance, 210–213
  literacy skills, influence on, 13–14,
    31–32
  long-term care costs, 15
  managed care, 204–206, 213, 214,
    219, 251, 253n3
  medical model for describing disabili-
    ties, 23n1, 73, 206, 223
  need for epidemiological data, 14–15,
    16, 223
  need for improvements, 15–16, 223
  prescriptions, 14
  prevention, 15–16, 68
  public health model, 69
  recommendations for improvement,
    364–365
  residential institutions, 206–207
  secondary conditions, 223, 230–233,
    243–246
  self-health care, 253–254, 364
  Title IX trend toward managed care,
    45
  vulnerable populations, 56–57, 68–69
  women's issues, 41, 217–218
  see also Public health issues
Health Care Financing Administration,
    mandatory managed care, 204–205

Health Insurance Portability and
    Accountability Act (HIPPAA) of
    1996 (PL 104-191), 236–237
Health maintenance organizations
    (HMOs), *see* Managed care
*Healthy People: The Surgeon General's
    Report on Health Promotion and
    Disease Prevention*, 223–224
Healthy People 2000, 224, 253, 269, 364
Healthy People 2010
    Behavioral Risk Factor Surveillance
        System (BRFSS), 229
    disability-specific objectives, 241–242
    failure to address needs of individuals
        with mild cognitive limitations, 22,
        225, 253–254
    health indicators, 224–225
    Healthy Families, 253–254
    objectives related to secondary condi-
        tions, 243–246
    overview, 224–225
    self-health care, 253–254, 364
Hearing disorders, 207, 246, 290
Heart disease, *see* Cardiovascular disease
Hemorrhoids, 207
HIPAA, *see* Health Insurance Portability
    and Accountability Act of 1996 (PL
    104-191)
Hispanics, *see* Latinos
HIV infection, 213
Homebuyers' coalitions, 163, 164t
Homelessness
    increase in, 252
    likelihood of, 26, 349
Housing
    community-based living arrangements,
        48
    Consolidated Plan (ConPlan), 152–153
    costs, 147–148
    demand for residential services, 48–49
    demographic data, 42–43
    developers of affordable housing, 150
    discrimination, 142, 148, 155–156
    documentation of need, 153–154
    federally subsidized housing, 141–142,
        147, 149–153
    frequent changes in residence, 258
    homebuyers' coalitions, 163, 164t
    homeownership, 156–165, 159t, 164t
    individual development accounts
        (IDAs), 161–162

low-income families, 143–148
mortgage assistance, 159–161, 160t,
    163–164
obstacles for individuals with disabili-
    ties, 148–149
recommendations, 361
rental assistance, 150, 151–152
Section 8 vouchers, 150, 151–152
trends, 48
worst case housing needs, 145–146
Housing Act of 1937, 149, 331n39,
    332n47
Housing Act of 1964, 40
HOYA, *see* National Home of Your Own
    Alliance
HUD, *see* U.S. Department of Housing
    and Urban Development

ICF/MR, *see* Intermediate Care Facili-
    ties/Mental Retardation regulation
IDAs, *see* Individual development
    accounts
IDEA, *see* Individuals with Disabilities
    Education Act and amendments
Identification, *see* Assessment
IEPs, *see* Individualized education
    programs
Illiteracy, *see* Literacy
Imprisonment, *see* Prisons
Incidence, *see* Demographic data
Inclusion
    barriers to, 191–192, 196–197,
        277
    in Code of Federal Regulations
        (C.F.R.), 320, 329nn29, 30,
    community, 141, 169–174, 192–198
    Healthy People 2010 goals, 242
    least restrictive environments, 329,
        329n30
    negative aspect of the term, 193–194
    public policy, 170, 196–197, 312–316,
        329, 340
    recommendations for, 131
    in spiritual communities, 303, 307,
        310, 312–316
    in tech-prep programs, 127
Incontinence, 207
Independent living
    assistive technology, 330, 330n35, 341
    public policy, 330–331, 341

Independent living—*continued*
　　Rehabilitation Act of 1973 (PL 93-
　　112), 336*n*73
　　see also Housing
Individual development accounts (IDAs),
　　161–162
Individualized education programs
　　(IEPs), and career development, 130
Individuals with Disabilities Education
　　Act (IDEA) and amendments
　　accountability, 334*nn*58, 62
　　confidentiality and parental consent,
　　　237, 335*n*66
　　definition of children's disabilities,
　　　327*n*15
　　early intervention, 335*n*64
　　ensuring meaningful opportunities,
　　　328*n*23
　　focus on "new paradigm," 324*n*8
　　funding, 92, 336*n*70
　　individual procedural rights,
　　　333*nn*52–57
　　interagency cooperation, 334*n*63,
　　　335*n*64
　　parent training and information cen-
　　　ters, 334*nn*60, 61
　　personnel standards and development,
　　　335*n*68
　　precept, 326*n*12
　　purpose, 326*n*11
　　remedies for discrimination, 333*n*51
　　report to Congress, 227
　　school-to-work transition plans, 119
　　selection of service providers, 329*n*32
　　state funding schemes, 335*n*65
　　timely basis of assessments, 328*n*20
Infant mortality rate
　　Healthy People programs goal to
　　　reduce, 224
　　low-income families, 41
Infectious diseases, 213, 244
Information management, need for cross-
　　system data management, 51–53,
　　235–236, 237, 269
Injuries
　　increased risk of, 26, 217
　　prevention models, 267*f,* 268*f*
　　self-injury, 279–280
　　from violence, 252
Inner-city residents
　　grade level achievement of, 41

school-to-work transitions for, 6–7
Institutionalization
　　decline in, 4, 48, 170, 193
　　reinstitutionalization, 4–5, 5–6
　　seen as rejection, 283–284
　　of individuals with severe behavior
　　　disorders, 279
　　stigma of, 193
Insurance
　　disability insurance, 47, 93–94,
　　　331*n*37, 332*n*45
　　health care, 45, 94–95, 233–234,
　　　236–237, 253, 358
　　lack of among individuals with disabil-
　　　ities, 45, 233–234, 253, 358
Integration, *see* Inclusion
Intellectual disabilities, *see* IQ score;
　　Mental retardation; Mild cognitive
　　limitations
Intermediate Care Facilities/Mental
　　Retardation (ICF/MR) regulations,
　　206–207
IQ score
　　classification of mental retardation,
　　　225–226
　　clinical judgment in assessing, 58
　　diagnostic overshadowing and, 291
　　individuals receiving federal assis-
　　　tance, 204
　　linked to adaptive behavior, 50–51,
　　　57–58, 225, 226
　　longitudinal research, 12
　　maladaptive behavior and, 278
　　mental health disorders and, 278–279
　　normal distribution of scores, 28, 29*f,*
　　　225–226
　　posttraumatic stress disorder (PTSD)
　　　and, 278
　　ranges associated with educational
　　　placements, 30*f*
　　scores in prisons and correction facili-
　　　ties, 348
　　validity of standardized measures, 58, 60

Job Training Partnership Act of 1982 (PL
　　97-300), 95, 96
Johnson, Lyndon Baines, Great Society
　　programs, 40–43, 41*n*1, 42*n*2
Joint Center for Housing Studies, Har-
　　vard University, 156

Joint Council on Accreditation of Health-care Organizations, need for dissemination of information, 360
Judicial system, *see* Criminal justice system
Justice, concept of, 347–348

Kidney disease, and Healthy People 2010 goals, 243

Labeling
  effects on individuals with mild cognitive limitations, 53, 58–60
  institutionalization as, 193
  loss of data from, 230
  risk factor for mental health disorders, 283
  warning against, 42
L'Arche communities, 311, 311*n*1
Latinos
  demographic data for, 61
  informal care of individuals with disabilities, 76
  prevalence of developmental disabilities, 62
Learning disabilities, diagnostic overshadowing, 290
Least restrictive environments, Code of Federal Regulations (C.F.R.), 329, 329*nn*29, 30
Legal system, *see* Criminal justice system
Legislation, *see* Public policy; *see also* *specific laws*
Life expectancy, *see* Life spans; Mortality
Life satisfaction, *see* Quality of life
Life spans, 32, 33*f*, 49
  see also Mortality rates
Literacy
  effect on parenting, 259–260
  grade level expectations, 29, 31, 31*f*, 259
  influence on health care, 13–14, 31–32
  likelihood of illiteracy, 349
  of mothers, 259–260, 260*f*
  parenting skills and, 31, 259–260
Living arrangements, *see* Housing; Independent living

Loneliness
  increased risk of, 358
  among those with mental retardation, 284, 285
Longevity, *see* Life spans; Mortality rates
Long-term care
  cash and counseling program, 176–177
  costs, 15
Low-income families
  challenges to, 249–252
  demographic data, 41–42, 44–45, 61–62, 203–204
  fear of government, 254
  housing crisis, 143–148
  individuals with disabilities in, 61–62, 144, 203–204
  risk factors, 41–42
  Urban Institute survey, 44–45
  see also Poverty

Maladaptive behavior
  defined, 275
  effects on community access, 277
  mental retardation and, 278–281
  negative reinforcement contingencies, 282–283
  Reiss Screen for Maladaptive Behavior, 280
  related to IQ score, 278
Managed care, 204–206, 213, 214, 219, 251, 253*n*3
Manpower Development and Training Act of 1962, 40
Marriage, individuals with mental retardation, 6, 249*n*2–250*n*2, 284, 351
Means-tested benefits, reliance on, 43–44
Medicaid
  buy-in program, 95
  child services, 45*n*3
  combination with state programs, 178–181
  eligibility, 145, 209, 234, 332*n*45
  establishment of, 40, 331*n*38, 332*n*46
  family reliance on, 44
  federal expenditures, 46–47
  fluctuating eligibility, 209
  funding for individuals with cognitive disabilities, 88
  managed care, 204–206, 219
  Medi-Cal program, 13

Medicaid—*continued*
  personal assistance services, 331*n*36
Medical Information Privacy and Security Act of 1999, 237
Medical Information Protection and Research Enhancement Act of 1999, 237
Medical issues, *see* Health care; Public
  health issues
Medical model for describing disabilities, 23*n*1, 73, 206, 223
Medi-Cal program, 13
Medicare, 13
  buy-in program, 95
  establishment of, 40
  federal expenditures, 46–47
Mental health disorders
  causes of, 282–289
  distinguished from mental retardation,
    275–276
  elderly adults, 281–282
  environmental risk factors, 283–286
  Healthy People 2010 goals, 244
  increased risk of, 26, 233
  individuals with mild cognitive limita-
    tions in mental health service sys-
    tems, 50–51
  mental illness, defined, 275
  persistence of, 277
  relationship to IQ score, 278–279
Mental retardation, individuals with
  age-related variation in prevalence,
    227, 228*f,* 234
  attitudes about, 351
  basic desires, 286–287, 287*t,* 288*t*
  behavior disorders, 279
  borderline, 351–352
  classification systems, 225–226, 235,
    351–352
  definition, 57–58
  demographic data, 41, 52, 61–62, 204,
    225–227, 228*f,* 229–230, 277–282
  diagnostic categories, 30*f*
  distinguished from mental health dis-
    orders, 275–276
  effects of cutoff criteria on prevalence,
    226, 352
  emotional disorders, 279
  loneliness, 284
  as parents, 249*n*2–250*n*2, 254–257,
    254*n*5
  personality disorders, 278–279, 280–281

prevalence in children, 229–230
in prisons, 348
relationship to mental health disorders,
  278–279
risk factors for mental health disorders, 283–286
"six-hour retarded child," 3, 39–40,
  222
social inadequacy, 279, 280
socioeconomic status, 41–43,
  143–144, 203–204
sterilization, 250*n*
stress levels, 285–286, 288–289
victimization, 284
see also Disabilities; Mild cognitive
  limitations
Metropolitan Atlanta Developmental Disabilities Study, 28, 226
Mild cognitive limitations, individuals
  with
  attitudes about, 351
  career development services, 121–122
  challenges, 249–252, 358–359
  classification, 23, 23*n*1, 57, 225–227,
    229–230, 235
  "cloak of competence" behavior, 59,
    288
  continuity and coordination of ser-
    vices, 32, 34–35, 51–53, 208–209,
    334, 334*nn*62, 63
  criminal justice system, 348–350
  functional approach, 23–24,
    23*n*2–24*n*2, 34, 57–60, 223
  grade level expectations, 259
  health care issues, 205–219, 230–234,
    235, 363–364
  health risks, 26, 209–210, 213, 217,
    223, 230–233, 235
  hypothetical accomplishment curve,
    33*f*
  ineligibility for Supplemental Security
    Income (SSI), 143, 205
  invisibility of, 349, 357, 365
  as involuntary minority group, 59
  lack of information about, 27, 60–63,
    205, 210, 222, 227, 235–237,
    348–349
  life-span issues, 32
  national surveys to determine preva-
    lence, 227, 229–230, 234–235, 236
  need for data, 354

as parents, 258–262
psychological health, 363–364
public policy shifts, 24–25
representative models, 32, 33f, 34
spirituality, 302–303, 305–307, 313
strategies and recommendations for increasing support, 32–35, 51–53, 235–237
terminology and assumptions, 57–58, 60, 249n1, 365–366
unemployment, 87, 284, 349, 358
Military service, 6, 42
Minority groups
attitudes about in 19th century, 351
demographic data for, 61, 62, 78, 203
dropout rates of, 29
effects of public policy shifts, 24–25
and fear of government, 254
identity issues among, 59
means-tested benefits for, 43
prevalence of developmental disabilities among, 62, 63
reduced entitlements of, 56
risk behaviors, 233
school-to-work transitions, 6–8, 12
self-identification of mild cognitive limitations, 229
socioeconomic status and, 42, 203
special education programs for, 222
voluntary versus involuntary, 59
Monadnock (New Hampshire) self-determination project, 178–179
Montefiore Ambulatory Network, identification of individuals with disabilities as underserved, 219
Mood disorders, 275, 276–277
Mortality rates
Healthy People programs goal to reduce, 224
individuals with cognitive limitations, 231
see also Life spans
Mortgage assistance, for individuals with disabilities, 159–161, 160t, 163–164
Mothers
education of mothers with mild cognitive limitations, 259–260
effects of social support on adequacy of child care, 261
injury prevention models, 267f, 268f
psychological characteristics, 260–261

reading skills, 259–260, 260f
risk of report to child protection services, 259
social support and stress level, 285–286
see also Parenting
Multiculturalism, 78

National Assessment of Vocational Education (NAVE) report, special population students in tech-prep programs, 127
National Council on Aging, funded by Robert Wood Johnson Foundation, 176
National Health and Nutrition Examination Survey, 229–230
National Health Interview Survey, 227, 229
National health surveys, 227, 229–230, 234–235, 236
National Home of Your Own Alliance (HOYA), 156, 165
National Institute on Consumer-Directed Long-Term Services, 175
National Institute on Disability and Rehabilitation Research, 323n3, 337n75, 362
National Longitudinal Survey of Youth
grade level expectations, 29, 31, 31f
parenting variable, 256n7
National Longitudinal Transition Study of Special Education Students, school-to-work transitions, 8
National Occupational Information Coordinating Committee (NOICC), guidelines for career development, 121
Native Americans, see American Indians and Alaskan Natives
Natural supports
circles of support, 172–173, 186
workplace supports, 100–101, 113, 114t
NAVE, see National Assessment of Vocational Education
NOICC, see National Occupational Information Coordinating Committee
Normalization
negative aspect of the term, 193–194

Normalization—*continued*
origin of term in Nordic countries, 197
Nursing homes, *see* Long-term care

OASDI, *see* Old-Age, Survivors, and
Disability Insurance
Obesity
Healthy People 2010 goals, 244–245
individuals with mental retardation,
231–232
Office of Special Education and Rehabil-
itative Services (OSERS), school-
to-work transitions, 121
Office of the Assistant Secretary for
Planning and Evaluation (ASPE),
cash and counseling demonstrations,
176
Office of Vocational Education, 361
Old-Age, Survivors, and Disability Insurance (OASDI), growth in number of
recipients, 47
Older Americans Act Amendments of
1987 (PL 100-175), funding needs,
16
One-Stop career centers, 95–96, 132
OSERS, *see* Office of Special Education
and Rehabilitative Services
Osteoporosis
Healthy People 2010 goals, 243
individuals with mental retardation,
232

Parenting
child abuse, 363
components of successful family life,
265t
effects of social support on adequacy
of child care, 261
injury prevention models, 267*f,* 268*f*
likelihood for individuals with mental
retardation, 284
mental retardation, individuals with,
249*n*2–250*n*2, 254–257, 254*n*5
mild cognitive limitations, individuals
with, 258–262
negative view of, 362
parent training, 334*n*61
psychological characteristics, 260–261
roles, 255–257, 255*n*6–256*n*6

skills linked to reading ability, 31,
259–260
PAS, *see* Personal assistance services
Paternalistic model of services, 69–70
Patient Self-Determination Act of 1990,
22
*Pennhurst State School & Hospital v.
Halderman,* 170
Personal assistance services (PAS),
174–176, 330–331, 331*n*36, 332*n*45
Personal Responsibility and Work
Opportunity Reconciliation Act of
1996 (PL 104-193)
changes in eligibility of children, 143
individual development accounts
(IDAs), 161
Personality disorders
defined, 275, 277
diagnostic overshadowing, 290
mental retardation and, 278–279,
280–281
PHAs, *see* Public Housing Authorities
Physicians
disabilities, need for training about,
208
dual diagnosis, need for training about,
276, 291–292
pediatricians as providers for individuals with cognitive limitations,
207–208
PL 74-271, *see* Social Security Act of
1935
PL 88-352, *see* Civil Rights Act of 1964
PL 88-525, *see* Food Stamp Act of 1977
PL 90-576, *see* Vocational Education Act
Amendments of 1968
PL 93-112, *see* Rehabilitation Act of
1973
PL 93-579, *see* Privacy Act of 1974
PL 94-142, *see* Education for All Handi-
capped Children Act of 1975
PL 97-300, *see* Job Training Partnership
Act of 1982
PL 99-319, *see* Protection and Advocacy
for Mentally Ill Individuals Act
PL 99-345, *see* Air Carrier Access Act of
1986
PL 99-457, *see* Education of the Handi-
capped Act Amendments of 1986
PL 99-506, *see* Rehabilitation Act
Amendments of 1986

PL 100-175, *see* Older Americans Act Amendments of 1987
PL 100-403, *see* Fair Housing Amendments Act of 1988
PL 100-503, *see* Computer Matching and Privacy Protection Act of 1988
PL 101-336, *see* Americans with Disabilities Act (ADA) of 1990
PL 101-392, *see* Carl D. Perkins Vocational and Applied Technology Education Act Amendments of 1990
PL 102-569, *see* Rehabilitation Act Amendments of 1992
PL 103-239, *see* School-to-Work Opportunities Act of 1994
PL 104-191, *see* Health Insurance Portability and Accountability Act
PL 104-193, *see* Personal Responsibility and Work Opportunity Reconciliation Act of 1996
PL 105-285, *see* Assets for Independence Act (AFIA)
Population statistics, *see* Demographic data
Posttraumatic stress disorder (PTSD)
    relationship to low IQ score, 278
    sexually abused women, 285
Poverty
    Great Society programs, 40–43, 41*n*1
    increase in number of children in, 251
    influence on participation in spiritual activities, 308
    relationship to mental retardation, 41–43, 143–144, 203–204
    relationship to race, 203
    see also Low-income families
Prader-Willi syndrome, 287
Pregnancy, unplanned, 213, 243, 252
Prejudice, *see* Discrimination; Stigmatization
Premature births, low-income women, 41
Prenatal care, low-income women, 41
Prescriptions, lack of education regarding, 14
President's Committee on Mental Retardation (PCMR)
    association between mental retardation and socioeconomic status, 143–144
    employment summit recommendations, 92–95

leadership role in provision of support services, 236
    report on family support services, 262–263
    report on the "six-hour retarded child," 39–40
Prevalence, *see* Demographic data
Preventive health care, 15–16, 52–53
    cost-effectiveness of family education, 267
    effects of spirituality on, 303
    injury prevention, 267*f*, 268*f*
    prevention model, 68
    screening guidelines, 216, 217
    secondary conditions, 223
    UCLA Parent/Child Health & Wellness Project, 263–264
Prisons
    DNA testing, 350
    individuals with mild cognitive limitations in, 50
    IQ scores of individuals in, 348
    likelihood of imprisonment, 349
    mental retardation in, 348
    prediction regarding imprisonment of individuals with mild cognitive limitations, 4–5
Privacy, *see* Confidentiality issues
Privacy Act of 1974 (PL 93-579), 236
Professionals
    advocacy role, 74, 193
    circles of support, competence in creating and maintaining, 186
    dual diagnosis, lack of training about, 276, 291–292
    educators, professional development, 132
    empowerment of communities, 71–72, 193
    ethnocentrism, 75–76
    health care consent issues, 216
    lawyers, judges, and law enforcement personnel, 354
    need for cultural information, 56, 66–67, 71, 78
    pediatricians as providers for individuals with cognitive limitations, 207–208
    role in serving individuals with mild cognitive limitations, 60
    service/support brokers, 173–174

Professionals—*continued*
  spiritual support coordinators,
      314–315
  spirituality supports, training in, 313
Protection and Advocacy for Mentally Ill
    Individuals Act (PL 99-319),
    334*n*60
Psychiatric disorders, *see* Mental health
    disorders
Psychological characteristics, parents
    with mild cognitive limitations,
    260–261
Psychological health, 363–364
PTSD, *see* Posttraumatic stress disorders
Public health issues
  children, prevalence of mental retarda-
      tion in, 229–230
  identification and prevalence of cogni-
      tive limitations, 223, 225–227, 228*f*,
      229–230, 234
  national health surveys, 227, 229–230,
      234–235, 236
  public policy shifts, 221–225
  see also Health care
Public Housing Authorities (PHAs), 149,
    150
Public policy
  corporate workforce diversity, 90–91
  deinstitutionalization, 207
  economic self-sufficiency, 331–332,
      341
  effects of changes on individuals with
      mild cognitive limitations, 24–27,
      185–186
  emerging disability framework,
      325–337
  equality of opportunity, 327–329,
      339–340
  ethnocentrism in, 67
  failure to address needs of individuals
      with mild cognitive limitations,
      22–23, 43, 185
  federal government role, 40–41
  full participation, 329–330, 340
  funding, 335, 335*n*65, 336, 336*nn*70,
      72
  historical perspective, 21–22, 39–43,
      50–51
  housing, 141–142
  inclusion, 170, 196–197
  independent living, 330–331, 341

  need for federal leadership, 92
  public health issues, 221–225
  recommended initiatives, 185–186
  role of senior citizens in shaping,
      46–48
  shifts in focus, to eliminate barriers,
      324
  spiritual development and inclusion,
      312–316
  traditionally targeted to individuals
      with severe disabilities, 50–51, 185
  trends, 49–50, 90
Public policy framework
  administration, 332–336, 341–345
  avoidance of discrimination, 328,
      328*n*18, 19, 22, 333*n*51
  core policies, 327–332, 339–341
  definitions of disability, 326–327,
      327*nn*14, 15, 328, 338–339
  precept and goals, 326, 326*nn*12, 13,
      338
  program support, 336–337, 345
  statement of findings and rationale,
      325–326, 326*n*11, 337–338

Quality of life
  assessing, 8–11, 74
  career development and, 124
  importance of social support, 11–13,
      74
  longitudinal research, 10–13
  negative aspect of the term, 193–194
  spirituality and, 303
  subjective variables, 9–10
  temperament as predictor, 10–11
  well-being, 256*n*, 303–304

Race issues, *see* Minority groups
Reading, *see* Literacy
Regressions, 275, 276
Rehabilitation Act Amendments of 1986
    (PL 99-506), 324*n*6
Rehabilitation Act Amendments of 1992
    (PL 102-569), 324*n*8
Rehabilitation Act of 1973 (PL 93-112)
  accessibility, 329*nn*27, 28
  advocacy, 334*n*60
  complaints and redress, 333*nn*54,
      57

description of protected individuals, 327*n*14
employment-related services, 331*nn*41–43
focus on "new paradigm," 324, 324*nn*5, 6, 8
full participation, 329*nn*31, 32
funding for employment alternatives, 92, 119
independent living centers, 336*n*73
individualized plans for employment, 328*n*21
interagency cooperation, 334*n*63
joint sign-off of agencies, 330*n*34
minority participation, 335*n*69
ongoing supports defined, 100
personal assistance services, 331*n*36
precept, 326*n*12
rationale, 326*n*11
research funding, 337*n*75
Section 504, 155, 327*n*14, 329*nn*27, 28, 339
self-advocacy training, 334*n*61
standards of care, 335*n*68
state plans, 333*n*50
timely basis of assessments, 328*n*20
Reinstitutionalization of individuals with mild cognitive limitations, prediction about, 4–5
Religions, *see* Spirituality
Residential institutions
decline in, 4, 48, 170, 193
health care, 206–207
Healthy People 2010 goals, 242
litigation against, 207
Pacific State Hospital, Pomona, California, 5–6
placement in seen as rejection, 283–284
reinstitutionalization rates, 4–6
severe behavior disorders and, 279–280
Residential services, community-based, 48–49
Resources and services
consumer direction, 175
exemplary practice approach, 174–180
gaps in, 25–27, 53
need for cross-system links, 51–53, 235–236, 237, 269, 334–335, 343
need for improved information management, 51–52

personal assistance services (PAS), 174–176
recommendations for enhancing, 185–187
residential services, 48–49
service sectors, 257–258
spiritual supports, 302–303, 304–307, 313
supported employment, 100–116, 177–178
waiting list reduction initiatives, 49–50, 184, 184*n*7
Risk factors
child abuse, 358, 363
crime, 6, 7, 26, 349, 350
depression, 358
disease model of health care based on, 67–68
environmental risk, 68–69, 283–286
health care needs, 26, 209–210, 213, 217, 223, 230–233, 235
injuries, 26, 217
loneliness, 358
low-income families, 41–42
mental health disorders, 26, 233
stress, 358
victimization, 358
violence, 26, 217, 250*n*
Robert Wood Johnson Foundation
cash and counseling program, 174, 176–177
Faith in Action Initiatives, 314
Self-Determination demonstrations, 174

Schizophrenia
diagnostic overshadowing, 290, 291
dual diagnosis and, 275, 277
legal protections, 350
School-to-Work Opportunities Act of 1994 (PL 103-239), 119, 121, 124, 125, 360
School-to-work transitions
effect on quality of life, 9–10
examples of successful programs, 125–126
mental health disorders, individuals with, 284–285
minority groups, 6–8
as national priority, 121

School-to-work transitions—*continued*
    need for new models, 360–361
    program benefits, 88
Secondary conditions
    associated with cognitive limitations,
        230–233
    defined, 223
    Healthy People 2010, 243–246
Section 504, *see* Rehabilitation Act of
    1973 (PL 93-112)
Section 8 housing vouchers, 150, 151–152
Self-actualization, *see* Spirituality
Self-concept, 59, 258, 288
Self-determination
    influence on social supports, 172
    managed care and, 205
    Monadnock (New Hampshire) demon-
        stration project, 178–179
    personal assistance programs (PAS), 175
    public policy, 329
    Rehabilitation Act of 1973 (PL 93-
        112), 329*n*31
    Robert Wood Johnson Foundation ini-
        tiatives, 178–180
    supported employment demonstra-
        tions, 178
Self-health care, focus on, 253–254
Self-injury, 51, 275, 277, 279–280
Seniors, *see* Aging
Sensitivity theory
    causes of dual diagnosis, 282–289
    negative environments, 283–286
    negative reinforcement contingencies,
        282–283
    unusual motivation, 286–289
Severe behavior disorders, *see* Behavior
    disorders, severe
Sexually transmitted diseases, 213
Sheltered workshops, 91
Single-parent households
    case study about, 214–215
    income levels among, 43
    women in, 258
SIPP, *see* Survey of Income and Program
    Participation
"Six-hour retarded child"
    defined, 3, 222
    President's Committee on Mental
        Retardation report, 39–40
Social competence
    effects on health care, 214–215

effects on quality of life, 9–10, 11–13
    longitudinal changes in, 12–13, 60
    social inadequacy, 279, 280, 283
Social policy, *see* Public policy
Social Security
    benefits data used to identify individu-
        als with mental retardation, 227
    fiscal dilemma, 46–47
    shortcomings, 88, 93–94
    statistics, 47*n*4, 61–62
Social Security Act of 1935 (PL 74-271)
    cash assistance, 332*n*45
    disability insurance, 331*n*37, 332*n*45
    employment-related services, 331*n*44
    federal funding, 92
    Title XVI, 332*n*45
    waiver provisions, 333*n*50
    workplace supports, 102*t*
Social Security Disability Insurance
    (SSDI)
    federal expenditures, 93
    increase in recipients, 47
    need for reform, 93–94
Social supports
    circles of support, 172–173, 186
    consumer direction, 175
    effects on adequacy of child care,
        261
    exemplary practice approach, 174–180
    health care providers as, 214–215
    inclusion, 169–174
    lack of for individuals with mental
        retardation, 285
    personal assistance services (PAS),
        174–176
    recommendations for enhancing,
        185–187
    self-determination, 172
    service/support brokers, 173–174
    sporadic need for, 171
    state programs, 177–184
    supported employment, 100–116,
        177–178
Socioeconomic status
    relationship to mental retardation,
        41–43, 143–144, 203–204
    relationship to race, 42, 203
    see also Low-income families; Poverty
Somatoform disorders, 275
Special education
    career development, 124–128

enrollment data to identify individuals
with cognitive limitations, 28–29,
30*f,* 31, 225, 227, 230
physical education and fitness programs, 232
relationship of placement to race and
socioeconomic status, 42, 59, 63,
222
role in development of adaptation
skills, 6–8
treatment of individuals with mild cognitive limitations, 222–223
Specialized services, *see* Resources and
services
Specific learning disabilities, 28
Spiritual communities, circles of support,
186
Spirituality
case studies, 299–300, 301, 304–307
challenges for individuals with cognitive limitations, 307–309
defined, 300
development of, 301–302
effects on health, 303
initiatives for meeting spiritual needs,
309–312
SSDI, *see* Social Security Disability
Insurance
SSI, *see* Supplemental Security Income
State programs
Arc projects, 177, 353
California, UCLA Parent/Child Health
& Wellness Project, 263–264
Colorado, systems reform plan,
183–184, 183*n*6, 184*n*7
faith-based collaborations, 312, 314
Florida, supported employment, 177
initiatives to reduce waiting lists for
services, 49–50, 184, 184*n*7
Medicaid managed care, 204–206
need for incentives to expand integrated employment opportunities,
92–93
New Hampshire, Monadnock self-
determination project, 178–179
personal assistance services (PAS),
175
Rehabilitation Act of 1973 (PL 93-
112), 333, 333*n*50
Rhode Island, Choices waiver,
180–181

Robert Wood Johnson Foundation self-
determination initiatives, 179–180
school-to-work transitions, 121
Vermont, Designated Service Agencies
(DSAs), 182–183
see also Devolution of services
Stereotypic behavior, 275
Stereotyping, *see* Labeling; Stigmatization
Sterilization, 351
Stigmatization
associated with identification, 60–61,
185, 205
as barrier to homeownership, 159*t*
of disabilities, 56, 58–60, 192–193
increased for individuals with mild
cognitive limitations, 58–60, 171
Stress
increased risk for, 358
mental retardation, individuals with,
285–286, 288–289
Structure of Scientific Revolutions, 302
Substance abuse
cognitive limitations, individuals with,
213, 233, 259
increased use, 358
Supplemental Security Income (SSI)
cash assistance, 331*n*37
changes in eligibility of children,
143
definition of disability, 327*n*15
demographic data, 47*n*4, 143, 147–148
eligibility, 142–143, 234
federal expenditures, 93
growth of working-age recipients, 47
inadequacy for housing costs, 147–148
incentives to work, 332*n*45
Medicaid managed care, 205
need for reform, 93–94
reliance on, 44
tightening of eligibility for children,
47
Support services, *see* Family support;
Resources and services; Social supports; Supported employment;
Workplace supports
Supported employment
assistive technology, 102*t,* 114*t,* 115
corporate liaisons, 102, 104–111
defined, 100
employer education topics, 109*t*

Supported employment—*continued*
  exemplary practice demonstrations,
    177–178
  income from, 91
  mentoring, 102*t*, 111–113
  as rehabilitation alternative, 88, 90–91
  tax credits, 101, 102t
  United Cerebral Palsy (UCP) Choice
    demonstration projects, 174,
    177–178
  workplace supports, 101–104, 102*t*,
    103*t*, 113–116, 114*t*
  see also Career development; Employ-
    ment; Vocational education
Survey of Income and Program Participa-
    tion (SIPP)
  increased age of primary caregivers,
    49
  trends in housing, 42–43

TAC, *see* Technical Assistance Collabo-
    rative, Inc.
TANF, *see* Temporary Assistance to
    Needy Families
Tax credits
  for small businesses, 332*n*49
  Work Opportunities Tax Credit, 361
Teachers, *see* Educators; Professionals
Technical Assistance Collaborative, Inc.
    (TAC), and housing affordability
    problem, 146–147
Tech-prep programs, 127
Teen pregnancy, *see* Pregnancy,
    unplanned
Temple University, criminal justice train-
    ing materials, 353
Temporary Assistance to Needy Families
    (TANF), 44, 143, 162, 204, 205
Ticket to Work and Self-Sufficiency Pro-
    gram, selection of service providers,
    330*nn*32, 33
Ticket to Work and Work Incentives
    Improvement Act of 1999, 94
  advocacy, 334*n*60
  focus on "new paradigm," 324*n*8
  funding for public agencies, 336*n*72
  health care benefits, 332*n*45
  joint sign-off of agencies, 330*n*34
Tobacco use
  case study about, 209–210

Healthy People 2010 goals, 246
  mild cognitive limitations, individuals
    with, 213
Transitions, life
  effect on quality of life, 8–13
  individuals with developmental dis-
    abilities, 3–8
  institution to community, 4–6
  rites of passage, 3–4
  school to work, 6–8
Transportation issues
  as disincentive to health care, 206
  for individuals with disabilities, 144

UCLA Parent/Child Health & Wellness
    Project, 263–264
United Cerebral Palsy (UCP) Choice
    demonstration projects, 174,
    177–178
Urban Institute, survey of households,
    44–45
U.S. Civil Rights Commission, establish-
    ment of, 40
U.S. Code (U.S.C.)
  access to records, 335*n*67
  personnel training, 337*n*74
  record keeping, 336*n*71
  technological assistance, 336*n*72
  technical assistance, 336*n*75
  training centers, 336*n*73
U.S. Department of Housing and Urban
    Development (HUD)
  contracting agencies, 149–151
  web site, 149
  worst case housing needs, 145–146
U.S. Preventive Services Task Force Rec-
    ommendations, 216

Victimization
  individuals with disabilities seen as
    victims, 195–196
  likelihood of, 26, 217, 250*n*, 252, 284,
    349, 350, 358
  of women, 217, 250*n*
Vietnam War, effects on Great Society
    programs, 42, 42*n*2
Violence
  increase in domestic violence, 252
  likelihood of, 26, 217, 250*n*, 349, 358

Vision disorders, 207, 246
Vocational education
    effect on employment rates, 8
    evolution of, 120–122
    recommendations for educators,
        131–132
    see also Career development
Vocational Education Act Amendments
    of 1968 (PL 90-576), 120
Vocational rehabilitation professionals
    advantages of business partnerships,
        103t
    corporate liaisons, 104–106
    guidelines for, 106–111, 109t
    preemployment support, 102–103
Vocational special needs programs, see
    Career development
Vouchers for housing, Section 8, 150,
    151–152

Welfare
    reduction in caseloads, 44
    reform, 204, 251, 253
Well-being, see Quality of life
WHO, see World Health Organization
Women's health care, 217–218

    see also Gender issues
Work Opportunities Tax Credit, 361
Workforce Investment Act
    accountability, 334n59
    block grants, 129
    career development, 124
    as example of generic employment
        program, 324n10
    overview, 95–96
Workplace supports
    accommodations, 101–102, 113–114,
        114t
    assistive technology, 102t, 114t, 115
    community supports, 114t, 115
    compensatory strategies, 114t, 115
    individualized training, 114, 114t
    job coaches, 113, 114t
    long-term supports, 114t, 115–116
    natural supports, 100–101, 113, 114t
    supports to enhance job retention, 102t
World Bank, emphasis on sustainability
    of programs, 72–73
World Health Organization (WHO)
    health promotion, 71
    International Classification of Func-
        tioning, Disability, and Health
        (ICIDH-2), 226, 230, 235